Ex Líbrís

Randy Manning

If It Takes
All Summer

If It
Takes All
Summer

The Battle of Spotsylvania

by William D. Matter

The University of North Carolina Press

Chapel Hill & London

The paper in this book meets the guidelines for permanence and durability of the Committee on Production Guidelines for Book Longevity of the Council on Library Resources.

92   5 4 3 2

Library of Congress Cataloging-in-Publication Data

Matter, William D.

  If it takes all summer: the battle of Spotsylvania / by William D. Matter.

    p. cm.

  Bibliography: p.

  Includes index.

  ISBN 0-8078-1781-3 (alk. paper)

  1. Spotsylvania, Battle of, 1864. I. Title.

E476.52.M38   1988   87-31950

973.7′36—dc19   CIP

TO MY PARENTS

Lawson and Elizabeth Matter

CONTENTS

PART IV: *North-South Becomes East-West, 13–21 May*

MAPS

ILLUSTRATIONS

PREFACE

This work is an account of the tactical military operations conducted in the vicinity of Spotsylvania Court House, Virginia, between May seventh and May twenty-first, 1864. These operations were the second in a series of confrontations between Union and Confederate forces north of Richmond during the initial phase of the 1864 campaign in Virginia.

Following these actions the armies continued to march and fight their way southward, crossing the James River, and confronting each other by mid-June near Petersburg, where siege operations were initiated by the Federals. It is hoped that someone will provide an account of the operations between Spotsylvania and Petersburg.

Using material from official reports and correspondence and other published and unpublished sources, I have attempted to present an account that is as complete as possible. Much of the source material proved to be vague, incomplete, conflicting, or unreliable. For example, Federal battle reports were written three, four, or five months after the event, with much marching and fighting occurring between. Many of the officers who would have submitted these accounts had become casualties in the interim, and the information was composed by surviving junior officers. Most of the few surviving official Confederate reports were composed after 1864. As a result, there are blank spots in the picture. Such usually identifiable factors as times or routes of march remain mysteries in some cases. Thus, I have been obliged to revert occasionally to conjecture, but I inform the reader when doing so. Such words as "possibly," "probably," and "approximately" appear often. I regret their use but believe that the alternatives of omitting episodes from the narrative altogether because of the dearth of precise information or of boldly presenting the interpretation of an event as being factual without mentioning the uncertainty involved are less satisfactory.

This work does not address such questions as, for example, whether or not Ulysses S. Grant should be considered a "heads down" frontal-attack general who relied upon attrition to defeat his opponents. I believe that, before addressing such issues, one should completely understand not only the decisions made back at the headquarters tents but also the conditions in the front lines and the details of the fighting there. This work, it is hoped, will supply some of this information for a two-week period in May 1864.

I hope that the narrative will enhance the reader's appreciation of the devotion to duty and personal courage exhibited by the American soldier, North and South, during the nation's Civil War. Generals are awarded praise and promotion, but not without enlisted men.

ACKNOWLEDGMENTS

One of the major benefits derived from performing a work such as this is that one becomes acquainted with many fine people while searching for information. Most of these people work in libraries or historical societies. Without their expertise and assistance very little could be accomplished by researchers. This inadequate acknowledgment cannot begin to repay the debt which I owe to each of them.

I particularly wish to record my gratitude to the following individuals. From the National Park Service: Robert K. Krick, Chief Historian, James H. Ogden III, Park Historian, and the late David A. Lilley of the Fredericksburg and Spotsylvania National Military Park; Edmund Raus of Manassas National Battlefield Park; Christopher M. Calkins of Petersburg National Battlefield Park; Kathleen R. Harrison, Research Historian at Gettysburg National Military Park.

From the United States Army Military History Institute: Dr. Richard J. Sommers, Archivist of Manuscripts, and his competent staff. Dr. Sommers shared his vast knowledge and expertise concerning Civil War matters and suggested valuable sources of information; Norma Umbrell of the library staff; Michael J. Winey, Curator.

In addition, I owe thanks to Diane C. Ansley, Office of the Registrar, National Museum of American History, Smithsonian Institution, who kindly furnished information pertaining to the oak tree stump on display at the Smithsonian; Dr. Gerald S. Brinton of New Cumberland, Pennsylvania; William C. Davis of Mechanicsburg, Pennsylvania, Civil War author and editor, for helpful advice; James A. Kegel of Mechanicsburg; Charles J. Kelly, Gary J. Kohn, and Marianne Roos of the Manuscript Division, Library of Congress; Loni Lindeman of Gettysburg, Pennsylvania; Patricia Morris of St. Augustine, Florida, and Ruth E. Potter of Harrisburg, Pennsylvania, who typed the manuscript; Michael P. Musick, Military Records Division of the National Archives, for his many favors and assistance; Edwin H. Olmstead of Mount Holly Springs, Pennsylvania; Jeanette C. Parson, Pattee Library, Pennsylvania State University; Richard A. Saurers, of Harrisburg, who provided leads to many obscure sources; Bryce A. Suderow, of Cotati, California, who made available applicable portions of his study of Confederate casualties; Charles and Rosemary Walker of Woodstock, Virginia, for their warm hospitality and assistance. Finally my gratitude to Agnes V. McGee of Bloomsbury Farm, Virginia, for kindly permitting repeated access onto her property, which is the site of the Harris farm.

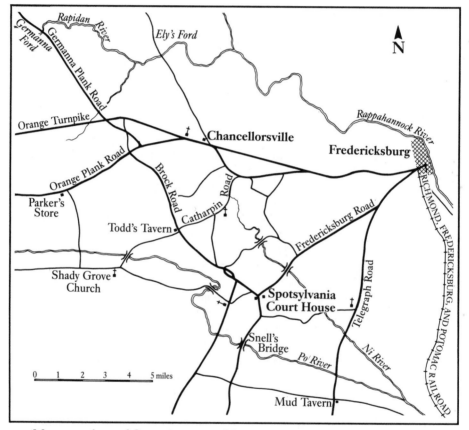

MAP 1-1. Area of Operations, ca. 1864

Initial Encounter

As darkness settled over the portion of northern Virginia known as the Wilderness of Spotsylvania on the evening of 6 May 1864, the two-day series of military engagements that would become known as the battle of the Wilderness came to a close. During the next day skirmishing would occur between elements of both armies, but the major efforts of Gens. Ulysses S. Grant and Robert E. Lee to gain victory here had ended.

What were the results of this fighting? Some immediate results could be determined by sight, sound, and smell. Portions of woodland on the field had been ignited by small arms and artillery fire, and some of the wounded, unable to walk or crawl to safety, had been burned alive. These men and their more "fortunate" comrades who lay in unburned areas rent the darkness with their cries of pain and their pleas for help and water. Amid the suffering and destruction, it was not obvious which army was victorious.

Grant's strategic plan for the campaign of 1864 required the Army of the Potomac under Maj. Gen. George G. Meade and the independent Ninth Army Corps under Maj. Gen. Ambrose E. Burnside to move against Lee's Army of Northern Virginia (see the Order of Battle, Appendix A). The Army of the James, commanded by Maj. Gen. Benjamin F. Butler, would advance toward Richmond via the south side of the James River and attempt to capture the Confederate capital city. If Lee retired his army immediately to the defense of Richmond, Meade and Burnside would follow and unite with Butler to invest the city.[1]

Simultaneously, an army commanded by Maj. Gen. Franz Sigel would advance south in the Shenandoah Valley. Farther west the troops of Maj. Gen. William T. Sherman would leave the vicinity of Chattanooga, Tennessee, advance into central Georgia, and attempt to destroy the army of Gen. Joseph E. Johnston. Finally, an army commanded by Maj. Gen. Nathaniel Banks would capture the city of Mobile, Alabama, and move on Montgomery, the state's capital city.

Grant hoped that the simultaneous activity of all his armies would prevent the Confederate forces from assisting each other with reinforcements or diversions. There were to be no quiet areas in the vicinity of any Confederate army.

Grant's subordinate commanders presented a variety of abilities and temperaments. Irascible Meade was competent and safe if not spectacular. Burnside's reliability, even for corps command, was questionable in view of his performance as commander of the Union army at Fredericksburg in December 1862 and January 1863. Sherman, one of Grant's staunchest friends, was reliable. Butler, Sigel, and Banks were incompetents who had been placed in command positions by President Abraham Lincoln because of their political clout throughout the North. The record of Banks, in particular, was pathetic. He had earned the sobriquet of "Stonewall Jackson's Commissary General" in the Shenandoah Valley in 1862 as he fled precipitately from Confederate troops, leaving behind his supply trains.

Across the lines, Lee had not changed his corps commanders since his reorganization of the Army of Northern Virginia following the loss of Jackson in the spring of 1863. Lt. Gen. James Longstreet was solid and reliable. Lt. Gen. Richard S. Ewell's ability as a corps commander was suspect. Lt. Gen. Ambrose P. Hill, always a fiery combat leader, was in questionable health. Maj. Gen. J. E. B. Stuart was an excellent commander of cavalry.

Grant and Meade had not planned to fight in the Wilderness. They had hoped instead to march through it and establish a position in more open terrain farther south, where they could face the west and await Lee's reaction. Lee, with three divisions of his army not yet present, had marched east into the Wilderness via the Orange Turnpike and Orange Plank Road, and his lead elements had collided on 5 May with the Army of the Potomac before he was fully prepared to offer battle. When contact was established, Grant discarded his original plan and ordered Meade to attack with whatever Federal units were in contact with the enemy. Later in the day the Federals attempted simultaneous attacks with units extending from south of the Orange Plank Road north to the turnpike, but with little success. On that first day of battle Lee attempted merely to hang on until the expected arrival of Longstreet's absent corps and a division of Hill's Third Corps early in the morning of the sixth.

During the march of the Army of the Potomac to its positions south of the Rapidan River, Meade had assigned two of the three divisions of his Cavalry Corps the duty of guarding the trains that accompanied the army. This decision had not pleased the fiery cavalry commander, Maj. Gen. Philip H. Sheridan. The Third Division of cavalry, commanded by the inexperienced Brig. Gen. James H. Wilson, which screened the infantry advance, had performed its reconnaissance function poorly on the evening of 4 May and had been battered on the fifth in an engagement with Confederate cavalry some miles south of the battlefield. Indeed, Meade had been informed of the nearby presence of Confederate infantry on both the Orange Turnpike and Orange Plank Road by elements of his infantry force, not by his cavalry.

The Federal plan for the morning of 6 May entailed an attack all along the line before Lee's three absent divisions arrived. The force under the command of Maj. Gen. Winfield S. Hancock, who was commanding the Union Second Corps and other units, advanced successfully westward along the Orange Plank Road, driving the two divisions of Hill's corps before it. Longstreet, known as "Old Pete" and as Lee's "War Horse," arrived with his two divisions on this front just in time to halt the Federal advance. Later he unleashed a brilliant flank attack against Hancock and drove the entire advanced left element of the Union army back into its works along the Brock Road. Personnel at the headquarters of the Army of the Potomac erroneously interpreted the report of this action to mean that Hancock's left flank had been destroyed. As a result, Meade ordered Sheridan to withdraw his two divisions which had been engaged with Confederate cavalry at Todd's Tavern to the vicinity of the Catharine Furnace and to Alrich's farm on the Orange Plank Road in order to protect the trains.

Lee was unable to take advantage of this success because Longstreet had been accidentally but seriously wounded by members of one of the Confederate flanking units, and his troops were disorganized from fighting in the thick woods. Lee did mount an attack along the plank road with some of Longstreet's troops and others later in the afternoon. However, Hancock had used the respite to reorganize his force and successfully repulsed this effort.

Just before darkness Brig. Gen. John B. Gordon of Ewell's Second Corps attacked the right flank of the Union infantry line, which was manned by Maj. Gen. John Sedgwick's Sixth Corps. The Confederates captured approximately five hundred Yankees, including two brigade commanders. The approaching darkness compounded the confusion generated by the surprise attack, and Gordon withdrew his force.[2] This action marked the end of the battle, although neither commander realized at the time that the other had decided to forgo any more offensive operations. Each would await daylight to see what his opponent chose to do next, and each would spend the night of 6 May evaluating the results of the fighting.

Lee was obviously aware that his army had been hit very hard. His casualties totaled ten thousand.[3] Longstreet, his most capable corps commander, was seriously, perhaps mortally, wounded; at any rate he would be unavailable for months to come. A. P. Hill was beginning to show symptoms of illness. Ewell, as always, would require relatively close supervision. Most of Maj. Gen. Wade Hampton's division of cavalry had not yet arrived, although it was expected the next day. Given these conditions, Lee deemed it prudent to strengthen his defensive position and to await action by Grant. He knew that his army had once again inflicted severe losses upon the Army of the Potomac. In the past this had usually been sufficient to ensure that the Federal army would retire across the river, replenish its ranks, possibly receive a new commander, and try again later in the spring or during the summer months. In reviewing the fighting of the past two days, however, Lee must have realized that he had spent much of his time reacting to Federal attacks. Moreover, but for Longstreet's opportune arrival on the morning of 6 May, two divisions of Hill's corps along with the corps trains might very well have been destroyed. Lee retained confidence in his splendid army, but he would have to be extremely vigilant.

Grant's introduction to warfare in the eastern theater had been startling. He could count fifteen thousand to seventeen thousand casualties in Meade's army and Burnside's corps in the two days' fighting. Appraising his first encounter with Lee, he reportedly told Meade that Confederate Gen. Joseph Johnston would have retreated after experiencing two days of such punishment.[4]

Thus, the first encounter between the war's two most prominent commanders ended with a total of approximately twenty-six thousand casualties and generated in each general a healthy respect for his opponent.

At 10:00 A.M. on May seventh, Grant wrote to Maj. Gen. Henry W. Halleck, chief of staff, in Washington, D.C., "At present we can claim no victory over the enemy, neither have they gained a single advantage."[5] He had ensured that every Federal enlisted man equipped with a musket, with the possible exception of Burnside's Fourth Division of Colored Troops, was given an opportunity to participate in the fighting, but even this had been insufficient to gain the victory.

Grant was undoubtedly disappointed by this result, but he realized he had little tactical opportunity now that Lee's army was concentrated in a strong defensive position. Sometime during the night he reached a decision to move his troops. In his memoirs, he stated that this move was prompted by two objectives. First, he wanted to ensure that Lee would not retire rapidly to Richmond and destroy Butler's army before it could be reinforced. Second, he wanted to position the forces of Meade and Burnside between Lee and Richmond, and if this were not possible, at least to threaten Lee's access to Richmond, forcing him to leave his entrenchments so they could engage him in the open field.[6] In other words, his plan remained unchanged, despite the two days of fighting and the devastating losses.

Whether Meade shared in the decision to move farther south is not known. A rumor, never substantiated, soon ran through the army that Meade had counseled retirement across the Rapidan but had been overruled by Grant. The story later appeared in print, and Meade had the newspaper correspondent responsible for it labeled "libeller of the press" and drummed from the area in disgrace. Because of this all other correspondents combined in a conspiracy against Meade, withholding his name from all of their reports unless it could be presented in an unfavorable light. Grant refuted the rumor in a wire to Secretary of War Edwin M. Stanton and explained to everyone who asked him that there was no truth to the allegation.[7]

A British student of Grant's military career has suggested that, with the full responsibility resting upon Grant's shoulders, Meade probably agreed with the move forward but might have recrossed the river had the choice been his.[8] Be that as it may, the episode is an illustration of the peculiar command arrangement which existed in the Army of the Potomac from the opening of the 1864 campaign until the army was in position at Petersburg.

Grant, as commander of all the armies of the United States, accompanied the Army of the Potomac. He never fully explained why, other than to say that he had realized after one visit to Washington, D.C., that he must be relatively close to the national capital in order to prevent interference with his direction of the war.[9] Another reason may have been his belief, which he shared with some officers in the western armies, that the nation's principal army in the east had never been worked to its full potential, had never fought "all out." He would see about this. A third reason was that Burnside outranked Meade, who theoretically could not issue orders to his superior. Thus, Grant's presence was necessary to coordinate the operations of Burnside's Ninth Corps with those of the main army.

Needless to say, Grant's presence with his staff at army headquarters fostered a form of dual command over the army no matter how diligently Grant and Meade strove to prevent it. Problems arose when Grant issued orders directly to Meade's subordinates and when Meade hesitated to take an unplanned course of action without first obtaining Grant's approval. A student of the Wilderness battle has said that the first instance of Grant's interference occurred on the morning of 5 May before any heavy fighting had begun.[10] This state of affairs boded ill for Federal command and control in the future.

But for ill or for good, Grant was making the decisions. At 6:30 A.M. on May the seventh, he issued a directive to Meade which ranks as one of the most significant of his military career. It began, "General: Make all preparations during the day for a night march to take position at Spotsylvania Court-House. . . ."[11]

This time there would be no turning back.

I Disengagement and Reengagement 6–8 May

1

Feel with Your Pickets

6–7 May

During the first hours of darkness on 6 May, the infantry-men of Sedgwick's Sixth Corps lay tensely behind their fieldworks, waiting. Behind them army engineers were reconnoitering and marking a new line to be occupied by these troops, who constituted the right flank of the army. Finally, shortly after midnight, the word was passed, and the tired soldiers moved to the rear.

Two brigades of Brig. Gen. Horatio G. Wright's First Division, located closest to the Orange Turnpike, proceeded quietly eastward along the pike for approximately one mile, turned to the left, and assumed their new posi-tion north of the road. The Second Brigade, under Col. Emory Upton, occupied the division's left flank, facing west-northwest approximately three hundred yards from the road. To Upton's right was Col. Henry W. Brown's First Brigade of New Jersey regiments facing due north.[1]

Next was the Third Brigade, under Brig. Gen. David A. Russell, facing to the northwest. When Russell's men had received the order to fall back, they had groped and stumbled through the thick undergrowth in the darkness for more than a mile to their assigned position. The Fourth Brigade of Wright's division was one of the units that had been routed by the Confederate flank attack just before dark. Its commander and many of its members had been captured. The remainder, dazed and demoralized, were placed to the rear of Upton's and Brown's brigades as a reserve under the command of Col. Nelson Cross.

To Russell's right was Brig. Gen. James B. Ricketts's Third Division. Three regiments of his First Brigade, which was commanded by Brig. Gen. William H. Morris, extended nearly to the Germanna Plank Road. Ricketts's Second Brigade had been the other unfortunate unit in the path of Gordon's attack and had also sustained a considerable number of casualties. It was placed in reserve behind the left of the corps line under the command of Col. Benjamin F. Smith, succeeding Brig. Gen. Truman Seymour, who had been captured.

The new Federal line crossed the Germanna Plank Road approximately three-quarters of a mile northwest of the intersection with the Orange Turn-

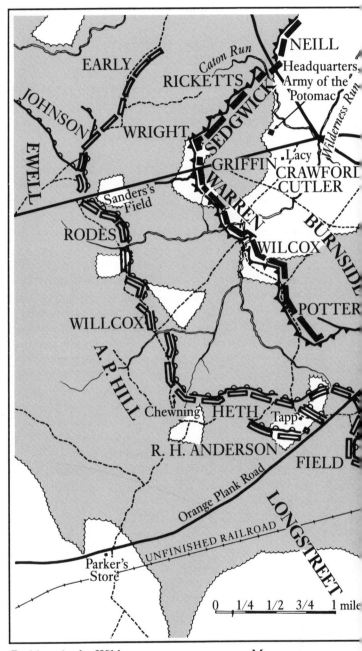

MAP 1-2. Infantry Positions in the Wilderness at 5:00 A.M. on 7 May

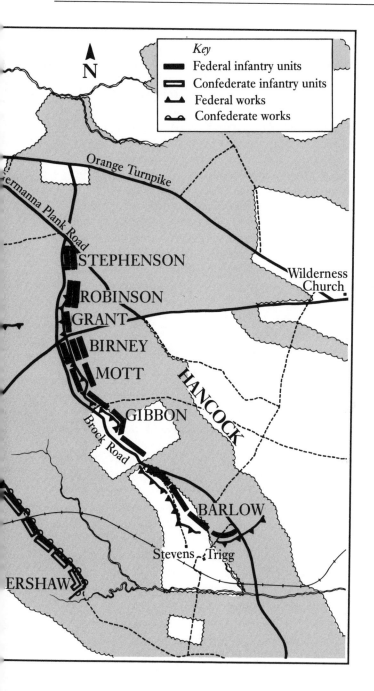

Key
- Federal infantry units
- Confederate infantry units
- Federal works
- Confederate works

N

Orange Turnpike

ermanna Plank Road

STEPHENSON

Wilderness
Church

ROBINSON

GRANT

BIRNEY

MOTT

HANCOCK

GIBBON

Brock Road

BARLOW

Stevens Trigg

ERSHAW

pike. Here to Ricketts's right was stationed the Second Division's Third Brigade of Brig. Gen. Thomas H. Neill, with its left along the road. The remaining three brigades of the Second Division, with its commander, Brig. Gen. George W. Getty, were on detached service under Hancock on the southern portion of the battlefield. Getty had been wounded in the fighting on 6 May, and Neill was now technically in command of the division, although he could exercise no control over it from the opposite end of the field. At 9:00 P.M. Hancock had released two of these Sixth Corps brigades, Brig. Gen. Frank Wheaton's First and Brig. Gen. Henry L. Eustis's Fourth. These troops had plodded north through the smoky darkness and were positioned on Neill's right, east of the Germanna Plank Road, at approximately 3:00 A.M. Hancock kept the remaining brigade, the Vermont troops of Col. Lewis A. Grant, near the Orange Plank Road, perhaps because of the importance of that position and the proven courage of the brigade, which had sustained nearly twelve hundred casualties in the two days' fighting, including twenty-three commissioned officers killed outright or mortally wounded.[2]

The new line of the army's right flank was defensively superior to the old. It was located on slightly elevated ground overlooking Caton Run, which an attacking Confederate force would have to cross. The withdrawal offered Lee ready access to the Germanna Ford by way of the Germanna Plank Road and the opportunity to sever Federal use of the Orange and Alexandria Railroad at Brandy and Rappahannock stations if he so desired. Lee did not so desire—a decision which proved to be correct, because Grant had abandoned the railroad upon crossing the river and never intended to maintain contact with it.[3] At 11:00 P.M. on 6 May, Meade had directed the Army Engineers to dismantle the pontoon bridge remaining at Germanna Ford, transport it downriver to Ely's Ford, and re-lay it at that point.[4]

Beyond the infantry line one and possibly two of Burnside's Ninth Corps cavalry regiments were positioned on the east side of the Germanna Plank Road approximately 1½ miles toward the river from the new line of works.[5] In addition Brig. Gen. Edward Ferrero's Ninth Corps Division of Colored Troops was scattered between the cavalry's position and the river. This division had received a bewildering series of orders from Grant and Sedgwick during the entire day and night of the sixth. At 9:30 P.M. Grant, fearing that it might be cut off, had ordered Ferrero to move his division along the Germanna Plank Road to the vicinity of army headquarters near the Orange Pike intersection. Due to the difficulties of executing such an order in darkness with inexperienced subordinate officers and men, Ferrero did not get the division moving as a unit until 6:00 A.M. of the seventh. One regiment near the river did not receive the word to fall back until 4:00 A.M.[6]

When Sedgwick's units had retired to occupy the newly assigned positions, their neighbors to the left had also moved. These troops consisted primarily of the three brigades of Brig. Gen. Charles Griffin's First Division of Maj. Gen. Gouverneur K. Warren's Fifth Corps. Griffin's Third Brigade, under Brig. Gen. Joseph J. Bartlett, was stationed immediately north of the turnpike. Between Bartlett and Upton was a battalion of U.S. Engineers, approximately 350 men commanded by Capt. George H. Mendell and assigned to Warren on the sixth for duty as infantry. They had been engaged that evening in constructing earthworks along Warren's line near the pike when Gordon's attack had struck the right flank of the Union line. The battalion had immediately been placed in a defensive position on Bartlett's right and had fallen back to the new line simultaneously with his brigade.[7]

Col. Jacob B. Sweitzer's Second Brigade was positioned south of the pike with its right adjacent to the road. Near its left was another unit of engineers, the Fiftieth Regiment of New York Engineers under the command of Lt. Col. Ira Spaulding. The battalions of this regiment had initially been separated on detached service handling pontoon bridges and repairing roads. Like the battalion of U.S. Engineers, these New Yorkers had been assigned on 6 May to the Fifth Corps as infantry, and dawn of 7 May found most of the regiment, approximately one thousand strong, in the rifle pits.

Next, to the south, was located the First Brigade under Brig. Gen. Romeyn B. Ayres. To its left was the First Brigade, Artillery Reserve. This unit, commanded by Col. J. Howard Kitching, consisted of two large regiments, the Sixth and Fifteenth New York Heavy Artillery. These former gunners had been assigned to the Army of the Potomac to serve as an infantry guard for the twelve field batteries which constituted the Artillery Reserve of the army. However, these batteries were now parked approximately four miles to the rear, and their guards were manning rifle pits on the left of the Fifth Corps line.[8]

All these redeployments of Warren's and Sedgwick's men were the results of Gordon's attack at dusk and Grant's decision to end offensive operations in the Wilderness area. The remainder of the Federal force, with a few minor exceptions, maintained the positions held when darkness fell on 6 May.

On the Confederate side the only major change of position after dark was the movement of Brig. Gen. Joseph B. Kershaw's division from the vicinity of the Orange Plank Road to a good defensive position south of the unfinished railroad bed,[9] near the crest of a wooded rise approximately three-quarters of a mile from the left of Hancock's line.

Kershaw's troops constructed crude breastworks in their new position during the night. This activity was heard by the pickets of Hancock's left flank unit, the First Division (four brigades) under Brig. Gen. Francis C. Barlow. Picket officers reported through Barlow to Hancock having heard commands to infantry forces and the sounds of artillery moving. Sometime after midnight Hancock forwarded these reports, and the message was received at 4:30 A.M. on the seventh.[10] For the past two days, Barlow, Meade, and Hancock had used no mounted troops to scout this Confederate infantry flank, so Barlow uneasily awaited a possible attack at dawn.

Meade asked Grant whether Burnside could spare any units with which to reinforce Hancock. Grant replied that, since Burnside was occupying his assigned sector with only two of his divisions, it would be better to wait until Hancock was actually attacked before committing any of Burnside's troops to another area. Here was an example of the weakness of the chain of command within the Federal force: Meade, with little knowledge of the Ninth Corps units' precise locations and battle formations, was required to query Grant for this information and to ask if any of these troops could be relocated safely. Meade was also uncertain of the whereabouts of some of his own army's units early on this morning of 7 May.[11]

As of sunrise Hancock still commanded units of the Fifth, Sixth, and Ninth corps as well as his own Second Corps. Throughout the day these units would be grudgingly returned to their parent corps.

Daylight Brings Action by the Confederates

At about sunrise on 7 May Lee sent for Longstreet's chief of staff, Col. G. Moxley Sorrel, to discuss with him the choice of a commander for the First Corps. Lee appeared to favor Maj. Gen. Jubal A. Early of Ewell's Corps. Sorrel, however, had reservations about Early and suggested instead Maj. Gen. Richard H. Anderson, who was presently commanding a division in Hill's Third Corps but who earlier in the war had served in the First under Longstreet. Later in the day Colonel Sorrel and the remainder of Longstreet's troops were gratified to learn that Anderson had been selected for the command. Brig. Gen. William Mahone was chosen to command Anderson's division, and Col. David A. Weisiger assumed command of Mahone's brigade.[12]

At first light, skirmishers from the Confederate Second Corps were sent forward to locate the enemy's position. North of the Orange Turnpike, Early's men warily approached the Sixth Corps's works and were surprised and relieved to find them vacant. A member of the Forty-fourth Virginia remembered forty years later the trepidation which he felt while approaching these works: "Several times I put my hand up to see if my cap was on my head. I think my hair must have been standing straight up."[13]

Toward the northern end of the vacant line, the Southerners found much Union equipment that had been abandoned during Gordon's attack. Each Reb gratefully confiscated what he needed. Some of these troops continued forward all the way to the Germanna Plank Road and discovered it to be undefended along that section. This information was forwarded through division and corps headquarters to General Lee.[14]

Farther south at approximately 5:30 A.M. a strong line of Confederate skirmishers advanced to the east on both sides of the pike to discover what had become of the Federal troops formerly there. This movement was suddenly reversed by canister fire from Warren's artillery batteries positioned in the rear of the new rifle pits. A member of the 155th Pennsylvania of Ayres's brigade was in front on picket and was driven in by this Confederate advance. When he and his companions neared their works, the artillery men shouted at them to get out of the way, so that the guns could open fire. The Pennsylvanian tumbled over the works directly under the muzzle of a piece which immediately fired on the Confederates. He was obliged to lie in this uncomfortable location until the firing had ceased. His hearing was permanently impaired by this experience.[15]

The troops of the Confederate First Corps who were astride the Orange Plank Road had fought to a state of near exhaustion on the sixth and had spent most of the night strengthening their works. At daybreak they lay patiently waiting for a Yankee attack. A member of the Fifteenth Alabama of Brig. Gen. E. McIver Law's brigade recorded that details had been sent out in front during the night to gather abandoned muskets and that at daylight each Alabamian had from three to five loaded muskets by his side. Some hoped that the Yankees would attack.[16]

Upon being notified that the Germanna Plank Road was no longer being defended all the way to the river, Lee realized that the Federals were changing their supply base. He left his headquarters camp near the Orange Plank Road and rode north behind his infantry line, picking up Gordon north of the Turnpike. They examined the area of the Confederate attack of the previous evening. In his reminiscences Gordon said that, during this morning ride, Lee mentioned the hamlet of Spotsylvania Court House, approximately twelve miles to the southeast, as Grant's possible destination.[17] Much has been written about this remarkable intuition. It was intuition bolstered by clear, logical calculation. If Grant neither continued to attack in the Wilderness nor recrossed the Rapidan, the only remaining directions for him to take were (1) to move east to Fredericksburg, from where he could do a number of things, including marching south along the Telegraph Road and railroad toward Richmond, or (2) to move southeast along the Brock Road through Todd's Tavern to Spotsylvania Court House and then toward the Confederate capital city. In either case Spotsylvania Court House would be an excellent location for the Army of Northern Virginia.

During this seventh day of May, Lee would be unable to determine precisely what Grant intended to do. His suspicions and hunches were reinforced to a small degree as more information, limited as it was, came in during the day, but he was never sure. Indeed, as will be seen, as of nine o'clock the next morning, after the infantry fighting had begun in the general vicinity of the courthouse, he was still uncertain which destination Grant had chosen.

Sometime during the morning Lee instructed his chief of artillery, Brig. Gen. William N. Pendleton, to supervise the opening of a road south from the infantry's right flank, in case a rapid movement in that direction became necessary. Pendleton detailed artillerymen from the First or Third corps for this assignment.[18]

At 9:30 A.M. Maj. Gen. J. E. B. Stuart, chief of cavalry, informed Lee that Union cavalry had returned to the Brock Road from the east and now occupied it from the left of the Union infantry line south as far as Todd's Tavern.[19] This movement did not signify anything definite to the Confederates. Late on the previous afternoon these Yankee horsemen, after skirmishing all day, had retired from this area for no apparent reason that the Southerners could see, and now they had returned; that was all.

Thus, by noon, Lee had learned that the Yankees were disinclined to conduct any more infantry assaults along the line and that they had voluntarily relinquished control of the road leading to Germanna Ford on the Rapidan. Moreover, Federal cavalry had returned to the Brock Road south of their infantry line. Some wagons formerly visible to the rear of the Union lines had disappeared by midmorning. In addition, there had been a small number of scouting sorties by groups of Northern skirmishers similar to those made by the Southerners. Given this limited amount of information Lee could only await further developments. His sole act had been to order the opening of the road south from his lines in case it should be needed.

Morning Action by the Federals

In the Wilderness fighting, limited visibility had obliged unit commanders, as well as army commanders, to rely for current information primarily on the sounds of gunfire and on messages (delivered by mounted couriers) which were often obsolete upon receipt. This uncertain method of conducting operations had created a mental strain for all concerned, especially for the Federals after the Confederates had seized the initiative on the sixth, culminating in the shattering surprise of Gordon's attack.

Meade and his corps commanders, especially Hancock and Warren, appear to have been nervous and apprehensive during the first hours of daylight on the seventh. Meade was desperate to learn the exact whereabouts of the Army of Northern Virginia. He was especially nervous about his flanks, both of which had been viciously assaulted on the previous day. Barlow, commanding the left flank, feared a Confederate attack at daylight. His pickets were stationed just forward of the works, watching the hillside across the unfinished railroad bed, and were extended as far south as the point where that bed crossed the Brock Road. A few of them were lying behind the railroad embankment. Most of the corps's artillery batteries were located at this end of the line because of the excellent visibility. Those batteries that were positioned for possible action faced to the south-southwest across the railroad bed and south down the Brock Road.

At about 7:45 A.M. Meade asked Hancock to send skirmishers out to the west and south to find the enemy, whom Burnside reported to have left the Ninth Corps's front. Hancock reported that an officer sent west on the Orange Plank Road one mile from the Union works had encountered no enemy. Furthermore, a skirmish party was already being formed to advance farther until it made contact with the enemy. He asked and was given the location of the Federal cavalry on the left.[20]

Soon after daylight Barlow ordered his First Brigade commander, Col. Nelson Miles, to send a reconnoitering party down the Brock Road. Miles selected two companies from the 140th Pennsylvania. They scouted as far south as the Furnace Road intersection without encountering any enemy and established communication with Federal cavalry near Todd's Tavern.[21] Meanwhile, a Confederate horse artillery piece suddenly pushed forward and opened fire from a clearing on the hilltop across from Barlow's position. Federal artillery answered, and the piece disappeared. The commander of the Twenty-sixth Michigan asked for volunteers to attempt to capture it. Shortly thereafter eight companies of the regiment double-timed down the slope on a farm road, crossed the railroad embankment and roadbed, and ascended the opposite hill into the trees. After a minute or two Miles became concerned for the volunteers' safety and sent his aide-de-camp, 1st Lt. Robert S. Robertson, to bring them back. Although mounted, the lieutenant did not overtake the Michiganders until he had ridden nearly one mile. He found them approaching a body of enemy troops, probably dismounted cavalrymen belonging to the brigade of Brig. Gen. Thomas L. Rosser. Robertson led the Federals back to their works expecting to be attacked at any moment, but the Confederates did not pursue.[22] Brig. Gen. John Gibbon, Second Division commander, notified Hancock of the results of these two missions. This information, forwarded to Meade at 11:25 A.M., should have lessened his anxiety for the safety of his extreme left flank.[23]

To the north Hancock decided to use an entire brigade for his reconnaissance along the Orange Plank Road. He selected the one formerly commanded by Brig. Gen. Alexander Hays (who had been killed in action on 5 May) and now commanded by Col. John S. Crocker. The First Regiment United States Sharpshooters led off the movement along the road in marching formation, preceded by approximately twenty skulkers whom the provost guard had discovered hiding unwounded in the rear and had sent to the front line. The Sharpshooters had orders to shoot on the spot any of these men who attempted to run away again.

After moving a short distance, the Sharpshooters deployed into a line on both sides of the road. Once off the road they passed among the bodies of many dead and wounded from the Wilderness fighting. Approximately one-half mile from their breastworks they flushed some Confederate pickets who disappeared into the gloom of the forest. One-quarter of a mile farther they were suddenly racked by a heavy volley of musketry and canister from a force behind fieldworks. They had struck the main Southern line where it crossed the road. One Confederate battery had been masked with tents and blankets. When the advanced line of Yankees came well into range, the gunners dropped the coverings and surprised their antagonists with a deadly dose of canister. The Federal troops retired a short distance to a more protected position and began long-range firing. The remainder of the brigade was eventually withdrawn to the Brock Road, leaving the Sharpshooters skirmishing.[24] Some troops of L. A. Grant's Vermont brigade participated in this action or in an independent reconnaissance at approximately the same time. They discovered piles of abandoned muskets, which the Confederates had been collecting, and retrieved these guns for themselves in wagons.[25]

Two divisions of Burnside's Ninth Corps occupied the position to the right of Hancock's troops. Their left flank was nearly one mile directly in front of Hancock's line north of the Orange Plank Road, evidence of the confused and uncoordinated fighting here on the previous day. Soon after sunrise Burnside informed Grant that his pickets had reported the sounds of enemy infantry and wagon movements during the night. He also reported that there were no Confederates in front of him. He based this statement solely on the fact that his skirmishers had just advanced a short distance to the front and had found no enemy troops there.[26] This information was certainly false, but Meade, with little else to go on, assumed that the Southerners withdrawn from Burnside's front would possibly be used for an attack on some other segment of the Union line, hence his incessant querying of Hancock for information from the left flank, and, as will be seen, of Sedgwick concerning the right.

To the right of Burnside's line, Warren, after the repulse of the Confederate reconnaissance along the Orange Pike at 5:30 A.M., had begun to sort out his corps line, which was infused with engineer and heavy artillery units. At 7:40 A.M. he told Meade that he was worried about the relative weakness of his left front. He suggested that works for an artillery line be constructed and manned behind his infantry on the northern bank of Wilderness Run for use if his men were forced from their position. The engineers and heavy artillery troops that he would replace in the line with troops from his corps could be used for this labor.[27] Headquarters agreed to and acted upon this logical suggestion. Warren, however, did not stop there, and the remainder of the message is an excellent example of his maddening propensity to forward to headquarters unsolicited opinions and advice concerning both tactical and strategic matters that lay outside of his own immediate area of operations and knowledge. He informed Meade of his belief that the enemy were all leaving Burnside's front and that they might also be leaving Hancock's. Moreover, he suggested that since Hancock had such a large force at his disposal, he should attack and find out. Warren also pointed out that Meade knew how much more important the right was at that time than the left.[28]

At approximately 10:00 A.M. Warren ordered Brig. Gens. Griffin and Samuel W. Crawford to advance heavy forces of skirmishers to drive back Confederate skirmishers and sharpshooters and to locate the Southerners' main line of battle opposite Warren's position. Crawford's division, which was composed of two small brigades of Pennsylvania Reserves, had replaced the two heavy artillery regiments on the left of Ayres's brigade at approximately 8:00 A.M.[29]

Griffin selected the Twentieth Maine, Sixteenth Michigan, and 118th Pennsylvania from Bartlett's brigade and the Twelfth and Fourteenth U.S. Regular regiments from Ayres's, all under the command of Lt. Col. Charles P. Herring of the 118th. This force advanced to the left of the pike with the Sixteenth Michigan skirting the road and the two Regular regiments on the left of the line with the Twentieth and 118th between.[30] According to a member of the 118th, "the instructions were to feel and drive the enemy. The latter part of the direction was inserted more in hopefulness than as a command. It was easy to feel, but the driving was not so readily accomplished."[31] The Regulars became separated from the Volunteer regiments in the forest and returned to the main line. The remaining three regiments advanced to the rifle pits on the eastern edge of Sanders's field, displacing Confederate pickets. Starting across the field, the Yankees received a volley of musketry and artillery fire from Ewell's troops, who were entrenched in the trees bordering the western edge of the field. The Federals fell back to the crest of a low hill and constructed an advanced line of crude rifle pits.[32]

Farther to the left, the two regiments Crawford had selected from Col. William McCandless's brigade, the Sixth and Thirteenth Pennsylvania Reserves (the "Bucktails"), advanced along a woods road to the southwest. This road connected with the Chewning farm and eventually Parker's Store on the Orange Plank Road. The Thirteenth took the road in deployed formation, and the Sixth scrambled through the trees and underbrush on the flanks of its sister unit. After about one-half mile they encountered Southern pickets who fired once and retired to a small field where another small group of Confederates waited. The Pennsylvanians charged and drove the enemy back into some rifle pits. Behind these pits a battery on a slight knoll opened fire with canister, whereupon Crawford recalled the two regiments. They had located the enemy's main line in this area.[33]

General Meade's well-known temper had been aroused at about sunrise when a courier informed him that the pontoon bridge at Germanna Ford was still in place despite his orders of the previous evening. Meade had vented his rage upon Capt. James C. Duane, chief engineer on the staff. Duane was having a bad time of it. Earlier, his rearing horse had fallen over backward, depositing him in the mud. Now he was being unfairly blamed for the bridge delay, for which he had no responsibility.[34] (Engineers' reports state that the bridge was up and being transported downstream at 6:00 A.M., but this may not have been the case.[35])

North of the Orange Turnpike, John Sedgwick and his Sixth Corps had endured a fatiguing night moving to the rear, and the infantrymen were still throwing dirt up in front of their new works when daylight arrived. The reputation of Uncle John Sedgwick for amiableness would be tested by Meade that morning. At 8:45 A.M. Meade informed Sedgwick that he could not understand why Sedgwick's cavalry was not forwarding intelligence reports. He urged his subordinate to "feel with your pickets, and ascertain if you can anything of the position of the enemy."[36] Sedgwick was temporarily in command of two regiments, Twenty-second New York and Second Ohio, attached to the Ninth Corps. They were assigned the duty of picketing the Germanna Plank Road and the area immediately west of it from the point where the Sixth Corps's works crossed the road to the river. The Twenty-second New York was composed primarily of new recruits who had left their home state as a unit on 8 March.[37] Their commander, Col. Samuel J. Crooks, was responsible for the cavalry picket operation. The Second Ohio was a veteran regiment from the west, newly assigned to the eastern theater. A third Ninth Corps regiment, the Third New Jersey Cavalry, nicknamed the "Butterflies" because of their elaborate Hussar uniform adorned with yellow trim, was patrolling the north bank of the river and downstream from Germanna Ford.

Sometime during the morning the Fifth New York Cavalry, commanded by Lt. Col. John Hammond and belonging to Wilson's division, was added to Crooks's small command. Sedgwick ordered Hammond to position his regiment immediately south of the ford.[38] The Twenty-second New York occupied the line to the left of the Fifth and extended as far as the Beale house, approximately two miles from the river. The Second Ohio was on the left of the Twenty-second. The Fourth Division of Colored Troops from the Ninth Corps no longer served with the horsemen. At 7:30 A.M., it had been ordered to proceed to Dowdall's Tavern on the Orange Pike to protect the army trains then assembling between the tavern and Chancellorsville.[39]

After receiving Meade's message about the cavalry's lack of reporting, Sedgwick sought information from Crooks, who answered that no enemy troops were in evidence in the vicinity of the road. At 9:30 A.M. Meade passed this information to his commander of cavalry and hinted that Sheridan should send a force to watch the Germanna Plank Road. He also placed Ferrero's Colored Troops under Sheridan's orders as train guards and said that Sheridan was free to execute offensive operations consistent with the safety of those trains. At 10:00 A.M. Sheridan grudgingly ordered Wilson to detail a brigade for the assignment suggested by Meade. Wilson selected the brigade commanded by Col. John B. McIntosh, consisting of the First Connecticut, Second and Fifth New York, and Eighteenth Pennsylvania. The Fifth New York, of course, had previously been detailed for this duty and was at the ford. Wilson accompanied the brigade on its march from near cavalry headquarters at Alrich's on the Orange Plank Road toward the Germanna Ford.[40]

Meanwhile, at 10:15 A.M. or shortly thereafter, Meade received word from Sedgwick that Crooks had just reported that his regiment's skirmishers were then engaging Confederate cavalry about one mile from the river. This report appears to have been a false alarm based on some picket firing. Nonetheless, it did nothing to calm Meade's nerves. He suggested at 11:00 A.M. that Sedgwick might send an infantry force out the road to support the Ninth Corps cavalry if he believed Crooks's report, but he could await the arrival of McIntosh to be certain. He also chided Sedgwick again for the lack of information from the army's right front. This exasperated Uncle John, who had enjoyed little or no rest in the past thirty hours. He replied testily: "I sent the commanding general all the reports I received from the Commanding Officer of the cavalry in front. I could not judge how reliable they were. My infantry was marching from 12 midnight till daylight. Since that time they have been engaged in throwing up rifle pits. A brigade is now ready to go out to support the cavalry, if necessary. My infantry pickets now reach from the Rapidan to General Warren's right."[41] Coming from the easygoing Sedgwick, this could be considered a furiously angry response.

At approximately this same time Meade sent orders to his three infantry corps commanders and to Sheridan directing the evacuation of the more than ten thousand Federal wounded.[42] (Burnside was notified separately by Grant.) The plan required Sheridan to provide a mounted escort for the ambulance train, which would cross the Rapidan River at Ely's Ford and proceed to Rappahannock Station, from which the wounded would be transported by rail to Washington.[43]

Three hundred twenty-five wagons were detailed from the general army and corps trains to augment the 488 ambulances available. Even with this amount of transportation, 960 wounded from the Army of the Potomac would be left behind in the Wilderness because of the lack of space in the wagons or because the seriousness of injury precluded movement.[44]

It is obvious that Meade and the members of his staff were kept busy from sunrise until noon dealing with the tactical situation in the Wilderness. However, they had other matters on their minds as well.

2

Make All Preparations
7 May

Grant's Preliminary Order

After approximately 8:00 A.M., Humphreys's signature no longer appears on messages from army headquarters. Meade had put him to work planning the details of the complicated movements required by Grant's order of 6:30 A.M. to move the Federal force southeast and lure Lee from his position. Grant hoped to engage Lee along the line of the North Anna River. The movement would be conducted in two stages: (1) to the area from Todd's Tavern to Spotsylvania Court House on the eighth and (2) to the line of the North Anna on the ninth, assuming tactical deployment there to await Lee's arrival on the tenth or later.[1]

Grant's order in its entirety read:

> HEADQUARTERS, ARMIES U. S.
> May 7, 1864 6.30 A.M.
>
> MAJOR-GENERAL MEADE, Commanding Army of the Potomac
>
> Make all preparations during the day for a night march to take position at Spotsylvania Court-House with one army corps, at Todd's Tavern with one, and another near the intersection of Piney Branch and Spotsylvania road with the road from Alsop's to Old Court House. If this move is made the trains should be thrown forward early in the morning to the Ny River.
>
> I think it would be advisable, in making the change to leave Hancock where he is until Warren passes him. He could then follow and become the right of the new line. Burnside will move to Piney Branch Church. Sedgwick can move along the pike to Chancellorsville, and on to his destination. Burnside will move on the plank-road to the intersection of it with the Orange and Fredericksburg plank-road, then follow Sedgwick to his place of destination. All vehicles should be got out of hearing of the enemy before the troops move, and then move off quietly.
>
> It is more than probable that the enemy concentrate for a heavy attack on Hancock this afternoon. In case they do we must be prepared to

resist them and follow up any success we may gain with our whole force. Such a result would necessarily modify these instructions.

All the hospitals should be moved to-day to Chancellorsville.

Respectfully, etc.,

U. S. Grant

Lieut.-General[2]

(Copy to General Burnside.)

The Problem of Maps

In general terms the order directed the army corps with their assigned artillery batteries to relocate as follows: Fifth Corps (Warren) at Spotsylvania Court House, Second Corps (Hancock) at Todd's Tavern, Sixth Corps (Sedgwick) at an intersection to be discussed shortly, and Ninth Corps (Burnside) at Piney Branch Church. Corps commanders and the members of Grant's and Meade's staffs were provided with copies of the map which Grant used to formulate his preliminary order for the movement.

The quality of this map is well described by Maj. Nathaniel Michler, Corps of Engineers. In his report of the summer campaign, Michler wrote: "the experience gained in the memorable campaign of the Army of the Potomac during the months of May and June of 1864 showed very conclusively that however well the only accessible maps might have served the purposes of general knowledge, still they furnish but little of that detailed information so necessary in selecting and ordering the different routes of marching columns, and were too decidedly deficient in accuracy and detail to enable a general to maneuver with certainty his troops in the face of a brave and everwatchful enemy."[3]

Useful information concerning primary roads and topography had been obtained during the Mine Run campaign the previous November. These data, however, were limited primarily to the area between the Rapidan River and the Orange Turnpike west of Chancellorsville, the Orange Plank Road west from Dowdall's Tavern, and the Catharpin Road from Todd's Tavern to Shady Grove Church and west from there. Documentation of the area south of the Orange Plank Road was based primarily on guesswork.[4]

Grant's order specified that Sedgwick's Sixth Corps should stop "near the intersection of Piney Branch and Spotsylvania road with the road from Alsop's to Old Court-House."[5] Neither of these roads existed except upon that map. The intention appears to have been to position the Sixth Corps within supporting distance of the Fifth, which would have been possible had the map been accurate, because the fictitious intersection was approximately 1 1/2 miles north of the courthouse. Burnside at Piney Branch Church could,

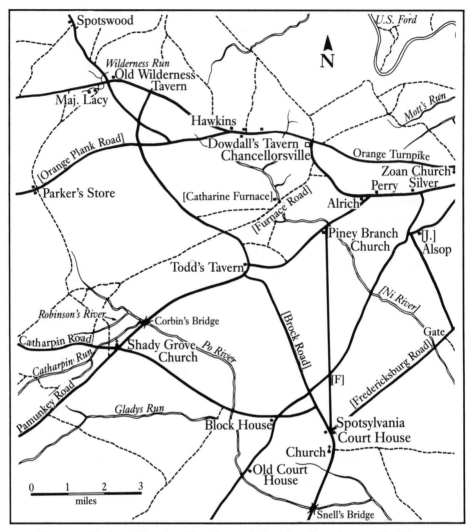

MAP 2-I. Federal Planning Map. Items in brackets have been added for clarification. [F] denotes the fictitious intersection.

if necessary, have supported Hancock at Todd's Tavern or Sedgwick and Warren to the south.

By suggesting that Hancock remain in position until Warren had passed behind him, Grant was ensuring that a nearly continuous line would be maintained in case of a Confederate attack during the initial stage of the movements down the Brock Road. This maneuver would be repeated by the

Federals throughout the summer. In this instance, Lee did not exercise similar care.

After the Fifth Corps had passed behind Burnside on the Brock Road, the Ninth was to fall back to the Germanna Plank Road between the Orange Pike and the Orange Plank Road and move east on the Orange Plank Road, entering the pike after the Sixth Corps had passed and following it to Chancellorsville. From there Sedgwick would proceed to just beyond Silver's farm on the Orange Plank Road and there turn right onto the road from "Alsop's to Old Court-House." Burnside would turn just short of Perry's farm and proceed to Piney Branch Church.

This, then, was the information with which Humphreys was to fashion detailed movement orders for three infantry corps and one cavalry corps. Burnside received a copy of Grant's order along with the instruction to govern himself accordingly. He apparently requested more detailed information and a reply from Grant at 2:00 P.M. said that Sedgwick would move immediately after dark and that Burnside should follow the Sixth Corps closely by the same road, stopping at Piney Branch Church. In addition he should send his cavalry by the Brock Road to Meade, who would issue it proper instructions.[6]

Afternoon Action

At 10:00 A.M. Sheridan had detailed a cavalry brigade to reconnoiter the Germanna Plank Road to the river. Colonel McIntosh probably led his three regiments from Alrich's farm through Chancellorsville to Ely's Ford and thence upriver to Germanna Ford.[7] As the troopers rode along the banks of the river, they stirred up clouds of dust, which were seen by the alert but unlucky Colonel Crooks of the Twenty-second New York Cavalry, who reported the sighting to Sedgwick. He also said that he had found Confederate pickets on the Germanna road itself. Sedgwick faithfully passed this information on to Meade. Crooks had sighted the dust between 11:00 A.M. and noon. At approximately 1:00 P.M. Sedgwick received a message from McIntosh, written at 12:45 P.M. from the Germanna Plank Road 1½ miles from the river, stating that everything was perfectly quiet, with no sign of the enemy to the west of the road.[8]

When Meade received Crooks's report from Sedgwick, his temper flared again. He asked Sedgwick who Colonel Crooks was. Sedgwick replied, laconically it seems, that he did not know, but that Crooks said he was a senior officer of cavalry and that he had just sent another verbal report that his skirmishers were engaging the enemy one mile south of the ford. As Sedgwick was composing this message, McIntosh reported to him and described his route of march, thus clarifying the dust sighting.[9] Just then another courier from Meade arrived with a message containing three enclosures for Sedgwick. The first ordered Colonel Crooks to consider himself under arrest for having forwarded false information concerning the enemy and to turn his command over to the next officer in rank, who would report to Lieutenant Colonel Hammond, Fifth New York Cavalry, for orders. The second enclosure ordered Hammond to assume command of the Twenty-second New York and Second Ohio Cavalry regiments and to patrol the area properly under Sedgwick's orders. The third ordered the commanding officer of the Second Ohio to consider himself under the command of Hammond while on detached duty with the Army of the Potomac. Sedgwick acknowledged receipt of this message, reported McIntosh's route of march, and verified that he was informing Colonel Crooks of his change in status.[10] He dispatched a courier up the Germanna Plank Road to distribute these latest orders. As the courier passed the vicinity of the Spotswood house, he noticed that most of the Second Ohio were there guarding the evacuation of wounded personnel from a Sixth Corps hospital on the grounds about the house. Moving on, he heard light musket firing ahead.[11]

One mile farther, in the vicinity of the Beale farm, he found the Twenty-second New York drawn up on the east side of the road. A squadron of vedettes commanded by a major was crossing the road from left to right to join the remainder of the regiment. Discovering that the major, Peter McLennan, was the next ranking officer after Colonel Crooks, the courier handed him the message placing him in command of the regiment. McLennan immediately reported to Hammond, who ordered him to withdraw his regiment toward Sedgwick's works. Suddenly, their conversation was interrupted by a salvo of artillery fire from the woods west of the road. Hammond and McLennan parted company immediately.[12] Most of the Twenty-second took off at a gallop down the road toward the army and safety. A member of the Second Ohio at the Spotswood house recorded that he heard the firing and presently saw a great cloud of dust rising above the trees. Soon the Twenty-second came tearing past with men and horses equally panic-stricken, followed by exploding shells. Some of the horses were riderless, with saddles slipped under their bellies.[13] The New Yorkers apparently did not slow down at the Sixth Corps's works across the road but continued on toward army headquarters. There they were halted by the mounted contingent of Meade's provost guard, which consisted of the Third Pennsylvania Cavalry and two companies of the First Massachusetts Cavalry.

The army's provost marshal, Brig. Gen. Marsena Patrick, seldom had anything good to say about anybody or anything during the war. The panic of the Twenty-second New York did nothing to alter his opinions. With disgust he entered in his diary that one of the rookie cavalrymen was so terrified that he could not even remember his name, let alone his regiment. The errant horsemen were placed under the jurisdiction of the commander of the Third Pennsylvania Cavalry, Maj. James W. Walsh.[14]

The flight of the Twenty-second exposed the left flank of the Fifth New York to enemy fire. These veterans retired rapidly down the right bank of the river almost as far as Ely's Ford but soon rode back, perhaps sheepishly, in the direction of the Germanna road. When they neared the road, Sedgwick's courier found them and delivered to Hammond his third message. If this courier survived the war, he certainly should have written an account of his errand on the afternoon of 7 May 1864.[15]

The artillery fire upon the cavalry pickets must have occurred sometime between 2:00 and 2:15 P.M. At 2:30 Sedgwick informed Meade's headquarters that the cavalry reported enemy infantry advancing on the Germanna road and he also reported the artillery fire.[16] Meade requested assistance from Grant, who ordered Burnside to send either the division of Brig. Gen. Robert B. Potter or that of Brig. Gen. Orlando B. Willcox to reinforce Sedgwick.[17] Potter's troops moved north to the vicinity of the Wilderness Tavern,[18] while Willcox's division extended to its right to fill in the Ninth Corps's line.[19]

The Confederate force which had caused all of this commotion consisted of the brigade of infantry formerly under John M. Jones, accompanied by a few pieces of artillery, all under the command of Ewell's chief of artillery, Brig. Gen. Armistead L. Long.[20] This was the reconnaissance mission that Lee had ordered simultaneously with his order to open a road to the south, probably about 10:30 A.M.[21] Long's orders from Ewell had directed him to reconnoiter in the general area of Germanna Ford. Leaving the Orange Turnpike, the Confederate force had marched north in the rear of the infantry line and then had entered a woods road by which it had arrived just west of the Beale farm. Advancing infantry skirmishers had reported two or three enemy cavalry units near the road. Long had ordered the artillery into position, and it had fired upon the Federal horsemen. The gunners had apparently used the head of the dust column as an offset aiming point and had achieved excellent results, although they probably never learned of this until after the war. General Long advanced scouting parties north to within sight of the ford and south nearly to the Spotswood house. As a result of these sorties, he reported that the pontoon bridge formerly at the ford was now gone and that the Germanna road in that area was devoid of enemy troops. The force was recalled and the troops rejoined their division in line near the turnpike.[22]

Lee already knew about the bridge. At 2:00 P.M. the commander of the First North Carolina Regiment of Maj. Gen. William H. F. ("Rooney") Lee's division had informed Ewell that, at approximately 1:00 P.M., the Federals had finished taking up the bridge and had hurried downstream with it. This report assured Lee that soon the Union forces would at least move, if not attack.[23]

Operations at the South End of the Field

At approximately 1:30 P.M. Jeb Stuart forwarded to Lee word that Maj. Gen. Fitzhugh Lee was withdrawing his division from the immediate vicinity of Todd's Tavern and was moving down the Brock Road approximately two miles toward Spotsylvania Court House.[24] Lee's troopers had been skirmishing with Union cavalrymen near the tavern since midmorning, which led the army commander to suspect an enemy move in that direction. He instructed Stuart to acquaint himself with the road network to the south of the army, in case the enemy moved toward Spotsylvania Court House or Fredericksburg, and he mentioned his suspicion that the Federals would move toward Spotsylvania rather than toward Fredericksburg.[25] At 3:00 P.M. Stuart replied that he would examine the roads to the south and that a cavalry scout had managed to get close enough to Todd's Tavern to be certain that there was no movement of Yankee infantry south of it. Enemy cavalry, however, were skirmishing as far west as Corbin's Bridge on the Catharpin Road.[26] This important information may have reassured Lee that there would be no sudden Federal infantry movement.

At 1:45 P.M. Meade ordered Hancock to return all detached troops to their parent commands.[27] These totaled six brigades: three from the Fifth Corps, one from the Sixth, and two from the Ninth. All but that of Brig. Gen. James C. Rice were positioned north of the Orange Plank Road. Hancock asked whether he should close to his right or left when refilling the gap caused by this order.[28] He was reluctant to abandon the ridge occupied by Barlow's division south of the Brock Road. This position anchored the Union infantry's left flank and was probably the strongest defensive position of the entire line. Hancock sent most of Brig. Gen. Gershom Mott's Fourth Division to occupy the vacated works north of the Orange Plank Road. Gibbon's and Barlow's divisions then sidled to their right to maintain a continuous line. Barlow left strong skirmish parties on the ridge and just to the south of it.[29]

By early afternoon the area to the front of Miles's brigade on the extreme left was covered by dense smoke. A reconnoitering party reported that squads of Confederates in the area were setting fire to trees and fences and that the Federal cavalry pickets who had extended north along the Brock Road from the Furnace Road intersection were gone.[30]

Hancock ordered another reconnaissance at about this time, an advance west along the unfinished railroad bed, to discover the location of the Confederate infantry's right flank—an operation which would have been more useful had it been conducted earlier. The Twenty-sixth Michigan of Miles's brigade, accompanied by the busy Lieutenant Robertson of Miles's staff, marched down the slope, crossed the railroad bed and embankment, and formed a battle line with its right flank adjacent to the embankment. The troops advanced along the foot of the embankment for about a mile, to the point where the roadbed began a left turn. There Robertson halted the unit and with a major from the regiment rode to the top of the embankment to scout ahead. Looking to their left front they saw what appeared to be an entire division of Confederate infantry at rest with muskets stacked. The Southerners, who belonged to Kershaw's division, spotted the two Yankees, and the scene that followed would have appeared comical to a disinterested spectator. Robertson and his partner galloped back down the bank, got the Michiganders turned around, and conducted them rapidly to the safety of Barlow's line. Some Confederates seized their muskets and fired ineffectual shots at the retiring Yankees from the top of the embankment. Hancock reported the results of this reconnaissance to Meade at 5:10 P.M.[31]

This report should have alleviated once and for all Meade's apprehension about the safety of his left flank. The fact that Kershaw's men were discovered at rest with their arms stacked seemed to nullify Grant's contention that Hancock would probably be attacked during the afternoon.[32] Meanwhile, the time for the initial movements of the Federal force had arrived.

Meade's Movement Order

HEADQUARTERS ARMY OF THE POTOMAC
May 7, 1864—3 P.M.

The following movements are ordered for to-day and to-night:

1. The trains of the Sixth Corps authorized to accompany the troops will be moved at 4 p.m. to Chancellorsville and parked on the left of the road, and held ready to follow the Sixth Corps during the night march.

2. The trains of the Fifth Corps authorized to accompany the troops will be moved at 5 p.m. to Chancellorsville, following the trains of the Sixth Corps and parking with them, and held ready to follow those trains in the movement to-night.

3. The trains of the Second Corps authorized to accompany the troops will be moved at 6 p.m. to Chancellorsville and park on the right of the road, and held ready to move at the same hour with the other trains by way of the Furnaces to Todd's tavern, keeping clear of the Brock Road, which will be used by the troops.

4. Corps commanders will send escorts with these trains.

5. The Reserve Artillery will move at 7 o'clock by way of Chancellorsville, Alrich's, and Piney Branch Church, to the intersection of the road from Piney Branch Church to Spotsylvania Court-House and the road from Alsop's to Block house, and park to the rear on the last-named road, so as to give room for the Sixth Corps.

6. At 8:30 p.m. Major-General Warren, commanding the Fifth Corps, will move to Spotsylvania Court-House by way of the Brock road and Todd's Tavern.

7. At 8:30 p.m. Major-General Sedgwick, commanding Sixth Corps, will move by the pike and plank roads to Chancellorsville, where he will be joined by the authorized trains of his own corps and those of the Fifth Corps; thence by way of Alrich's and Piney Branch Church to the intersection of the road from Piney Branch Church to Spotsylvania Court-House and the road from Alsop's to Block house. The train of the Fifth Corps will then join its corps at Spotsylvania Court-House.

8. Major-General Hancock, commanding Second Corps, will move to Todd's Tavern by the Brock road, following the Fifth Corps closely.

9. Headquarters during the movement will be along the route of the Fifth and Second Corps, and at the close of the movement near the Sixth Corps.

10. The pickets of the Fifth and Sixth Corps will be withdrawn at 1 a.m., and those of the Second Corps at 2 a.m., and will follow the routes of their respective corps.

11. The cavalry now under the command of Colonel Hammond will be left by General Sedgwick at the Old Wilderness Tavern, and, upon being informed by General Hancock of the withdrawal of his corps and pickets, will follow that corps.

12. Corps commanders will see that the movements are made with punctuality and promptitude.

13. Major-General Sheridan, commanding Cavalry Corps, will have a sufficient force on the approaches from the right to keep the corps commanders advised in time of the appearance of the enemy.

14. It is understood that General Burnside's command will follow the Sixth Corps.

By command of Major-General Meade:

S. WILLIAMS
Assistant Adjutant-General[33]

The order was probably not issued until the latest possible time, 3:00 P.M., for reasons of security. At 8:45 that morning the corps trains had been ordered to move south of Wilderness Run and east of the Brock Road after they resupplied the troops with ammunition.[34] These trains, which carried entrenching tools as well as ammunition, were composed of ordinary supply wagons, ambulance wagons, a few light spring wagons, and some mules.[35] They were to lead off the movement, each with an infantry escort, proceeding to Chancellorsville to await the arrival of the Sixth Corps. Burnside's corps trains apparently accompanied his troops. The main army trains had been shunted during the day farther east from Alrich's farm nearly to Tabernacle Church to clear the way for the traffic that would come as far as Alrich's before turning southwest onto the Catharpin Road.

The first element of this traffic was to be the Artillery Reserve, whose twelve batteries were to be rejoined by their infantry guard, the Sixth and Fifteenth New York Heavy Artillery regiments, by the designated departure time of 7:00 P.M. The six batteries of Burnside's Ninth Corps Artillery Reserve would travel with this caravan of field guns to join the Sixth Corps at "the intersection of the road from Piney Branch Church to Spotsylvania Court-House and the road from Alsop's to Block house" ("Old Court-House" in Grant's preliminary order).[36]

Why the Artillery Reserve was chosen to be the vanguard on this route is a mystery. It would not have been in anyone's way at its park in the western angle formed by the junction of the Orange Pike and Orange Plank Road. Nor would there be any pressing need for it at the end of the movement, because each army corps would be accompanied by its own artillery complement. Whether or not they would be needed, between eighty-six and ninety-eight field artillery pieces, escorted by approximately three thousand inexperienced infantrymen, were scheduled to arrive a minimum of 1½ hours ahead of the Fifth Corps, which was to provide support. Theoretically, though not realistically, support might be expected from the two divisions of Federal cavalry that had been operating in the vicinity of Todd's Tavern during the day. Perhaps the explanation for the sequence of march lies in the Federal belief that the move would surely be completed before Lee could react.

Army headquarters did exhibit considerable concern for the safety of the Artillery Reserve in a message sent around 6:00 P.M. to Col. Henry S. Burton, commander of the Reserve: "I am directed to advise you that a division of infantry has been ordered to reinforce you and protect your Command from an attack of infantry which the enemy have sent down the other side of the Rapidan, and are now at Ely's Ford. In what force is not known."[37]

Brig. Gen. Henry J. Hunt, Meade's chief of artillery, said he received a report (the source of which is undocumented) of a body of enemy troops, including infantry, marching down the north bank of the river. In response he sent a battery from the Reserve to Ely's Ford. Perhaps this enemy force was a group of Rooney Lee's horsemen, who followed the Third New Jersey downstream and skirmished with them briefly near Ely's. There was no organized Confederate infantry north of the river at this time.[38]

Meade ordered Hancock to supply the reinforcing division, and soon Maj. Gen. David B. Birney's two brigades were marching east on the Orange Plank Road toward Dowdall's Tavern, planning to escort the guns as far as Piney Branch Church, from which they would turn west and rejoin their corps at Todd's Tavern. Meade soon had second thoughts about weakening the Second Corps line by a complete division and suggested that Hancock might send only a part of a division. Hancock replied that it was too late, because the entire division had gone, and its lead element had probably reached the turnpike. Before receiving this message Meade had decided to cancel the reinforcement mission and ordered Hancock to recall Birney's men.[39] This unnecessary maneuvering illustrates again the degree of apprehension and uncertainty which Robert E. Lee continued to create in Meade and the members of his staff. Whether Grant shared in this concern is not known.

As a result of this alarm, the ambulance trains were sent to Fredericksburg rather than to Rappahannock Station. This decision was probably made between 6:00 and 7:00 P.M. Burnside was notified by Grant's staff at 7:15 P.M.[40] The gathering of the wagons and the loading of the wounded men did not proceed smoothly. The medical inspector of the Fifth Corps claimed that the wagons allotted for that corps's wounded did not report to the hospitals until between 8:00 and 9:00 P.M.[41] A soldier with the Second Corps's ambulance train said that the train had crossed the Rapidan River at Ely's Ford and had gone into camp by approximately 10:00 P.M., when the change of orders arrived. The wagoneers and escort troops wearily recrossed the river and turned east onto the Orange Turnpike, which by then was jammed with traffic.[42]

Lee Also Decides upon a Movement

Late in the afternoon Lee visited A. P. Hill's headquarters at the Chewning house. Members of Hill's staff had broken a hole in the roof of the house, through which they were observing the area around the intersection of the Orange Pike and Germanna Plank Road through a marine telescope. From the large number of mounted couriers arriving and departing, the Confederates concluded that Grant's headquarters were located nearby. As Col. William H. Palmer, Hill's chief of staff, was using the glass, he noticed increased activity within a group of heavy guns in a field. Suddenly all of these guns left the field and took a road which led in the general direction of the Confederate right. He reported this event to Hill and Lee.[43]

Sometime before 7:00 P.M. Lee instructed Richard H. Anderson, who now commanded the First Corps, to withdraw his troops a mile or so from their works after dark and allow them to get some rest. They were to move quietly and to have no camp fires, to avoid detection by the Federals. At 3:00 A.M. they were to begin their march to Spotsylvania Court House, led by a guide Lee would send him.[44]

Thus, as the sun began to sink behind the trees that marked the western edge of the Wilderness, the fighting components of both armies prepared to depart from the area of their initial encounter in the campaign. After the war, writers and orators would try to explain why either the Confederates or the Federals had been victorious there, some of these explanations being heavily dependent upon later events. Lee and Meade and Warren and Anderson, whatever their assessments of the Wilderness fighting, were concerned primarily that some of their troops reach a small hamlet named Spotsylvania Court House before the enemy.

Before following the troops on their night march, it is useful to examine the operations of those cavalry forces that were active south of the main battlefield area on that seventh day of May. The results of their fighting would determine which routes would be available to the foot soldiers and artillerymen during the night.

3

The Enemy Came, Yelling As Only They Could

7 May

During the afternoon of 6 May, Sheridan, at Meade's direction, had withdrawn the divisions of Brig. Gen. Wesley Merritt and Brig. Gen. David McM. Gregg from their positions on the Brock Road to camp for the night at the Catharine Furnace and between Piney Branch Church and Alrich's farm. As the Federals withdrew, Confederate cavalrymen followed and established pickets out to the east from Todd's Tavern and near the intersection of Brock and Furnace roads. In his report Sheridan stated: "On the 7th the trains of the army, under directions from headquarters Army of the Potomac, were put in motion to go into park at Piney Branch Church. As this point was held by the enemy, I was confident that the order must have been given without fully understanding the condition of affairs, and therefore thought the best way to remedy the trouble was to halt the trains in the vicinity of Alrich's, attack the enemy, and regain the ground."[1]

No copy of these orders from Meade's headquarters has been found. Whoever was responsible for them misinterpreted Grant's loosely worded phrase in his preliminary movement directive to Meade at 6:30 A.M. ("If this move is made, the trains should be thrown forward early in the morning to the Ny River") to mean the morning of the seventh rather than the morning of the eighth.[2] The trains in question were the general army trains, which were located just off the Orange Turnpike between Chancellorsville and Dowdall's Tavern.

The wording of Sheridan's report conveys the misleading impression that the cavalry commander stopped the trains and immediately tried to regain possession of the areas from Piney Branch Church and Catharine Furnace to the Brock Road and Todd's Tavern. Just before 7:10 A.M. Sheridan did indeed order Brig. Gen. George A. Custer to advance his brigade on the Furnace Road and to resume his former position at the intersection of Brock Road and Furnace Road.[3] This order was issued, however, before the officer in charge of the trains could have received the order to move. Later, the trains were started in obedience to the erroneous order and moved east of

Chancellorsville before being halted, probably by Sheridan, who spent most of the morning there at his headquarters, but all of this activity could not have occurred between 6:30 and 7:00 A.M. Sheridan ordered Custer's mission on his own initiative apart from any movement of trains and apparently informed army headquarters of his actions.

Col. Thomas C. Devin's brigade accompanied Custer's and led the advance.[4] Merritt's reserve brigade, now commanded by Col. Alfred Gibbs of the Nineteenth New York, remained in the vicinity of Alrich's as an additional guard for the trains. Meade, in a message written at 10:00 A.M., had informed Sheridan that General Ferrero's division of Colored Troops from the Ninth Corps had been ordered to report to him and to assist in the guarding of the trains and that Sheridan was authorized to conduct local offensive operations.[5]

By this time Devin and Custer had arrived, with little or no opposition, at the intersection of Brock Road and Furnace Road and had reestablished the Federal position there.[6] Custer sent his First Michigan Regiment south along the Brock Road, where they were fired upon by Confederate cavalry pickets approximately three-quarters of a mile from the intersection. With two squadrons dismounted and deployed in the forest on either side of the road and with a mounted squadron remaining on the road, the regiment continued the advance with another regiment, probably Devin's Sixth New York, on its right flank and still another in its rear. The Confederates withdrew in the direction of Todd's Tavern.[7]

Devin followed the retiring Confederates toward the tavern, and when they turned to offer battle, he sent a portion of his Sixth New York in on a charge. The Yankees were stopped in their tracks with some loss. This action occurred a short distance north of the site at Confederate barricades where the Catharpin Road enters the Brock from the east. Devin and Custer then reported to Sheridan, who forwarded their reports to army headquarters at 11:30 P.M. At noon the reserve brigade was relieved of its train-guarding assignment by Col. George H. Chapman's brigade of Wilson's Third Division and was ordered to join Devin and Custer on the Brock Road.[8]

Sheridan probably rode to the front between noon and 1:00 P.M. and joined Devin and Custer on the Brock Road just south of the Furnace Road intersection. Since receiving Meade's clearance to resume offensive operations, the cavalry commander had formulated a plan of action. Before leaving his headquarters near Chancellorsville for the front, he ordered Gregg to advance his Second Division along the Catharpin Road to Todd's Tavern and to reestablish a position west of the tavern. During his advance Gregg dropped off Brig. Gen. Henry E. Davies's brigade in the vicinity of Piney Branch Church to reconnoiter the road leading south from there. Members of Col. J. Irvin Gregg's brigade had picketed this area the preceding night, and they now rejoined their regiments and rode toward the tavern.[9] The reserve brigade under Gibbs arrived at the Brock Road and reported to Sheridan at approximately 2:00 P.M. Sheridan ordered the brigade down the road with Devin's troopers following. Custer's brigade was retained at the intersection and picketed north toward the left of the infantry line. As Gibbs's men moved south, they raised clouds of dust from the dry road.[10]

Fitz Lee had been at Todd's Tavern all morning. By about 11:30 A.M. he had become aware that a Federal cavalry force was located north of his position, and he later learned of Gregg's approach from the east. His two brigades were stationed at the tavern and down the Brock Road in the direction of Spotsylvania Court House. He knew that Stuart was with Brig. Gen. Thomas L. Rosser's depleted brigade on the Catharpin Road near Corbin's Bridge. Realizing the odds against him, Lee, sometime before 1:00 P.M., retired his force down the Brock Road approximately two miles from the tavern to a good defensive position where fieldworks had been constructed earlier. Along the way, Brig. Gen. Lunsford L. Lomax dropped off some skirmishers approximately one mile from the tavern, where some light fieldworks had been thrown up on 5 May.[11]

Action on the Catharpin Road

J. Irvin Gregg's brigade arrived at Todd's Tavern shortly after noon. It encountered Confederate cavalry pickets behind barricades who conducted a brief resistance and then retired west on the Catharpin Road across a small stream and disappeared into some woods that began approximately one mile west of the tavern.[12] These pickets were from Rosser's brigade. Most of this brigade was positioned a mile or so east of Corbin's Bridge awaiting the Federal advance. Company A of the Thirty-fifth Virginia Battalion was at the bridge.[13]

Gregg left his First Maine[14] and Sixteenth Pennsylvania[15] regiments at the tavern as a reserve. The remainder of the brigade, the Second, Fourth, and Eighth Pennsylvania and the Tenth New York regiments advanced west on the Catharpin Road. It is difficult to determine from the available evidence the sequence of events in the ensuing encounter. Apparently the two dismounted cavalry forces became engaged in the woods on both sides of the road between one mile west of the tavern and Corbin's Bridge. At one time the Federal line wavered, and Colonel Gregg appeared among the front line troopers and steadied the men.[16] The Eighth Pennsylvania reported driving Confederate skirmishers across the Po River.[17] Confederate accounts speak of fighting near Corbin's Bridge.[18]

At approximately 3:00 P.M. the Federal line withdrew to a defensive position one-half mile to the west of Todd's Tavern on the western brow of a hill looking down upon the stream and across to the edge of the woods about two hundred yards away, where they had left pickets. The two reserve regiments came forward from the vicinity of the tavern, and the line was formed across the road. Two Napoleons of Lt. Rufus King's Battery A, Fourth United States Regular Artillery, were placed on the line pointed through the openings in the breastworks, which had been hastily constructed from nearby fence rails and posts.

At this time some badly needed Confederate reinforcements arrived at Shady Grove Corner: Wade Hampton brought portions of the brigades of James B. Gordon and Pierce M. B. Young. At approximately 3:00 P.M. Hampton reported to Stuart at Mrs. Rowe's, 1½ miles north of Corbin's Bridge. Stuart sent him back to Shady Grove, where he began to organize his two small brigades with Rosser's into a position near the bridge. This may have been why Gregg's division left that area.

Action on the Brock Road

Meanwhile, Gibbs's reserve brigade, followed by Devin's brigade, had been advancing toward Todd's Tavern from the north. They arrived at the tavern at approximately 3:00 P.M. and were given a short rest, following which Gibbs sent the Sixth Pennsylvania, now only about three hundred troopers, ahead down the Brock Road.[19] Less than a mile from the tavern the Pennsylvanians were racked by a volley from dismounted Confederate skirmishers, invisible in the trees on both sides of the road, who had been advancing toward the tavern. The Federal cavalry fanned out, with one squadron on the right of the road, dismounted because of the dense forest, another squadron on the left of the road, and a third remaining on the road.[20] The advance continued against stiffening opposition, and Gibbs called for more support from the rear. It is possible that Fitz Lee was feeding portions of Lomax's regiments forward at this time.[21]

When Gibbs's request for reinforcements arrived at the tavern, his own regiment, the Nineteenth New York (First New York Dragoons), now commanded by Lt. Col. Thomas Thorp, immediately dismounted and proceeded on the double-quick to the scene of the action. The New Yorkers positioned themselves on the left of the Pennsylvanians in the woods. The Sixth Pennsylvania squadron, which had been in reserve on the road, now joined its sister squadron on the left of the road. All were now dismounted. In the meantime the remainder of the brigade had arrived. The Fifth U.S. took a position on the right of the road, the First U.S. was stationed to the left of the Nineteenth New York, and the Second U.S. remained to the rear of the left

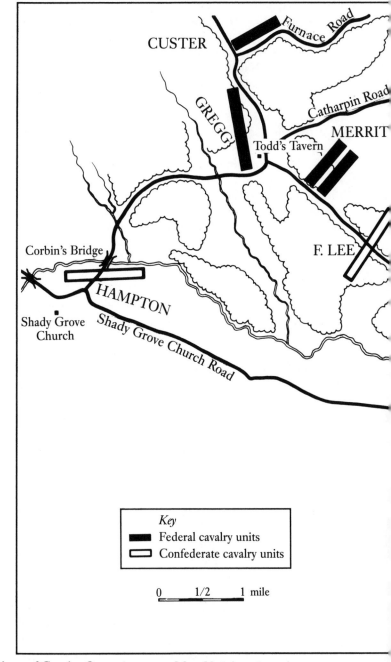

MAP 3-1. Area of Cavalry Operations on 7 May. Unit locations shown are those assumed when the fighting ended at nightfall.

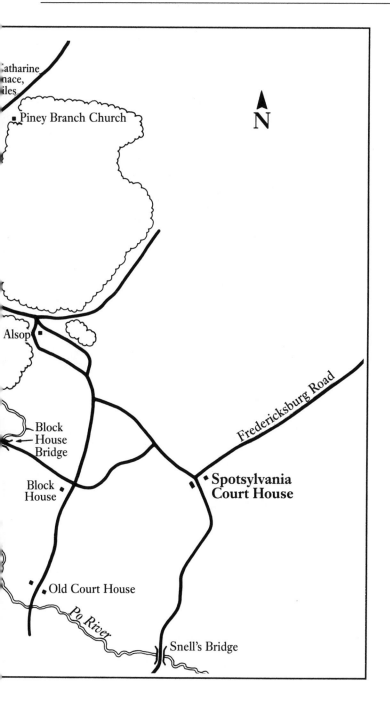

end of the line. Lt. Edward B. Williston's Battery D, Second U.S. Artillery, composed of four Napoleons, was positioned on a ridge to the left rear and began to shell the woods ahead of the Federal line, which once again moved forward. The firing now became more intense.[22]

The two squadrons of the Sixth Pennsylvania and the Nineteenth New York immediately north of the road advanced more rapidly than the remainder of the brigade and soon ran into trouble with Confederate troopers, who had worked around through the thick forest to the Yankee left flank and rear. When the Yankees realized this, they elected to stand and fight rather than run for it, and this decision cost them dearly. Firing Confederates swarmed in from all sides. The Nineteenth sustained nearly ninety casualties that day, most of them in this engagement, including the capture of four officers and over thirty enlisted men.[23] The Sixth suffered approximately thirty casualties, including a captain and a lieutenant who were captured while attempting to move a wounded lieutenant to safety. The Confederates rifled the wounded lieutenant's pockets, removed his boots, and then fell back with their prisoners, leaving him lying on the field.[24]

The remaining regiments of the brigade arrived and extricated their comrades, but the damage had been done. The brigade had experienced the same difficulties as its infantry comrades in the Wilderness area, the result of attempting to maintain a line of battle in heavy woods while under fire.

The advance continued, and Fitz Lee's troopers fell back to the works two miles from the tavern. The fighting here was especially severe. Available accounts are sketchy. Toward the end of the day's fighting the Nineteenth New York and other Federals made a final dismounted charge up to the breastworks and fired over and between the logs before they were repulsed. During this melee the logs were engulfed in flames, and the Confederates withdrew one-half to three-quarters of a mile to another position of log works.[25]

During the fighting at the burning works Col. Charles R. Collins, a former Pennsylvanian who commanded the Fifteenth Virginia Regiment of Lomax's brigade, was killed. A confederate private remembered years after the war that he and a major were ordered by Fitz Lee to retrieve Collins's body. They rode forward, dismounted amid a hail of bullets, and attempted to place the body onto the private's horse but had difficulty lifting it. Finally they gave up, remounted, and dashed for the works. They leaped the works and arrived safely, but the private's horse was hit and killed during the leap over the works.[26]

Devin's brigade was sent forward as support near the end of the day. The Ninth New York reported, joining the two Regular regiments, who promptly retired. The Ninth pressed forward and had begun to cross a field near the burning works when they were greeted by a salvo of canister fire from artillery located in the edge of the trees at the other side of the field. They fell back beyond the field and lay on the ground listening to the canister balls tear through the trees above them.[27] Davies's brigade had been posted in the early afternoon at Piney Branch Church with orders to reconnoiter the road south. Part of the brigade joined Devin's left flank in action at dusk.[28]

The final Confederate position was a short distance southeast of the intersection of the road from Piney Branch Church and the Brock Road. Gibbs sent skirmishers forward to probe the Confederate line, but the major fighting on the Brock Road that day was over. Once again the Federal flank regiments had failed to keep pace with those near the road. With darkness approaching, Gibbs, following orders from Sheridan, withdrew his force in the direction of Todd's Tavern, and Davies withdrew north toward Piney Branch Church. While neither Sheridan, Merritt, Gibbs, nor Davies was aware of it at the time, every yard which the Federal cavalry yielded would be significant in determining the outcome of events on the next morning.

Catharpin Road

During the fighting, Fitz Lee had sent a message asking Rosser to reinforce him on the Brock Road if not engaged. Stuart reported that night to the army commander that, when he had become aware of Fitz Lee's engagement, he had attacked the Federals on the Catharpin Road with Rosser's, Young's, and Gordon's brigades in an attempt to relieve the pressure on Fitz. This attack had occurred at approximately 5:00 P.M.[29]

Between 3:00 and 5:00 P.M. the forces of Gregg and Hampton had engaged in skirmishes at different locations along the road west of the tavern. Just before the Confederate attack of 5:00 P.M., a strong Federal skirmish line had advanced into the trees west of the Union defensive line. The Confederate attack collided with these Yankee skirmishers and sent them scurrying back to their works. Their comrades waited until the Southerners were in the open area between the edge of the woods and the small stream before opening fire. A cavalryman from Maine remembered, "Out of the woods the enemy came, yelling as only they could yell, and they had but fairly got into the open field when cannon and carbines opened a terrible fire, and the rebel yell turned into a whine as they quickly disappeared in the woods. The sight was enough to make the boys laugh, so suddenly did the enemy turn."[30] From the edge of the woods the Confederates fired across the open space between the lines until darkness arrived. This ended the fighting for the day.

Cavalry Dispositions after Dark

With the advent of darkness, J. Irvin Gregg's brigade was withdrawn to Todd's Tavern, where it went into bivouac, leaving a picket force in the defensive works one-half mile to the west. Davies's brigade regrouped at Piney Branch Church, then marched west on the Catharpin Road and camped with Gregg's brigade near the tavern.

Hampton stationed pickets, probably in the eastern edge of the woods across the stream opposite Gregg's pickets. The Jeff Davis Legion picketed Corbin's Bridge. The remainder of Young's brigade camped in the vicinity of Shady Grove Corner. Rosser's men bivouacked north of the bridge in the direction of Mrs. Rowe's.[31]

On the Brock Road, Devin's and Gibbs's brigades retired to some open fields approximately one mile east or southeast of the tavern. Custer remained near the intersection of the Brock and Furnace roads north of the tavern. Fitz Lee returned the brigades of Lomax and Brig. Gen. William C. Wickham to the burned fieldworks two miles from the tavern.

Jeb Stuart, from midday on, had received orders from Robert E. Lee to watch for indications of a movement by Federal infantry in the direction of Spotsylvania Court House via the Brock Road. He was also directed to locate roads by which the Army of Northern Virginia could move expeditiously to Spotsylvania, should it become necessary. Jeb had few days of life remaining in which to serve the Confederacy; his efforts on that day and night and on the succeeding day would be among the most important of his career.

In contrast to Stuart, Sheridan's whereabouts throughout the afternoon and early evening cannot be determined, nor can the extent to which he personally directed the fighting. As a result of the alarms caused by the reports of Colonel Crooks on the Germanna Plank Road beyond the right flank of the infantry line, Meade had sent a message to Sheridan at 2:50 P.M. ordering him to make immediate dispositions for the protection of the trains in that direction. Sheridan may have acknowledged receipt of this order, but he certainly did nothing about it. He seems to have fought his two divisions unencumbered by distractions.[32]

During the first hours of darkness, Stuart reported the results of the action to headquarters and volunteered his opinion that no Federal infantry were in the vicinity of Todd's Tavern, despite the contrary opinions of his subordinates. He also coordinated the establishment of guides for the intended march of the Confederate infantry that night and ensured that his commanders were kept informed of these plans.[33]

Sheridan reported the results of the day's action in messages to Meade, written at 6:15 and 8:00 P.M., that implied complete victory, containing such phrases as "drove them in confusion toward Spotsylvania Court-House."[34]

The second message was written at Todd's Tavern, where he apparently congratulated his two division commanders for their achievements of that day, bade them goodnight, turned, and rode off into the darkness. He did not inform Merritt and Gregg of the intended infantry movement, scheduled to begin in less than half an hour. It is entirely possible that he was still unaware of the movement himself. Members of his staff may not have forwarded the movement order of 3:00 P.M. when it arrived at cavalry headquarters at Alrich's but may have held it there until his return. If so, this staff action would also affect the outcome of operations on the following day.

4 Press On   7–8 May
and Clear
This Road

Throughout the war the extraction of an army from its position facing an enemy force was always a ticklish endeavor. The withdrawing troops were always vulnerable to attack when moving from their line to their marshaling point for the beginning of the march proper. As they pulled back they depended on their pickets to detect and report any advance of enemy forces opposite to their positions. The pickets often sacrificed their lives or freedom when sounding the alarm. If the movement was executed during the hours of darkness, the likelihood of enemy detection was diminished, but the mental strain upon the pickets was increased. Although each man knew that he could usually rely completely upon his fellow pickets, he was also aware that the army was pulling out from behind him and that he would be virtually on his own until he was called in and once again was marching in the ranks. Moreover, physical fatigue was a burden for night pickets, who usually enjoyed little or no rest during the day before their night duty.

Most of the Fifth Corps pickets were exhausted on the night of 7 May. The detail was composed of the Twentieth Maine, Sixteenth Michigan, and 118th Pennsylvania, who had executed the reconnaissance just south of the Orange Turnpike at 10:00 A.M. and had remained in their advanced positions since then.[1] At 6:00 P.M. six companies of the Twenty-second Massachusetts and one company from the Ninth Massachusetts, all from Sweitzer's brigade, were sent forward to augment the others, under the command of Lieutenant Colonel Herring, corps officer of pickets.[2] As darkness settled over this small contingent of troops on their lonely vigil west of the Lacy house, their comrades of the Fifth Corps were taking up the march toward Spotsylvania Court House.

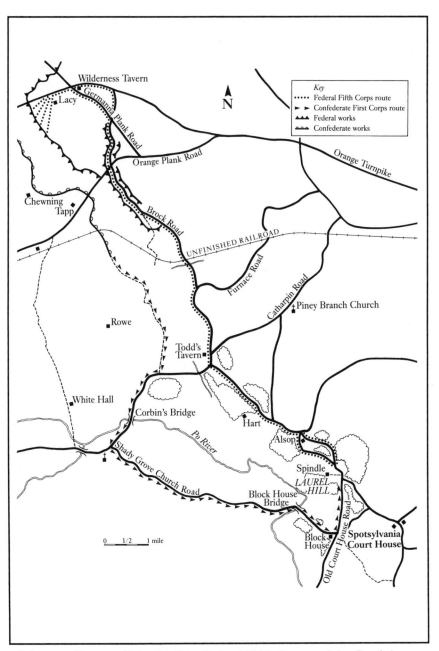

MAP 4-1. Routes of March of the Federal Fifth Corps and the Confederate First Corps on the Night of 7–8 May

Federal Movement—Fifth Corps

The Fifth Corps order of march probably began with Brig. Gen. John C. Robinson's division with two artillery batteries, followed by Griffin's division with two batteries, Brig. Gen. Lysander Cutler's division with two batteries, and Crawford's division with one battery.[3] With the Maryland brigade leading, Robinson's division struck the pike less than one-quarter mile west of the Germanna Plank Road crossing[4] and continued on the pike to the intersection with the Brock Road. Here they turned south.[5]

It is not known why the van of the column did not use the Germanna Plank Road to get to the Brock Road. Perhaps the members of Warren's staff mistakenly chose this route, and Robinson followed them. Warren himself remained in the vicinity of the Lacy house to oversee the withdrawal of his men, a choice of location which would have an effect upon future events.[6] Griffin's division did turn onto the Germanna Plank Road, followed presumably by the remaining two divisions of the corps.[7]

At about the time the head of Robinson's division passed the Wilderness Tavern, cheering was heard far off to the southwest. A Confederate unit near the right of Lee's infantry line had, on a sudden impulse, raised a shouting cheer. The next unit to the left picked it up, and it passed then from Anderson's corps through Hill's and finally ended on Ewell's left. Twice more the cheer was repeated in the same sequence. The troops of the Fifth Corps listened to these sounds as they marched, no doubt wondering about the cause of the cheering.[8]

Grant and Meade, with their staffs, left their headquarters at approximately 9:00 P.M., shortly after the beginning of the Fifth Corps's march.[9] They followed Robinson's route to the Brock Road and reportedly passed the head of the Second Division column immediately after it had turned from the pike onto the Brock Road. These troops, who suddenly realized that this march was to be an advance and not a retreat, loudly cheered their commanding generals as they passed.[10] The headquarters group continued on to Hancock's headquarters near the intersection of the Brock and Orange Plank roads. Here they halted for Meade to confer with Hancock and to await the arrival of the head of the Fifth Corps column before proceeding.

Members of this corps who left written accounts of their participation in the movement universally agreed that it was one of their worst night marches during the war. There had been no rain for days, and the roads were dusty. The night was very dark, with stars visible but no moon. The columns moved along in stops and starts, the stops never being long enough for the exhausted infantrymen to get any restful sleep. Some fell asleep while standing, leaning on their muskets, and a few claimed to have dozed while marching.

Sometime during the march a disturbance arose near the head of Griffin's division, and the men farther back in the line heard the sound of pounding hooves. Soon they could dimly see the forms of men ahead leaping or being driven off of the road into the ditches. The culprit was a driverless runaway artillery team, whose legs and sides were being lashed by their chain traces, with the resulting pain and noise frightening them into increased speed in the darkness. Somewhere along the line the horses ran into some fully laden pack mules, who broke loose and followed the runaways at full speed, cutting an even wider swath along the narrow road.

A member of the 140th New York Regiment of Ayres's brigade, who had been knocked down, rolled on, and trampled in the ditch before the horses had even passed his position, remembered that most of his nearby comrades, after realizing what had happened, stood perfectly still by common consent and listened. They could hear pandemonium and confused shouts receding for about a mile. Many of the soldiers had cocked their muskets at the first sound of trouble, but not a shot was fired along the entire line. This was fortunate considering the exhausted mental and physical condition of the men and the fact that equally exhausted troops of the Second Corps were sleeping close to the Brock Road.[11]

Col. Charles B. Wainwright, Fifth Corps chief of artillery, had remained behind by Warren's order to ensure that the batteries were removed safely from the battle line and that each assumed its proper place in the column. The colonel said that the last battery did not pull onto the Orange Pike until after midnight and that he personally did not leave the Lacy house until about 1:00 A.M. He tried to pass the marching troops to gain the head of the column where Warren supposedly was, but on the narrow, crowded road, he was unable to bypass the infantrymen.

Wainwright remembered that the speed of the infantry appeared to be not more than one-half mile per hour. Every lighted pipe shone distinctly in the darkness. When the cavalcade of runaway animals approached him near the rear of the column, his horse reared up onto a bank (of which he had been unaware) and fell over backward. Horse and rider were unhurt in the fall, and he managed to hold on to the reins, preventing his mount from joining the runaways. He rode on and, upon entering the Brock Road, noticed Hancock's infantrymen sleeping on both sides of the road. Even the passing of the artillery pieces and caissons within two or three feet of their heads did not rouse the exhausted troops.[12]

Meanwhile, at approximately 10:30 P.M. the head of Robinson's division had approached the Orange Plank Road crossing on the Brock Road and discovered Meade's mounted provost guard blocking the intersection. The column halted, and many of the troops immediately fell asleep. Presumably after waiting for fifteen or twenty minutes with Warren still absent, Robinson or perhaps members of his staff moved forward through the mounted headquarters escort to see about the delay. When the commanding generals realized that their escort was holding up the Fifth Corps, they decided to clear the route by moving forward to Todd's Tavern, approximately 4½ miles ahead. They soon moved off. One wonders whether Grant noticed and tucked away in the back of his mind the fact that Warren was not at the head of his command during this critical movement.[13]

Where and when Warren arrived at the head of his corps are not known. He reported that his troops were delayed at the Orange Plank Road crossing for 1½ hours, which would mean that Robinson's division left that point at about midnight. Perhaps Robinson and the members of Warren's staff decided to wait there for Warren before resuming the march.[14]

As the headquarters contingent rode south, Birney's troops on both sides of the road raised a cheer. After proceeding a little more than a mile, the Federal generals and staffs mistakenly left the Brock Road at a point where it veers left toward the southeast. They missed this turn and continued straight ahead onto a narrow woods road which lay along the ridge formerly occupied by Barlow's division. Barlow had left a considerable number of pickets there when he complied with Hancock's order to close to the right in the afternoon. At that time the refused portion (that part turned toward the flank rather than the front) of the southern end of the line perpendicular to the Brock Road had also been moved a short distance to the north, and many of the troops assigned to Barlow's picket detail here were now sleeping across and on both sides of the narrow road.

With Meade leading, the mounted party was suddenly approached by a soldier who asked the group to halt. Meade, gruffly demanding the man's identity, asked if the man knew who he was. The soldier referred to Meade by name and identified himself. He was the busy Lt. Robert S. Robertson of Miles's staff. His assignment for the night was to monitor the passage of the Fifth Corps along the Brock Road and to notify his superiors when it had passed, so the Second Corps could follow promptly as ordered. He had been commuting between the Brock Road and the ridge road periodically in an effort to remain awake. He told Meade that a few more steps would bring the party among Barlow's sleeping troops and that if they proceeded very much further, they would pass through the picket line and possibly enter that of the enemy. Meade was finally convinced that the group was on the wrong road and asked Robertson to lead them back to the Brock, which he did.[15]

As the mounted column returned to the Brock Road, an incident occurred which may have been what Provost Marshal Marsena Patrick had in mind when he entered in his diary that this night march was one of the most disgraceful rides in which he had ever participated.[16] Presumably after the generals and their staffs had regained the Brock Road, the Third Pennsylvania Cavalry regiment, following them, passed the portion of the Twenty-second New York which had been assigned to the care of the Third after the

Intersection of Orange Turnpike and Germanna Plank Road, looking west, with Wilderness Tavern at left. The Federal Fifth, Sixth, and Ninth corps passed here at the beginning of their marches toward Spotsylvania Court House.
(Mass. MOLLUS Collection, MHI)

panic earlier in the day.[17] Suddenly the Pennsylvanians leaped from their saddles, pulled the New Yorkers from their comparatively fresh horses and new saddles, mounted, and rode off into the darkness. There were a few fist fights on the ground, but before long the victorious veterans were out of sight, and the disgruntled recruits were rounding up the mounts left behind. Soon both detachments were trotting dutifully behind the commanders and their staffs.[18]

Near midnight the group arrived at Todd's Tavern. Here the generals

Segment of the Brock Road immediately south of the Orange Plank Road crossing
(Charles D. Page, *History of the Fourteenth Regiment, Connecticut Vols. Infantry,* p. 236)

discovered the two cavalry brigades of Gregg's division encamped. They were informed that two brigades of Merritt's division were in camp about a mile to the southeast in a field just off of the Brock Road. Meade also surmised, much to his exasperation, that neither division commander had received any orders from Sheridan for support of the army movement now in progress. As has been suggested, it is probable that the two cavalry leaders were still unaware that a move by the army was even being contemplated, let alone that it was currently underway. At 1:00 A.M.[19] Meade personally wrote and signed separate orders to Merritt and Gregg. He ordered Merritt to move down the Brock Road beyond Spotsylvania Court House, clearing the road for the Fifth Corps, which would be following to occupy that area. He was to position a brigade 1½ miles west of the courthouse at the Block House, where Shady Grove Church and Old Court House roads intersected. In addition, he was to picket all of the roads approaching Spotsylvania and to use his other two brigades for the protection of the trains in the general direction of Alrich's, north of the Ni River.[20] Meade ordered Gregg to advance his two brigades westward to Corbin's Bridge and to watch the roads to the north in the direction of Parker's Store on the Orange Plank Road. When the Second Corps of infantry arrived at Todd's Tavern, he was to position a force on the Brock Road north of the tavern to watch for any

Todd's Tavern
(Mass. MOLLUS Collection, MHI)

Confederates who might have followed Hancock from the Wilderness battle-field.[21] At 1:00 A.M. Meade also wrote a message to Sheridan. Having found Gregg's and Merritt's divisions at Todd's Tavern without orders and in the way of the approaching Fifth Corps and having no time available for consultation, Meade had issued certain orders (he sent copies) which Sheridan could modify after the infantry corps had arrived at their destinations.[22]

Coincidently Sheridan was also composing orders at this time. The contents of only one order, to Gregg, are known. It required Gregg's division, followed by Merritt's, to move west on the Catharpin Road across Corbin's Bridge to Shady Grove Church. At that point Merritt would take the lead, moving east and taking a position at the Block House. Gregg was to follow and to assume a position near the bridge over the Po River (which will henceforth be designated Block House bridge). Wilson's division was to move from Alrich's via J. Alsop's and the Fredericksburg Road through Spotsylvania Court House south to Snell's Bridge over the Po River. Each of these three movements was to begin at 5:00 A.M. The final sentence of the order read, "The infantry march to Spotsylvania Court-House to-night," meaning apparently the night of the seventh.[23]

Whether Gregg and Merritt received copies of these orders during the night is not known. It makes little difference, however, because by the time at

Spotsylvania Court House, the Union goal
(Mass. MOLLUS Collection, MHI)

which the orders would have been delivered to them, the cavalrymen were already operating under Meade's direction and had ordered their exhausted troopers roused.

Confederate Movement—First Corps

It is difficult to reconstruct the sequence of preparation for and execution of Anderson's movement toward Spotsylvania Court House. Available accounts are largely incomplete or contradictory, and Anderson's memory was unreliable.[24]

In a message marked 7:00 P.M. Lee informed Ewell that he had directed Anderson to start for Spotsylvania as soon as he could withdraw his First Corps from its present position. The message implies that Anderson had been granted some latitude as to when to start, so long as it was no later than 3:00 A.M.[25] Lee said that Anderson would proceed by way of either Todd's Tavern or Shady Grove Church as circumstances might determine and that Ewell should prepare his command to follow in case the Federals were discovered to be moving in that direction or any other Yankee change of position rendered it advisable. Lee added that his headquarters that night would be at Parker's Store on the Orange Plank Road.[26]

Also at 7:00 P.M. Lee sent a message to Stuart requesting that a guide be made available at Shady Grove for General Anderson's use in case that route was selected. Stuart offered to accompany Anderson personally if Lee thought it advisable.[27]

Sometime between 8:00 and 9:00 P.M. Pendleton, accompanied by a staff officer chosen to be the guide, reported to Anderson and briefed him on the road that had been opened to the south from Kershaw's right flank in the morning.[28] The chief of artillery reported that Anderson said the march would begin at 11:00 P.M.[29]

Kershaw's division and that of Maj. Gen. Charles W. Field withdrew quietly from their fieldworks, and, led by Anderson and the guide, they began the march south on the woods road. Some artillery was interspersed among the infantry, but most of the First Corps's guns were conducted by Brig. Gen. Edward Porter Alexander from the park at Parker's Store on a road to the south that intersected the Catharpin Road west of Shady Grove Church.[30] After proceeding a mile or so Anderson began to look for a site where the men could fall out and sleep for a few hours. The trees in all directions appeared to be on fire, however, so the march was continued.[31] Progress was slow in the darkness because of tree stumps along the edge of the road. Some of the felled trees had not been completely removed from the rough road-bed.[32] As he rode, Anderson conferred with his guide, who said that the entire road was in poor condition. After passing clear of the burning area, Anderson again watched for a suitable bivouac site but was unable to find one large enough for both of his divisions. He decided to continue moving until daylight, when he knew that the marching troops would have a better road and a suitable rest area.[33]

Kershaw's leading brigade struck the Catharpin Road and turned to the right toward Shady Grove. The commander of the Jeff Davis Legion of Hampton's division recalled that the head of the column passed Corbin's Bridge at approximately 1:00 A.M.[34] If this time is reasonably accurate, it would appear that Anderson's corps entered the Catharpin Road at a point a little more than a mile from Todd's Tavern. At Shady Grove Corner the head of the column turned left toward Spotsylvania Court House, slightly more than seven miles away.[35]

The Confederates marched for two more hours, until the first light of dawn became visible through the treetops ahead of them. Soon Anderson ordered a halt, and the grateful men of Kershaw's division fell out of ranks on both sides of the road. They were just west of the Block House Bridge, which crossed the Po River approximately three miles from Spotsylvania. There Alexander joined them with the remainder of the corps artillery.[36] Field's division was strung out behind, probably as far as Shady Grove. As Kershaw's troops prepared to search for firewood or to find a soft place to sleep, they could hear firing off to the north.

Federal Infantry Arrives at Todd's Tavern

Warren, riding in advance of his corps, reportedly arrived at Todd's Tavern at 1:00 A.M. Here the headquarters escort and provost marshal's trains again blocked the road.[37] While they were being moved, Warren conferred with Meade and was informed of Merritt's orders to precede the infantry on the Brock Road to Spotsylvania Court House. Ordering Robinson to follow with his division, Warren rode with his staff farther down the Brock Road to learn how Merritt's troopers were progressing.

About a mile and a half from the tavern, they arrived at Merritt's headquarters at 3:00 A.M. to discover that the cavalrymen were just mounting and starting out on their assignment. Even though Merritt's men were undoubtedly exhausted from having fought on foot for four or five hours the previous afternoon, this still appears to have been a rather slow response to Meade's order, which Merritt should have received not much later than 2:00 A.M. At 3:30 A.M. the van of Robinson's division arrived near Merritt's headquarters, and Warren ordered Robinson to rest the men there while the cavalry moved ahead on the road. Robinson's men gratefully collapsed along the sides of the road and were soon asleep.[38]

Meanwhile, Colonel Wainwright had been able to pass some of the infantry marching on the Brock Road just south of the Orange Plank Road crossing, and at earliest light (4:00–4:30 A.M.), he came upon Griffin's halted division. Ayres's entire brigade was lying on the ground. Moving ahead, Wainwright discovered the cause for the delay. Just south of the point at which the bed of the unfinished railroad crossed the Brock Road, a small stream named Poplar Run also crossed the road. Wainwright later said that the water was only one inch deep, but Griffin's men were falling out of ranks and picking their way across the run. Wainwright passed the head of this division and rode the final two miles to Todd's Tavern in good time, passing few troops on the way.[39] At the tavern he found all headquarters staff members asleep. He probably had not been told the reason for the army's movement, but he understood that a night march was usually an attempt to gain a location before the enemy did. From what he had seen since leaving the Lacy house, Union officers were not pushing themselves very strenuously. He awakened Meade's assistant adjutant general, Brig. Gen. Seth Williams, and voiced his concern for the slow pace of Griffin's division and the remainder of the corps. He then continued down the Brock Road to join Warren. On the way he passed Robinson's division sleeping along the road and upon arrival was exasperated to find Warren and his staff eating breakfast, still waiting for the cavalry to clear the road to the courthouse. Carbine firing could now be heard in that direction.[40]

The troopers of Merritt's two brigades soon encountered opposition. Merritt's own brigade, temporarily commanded by Colonel Gibbs, led the advance, followed by Devin's. The depleted Nineteenth New York and Sixth Pennsylvania regiments, in the advance on foot, soon came upon trees across the road, felled by Fitz Lee's men during the night. As they tried to remove these obstructions, they were fired upon by a strong picket force from Lomax's brigade.[41] The three United States Regular regiments were sent forward dismounted by Gibbs to assist the volunteers, and shortly thereafter the Ninth New York and Seventeenth Pennsylvania of Devin's brigade advanced and took positions on both flanks of Gibbs's line. The rate of advance remained extremely slow.[42] Until dawn, the fighting consisted primarily of firing back at muzzle flashes in the dark woods, always an ugly, unpleasant mode of combat.[43]

At 5:00 A.M. Warren told army headquarters what he knew of the situation along the road. He reported that Robinson's division had closed up in mass and was resting and estimated that the cavalry engagement was taking place approximately one mile down the road from his position.[44]

At 6:00 A.M. Merritt suggested to Warren that infantry could probably make better progress in this situation than could cavalry. Warren agreed and ordered Robinson to rouse his men and to start them moving again. Apparently, Col. Richard Coulter's brigade assumed the lead with the Twelfth Massachusetts and Eighty-third New York in advance. After proceeding a short distance, the lead regiments were met by Sheridan, who ordered them to deploy on both sides of the road. When a regimental adjutant asked by whose orders the infantrymen were to comply, the cavalryman raised the brim of his hat and answered merely "Sheridan." He then briefed the regimental commanders, biting off every sentence with the word "Quick!" This was the Fifth Corps's initial encounter with the chief of cavalry; it would not be the last. Continuing down the road, the van of Robinson's column arrived in the rear of Merritt's skirmish line, and the cavalrymen gave up the road to the infantrymen at the Hart farm.[45]

Col. Peter Lyle's brigade now assumed the lead, with skirmishers from the Thirteenth and Thirty-ninth Massachusetts regiments in advance.[46] Lomax's cavalrymen retired from a wooded rise to another about a half mile farther on, just to the northwest of the intersection of the road from Piney Branch Church and the Brock Road. Here the Southerners made a brief stand, supported by Capt. Philip P. Johnston's four-gun battery of Maj. James Breathed's battalion of horse artillery. As the Federals started up the rise, the Confederates fired a volley and retired from sight. When the Yankee skirmishers reached the position which the Rebs had just vacated, they paused to gain their breath and to permit the remainder of the division to close up to some degree.[47]

The Confederate troopers and their battery entered the clearing of the

Alsop farm. On a slight eminence along the road, Fitz Lee detached one section of Johnston's battery and a few dismounted skirmishers to delay the Federal advance so the remainder of Lomax's force could retire to the next position. Lee and Breathed remained near the guns. As the head of the Federal advance came into view, the guns fired. Lee reported that several salvos produced the desired effect of throwing the Yankee column into disorder and causing it to deploy into line of battle.[48]

The skirmishers of the Thirteenth Massachusetts, now in the lead and carrying the regimental colors, broke into a run at the first fire in an attempt to capture the two guns. A shot broke the flagstaff and wounded the color-bearer, but the advance continued. The dismounted Confederate skirmishers in front of the guns disappeared. Lee ordered Breathed to retire the guns. The major sent one to the rear but kept the other in action. Soon the battery commander was hit, and the Yankees were shouting for the battery to surrender. Breathed ordered the battery to limber up and retire. By the time it began to withdraw, only one driver remained on horseback, the others having fled or been shot. A volley shattered this last driver's arm. Breathed leaped from his own mount onto one of the wheel horses, but a lead horse went down thrashing, so he dismounted and cut the dying horse loose. Before he could remount, another horse was hit and Breathed also cut it loose. Remounting the wheel horse, he turned the gun and drove it away to safety.[49]

Major Breathed's heroic exploit was verified in postwar writings by members of the Thirteenth Massachusetts who witnessed it. One of these Yankee veterans, when asked after the war to contribute an experience for a collection of personal war sketches, chose this episode on the Brock Road. He referred to the Rebel who had saved the artillery piece as the bravest man whom he had seen during his three years of service.[50]

By this time most of Lyle's brigade had arrived at the intersection northwest of the Alsop farm buildings. The remaining two brigades of the division were not yet in sight. Robinson and Lyle led the First Brigade along the left-hand fork past the Alsop buildings. They were accompanied by the Fourth Maryland Regiment, which had been a part of the advanced skirmish line and had become separated from its parent Third Brigade.

At about this time Warren informed Meade of Robinson's progress with Lyle's brigade at the head of the advance. He said that he was following closely with columns of infantry and artillery. "If there is nothing but cavalry, we shall scarcely halt, if our troops can be made to move, but they are exceedingly hesitating, I think. General Robinson's orders are to use only the bayonet, and carry every battery the enemy shows."[51]

After following the left-hand fork for about half a mile, the head of Lyle's brigade entered a forested area. After a quarter mile the roadway turned to the south, and those in the lead could see the light of a clearing ahead. Robinson halted the head of the brigade just short of the point where the forks rejoined, at the southern edge of the trees. Looking down the road and across the clearing, the general saw an open space extending south for about four hundred yards and ending at a slight ridge. This was Laurel Hill. On a lower rise of ground, one-half to two-thirds of the way across the clearing, was the Spindle cabin. On Laurel Hill, Robinson could see some troops busily constructing fieldworks. These were Fitz Lee's cavalrymen.

At that time Warren rode up and urged Robinson to keep moving, as the orders were to go to Spotsylvania Court House. Robinson pleaded for a little time to enable the remaining two brigades to catch up. Warren reluctantly acceded to the delay. The strength of Lyle's brigade had been greatly reduced, many of the men having fallen out of ranks because of fatigue and even sunstroke, although it was only 8:00 or 8:30 A.M. Among the victims of the sun's rays was Col. Phineas S. Davis, commanding the Thirty-ninth Massachusetts. Lt. Col. Charles L. Peirson assumed command of the regiment. The troops were permitted a short rest and were ordered to stack their knapsacks.[52]

Confederate Action

When Fitz Lee realized that his troopers faced Federal infantry on the Brock Road, he knew he needed help. He notified Stuart, who was probably on the Old Court House Road north of the Block House. Stuart composed a dispatch addressed to either Lee or Longstreet requesting artillery support as soon as possible, and then he ordered the courier, a youngster from Baltimore named Pegram, to ride west on the Shady Grove Road, where he would eventually meet Anderson. Pegram saluted and galloped away in a cloud of dust.[53]

After a much-needed rest of an hour or more, Anderson ordered his troops to fall in for the final leg of the march to Spotsylvania. Maj. John C. Haskell and his artillery battalion of three batteries were resting a short distance in advance of Kershaw's infantrymen.[54] As the gunners waited for some of the infantry to pass before taking the road, Haskell saw the courier Pegram approaching rapidly. Pegram, who was acquainted with Haskell, stopped and showed him the unsealed message. After reading the contents Haskell endorsed upon the message that he was going ahead with his guns immediately. He probably told Pegram where he could find Anderson. The major then moved with two batteries of his battalion rapidly across the Block House bridge over the Po and up the hill to the Block House, where he met an anxious Stuart, who turned the column to the left and conducted it north toward the intersection of Brock Road and Old Court House Road at the Spindle farm.[55]

Pegram found Anderson and delivered the message. As Anderson digested

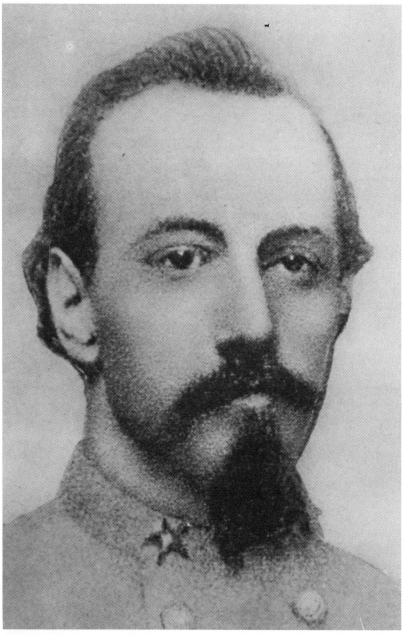

James Breathed
(National Archives)

its contents, he realized that the situation on this warm Sunday morning was becoming complicated. His orders were to take his corps to Spotsylvania. He could tell that Stuart's cavalrymen were engaged with a Federal force somewhere to the north of his own position at the bridge. As he led his command away from its rest area, he was doubtless pondering his priorities.

When the head of the infantry column arrived at the Old Court House Road intersection, between 7:00 and 8:00 A.M., Anderson halted the movement. Almost immediately a rider approached from the north, a hatless and shoeless elderly gentleman who breathlessly explained that Federal infantry were forming for an assault against Stuart's cavalry to the north on the Brock Road and that support was needed immediately if the position there was to be maintained.[56] Anderson ordered Kershaw to detach two brigades to Stuart's support. Kershaw selected his own former South Carolina brigade, now commanded by Col. John W. Henegan, and Brig. Gen. Benjamin G. Humphreys's four regiments of Mississippians and sent them up the road on the double-quick with orders to report to Stuart.[57]

Scarcely had these troops disappeared when another cavalry courier galloped up to the intersection from the east. He had been sent by Fitz Lee and reported that a force of Federal cavalry had been spotted approaching Spotsylvania from the east on the Fredericksburg Road. The Third Virginia Cavalry Regiment from Wickham's brigade had been sent to delay the Yankees but could not be expected to hold them for very long.[58] The Yankee horsemen were Wilson's Third Division, obeying Sheridan's instructions to proceed to Spotsylvania Court House and Snell's Bridge to the south.[59] Anderson ordered Kershaw to move with the brigades of Brig. Gen. William T. Wofford and Brig. Gen. Goode Bryan to Spotsylvania and sent an order back to Field to bring his division forward with all possible speed.[60] Before Kershaw had marched very far with his two brigades, he received the information that the badly outnumbered Third Virginia Regiment of Col. William R. Carter had been driven out of the village by Wilson's First Brigade, supported by the Second.[61] Kershaw decided to approach the village from the south and marched to the east to intercept the road from Snell's Bridge.[62]

Meanwhile, the brigades of Henegan and Humphreys had moved perhaps three-quarters of a mile north from the Block House when they met a cavalryman who urged them to hurry forward to some piles of fence rails. Rushing up a slight rise, the infantrymen met Stuart, who placed them into position on the cavalry's line, which crossed the Old Court House Road at its intersection with the Brock.[63]

The Third South Carolina took its post to the east of the road among some small pine trees, which the infantrymen immediately cut down to form abatis on the descending slope in their front. To their left, across the road and one hundred yards or more to the rear along a line of trees, were the remaining regiments of Henegan's brigade, beginning with the Second South Carolina along the edge of the road. Humphreys's brigade moved into the woods to the right of the Third South Carolina. Stuart withdrew some of the cavalrymen and sent them to Fitz Lee in the direction of Spotsylvania. The remainder he placed on the flank of Henegan's men. Haskell's two batteries, which had arrived earlier, may have already been engaged in this general area, but this is uncertain.[64]

Initial Infantry Engagement—Laurel Hill

Meanwhile, Warren had become impatient after waiting for perhaps five or ten minutes and had ordered Robinson to continue the advance with the available troops, Lyle's five regiments and the Fourth Maryland. All of these units were reduced in strength because of the casualties in the Wilderness, straggling during the night march, and the action since daylight.[65] Lyle, who assumed he was still facing only dismounted cavalrymen, formed his men into columns of regiments and started them forward on the left side of the road. The slight rise of ground in front of the Confederate works on the east side of the road was not as pronounced as on the west. Along the top of the rise a rail fence extended from the road almost to the trees at the eastern edge of the clearing. This portion of the clearing contained several small gullies that made it difficult for the advancing Yankees to maintain formation.[66] The soldiers of the Third South Carolina directly in front of Lyle's men withheld their fire until the Federals had nearly reached the rail fence. Some of the Carolinians became shaky as Lyle's men first came out of the trees, but Stuart held them to their work. Their opening volley was followed almost immediately by one from their sister regiment, the Second South Carolina, across the road and to their rear. These unexpected volleys of rifled musket fire staggered the exhausted Unionists, many of whom immediately retreated in disorder to the shelter of the trees in the rear. However, a portion of the brigade led by Lieutenant Colonel Peirson scaled the fence and advanced to the foot of the hill, where they were partially protected by the slope of the hill and the felled pine trees. They lay there panting with exhaustion.[67]

After ordering Robinson to move on, Warren rode back to the vicinity of the Alsop house to await the arrival of the two remaining brigades of his Second Division. The house sat on a slight hill that provided good visibility to the south. Soon the brigades of Cols. Richard Coulter and Andrew W. Denison marched into view. Warren exhorted them to hurry as they passed him. When the Seventh Maryland marched by, he exclaimed crisply, "Never mind cannon! Never mind bullets! Press on and clear this road. It's the only way to get your rations." The brigades continued to the edge of the woods, where Robinson halted them and formed them for an assault, putting the Marylanders on the right of the road in column by regiments, with the First and Eighth in front of the Seventh.[68] Capt. Augustus P. Martin's Third Massachusetts Battery of Napoleons, which had accompanied the infantry this far, took a position to the right of the Marylanders and fired upon the Confederate position. Lt. George Breck's Battery L, First New York Artillery, was placed in position back on the high ground in the vicinity of the Alsop house.[69]

Robinson and Denison, both mounted, led the movement forward from the right front of the Maryland brigade. Martin's gunners had time for only a few ineffective shots. Col. Charles E. Phelps, commanding the Seventh Maryland Regiment, remembered that his troops were so numb with fatigue that they did not realize that an advance was being contemplated until the command, "Battalions Forward, Guide Center, March," was given. Nonetheless, the three regiments of the brigade, about seven hundred strong, immediately stepped off with a hearty cheer. Time had not allowed the formation of a line of skirmishers to precede the brigade. Perhaps Coulter's brigade and some of Lyle's brigade (which had been retreating) advanced on the left of the Marylanders.[70]

Confederate artillery, probably Haskell's, fired from the left front. The South Carolina regiments west of the road also opened fire on the advancing Yankees. The Marylanders in the front rank soon halted and returned the fire. (If the assault had been less hurried, the men would have been briefed to keep moving and not to open fire until ordered.) The inevitable delay occurred within Denison's brigade in the middle of the clearing when the front rank halted to reload while the men behind pushed forward to fire. Soon the ranks and regiments commingled. As Henegan's troops increased the rate of their fire, the Yankee casualty list grew. The advance continued.[71]

Approximately fifty yards from the works, both Robinson and Denison were shot from their horses, Robinson hit in the left knee and Denison in the right arm. (The wounds would cost each man his limb.) With their fall, many of the men behind began to waver. Phelps assumed command of the advance. Pushing his horse to the front, he shouted to the men to hold their fire and to double-quick forward. He moved ahead, pointing his sword at the works. Suddenly he and his horse went down. Capt. Ephraim F. Anderson, commanding Company I of the Seventh Maryland, had been following Phelps closely. He tried unsuccessfully to drag the colonel from under his dying horse. Giving up, the captain took a step or two forward and was struck simultaneously by three balls.[72] This was the end of the advance. The Marylanders turned and fled across the clearing.[73]

Warren personally rallied the remnants of the brigade by seizing the ragged regimental flag of the Thirteenth Massachusetts of Lyle's brigade from the grasp of its bearer and using it as a rallying point.[74]

Every soldier assigned to the honorable duty of color guard in the three Maryland regiments had been either killed or wounded. Every mounted officer had been hit, including the division and brigade commanders.[75] Total casualties of the brigade for the day were 1 officer and 15 men killed, 7 officers and 110 men wounded, and 6 officers and 53 men missing for a total of 192.[76]

No detailed account describing the participation of Coulter's brigade has been found. A member of the Eighty-eighth Pennsylvania recorded that his brigade advanced along one side of the road to a position near the Confederate works, was outflanked, and retired along the road, which the Confederates were raking with artillery fire. This brigade reported a total loss of 231 for operations on 8 May.[77]

Because of the devastating losses in field officers in the Wilderness and at Laurel Hill on 8 May, Robinson's division was disbanded the following morning. Its First Brigade was attached to the Fourth Division and its Second Brigade to the Third Division. Warren retained the Maryland brigade as an independent command, operating under his direct orders, a decision which implied that its members had behaved poorly in the day's action.[78] During the next week Warren or perhaps some members of his staff were heard to utter disparaging remarks about the Marylanders. An embittered major in the Eighth Regiment asked Warren about these insults but received only an evasive reply.[79]

The men from Lyle's brigade who had been resting at the foot of the slope in front of the Third South Carolina had watched the repulse of the Marylanders. Nevertheless, they were willing to attempt to take the works before them when their officers insisted. As they rose to their feet and prepared to charge up the slope, they heard a shout behind them. Looking back, they saw a body of Confederate infantry emerging from the trees. This was Humphreys's Mississippi brigade. Realizing their perilous situation, the Federals retreated as fast as the exhausted men were able.[80]

Colonel Peirson was limping slowly along using his sword as a cane when he was struck in the shoulder by the three pellets of a buck and ball load. He stood helplessly in the open clearing until Isaac H. Mitchell, Company A, of the colonel's regiment, placed him upon his shoulder and carried him through the woods to the rear. As the two men waited for a stretcher to be brought forward, Robinson was carried by on his way to a field hospital where his leg was later amputated. Mitchell noticed that the general had been wounded and was "saying things."[81] Unfortunately the soldier chose not to record the object of Robinson's wrath, be it the Confederate who had shot him, the troops of his division who had stampeded to the rear, the superior officers who had insisted upon hurrying the assault without preparation, or perhaps army life in general. (Thirty-one years later Robinson would receive a Medal of Honor from the War Department for conspicuous gallantry at Laurel Hill.) Most of the men with Peirson retreated northwest. Some crossed the road and joined the Marylanders in the woods where the assault had begun.[82]

Casualty figures for Lyle's brigade are incomplete. The Thirty-ninth Massachusetts lost 131 and the Sixteenth Maine more than 50. Like their comrades from Maryland, the men of the color guard suffered severely, but no banners were lost.[83]

The Mississippians pursued the Yankees a short distance across the clearing but soon retired into the woods whence they had appeared. Confederate losses in this engagement were minimal, with the possible exception of Haskell's two batteries.

Arrival of the Remainder of the Fifth Corps

Sometime shortly after sunrise Griffin's division caught up with Robinson's on the march. Arriving at the fork in the road northwest of the Alsop buildings, the column took the right-hand fork, with Bartlett's brigade leading, followed by Sweitzer's and Ayres's. The troops soon learned that Confederate cavalrymen were making a stand ahead. Lt. Col. Freeman Conner, commanding the Forty-fourth New York, sent his adjutant to ask Bartlett whether the men could not stack their knapsacks before becoming engaged. The brigadier replied, "No, tell Colonel Conner there is no force in front but cavalry and to march right up the road in fours."[84] Likewise, a captain in the First Michigan, which was reduced to a strength of 124 officers and men, asked a major if some of the men could fall out of ranks at a spring to refill their canteens. Griffin, who was nearby, heard the request and told the major to keep his men in ranks, because there were only a few cavalry to be brushed out of the way before his troops could have breakfast.[85]

Half-way along the right-hand fork, open fields to the south revealed the Confederate position on Laurel Hill nearly half a mile away. The Southerners opened fire upon the head of the Yankee column with artillery and musketry, so Bartlett's men assumed battle formation, with the Forty-fourth New York and Eighty-third Pennsylvania constituting the front line and the First Michigan and Eighteenth Massachusetts the second. The remaining three regiments of the brigade had not yet returned from their picket assignment in the Wilderness. Two sections of Breck's battery opened fire on the Confederate position. As the troops of the four Federal regiments swung around to face the south, they received questionable encouragement from one of Bartlett's aides, who urged them to hurry or they would not get any shooting.[86]

The Federals advanced approximately one-quarter mile before receiving hostile fire. They were too tired to run or to yell. Somewhere along the way they were ordered to fix bayonets. They passed through a grove of trees on the northern edge of the Spindle farm clearing and entered the open area just as the Maryland brigade was beginning its advance a few hundred yards to the left of their position.[87]

Starting across the clearing, the Eighty-third Pennsylvania received scattered musket fire from Southern skirmishers located in some trees to the right. A company was detached to face in that direction. Another enemy skirmish line was sighted on the crest of a slight rise directly ahead of the Yankees. These Southerners rose and fired one volley before retiring to the main line in the edge of the trees, from which they fired heavily as the Federals followed over the crest. Dashing forward, the Yankees abruptly realized that the enemy force consisted of infantry behind crude breastworks. Some of the Pennsylvanians went over the works and used their bayonets. A few of the Confederates attempted to withdraw, but their officers forced them back with the points of their swords.[88]

The Forty-fourth New York was stopped approximately twenty yards from the works by fallen logs and brush entanglements. They stood and fired at this close range, with officers using their pistols. Soon they were flanked on their left by some Southerners who may have been pursuing the retreating Marylanders across the clearing. The Pennsylvanians were taking heavy losses when suddenly the formations of the two regiments dissolved, and the men retreated rapidly across the clearing and continued nearly to their starting point before halting. Losses were approximately 150 in the Eighty-third, including over 50 killed, and a total of 81 in the Forty-fourth, in which no field officer remained and a captain assumed command. The color guards of both units were nearly obliterated. During the withdrawal the last member of the Eighty-third's color guard, carrying the regimental flag, was wounded. Lying on the ground, he asked a passing New Yorker to take the emblem and deliver it safely to its regiment. This was done.[89]

The First Michigan may have advanced as far as the two leading regiments. It claimed ninety-eight casualties, which left the strength of the command at twenty-seven officers and men. The Eighteenth Massachusetts sustained a loss of ten.[90]

At the time when Bartlett's men trudged from the right-hand fork toward the south, Sweitzer's brigade, behind them, was ordered to follow in line of battle. The Thirty-second Massachusetts, however, was immediately detached to support Capt. Charles A. Philips's Fifth Massachusetts Battery of three-inch rifles near the Alsop house.[91] The five present companies of the

Twenty-second Massachusetts, eighty muskets, were detailed to support Martin's battery which was supporting the Maryland brigade's attack from the right. Col. William S. Tilden, commanding the Twenty-second, and his men took a position on a small knoll to the right of Martin's Napoleons and were soon reinforced by the Fourth Michigan Regiment of their brigade.[92]

Ayres's brigade was halted at a relatively low point along the right-hand fork, at the head of a ravine that led south-southwest and contained a small tributary of the Po River. A member of the 140th New York remembered that, after two or three minutes, the regimental commander shouted to his men to follow him and dashed ahead on horseback. His men gamely followed, still carrying their knapsacks and still in a column of four abreast. The exhausted troops soon began to suffer casualties. Eventually the colonel was shot, and the men became entangled with other rapidly retreating troops of the brigade. The New Yorkers, having suffered fifty-five casualties, fell back until Ayres rallied them near the road at the head of the ravine.[93]

When the Marylanders and Bartlett's men retreated across the clearing, they were pursued by some of Kershaw's troops. Captain Martin notified either Sweitzer or Griffin that he feared he would lose his weakly supported battery. The five companies of the Twenty-second Massachusetts were moved closer to the guns as he limbered up. The Fourth Michigan was also close by. These two regiments opened fire upon the Confederates who were pursuing Bartlett's men. The demoralized First Michigan and Eighteenth Massachusetts came running back through their ranks but soon rallied and helped to repel the Southerners.[94]

Suddenly, Humphreys's Mississippians reappeared in a flank attack from the trees east of the Brock Road, forcing Robinson's demoralized troops to retreat up the eastern fork as far as the Alsop house. Martin's battery was moving rapidly up the western fork when the commander was wounded. Martin was replaced by Lt. Aaron F. Walcott, who posted the guns on a knoll about halfway back to the house. The Federal regiments that had been firing across the clearing at Henegan's men broke to their right rear. Most of them went all the way back to the head of the ravine, where by this time Ayres's brigade had assumed a defensive position. Griffin, Bartlett, and Ayres all exerted strenuous efforts and finally halted the retreat.[95]

All of this action on the Spindle farm probably occurred between 8:30 and 9:45 A.M. At 10:00 A.M. the Third Division of Pennsylvania Reserves arrived at the fork in the road west of the Alsop house, where Warren ordered Crawford to march them down the left-hand fork for one-quarter of a mile and to prepare for action.

Wainwright also arrived at about this time with the remainder of the corps's batteries. (He had stayed behind near Merritt's headquarters and had sent forward batteries as Warren called for them.) Now he posted batteries to command both forks of the road to the southeast and the ravine to the southwest.[96]

It is impossible to determine accurately the time or, in some instances, even the sequence of events there during the next five or six hours. Warren sent a situation report to Meade at 10:15 A.M. in which he described the repulses of Robinson's and Griffin's divisions and the generally poor condition of their men. He also reported that both Crawford's and Cutler's divisions had arrived and were advancing. In addition to expressing his doubts that Longstreet's troops had yet arrived, Meade informed Grant that a division of Sedgwick's had joined Warren.[97] This was three brigades of Wright's division, which had been marching one mile south of Piney Branch Church when a request from Warren for support had reached Wright. Wright had forwarded his troops immediately, without consulting Sedgwick.[98] The New Jersey brigade led the advance of his column. They remembered that Warren met them at the fork near Alsop's in a very excitable state. He demanded the identity of the brigade and the whereabouts of its commander and exclaimed that he needed their services immediately.[99] Warren's agitation could perhaps be attributed to embarrassment that some of Robinson's demoralized troops were drifting to the rear in sight of Wright's men. In addition, Warren might have become edgy and irritable due to the manner in which operations were proceeding on this morning.

After Griffin's men had reformed, a portion of the First Division moved down the right fork as Crawford's Pennsylvanians advanced along the left. Wainwright wrote that the Federals encountered little opposition during this forward movement to the junction of the forks.[100]

Sometime after McCandless's brigade had established a position, members of the Thirteenth Regiment, on the right flank of the brigade, noticed a body of Confederates in front of them, apparently moving to get on the left of Griffin's left brigade. A squad from Company E was sent to outflank the flankers. They were armed with Spencer carbines, but they were outnumbered. Every member of the detail, including the captain, was hit. Simultaneously, a general advance was conducted by the Reserves across the northern portion of the field east of the road and into the trees along its eastern edge. Crawford had been injured by a falling tree limb and did not accompany his troops, who claimed to have driven a Confederate force through a swamp knee-deep in mud and water. McCandless was hit, and the men became disorganized and eventually retired to their starting point sometime after 2:00 P.M.[101]

The Confederates involved may have been Humphreys's troublesome Mississippians. On that Sunday two hundred officers and men of the Seventeenth Mississippi Regiment became cut off and hid in a ravine until darkness permitted them to sneak by a roundabout route to the safety of their lines. Their predicament may have been caused by this temporary advance of McCandless's brigade.[102]

Griffin's division established a line whose left was located at the junction of the forks of the Brock Road. The line extended southwest for approximately six hundred yards. Fifty to one hundred yards beyond the right of the line lay a body of trees that formed the western edge of the Spindle farm clearing. Some Confederates worked their way into this growth of timber and began to harass the right element of Griffin's division. These Southerners were Henegan's infantrymen and possibly some of Lomax's cavalrymen.

The Fifth Corps's Fourth Division, coming to aid Griffin, now arrived one-half mile to the north in the Alsop clearing. This unit had experienced some dramatic command changes as a result of the Wilderness fighting, and was now commanded by Cutler, replacing Brig. Gen. James S. Wadsworth, who had been mortally wounded on 6 May. Command of Cutler's Iron Brigade had been assumed by Col. William W. Robinson, formerly commanding the Seventh Wisconsin of that brigade. Col. Roy Stone had been disabled in an accidental fall on 6 May and had been replaced by Col. Edward S. Bragg, former commander of the Sixth Wisconsin. Brig. Gen. James C. Rice still commanded the Second Brigade.[103]

The division had been permitted to halt at Todd's Tavern and to have a breakfast of sorts. Upon arriving at the Alsop clearing, the troops were permitted to fall out of ranks to prepare coffee. A band near the Eighty-fourth New York Regiment was offering an arrangement of "Hail Columbia" when a Confederate shell burst directly overhead. The musicians and instruments disappeared in a twinkling. (At postwar gatherings the colonel of the Eighty-fourth loved to relate this incident, explaining how shells affect music.)

Suddenly the division was ordered into line, with Rice's brigade leading.[104] Arriving at the northern edge of the clearing, Rice ordered the Fifty-sixth Pennsylvania and Ninety-fifth New York regiments forward to clear Confederate skirmishers from an orchard immediately to the northwest of the Spindle farm house, which by now was burning from artillery fire. When the two units reached the orchard, Rice ordered his remaining three regiments forward to join their comrades. His troops hugged the ground on the northern crest of a slight rise as Confederate musket fire from the trees ahead on Laurel Hill increased in intensity.[105]

Next came the Third Brigade under its new commander, Colonel Bragg, followed by the Iron Brigade under Robinson. As the Pennsylvanians entered the clearing, a Confederate battery directly ahead on Laurel Hill began to fire case shot at them. Southern skirmishers lay in front along the same slight rise which Rice's men were hugging to the left. Bragg's men were in two lines. The front line suddenly swung around to face the woods on the right and began to fire in that direction. The second line closed up on the right, a maneuver which placed its members in the edge of the woods.[106]

The Iron Brigade moved into position on the right of the division, with the Sixth Wisconsin occupying the right of the line. Lt. Col. Rufus R. Dawes dispatched skirmishers on the right flank, who were immediately driven in and who reported that Confederates were moving around the right end of the line unmolested. Suddenly, everything on Cutler's line let go, and the troops came rushing back. Officers rallied them perhaps four or five hundred yards to the rear. The Confederates did not pursue them at this time. Later in the afternoon the Northerners would advance again and occupy a permanent defensive line.[107]

Arrival of Field's Division

These Confederates had been reinforced during the action by two regiments of Law's brigade, of Field's division, which had arrived at the Block House at about 10:00 A.M. The Fifteenth and Forty-eighth Alabama regiments, under the command of Col. William C. Oates, had been detached from their brigade by Stuart and had assisted in the repulse of Bragg's troops and probably Robinson's as well.[108] The remaining three regiments of the brigade were positioned on Henegan's right flank as a support to Humphreys's brigade and the Third South Carolina.[109] Meanwhile, Field led the remaining four brigades of the division east toward the Brock Road and Spotsylvania. Arriving at the Brock Road intersection, Field was informed that the enemy had retired from the village. He turned the column left onto the Brock Road and marched toward Henegan's position, picking up the three regiments of Law's brigade (who were supporting Humphreys) as he passed them. Col. John Bratton's brigade of South Carolinians was dropped out of line immediately to the right of the intersection to buttress Henegan's Third South Carolina Regiment. The remainder of the division marched across the Old Court House Road and then west behind Henegan's position, reaching Henegan's left flank at the end of the fighting with Cutler's division. To the left of Henegan's line, Field posted, from right to left, the brigades of Col. Dudley M. DuBose, General Law, Brig. Gen. George T. Anderson, and Brig. Gen. John Gregg. The left of Gregg's Texas brigade extended nearly as far as the Po River. Arriving at their new position, the troops dug in, using whatever implements were available, including knives, spoons, and canteens.[110]

Yankee Cavalry Capture and Relinquish
Spotsylvania Court House

Wilson's First Brigade, led by the First Connecticut Regiment, charged through the village, easily driving away the few Confederate pickets there. Colonel Carter's Third Virginia was probably positioned across the Brock Road a short distance northwest of the village. A portion of the Yankee brigade dismounted and flanked the Virginians on their left. The Southerners fell back half a mile or so to a wooded position near the junction of the Brock and Shady Grove Church roads. The pursuing Federals, both mounted and dismounted, charged and routed the outnumbered Virginians after a short struggle.[111]

Wilson was now little more than a mile to the right rear of Henegan's position at the intersection of the Brock and Old Court House roads. Forty-one Confederates were captured, from whom Wilson learned of the movement of Anderson's corps during the night and of Warren's engagement ahead on the Spindle farm. He prepared to move McIntosh's troopers forward against Henegan's rear instead of moving south as ordered. One of Wilson's batteries supposedly inflicted casualties among Haskell's gunners. Shortly after McIntosh's brigade started forward, Wilson received the information that a large enemy force was moving north toward Spotsylvania on the road from Snell's Bridge.[112] These were the brigades of Wofford and Bryan, led by Kershaw. Wilson retired to the vicinity of the village and prepared to fight, but he received an order from Sheridan, who had discovered that Wilson's three divisions were rather isolated and, fearing for their safety, recalled them.[113] Wilson led his two brigades back in the direction of Alrich's.

Grant Intends to Continue the Advance

Thus, with the arrival of midday, a lull in the fighting occurred in the area of the Spindle farm and Laurel Hill. From prisoners, Grant and Meade learned that Warren was opposed by only two divisions of Confederate infantry and some dismounted cavalry. Meade, possibly with some prodding from Grant, decided to advance the remaining two divisions of the Sixth Corps to Warren's location. From there the two corps would execute a combined assault against Laurel Hill, with the goals of destroying Anderson's corps and of gaining possession of Spotsylvania Court House.[114]

At 11:30 A.M. Grant composed a situation report to Halleck in which he stated his opinion that the results of the Wilderness fighting had been decidedly favorable to the Federals. He also listed the positions he planned for his troops at the end of the day's movements. Finally, Grant stated his intention to join with Butler as soon as possible and to be prepared at all times to meet any enemy force intervening.[115] It thus appears that the Federal high command still intended to follow the original timetable for movement, after defeating the Confederate corps it faced.

5

Our Advance Is   7–8 May
Now at Spotsylvania
Court House

Movement of the Sixth Corps

The Sixth Corps was scheduled to begin its march at 8:30 P.M. Sedgwick's designated order of march was First Division with one battery, Third Division with six batteries, and Second Division with one battery.[1] An immediate delay was caused by Robinson's Fifth Corps division, which continued across the Germanna Plank Road intersection to the Brock Road turnoff. Oliver Wendell Holmes, Jr., of Russell's brigade staff, stated that despite orders (presumably for his brigade) to move at 8:30 P.M., the move was postponed to 9:30.[2]

Once started, Sedgwick's troops made no better time than Warren's. Wright's division reached Chancellorsville at daylight, perhaps 4:15–4:45 A.M., having taken seven hours to travel approximately 5 ½ miles. Accounts of the march contain no references to the corps trains until the arrival at Chancellorsville, which suggests that the trains arrived, as planned, prior to the infantry. A large group of Confederate prisoners also marched east along the turnpike during the night, guarded by Patrick's infantry contingent.[3]

A private in Capt. John E. Burton's Eleventh New York Battery of the Artillery Reserve left a vivid description of some of the Sixth Corps troops as they marched that night. The artilleryman reported that the infantrymen were angry because they had been ordered to retire from the enemy's front without having been defeated. A sergeant from Vermont, whose face had been nicked by a minie ball, spoke bitterly about the poor manner in which the Union troops had been handled by their officers in the Wilderness fighting. All believed the rumor prevalent in the Sixth Corps that Meade had strongly urged Grant to retire across the Rapidan. No one expressed much confidence in Meade. The troops withheld judgment of Grant until they discovered the destination of that night's march. When the head of the column turned to the right at the Chancellorsville crossroads, the foot soldiers had their answer. They accepted it with relief and with rising spirits.[4]

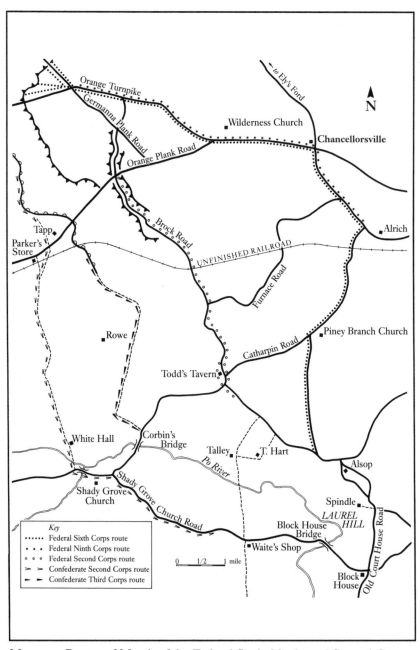

MAP 5-1. Routes of March of the Federal Sixth, Ninth, and Second Corps and the Confederate Second and Third Corps on the Night of 7–8 May

The Second Rhode Island Regiment was assigned to picket duty east of the Germanna Plank Road just before dark. The regiment was ordered to remain in advance and to maintain the appearance of a fighting front as the corps withdrew from the breastworks behind it. The officers were told to attempt to save the regiment but to expect that the unit most likely would be captured. At midnight orders were received to retire, and the men silently moved down the Germanna road until they arrived at the abandoned field-works. There the regimental adjutant was ordered to ride ahead to try to find the Sixth Corps officer of the day. After riding for half a mile, the lieutenant encountered the colonel, and the two officers exchanged greetings after trading challenges in the darkness. They moved off the road, and as they waited for the regiment to come along, the colonel said that he had come very close to shooting the lieutenant. The regiment marched for the remainder of the night and caught up with the rear guard of the army at daylight.[5]

In the vicinity of Chancellorsville at first light there was a profusion of wagons, including the corps trains and the conglomerations of wheeled vehicles being used to carry the wounded to Fredericksburg.[6] Sedgwick's troops turned onto the Orange Plank Road and moved in the direction of Alrich's, accompanied by the trains of the Sixth, Fifth, and Second corps. Hancock's train was to depart from the column at the Furnace Road and proceed to Todd's Tavern. The battered Vermont brigade of Neill's division, which brought up the rear of the infantry column, was assigned the duty of escorting its corps trains.[7]

Members of Wright's division remembered seeing Burnside and some members of his staff at Chancellorsville. They also saw Ferrero's Colored Troops for the first time.[8] The lead division turned at Alrich's onto the Catharpin Road and continued the march. As the sun climbed above the tops of the trees, the infantrymen realized that the day was going to be a hot one. Most of the troops were numb with fatigue, and a few began to fall out of ranks voluntarily or collapse involuntarily, unable to continue the march without rest.

At 8:00 A.M. Grant and Meade changed their headquarters from Todd's Tavern to Piney Branch Church. At this same time Sedgwick's destination was modified slightly and Burnside's was changed completely. Only the lead Sixth Corps division would now proceed to the original destination, that is, the fictitious intersection. The next in column would halt halfway between that intersection and Piney Branch Church, and the last would halt at the church. The Ninth Corps would now march only as far as the vicinity of Alrich's on the Orange Plank Road, supposedly to protect the army trains more adequately. The reason for spreading out Sedgwick's three divisions along the road is not known. It may have been to provide potential support for Hancock after his arrival at Todd's Tavern, but this is uncertain.[9]

Finally, as the head of Wright's division approached the vicinity of Piney Branch Church at approximately 10:00 A.M., a halt for rest and breakfast was ordered. Gratefully the men fell out of ranks and sought the shade of trees by the side of the road. Those near the head of the column could hear the sound of firing to the south.[10] An order to resume the march was apparently delivered to Wright shortly after the rest began. The First Division started south from the church toward the Brock Road. Warren's request for assistance reached Wright after a mile's march, and he went, as we have seen, to Warren's aid. The remaining two divisions continued their march toward the church.

Movement of the Ninth Corps

Burnside was ordered to move his three divisions up the Orange Plank Road to its intersection with the turnpike. (Ferrero's Fourth Division was at Chancellorsville under Sheridan's orders, guarding the army trains.) Burnside was expected to hold his troops short of the intersection until the Sixth Corps had passed on the pike and then to follow them in the direction of Chancellorsville. The heavily whiskered general obeyed the instructions for his First Division. Because his Second Division was near the Wilderness Tavern, however, he held it there. After dark he moved the Third Division and the Provisional Brigade out of line and positioned them near the Second so they could enter the turnpike at the beginning of the movement.[11]

The order of march of Burnside's three divisions cannot be determined definitely. Most available accounts indicate that the troops began to move between midnight and 1:00 A.M. and that they arrived at the Orange Turnpike entry points near daylight. By first light the rear element of the Sixth Corps left the Wilderness Tavern area, and Brig. Gen. Robert B. Potter's Second Division and the Provisional Brigade took the pike, followed by the First Division of Brig. Gen. Thomas G. Stevenson, at around 8:00 A.M.[12]

The head of Brig. Gen. Orlando B. Willcox's division departed from the area of the tavern at approximately 8:00 A.M. While waiting to move, some of the soldiers were detailed to destroy some abandoned ammunition by throwing it into Wilderness Run. On the march Col. Benjamin C. Christ's brigade brought up the rear, with the Twentieth Michigan and Fiftieth Pennsylvania regiments positioned a short distance behind on both sides of the road. These were prepared to defend the rear if that became necessary. At the site of the Fifth Corps hospital, one mile east of the tavern, the rear brigade halted while some of the remaining wounded were loaded into wagons for the trip to safety. Sadly, many had to be left behind.

The Third Division arrived at Chancellorsville at noon and joined its sister divisions and the Provisional Brigade for a welcome rest and some coffee. At approximately 3:00 P.M., Willcox's men fell back into ranks and marched along the Orange Plank Road a short distance beyond Alrich's where they went into bivouac for the night. Stevenson's division marched about half of the distance to Alrich's and halted there. Potter remained in the vicinity of Chancellorsville. The Ninth Corps infantry did nothing more that day.[13]

The true rear guard of the Ninth Corps was its cavalry. Grant had ordered Burnside to send his horsemen to Meade. Late on the seventh, Sedgwick had ordered Colonel Hammond of the Fifth New York, who commanded the cavalry contingent, to remain in the vicinity of the Wilderness Tavern until Hancock's pickets were removed, which was scheduled to occur at 2:00 A.M. The troopers were then to follow the Second Corps down the Brock Road to Todd's Tavern.[14] At 8:45 A.M. Meade asked that Hancock forward the Fifth New York to army headquarters when it became safe to do so and that he return to Burnside the Second Ohio and the portion of the Twenty-second New York that was still in the vicinity of Wilderness Tavern.[15]

As the rear of Burnside's infantry column departed, a detachment of the Second Ohio Cavalry scouted to the west of Wilderness Run but discovered only a few Confederate cavalry skirmishers. Recrossing the run, these Yankee horsemen destroyed the bridges which engineers had constructed for Warren on the morning of the seventh. While passing the Fifth Corps hospital along the pike, they gathered as many blankets as they could find for the unfortunate wounded who had to be left behind. Arriving at the western edge of the battlefield of Chancellorsville, the horsemen were detailed for picket duty to watch west and north for any Confederates who might have followed the march east on the turnpike.[16]

A Restless Night for the Confederate Second and Third Corps

Sometime during the early evening hours of 7 May, Lee ordered Hill and Ewell to close their corps to the right as Anderson's men abandoned their position south of the Orange Plank Road. Hill was to occupy the segment of the line evacuated by Anderson, and Ewell was to keep closed up on Hill's left and to follow Anderson toward Spotsylvania at daylight if there were no large enemy force in front at that time.[17]

The rear element of Field's division probably did not leave its position adjacent to the Orange Plank Road until midnight or later. This meant that Hill's troops were required to be ready to move during all of that time. A member of the Forty-second Mississippi of Brig. Gen. Joseph R. Davis's brigade recorded that, two hours after the beginning of Anderson's move, the Third Corps had not traveled more than two hundred yards. In addition, Hill had become ill during the fighting in the Wilderness, and his usefulness was becoming impaired.[18]

The infantrymen of the Second Corps got even less sleep that night than the Third. The orders were to follow the troops on the right along the rear of the breastworks, maintaining silence during the movement. Halts were frequent and too brief for anyone to get any sleep. Sometimes the connection between units was broken and useless countermarching resulted. The corps was halted at approximately 3:30–4:00 A.M. and permitted to rest. A member of the Thirteenth Virginia remembered that, by this time, he and his comrades were in vile moods and almost completely broken down. The lead element of the corps was probably now located on the Chewning farm north of the Orange Plank Road, behind the works vacated by the Third Corps.[19]

The Second Corps Leaves the Wilderness as Lee Shuffles Commanders

Sometime before 8:00 A.M. Lee ordered Ewell to move his command to Shady Grove Church via the road from Parker's Store to White Hall Mill and Catharpin Road. Lee planned to precede the corps and await its arrival.[20] The order of march by divisions would be Maj. Gen. Robert E. Rodes's, Maj. Gen. Edward Johnson's, and Early's. Rodes's troops began to move at approximately 8:00 A.M. and Early's by 10:00 A.M.[21]

Before leaving the Wilderness, Lee felt he must make more command changes. A. P. Hill was so ill that morning that he was unable to mount his horse. Lee decided to place Early temporarily in command of the Third Corps. Gordon was rewarded for his services in the Wilderness action by being given command of Early's division. Brig. Gen. Harry T. Hays and his brigade of Louisiana troops were transferred from Early's to Johnson's division and combined there with the Second Louisiana Brigade, whose commander, Brig. Gen. Leroy A. Stafford, had been killed in the Wilderness. To maintain a semblance of parity, the brigade of Brig. Gen. Robert D. Johnston was transferred officially from Rodes's to Gordon's (formerly Early's) division, with whom it had been serving since joining the army on 6 May.[22]

Lee, in a message to the Confederate secretary of war sent at 9:00 A.M., informed his government that the Federal army was abandoning its Wilderness position and was moving toward Fredericksburg, that his army was moving on the Federals' right flank, and that "our advance is now at Spotsylvania Court-House."[23] Some postwar writers, including Grant, maintained that this message proved Lee to be completely misled as to Federal intentions. The fact that Lee had dispatched an entire corps to the correct destination appears to refute these claims.[24]

Operations of the Federal Second Corps
and the Confederate Third Corps, 8 May

On 7 May Hancock had issued a circular to his corps with instructions for the intended march to Todd's Tavern that night. He had said that the move would probably not begin before 11:00 P.M. In fact, the lead division did not start until after daylight.[25] The probable order of march by divisions was Barlow's First, Gibbon's Second, Birney's Third, either preceded or followed by the Third Battalion of the Fourth New York Heavy Artillery, functioning as infantry, and lastly, Mott's Fourth Division. Artillery batteries marched with each infantry division.[26]

Barlow arrived at Todd's Tavern between 9:00 and 10:00 A.M. Hancock reported that Mott had passed the Furnace Road intersection, 1¼ miles north of the tavern, by noon. The First Division moved west on the Catharpin Road approximately one-half mile and began to construct fieldworks. Gibbon's division was positioned on Barlow's left extending perhaps as far as the Brock Road. Birney was placed in reserve, and when Mott's troops arrived, they were positioned so as to extend Barlow's right northeast across the Brock Road north of the tavern. Hancock expressed a desire to send a force west on the Catharpin Road as far as Corbin's Bridge to scout for Confederate forces. He had observed a large column of dust to the west, paralleling his route as he moved down the Brock Road toward Todd's Tavern. This dust probably was raised by Ewell's corps and by the trains of the Army of Northern Virginia on the road from Parker's Store to White Hall Mill.[27]

The part of the Catharpin Road in front of Barlow's position had already been the scene of skirmishing between the cavalry forces of Gregg and Hampton on this Sunday morning. Gregg had stationed part of the First Maine Regiment as a picket force about half a mile west of the tavern on the previous evening.[28] Anderson's infantry had entered the Catharpin Road a little less than one mile in advance of this picket line. Accounts of the morning action are sketchy. Most Federal accounts indicate that the earliest Union advance was at approximately 7:00 to 8:00 A.M. As Meade's order of 1:00 A.M. to Gregg had directed him to move immediately to the vicinity of Corbin's Bridge, obviously Gregg was even slower to respond than had been Merritt on the Brock Road.[29]

Apparently, a portion of Col. Irvin Gregg's brigade pushed Hampton's pickets back across Corbin's Bridge, where the Yankees encountered heavy opposition from dismounted cavalry and horse artillery. The Federals retired to the original picket line, followed by Hampton's men. Later in the morning a charge by two Federal regiments on the left side of the road pushed the Confederates back some distance, after which the Yankees retired again. As

Hancock positioned his divisions around Todd's Tavern, Gregg concentrated his troopers west and northwest of the intersection at the tavern.[30] They were picketing the area north of the road for a mile or more.[31]

Between 11:00 A.M. and noon Hancock sent Barlow's First Brigade out the Catharpin Road, accompanied by a battery of artillery. The five regiments, in line abreast on the right of the road, moved cautiously through areas of pine trees and thorny undergrowth. They were unopposed by any Confederates until they emerged from a patch of woods into the open on the crest of a hill about half a mile from the Po River. There they were fired upon by two Confederate artillery pieces on the hill across the river little more than a mile away. The firing occurred at 12:45 P.M. Miles formed his men into a line under cover of the trees, as the Federal battery took position and fired a few salvos in reply. The Yankee infantrymen enjoyed a spectacular view. The slopes of both ridges facing the river were devoid of trees, and behind the crest of the southern slope lay the Shade Grove Church Road to Spotsylvania Court House. The Federals could see that the road was jammed with enemy troops and vehicles moving in what appeared to Miles's men to be a southerly (actually southeasterly) direction. The Confederates they saw first were the rear element of Anderson's column, ambulances, and ammunition or supply wagons.[32] The van of Ewell's Second Corps soon came into view. When these troops passed to the east of Shady Grove Corner, they were suffering immensely from heat and fatigue. Their march had perhaps been the most difficult of that day and the preceding night. Moreover, some of these troops would become involved in an ugly infantry engagement before their work for the day was done.

The Third Corps Is the Last Major Unit to Depart from the Battlefield

In a postwar narrative of the conflict, Jubal Early claimed that, when he assumed command of the severely ill A. P. Hill's Third Corps on the morning of 8 May, it contained about thirteen thousand armed infantrymen. The field return for 20 April indicates that the corps contained 20,648 enlisted foot soldiers on that date. Hill's men had sustained cruel losses in the Wilderness fighting, but a total of six thousand to seven thousand casualties for the two days seems rather high.[33]

Lee's order to Early was to move the corps by Todd's Tavern along the Brock Road to Spotsylvania Court House as soon as the front was clear of the enemy.[34] Therefore, the Confederate scouting parties spent the morning and early afternoon probing the Federal lines. Scouts from the Forty-second Mississippi Regiment reconnoitered north of the turnpike all the way to the works of the Sixth Corps, where they discovered much abandoned equipment. They then moved down the vacated lines of the Union Fifth and Ninth corps to the Orange Plank Road and, rejoining their brigade, reported that the Yankees were gone.[35]

Another scouting party from Brig. Gen. Abner Perrin's brigade of Mahone's (formerly R. H. Anderson's) division had a more interesting adventure. One hundred men from the Eleventh Alabama Regiment, under the command of Capt. George Clark, were sent forward to reconnoiter the area to the south of the Orange Plank Road. After toiling through the heavily forested area for a time, they emerged from the trees into an old field of sassafras. On the opposite side of the field, the Southerners could see a group of horses tied to small sapling trees. They crept across the field expecting to be ambushed by dismounted Federal cavalrymen at any moment. They arrived safely among the horses, however, to find them well equipped with saddles and bridles, and no Yankees in the vicinity.[36]

The infantrymen, who had probably not been on horseback for months or even years, each confiscated a horse. Captain Clark sat on a fallen log and watched the show. One lanky Alabamian mounted a steed that refused to be pacified. After racing around the field two or three times, the soldier gained control of the animal and rode over to the officer where he halted and gasped out the explanation, "Captain, he tried to nullify, but damn him, I hilt him to it."[37] The men rode most of the afternoon, until they rejoined their brigade, which had moved to the south, and the animals were given to the artillery.

Knowledge of the movements of the Federal Second Corps picket force as they left the Wilderness area might explain how these horses came to be standing in the edge of the field unattended. Col. James A. Beaver, commander of the 148th Pennsylvania Regiment of Barlow's division, was the corps officer of the day.[38] He expected to enjoy the support of the brigade of Burnside's cavalry as rear guard, but Burnside had ordered the horsemen to follow his corps along the turnpike.[39] A number of the Twenty-second New York Cavalry Regiment did report to Beaver for orders, probably the portion of the regiment which had fled north to the Germanna Ford during the panic of the previous afternoon. The acting commander of the Twenty-second, Maj. Peter McLennan, was briefed thoroughly on the procedures to be followed on the march. The infantry pickets were withdrawn at approximately 10:00 A.M., and the march to Todd's Tavern began. Almost immediately, Confederates in trees to the west of the road fired on the rear of the column. The horsemen dashed ahead in terror and overran the rear element of the infantry. Major McLennan was advised to dismount most of his men and to detail horseholders to lead the mounts along near the rear of the column. After more Confederate firing, most of the led horses were discovered to be missing. A company of Vermont sharpshooters was then placed at the rear of the column, and the march continued to Todd's Tavern. McLennan sent volunteers from the regiment back to search for the missing horses and their keepers, but they were unsuccessful. Brig. Gen. Nathaniel H. Harris recorded that a reconnaissance party from his brigade encountered some Union cavalry in the morning south of the Orange Plank Road and captured 80 troopers, 107 horses, and 2 guidons. This was probably the first encounter, shortly after the movement had begun.[40]

Early started the Third Corps on its movement to Spotsylvania Court House in midafternoon. The order of march was Mahone's division followed by those of Maj. Gen. Henry Heth and Maj. Gen. Cadmus M. Wilcox. One battalion of artillery accompanied the infantry. The route was probably the one used by Anderson the previous night.[41] Meanwhile, in the morning an event occurred north of the Rapidan River, the significance of which extended beyond the spheres of military strategy and tactics.

On 7 May, the Ninth Virginia Cavalry Regiment of the brigade of Brig. Gen. John R. Chambliss, Jr., from Rooney Lee's division scouted from the town of Culpeper in the direction of Stevensburg. The troopers examined the abandoned winter camps of the Army of the Potomac and were amazed at the quantity of military stores the Yankees had left there. After camping for the night they resumed their march at daylight along the road leading to the Germanna Ford from the north. This roadway had been used by the Union Fifth, Sixth, and Ninth corps on the fourth, fifth, and sixth of May. The Virginia horsemen found many Federal stragglers limping along or lying on the road, all of whom surrendered without resistance. Most of these troops belonged to the Ninth Corps, which, at the beginning of the month, had been guarding various points along the Orange and Alexandria Railroad as far east as Manassas Junction. On 4 May they had been ordered to join the Army of the Potomac by forced marches. Ferrero's Fourth Division of Colored Troops, having been stationed at Manassas Junction, had the longest distance to travel and contributed its share of stragglers. These Negro soldiers were the first the Ninth Virginia had seen. (Indeed, the opening of this campaign had marked the first use of organized black units against the Army of Northern Virginia in the war.) They were gathered together along the side of the road and shot, their bodies left to lie where they fell. The Confederate cavalrymen then continued with approximately two hundred white prisoners to the ford, which they crossed at approximately 10:00 A.M., rejoining the army near Spotsylvania Court House on the morning of 9 May. This nefarious incident apparently never became known to the higher command of either army.[42]

Bitter Argument between Meade and Sheridan

At noon Sheridan reported to Meade's headquarters, where the army commander and some of his staff were having lunch. Meade rebuked the cavalryman, claiming that his men had blocked the way of the infantry at Todd's Tavern despite orders to leave the road clear. Sheridan angrily denied having received any such orders, whereupon Meade supposedly apologized for his accusation. Sheridan's anger had reached a furious pitch, however, and he proceeded to disparage the efforts of the Fifth Corps at Laurel Hill, declaring that the infantrymen had faced hardly any opposition at all.[43] This charge, in turn, infuriated Meade, and the two officers apparently engaged in an angry shouting match, during which Sheridan complained that Meade's contradiction of his orders had endangered Wilson's division at Spotsylvania. In addition, Sheridan said that the manner in which Meade had been using the mounted arm in the campaign would soon render it completely useless for any military duty. Sheridan concluded his tirade by stating that he could whip Stuart and his horsemen if Meade would only let him, but since Meade insisted upon issuing instructions to the cavalry corps without consulting with or informing its commander, henceforth Meade could command it himself.[44]

Sheridan apparently stalked off, and Meade went to tell Grant what had happened. As he listened to Meade, Grant realized that his two subordinates, neither of whom he wanted to lose, were no longer able to work together. When Meade repeated Sheridan's boast of being capable of whipping Stuart if permitted, Grant saw a temporary solution to the problem. Sheridan shortly received orders from Meade's headquarters directing him to concentrate his force with his loaded ammunition and supply wagons and to proceed against the enemy's cavalry.[45] Sheridan lost little time. At 1:30 P.M. he ordered Gregg to withdraw his division from west of Todd's Tavern, take it to Silver's house on the Orange Plank Road east of Alrich's, and prepare it for departure in the morning.[46]

Afternoon Action West of Todd's Tavern

In the middle of the afternoon, Miles sent a reconnaissance party of one hundred men down the slope in front of his advanced position, across the Po River, and up the opposite slope for a short distance. The party returned without loss, reporting that it had seen only enemy cavalry and artillery. Miles then withdrew three of his regiments one-half mile along the road, leaving the Twenty-sixth Michigan and Eighty-first Pennsylvania at the original position astride the road, with a picket line in the edge of the woods overlooking the river valley.[47]

Sometime before 3:30 P.M., Miles's busy aide-de-camp, Lieutenant Robertson, was sent out a woods road to the north to communicate with a squadron commander from Gregg's division, whose troopers were posted in the area. The cavalryman told Robertson that he had received orders to withdraw soon. Robertson returned to Miles with this unwelcome news, whereupon a picket detail of infantrymen was dispatched and posted there. At 3:30 P.M. five wagons of rations and two head of cattle were sent out to the brigade from Todd's Tavern.[48] When the cattle had been hamstrung to prevent their wandering away and the wagons had been partially unloaded, a volley of musketry erupted from north of the road in the vicinity of the newly positioned picket line. Miles quickly placed his three rear regiments, the Sixty-first New York, 140th Pennsylvania, and 183d Pennsylvania, north of the road and sent Lieutenant Robertson out to withdraw the north picket line slightly and post it in a different direction. While Robertson and the officer in charge of the pickets were performing this assignment, they were surprised and nearly captured by a Confederate infantry brigade advancing across a field toward them. These Rebels were from Mahone's division, which was leading the Third Corps.[49]

Meanwhile, the Twenty-sixth Michigan and Eighty-first Pennsylvania were withdrawn and placed across the Catharpin Road to the left of and nearly at a right angle to the line of the other regiments. Some of the rations were left on the ground in advance of the line of defense across the road. Soon firing began again north of the road when some of Rosser's dismounted troopers advanced on the right flank of Mahone's infantrymen. In addition, a force of Confederates was seen advancing across the river and up the slope west of the Catharpin Road. These were dismounted horsemen of Young's brigade, helping Early in an effort to destroy the Federal brigade. Horse artillery batteries supported these Confederate advances. Gordon's brigade of North Carolina cavalrymen (which had been returned sometime during the day to Rooney Lee's division, much to its and Hampton's chagrin) approached the Federal line on Catharpin Road. Col. H. Boyd McKeen, commanding the Eighty-first, permitted the Southerners to get among the abandoned rations before ordering the two regiments covering the road to fire. The Confederates quickly withdrew.[50]

Lieutenant Robertson was sent to the rear for reinforcements. He posted two regiments from Col. Thomas A. Smyth's brigade, one of which was the 116th Pennsylvania, near the right flank of Miles's three regiments fighting north of the road. Soon the brigade was recalled by Barlow, and the Federals returned to the earthworks west of Todd's Tavern. Early realized that he would have to fight his way past the tavern to reach Spotsylvania by that route. He decided instead to go by Shady Grove road. As it was nearly dark, he camped his troops along the Catharpin Road from a point 1½ miles west of Todd's Tavern to Shady Grove Corner.[51]

6

Went in Rough   8 May
and Tumble

Federal Operations along the Brock Road

Just before noon, when Crawford's two brigades moved down the left fork and a portion of Griffin's division moved down the right fork across the Alsop farm, Colonel Wainwright followed Griffin's men with Lt. James Stewart's and Walcott's (formerly Martin's) batteries (for the geography of this area, see Map 6-1 below). Arriving at the junction, the artillerymen were immediately fired upon by enemy sharpshooters about four hundred yards away, in the edge of the trees on the east side of the road. As the two Union batteries swung into position, they felt the fire of six artillery pieces that were immediately behind the small rise where the burning Spindle house stood.[1] These Confederate guns were the Napoleon sections of three different batteries of Col. Henry C. Cabell's battalion. Their crews had been detailed by Stuart to fire at the mass of Federal troops, artillery, and wagons which had begun to accumulate near the Alsop house. Wainwright positioned one section of Stewart's Battery B, Fourth U.S. Artillery, on each side of the road and the remaining pieces to the right. The Southern gunners shifted targets and began to fire at Wainwright's position. Both groups initially fired high, but Wainwright eventually persuaded his men to aim and fire so as to skim with their exploding shells the top of the rise in front of the Southern guns.

At the beginning of the artillery action, Wainwright, with his staff and some orderlies, were all mounted. They attracted the attention of some of Anderson's skirmishers, who began to fire by volley at the party. After some near misses, Wainwright ordered the rest of his party to move into the cover of some nearby woods, which, to his surprise, they did not wish to do. He insisted, promising them that they would have abundant opportunity to get shot before the campaign was over.[2]

As was the case with many artillery duels in this war, both parties claimed to have silenced or driven off the other. Wainwright said the two Union batteries were withdrawn from the position after dark. A Southern chronicler stated that Cabell's gunners were engaged for three hours before ceasing fire to rest. At any rate, Wainwright recorded that this action, which he said lasted for one-half hour, was the smartest engagement which he had seen up to that time.[3]

Meade Decides to Attack with Two Corps

At noon Meade informed Hancock of Warren's situation and directed him to be prepared to support the Fifth Corps if necessary. Warren also asked Hancock to send him a division if he could safely spare one. He explained that his troops were out of ammunition and might not be able to resist an attack. Hancock ordered Gibbon to move his division down the Brock Road to Warren's position, notified Meade, and reported that he had no ammunition to spare for the Fifth Corps.[4]

At 12:30 P.M. Warren sent to Meade a fairly complete situation report in which he stated that he faced two of Longstreet's divisions and that his own troops were out of infantry ammunition. He advanced his opinion that, given the condition of his command, he would be unable to attack, unsupported, unless the Confederates exhibited a great weakness on one of their flanks. He said he definitely could not gain Spotsylvania Court House with his present force. Meade answered that the entire Sixth Corps had been ordered to Warren's support and that when it arrived, he and Sedgwick should conduct a massive assault without delay.[5] This news and the later promise of a resupply of ammunition seem to have elevated Warren's spirits. At 2:00 P.M. he promised headquarters that he would do his best to smash the Confederates when Sedgwick's corps arrived. Moreover, he now felt less apprehension about an enemy attack, because after some reflection, he realized that the Southerners were just as exhausted as his own men. A short time later, Cutler expressed concern for the reliability of Bragg's brigade and requested two brigades to replace it on its segment of the front line. In reply Warren expressed his doubt that the Confederate force opposite Cutler was very strong or in good fighting condition and explained that when Sedgwick came up, the Rebels would be smashed.[6]

Meanwhile, at approximately 1:45 P.M., Grant and Meade moved their headquarters from Piney Branch Church south, close to the intersection of the road from the church with the Brock Road.[7] When Gibbon and his division approached this intersection from the direction of Todd's Tavern, Meade halted the unit and ordered its commander to keep it near army headquarters. He notified Warren of this action and explained that Warren was to use the detached division only in case of the most urgent necessity, because Hill or Ewell would probably make an appearance at Todd's Tavern, which had to be held.[8]

As the Federal commanders waited for Sedgwick to join Warren south of the Alsop clearing, Grant ordered preparations for the march the following day toward the North Anna River. Burnside was notified of his destination and route of march in a message sent at 12:45 P.M. The Army of the Potomac received its orders at approximately 4:30 P.M.[9]

The commanding generals grew impatient as they watched the weary men of the Second and Third divisions of the Sixth Corps march past headquarters and onto the Brock Road. At 3:20 P.M. they ordered Lt. Col. Theodore Lyman, a volunteer aide-de-camp of Meade's, to examine the lines ahead and find out from Warren or anyone else how the preparations for the assault were progressing. Lyman discovered Warren, Sedgwick, and Wright near the Alsop house and was struck by the troubled demeanors of the three generals. Neither Warren nor Sedgwick could provide an estimated time at which their attack would begin. Lyman reported this to Meade at 4:30 P.M.[10]

After a short interval, Lyman was sent down the road a second time, where he met another staff officer, Maj. William Biddle, who informed him that Warren had at last devised a plan for an immediate attack. Upon receiving this information, Grant, Meade, and their staffs moved to the front and halted to observe the situation from a wooded knoll near the junction. They were able to see very little more than some Union infantrymen lying behind fieldworks on the right of the road and some regiments moving into position on the left. They certainly saw nothing which looked like an attack by two army corps. Confederate riflemen fired at the mounted party sporadically, and soon the commanders returned to their camp back up the Brock Road. Humphreys remained behind and reconnoitered the lines until nearly dark.[11]

Initial Deployment of the Sixth Corps

When the three available brigades of Wright's First Division (Upton's remained behind) reported to Warren at about 10:30 A.M., the New Jersey brigade was positioned immediately to the east of the intersection north of Spindle's, on a wooded rise which sloped to the east.[12] Russell's and Cross's brigades were sent to the right flank of Warren's line to form a support behind the Iron Brigade after its hurried withdrawal. Upton's brigade rejoined early in the afternoon and assumed its position on the right of Russell's troops, with Cross being on Russell's left.[13]

Ricketts's Third Division arrived at Warren's headquarters near the Alsop house at approximately 3:00 P.M. Initially, it was positioned behind Russell's and Cross's brigades near the right of the line. Brig. Gen. William H. Morris, commanding the First Brigade, reported seeing an estimated fifteen thousand Federal troops drawn up in several lines in column of attack. Morris was instructed to coordinate his movements with those of Wright in front. Meade soon ordered Ricketts's command to the left, and after many sets of instructions from various staff officers, it was positioned immediately south of the junction, astride the Brock Road.[14]

Neill's division, without its Second Brigade, which was detached guarding the corps's trains, arrived on the scene at about 5:00 P.M. Like the Third Division, it was apparently positioned behind the right flank of the line and then moved to the left of the Brock Road.[15]

The Confederate Second Corps Moves toward Spotsylvania

Ewell's order of march by division from the Wilderness was Rodes's, Johnson's, and Gordon's, with Rodes beginning to move at approximately 8:00 A.M. Available accounts of the march all testify to the unusual heat. In the first few miles south of the Orange Plank Road, the troops also suffered from burning brush along both sides of the path and from great clouds of smoke caused by burning trees. After an hour or two, soldiers began to fall out of line as they were overcome by exhaustion.[16] The time at which the head of the column arrived at Shady Grove Church is not known. A reasonable estimate would be between noon and 1:00 P.M. General Robert E. Lee was not there. He had proceeded east on the Shady Grove Church Road toward Spotsylvania, probably after leaving instructions for Ewell to continue the march in that direction as rapidly as possible. At 2:30 P.M. Lee dispatched a message to Richmond from near Spotsylvania Court House informing the Confederate secretary of war that Anderson had repulsed the Union Fifth Corps and a division of cavalry with heavy slaughter and taken possession of the village of Spotsylvania. Lee expressed his gratitude that Confederate losses were small. He probably consulted Anderson and Stuart then waited anxiously for the arrival of his Second Corps.[17]

A short distance east of Shady Grove Corner, Brig. Gen. Stephen D. Ramseur rode down the line of regiments of his brigade, which led the corps's column of march. He distributed a dispatch from Anderson that stated that a heavy Union assault had been repulsed ahead by the First Corps and implored the Second to hurry on as a support force, in case there might be another enemy assault later. Ramseur asked his men whether they could continue, and those who were still able to shout answered affirmatively. The march was resumed at a more rapid pace. A member of the Fourth North Carolina Regiment held out until near the Block House Bridge, where he collapsed by the side of the road, exhausted and filled with shame. After lying on the ground for about an hour, he scrambled to his feet when he heard the sounds of artillery and musketry ahead. He discarded everything (including his rations) except his musket and ammunition and in fifteen minutes had caught up with his brigade, which was about to go into action.[18]

Brig. Gen. Junius Daniel's brigade marched behind Ramseur's, followed by those of Brig. Gen. George Doles and Brig. Gen. Cullen A. Battle. A member of Daniel's Forty-fifth North Carolina recorded that just before sunset, his brigade was halted, closed up, and ordered into line of battle (probably on the Brock Road between Old Court House Road and Shady Grove Church Road). Daniel hurriedly announced to each regiment the situation of Anderson's troops and exhorted the brigade to move forward rapidly in order to prevent the First Corps from being outflanked. Daniel's North Carolinians rushed forward with a shout on the right rear of Ramseur's brigade and were followed in turn on their right by Doles's and Battle's troops.[19]

Johnson's division was led by Brig. Gen. George H. Steuart's brigade, followed by that of Brig. Gen. John M. Jones (who had been killed in the Wilderness). An hour or so before sunset, the head of the column was located on the Shady Grove Church Road just west of its intersection with the Brock Road. Steuart's men were happily contemplating the latest word that they would soon be going into camp when the sound of firing was heard to the northwest. The column turned in that direction and was soon positioned in line of battle one hundred yards or so to the rear of Rodes's division.[20] Gordon's division, in turn, arrived on the scene at about sunset and was placed in reserve behind Rodes and Johnson.[21]

The Final Union Assault of 8 May

The combined attack of the Fifth and Sixth corps, which headquarters had planned for 1:00 P.M. against the Confederate position astride the Brock Road 1½ miles from Spotsylvania Court House, did not begin until 6:00–6:30 P.M., partly because the last division of the Sixth Corps did not arrive until 5:00 P.M. In addition, Sedgwick apparently insisted that Warren brief him thoroughly on the plan of attack before he deployed some of his units into their final positions. Moreover, the shifting of Sixth Corps brigades from behind the right of Warren's line to the left, astride and east of the Brock Road, consumed valuable time. Perhaps the most important reason was the physical and mental exhaustion of enlisted men and officers alike at the end of a strenuous day following a night without much sleep.[22]

Sometime late in the afternoon, before the main assault began, a portion of Brown's New Jersey brigade of Wright's division followed Warren's order to reconnoiter in force across the field just east of the road. The Third Regiment deployed as skirmishers and preceded the Fifteenth in the advance.

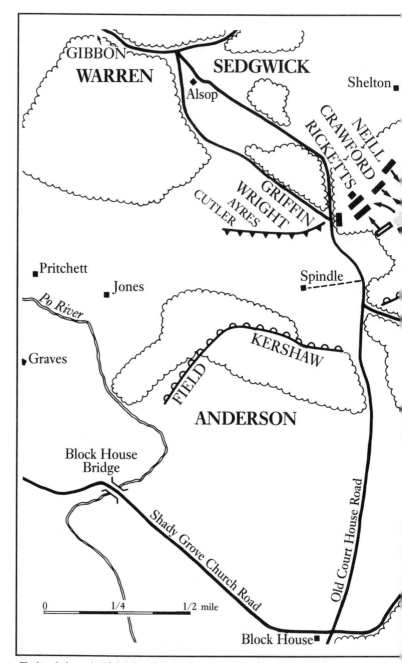

MAP 6-1. Federal Attack of 8 May Beginning at 6:00–6:30 P.M. and Ending after Dark. When the fighting ended, the opposing forces entrenched as indicated. At this time the Federal Second Corps was at

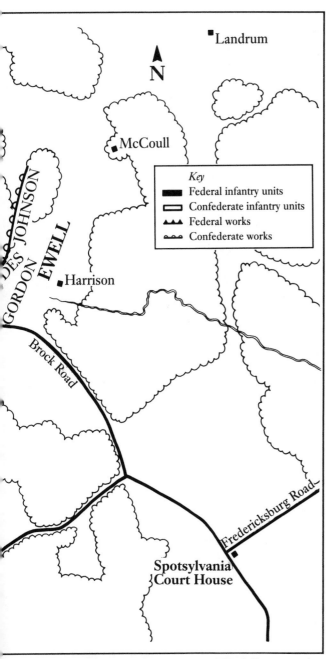

Todd's Tavern, the Confederate Third Corps was between Todd's Tavern and Shady Grove, and the Federal Ninth Corps was to the north on the Orange Plank Road.

The Confederates opposite them, probably the right element of Bratton's brigade and Humphreys's Mississippians, waited until the Unionists were within fifty yards of the fieldworks before opening fire. While sustaining heavy casualties, Brown's men went in over the first line of works, but receiving flank fire from two directions, they were compelled to retire. Halfway back, they met the First New Jersey advancing to their support. The three regiments lay down in the tall grass until dark and then crept back to their line. The Fifteenth Regiment sustained 101 casualties in this operation and brought back one enemy prisoner.[23]

It is difficult to obtain a clear picture of the main engagement from the sources available. The accounts of Federal units positioned to the west of the Brock Road claim that the attack was to begin on the left of the line and proceed to the right. None of these units participated in the action.[24]

The Union order of battle for the attack east of the Brock Road was, from left to right, Col. Daniel D. Bidwell's (formerly Neill's) and Eustis's brigades of the Second Division, Sixth Corps, with Crawford's two Fifth Corps brigades of Pennsylvania Reserves to their right. (As Bidwell's regiments waited for the order to move forward, Uncle John Sedgwick, riding in front of the line, informed his men that they would soon be able to fight in open country where they would have a better chance of success.[25]) Ricketts's division was positioned astride the Brock Road. A regiment from this command also reported participating in the attack.[26] The formation of Eustis's brigade was Tenth Massachusetts and Second Rhode Island in the front line and Seventh Massachusetts and Thirty-seventh Massachusetts in the second.[27] As the brigade prepared to move into position for the advance, it was observed by a nearby group of horsemen, which included generals Grant, Meade, Warren, and Sedgwick. Eustis appeared to be experiencing difficulty maneuvering the brigade properly, and Sedgwick became extremely embarrassed. Finally, he ordered a member of his staff to ask Col. Oliver Edwards, commander of the Thirty-seventh Massachusetts, the reason for this delay, which was disgracing the Sixth Corps. Edwards replied that Eustis was drunk, and he added that he could position his regiment properly for the attack in thirty seconds, given the authority. Sedgwick immediately ordered Edwards to assume temporary command of the brigade and to place it into line, which he did.[28] The Pennsylvania Reserves division was formed in two lines for the attack, with the First Brigade in the front line and the Third Brigade in the second. Both commands were being led by temporary commanders—the First Brigade by Col. William C. Talley and the Third Brigade by Col. Silas M. Bailey. They were to be supported by the picket detachment from the First Division, Fifth Corps, which was under the command of Lieutenant Colonel Herring.[29] This detail was composed of the Twentieth Maine, Sixteenth Michigan, and 118th Pennsylvania of Bartlett's brigade, along with six companies from the Twenty-second and one from the Ninth Massachusetts of Sweitzer's brigade. These troops had been withdrawn from their position in the Wilderness at 1:00 A.M. Following the rear of the Fifth Corps column, they had arrived near the Alsop house between 10:00 and 11:00 A.M. Herring had reported to Warren there, expecting the men to be returned to their parent units, but instead he was ordered to report with the group to General Crawford, who was located ahead along the left-hand fork of the road. Crawford ordered Herring to function as a support for his division. Late in the afternoon, the general directed the lieutenant colonel to place his small command two hundred yards to the rear of the Pennsylvanian's second line during the advance. Herring positioned seven companies of the Ninth and Twenty-second Massachusetts regiments behind the right of the Reserves and the Twentieth Maine and 118th Pennsylvania to their left. The Sixteenth Michigan constituted a reserve behind the Twentieth and 118th.[30]

The Federal assault force moved forward at about the same time that Rodes's four brigades opposite were moving ahead past the right flank of Humphreys's Mississippi brigade. On the right of the Union line, the Tenth New Jersey Regiment, which had become separated from its Sixth Corps brigade, marched alongside the First Pennsylvania Reserve Regiment. It was now dusk and rapidly becoming dark. The Tenth soon became separated from the line on its left in the thickly forested area and became disorganized under fire. The lieutenant colonel of the regiment led three or four companies forward to Humphreys's works and after a brief engagement there was obliged to surrender. The remainder of the regiment drifted back to the Union line.[31]

After advancing down a gentle slope three or four hundred yards, the first line of Pennsylvania Reserves crossed a small rivulet and had started up the opposite slope when they unexpectedly encountered Ramseur's brigade advancing from their right front. Both parties immediately commenced firing. The surprised Pennsylvania troops began to waver and soon broke for the rear. Colonel Talley, commanding the First Brigade of Reserves, rallied some of his men a short distance back. Some of Ramseur's men and Daniel's brigade swept past their left flank and, after gaining their rear, captured approximately four hundred of the Pennsylvanians, including Colonel Talley. The Palmetto Sharpshooters of Bratton's brigade also claimed to have participated in these captures.[32]

When the opening volley of the engagement was fired, Herring's men, who constituted the third line, were about halfway down the slope behind the small stream. They dressed their line and peered ahead through the gloom to see what was happening. On the right, members of the Pennsylvania Reserve regiments soon began to filter back through the line occupied by six companies of the Twenty-second Massachusetts. When urged to stop and fight, the

Pennsylvanians replied that the present location was not a proper place, which seemed very sensible indeed to the questioners. After the front became clear, a confused mass of Confederates appeared, yelling and firing. The Union companies fired with effect, and the Southerners recoiled a short distance before advancing again. Numerous volleys were exchanged at near point-blank range in the darkness.[33]

During a lull in the firing, the Federals withdrew one hundred yards. Soon the Confederates came on again, perhaps believing that they had broken the line. They were racked by another volley at close range, after which they retired for the rest of the evening. Capt. Frederick K. Field, commanding the six Union companies, reported casualties of ten wounded and four missing. He also reported the capture of approximately fifty prisoners and the regimental colors of the Sixth Alabama Regiment.[34]

The Confederates involved were from Battle's brigade. They had moved past Ramseur's right flank after the Federal front collapsed and had collided with Herring's troops. The Twelfth, Sixth, and Sixty-first Alabama regiments on the left of the brigade line were nearest to the Federals and thus became engaged first.[35] The collision between Battle's and Herring's men was sudden and deadly. Federal accounts of the action state that Crawford's line in front simply disappeared and that a mass of Confederates came roaring out of the darkness. A wild melee ensued. There was no time to reload, so officers and men used muskets, bayonets, pistols, and swords in hand-to-hand combat. A participant from the Twenty-second Massachusetts remembered that "it was a death-grapple; men even threw down their arms and went in rough and tumble, taking over sixty prisoners, including one captain. The latter, taking a survey of the field in the darkness, after passing over his sword, inquired, 'Which way is it to the rare?' "[36] The initial impact carried the Twentieth Maine back several yards, but they came charging back with fury. A chronicler of the regiment recorded that, in addition to being tired and hungry, the men were angry about having been detached from their brigade for nearly twenty-four hours. Now it appeared to them that they had been abandoned in the midst of the entire Confederate army. There seemed to be no front, rear, or flanks. Confederates were everywhere. The confusion was increased by the fact that everyone was shouting as loudly as possible. During the fighting, troops of the Twentieth Maine sent seventy-seven unescorted prisoners off in some direction, where they escaped. Members of both the Twentieth Maine and 118th Pennsylvania later designated this engagement as their most severe and desperate of the war (worse than Little Round Top at Gettysburg for the Twentieth and Boteler's Ford near Shepherdstown, West Virginia, in September 1862, for the 118th).[37]

The Sixteenth Michigan had assumed a position at the head of a small ravine on a flank. Two Confederate regiments attempted to get in the Federal rear by this route near the end of the action but were repelled by the

Michiganders. The fighting now ceased, and Herring set up a defensive line of sorts in the darkness. Out in front a body of men could be heard moving, and officers were shouting orders. General Battle was attempting to lead his men forward again, but the troops were reluctant to follow. Later Ramseur appeared and together they urged the men to advance, but the Confederates were just as exhausted as their opponents. Rodes soon ordered his troops to retire a short distance and to entrench. Herring sent three officers to the rear to request orders from Crawford. The three returned at midnight, reporting that they had been unable to find Crawford, but that General Neill of the Sixth Corps had suggested that they remain in their position until 3:00 A.M. and then retire. At that time, the withdrawal was performed gingerly but successfully, and later in the morning the members of the detachment were permitted to rejoin their parent brigades. They had many tales to tell.[38]

Left of the site of Herring's battle, Eustis's brigade, now commanded by Colonel Edwards, moved forward against little or no opposition. When Crawford's line to the right collapsed, Edwards continued a short distance with his Thirty-seventh Regiment, until several prisoners were reported captured behind the advance. Edwards withdrew the brigade to a defensive position on a slight elevation, leaving pickets in front who soon reported a Confederate line approaching. These Southerners, who may have been the members of the Third and Fifth Alabama regiments, retired after a volley from the Tenth Massachusetts and Second Rhode Island. Prisoners claimed that two Confederate brigades were in front of Edwards's position, which was entirely possible in the confusion of this night action. Federal stragglers migrated to Edwards's position until he eventually had a line of battle composed of nearly three thousand troops. During the night, Sedgwick officially assigned the command of Eustis's brigade to Edwards.[39]

On Edwards's left, a part of Bidwell's brigade had advanced down one side of a slight ravine and were ascending the opposite slope when a Confederate line of battle suddenly appeared out of the darkness directly in front. A Southern officer seized the flagstaff of the Sixty-first Pennsylvania's regimental colors and demanded the surrender of the regiment. The color-bearer retained his grip on the staff, and officers of the Sixty-first captured the brave Confederate. At this, the Southern infantry fired a volley, and the battle was on. The engagement was similar to Herring's but not as lengthy. No commands could be heard. Hand-to-hand combat prevailed, with officers using their pistols and swords. Then the Confederates withdrew, and the Sixty-first Regiment found itself alone in the inky darkness. Pickets were stationed in all directions, and the remaining members of the unit settled in for the night. At midnight the regimental adjutant was sent to the rear to locate brigade headquarters. He was shot and killed by a nervous sentry, who did not give the officer time to respond to his challenge.[40]

Troops in the Federal units west of the Brock Road listened tensely to the firing on their left, expecting at any moment to be ordered forward. These orders were never given. After dark, units from the Fifth Corps were advanced southward from near the Alsop clearing to the slight ridge which extended southwest from the junction. Portions of Griffin's and Robinson's divisions occupied the line beginning on the west side of the road. To their right was Wright's division of the Sixth Corps, without the New Jersey brigade. Next was Ayres's brigade, upon whose right flank were the Iron Brigade and Bragg's brigade of Pennsylvania troops. Pickets were advanced to the slight rise on which stood the burned Spindle building and peach orchard.[41]

On the Confederate side, the brigades of Rodes's division retired as ordered and established a line extending northeast from the right of Humphreys's brigade. The alignment from left to right was probably Ramseur, Daniel, and Doles, with Battle in reserve. In Daniel's brigade one man from each regiment was led forward in the darkness by an officer and stationed upon a crest of a low ridge with instructions to listen for a low call from the right. The soldier was to repeat the call and continue it until his regiment had moved up to his position, guided by the sound of his voice. In this manner the division was eventually formed into a line facing northwest and roughly parallel with the opposing Federal line, which was composed of Ricketts's and Neill's divisions of the Sixth Corps, approximately one-half mile away.[42]

Johnson's division, which had been supporting Rodes's, faced to the right and moved forward to take a position on Rodes's right. The order of march, if such it could be called, was Steuart, Jones, Hays, and the Stonewall Brigade under Brig. Gen. James A. Walker. The troops stumbled about in the darkness among the trees until nearly midnight before being permitted to rest. They were in a line that extended northeast from Rodes's right. At one point Walker's men were halted with the two lead regiments of the brigade standing in muddy water ankle deep. Walker moved the two units back a short distance without requesting permission from or notifying a superior officer. Ewell soon learned of Walker's action and berated the brigadier severely for acting without orders. At midnight Walker's troops were ordered to move again, and after another hour of marching in the darkness, they were halted and told to entrench where they were. They set to work digging and by daylight were sleeping comfortably. Gordon's division remained in reserve throughout the night.[43]

During the day, E. P. Alexander had positioned his batteries along or behind Anderson's infantry line, which now extended from near the Po River right to a short distance east of the Brock Road. Cabell's battalion covered the left of the line, Haskell's the center, and Lt. Col. Frank Huger's the right with Capt. William W. Parker's battery on the Brock Road. Alexander claimed that nearly every artillery piece of the First Corps had been engaged during the day. Now the artillerymen constructed lunettes around their gun positions and attempted to get some sleep.[44]

Nightfall found two sets of parallel fieldworks approximately five to six hundred yards apart across the Brock Road. What the Unionists had thought would be a rapid march into open country had stalled behind these works, still in the woods. The Battle of Spotsylvania Court House was under way.

II Thrust and Parry

9–11 May

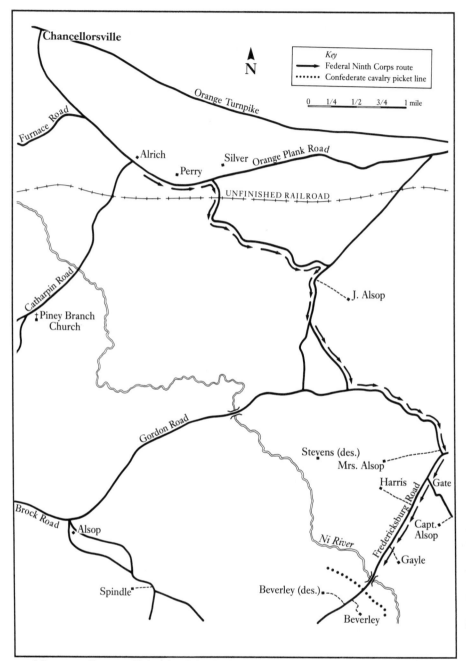

MAP 7-1. Route of March of the Federal Ninth Corps on 9 May

7 Couldn't Hit 8–9 May
an Elephant

Union Ninth Corps

Burnside had been notified early on the afternoon of 8 May that his route of march for the ninth should be from Alrich's on the Orange Plank Road via J. Alsop's to a point the map called "Gate" (on the Fredericksburg Road approximately four miles from Spotsylvania) and then south to Chilesburg.[1] At 9:00 P.M. Burnside learned that the movement was cancelled and that, if his march had already commenced, he should proceed no further than the "Gate." In any event, he was to have two of his divisions up to the "Gate" by 6:00 A.M., prepared to move directly toward Spotsylvania if so ordered.[2] Burnside ordered Willcox to lead off with his division at 3:00 A.M. and Stevenson to follow half an hour later. The Provisional Brigade was to replace Willcox's troops at Alrich's.[3]

At the scheduled hour Willcox's troops, led by Colonel Christ's brigade, took up the march east on the Orange Plank Road. Christ's men had traveled scarcely two hundred yards when they were forced to halt. The van of Sheridan's Cavalry Corps had entered the road ahead on the beginning of its raid toward Richmond. The horsemen, who had camped a short distance east of Willcox's bivouac, apparently took precedence over the foot soldiers. After waiting an hour or so for the cavalrymen to clear the road the men of the Ninth Corps's Third Division resumed their march.[4]

The Federal infantrymen proceeded past the J. Alsop farm to the Fredericksburg Road. There they turned southwest and moved directly toward Spotsylvania. A colonel remembered, "The road was now broad and good, and we marched with ease. We were out of the unbroken wilderness." Unknowingly they soon passed the position which the planning map designated at "Gate." Why the site was so named is unknown. It may have been merely a fence gate across a road leading to Captain Alsop's house, which was a short distance east of the main road. Willcox and Christ were probably watching for something more prominent. Willcox ordered Christ to deploy some skirmishers, and soon a few companies from the rookie Sixtieth Ohio and the veteran Twentieth Michigan were advancing in line on both sides of the road.[5] They sighted some Confederate vedettes ahead, which immediately retired in the direction of Spotsylvania. Willcox, reporting to Burnside at 7:15 A.M., said that this sighting of the enemy had occurred one-half mile before Gayle's house. This structure, whose name would contribute to the confusion of the Federal commanders that day, was located three hundred yards east of the road, about a third of a mile north of the Ni River.[6]

The troops of Willcox's division were halted for a rest. Willcox, accompanied by Colonel Christ and Lt. Col. Byron M. Cutcheon, commander of the Twentieth Michigan, rode over to the grounds of Gayle house to examine the topography. The ground in front of them sloped down to the Ni River and ascended from the far bank. Some buildings were visible to both sides of the road on the opposite slope. A small group of mounted Confederates could be seen on the opposite crest.[7] These troopers from Fitz Lee's division had been sent by Stuart to investigate the advancing Federal force. Stuart notified Lee of this Federal approach at 8:00 A.M.[8]

At around 9:00 A.M. Willcox ordered Christ to cross the river and to occupy the opposite crest. Col. John F. Hartranft was directed to advance his brigade to the north bank of the river after Christ was across and to offer support as necessary. The skirmishers of Christ's Sixtieth Ohio and Twentieth Michigan regiments double-timed down the slope, crossed the river, and ascended the opposite slope, encountering no opposition. They were followed at a distance of one hundred fifty yards by their regiments, which were in turn followed at a greater distance by the remaining three regiments of the brigade. The skirmishers crossed the crest and entered some woods a short distance beyond. The remainder of the Sixtieth Ohio halted on the crest. The Twentieth Michigan stopped about halfway up the slope and deployed to the left in a sunken road 2½ to 3 feet deep, which lay perpendicular to the main road and which led to one of the Beverley houses. The First Michigan Sharpshooters Regiment was stationed to the left of the Twentieth and the Fiftieth Pennsylvania on the right of the main road. The Seventy-ninth New York took a position near the house.[9] Suddenly, the advanced skirmishers were assaulted by three or four regiments of dismounted Confederate cavalrymen deployed on both sides of the road. Christ's brigade was hard put to maintain its position, but as Hartranft sent most of his regiments to its support, the Federal line was stabilized along the crest by noon, and the heavy firing ceased. The two batteries attached to Willcox's division had supported the infantrymen from positions on the crest north of the river. Stevenson's division arrived at the river crossing at midday.[10]

Because of the poor quality of available maps, Grant and Meade were unaware of the topography between the Alsop farm on the Brock Road and the position of Willcox's division on the Fredericksburg Road. At 8:45 A.M. Grant ordered Burnside, who had remained at Alrich's, to reconnoiter from Gate toward Spotsylvania and to attempt to discover if any roads existed there that led west toward the general location of the Army of the Potomac. Potter's division was to proceed to Piney Branch Church and Ferrero's Colored Troops would remain near Chancellorsville to guard the trains and the rear of the Ninth Corps.[11]

Burnside acknowledged receipt of these instructions at 9:25 A.M. and forwarded to Grant copies of Willcox's messages that reported the sighting of Confederate cavalry and perhaps infantry just short of the Gayle house. He also informed Willcox of Grant's desire for a reconnaissance mission.[12]

At 10:00 A.M. Burnside was told to be sure that Potter, at Piney Branch Church, became familiar with the locations of the Fifth and Sixth corps astride the Brock Road and the Second Corps at Todd's Tavern and the roads leading to these corps from the church. His division was designated as a potential support element for each of these commands and was to be prepared to march immediately.[13]

Willcox, at 11:45 A.M., reported the results of his engagement up to that time. He was worried, erroneously believing that he was engaging vastly superior numbers, and he asked for the location of Stevenson's division. He forwarded the false report that Hill's and Longstreet's corps were at Spotsylvania. In a message written at 1:15 P.M., he claimed to have taken prisoners from all three Confederate infantry corps, but it appears certain the the only troops he had faced were Fitz Lee's troopers.[14]

Union Sixth Corps

At approximately 3:00 A.M. on the ninth, Sedgwick ordered the commander of his Third Division, General Ricketts, to strengthen his line by constructing entrenchments as soon as it became light enough to see. Sedgwick explained that the army was to remain in position that day so the men could rest.[15] Ricketts's two brigades were positioned in the area of the Brock Road junction at the south end of the Alsop farm. Most of the regiments faced east, but one or two were positioned along the western road facing south-southwest.[16]

At 6:30 A.M. Meade ordered Sedgwick to extend his pickets well to his left and to ensure that they advanced close to the enemy's position. Meade also directed that, should the Sixth and Fifth corps engage in a combined action in his absence, Sedgwick should assume command of both corps. Warren received similar instructions. A short time later Sedgwick met one of Warren's staff and instructed the officer to advise Warren to go on commanding the Fifth Corps as usual, since Sedgwick had perfect confidence in him. Apparently he intended to comply with Meade's directive only as a last resort.[17]

At approximately 8:00 A.M., Crawford's two Fifth Corps brigades withdrew from their positions on Ricketts's left and marched to the west of the Brock Road, where they replaced the three brigades of Wright's Sixth Corps division in the line to Griffin's right. Wright's troops withdrew from the line and marched north to take their position on the left of Neill's division, becoming the left flank of the Sixth Corps's line.[18]

The remaining brigade of Wright's division, six New Jersey regiments, was still positioned immediately east of the Brock Road junction, where it was intermingled with or perhaps posted slightly in advance of Ricketts's troops in the edge of the woods.[19] At 9:00 A.M. a section of Capt. William H. McCartney's First Massachusetts Battery moved into position just to the east of the junction.[20] About fifteen minutes later, Sedgwick and members of his staff arrived in the area checking and making minor adjustments to the corps line. Sedgwick noticed that the New Jersey troops and Ricketts's men occupied the same segment of the line, so he ordered the Jerseymen to withdraw. As the color-bearer of the Fifteenth New Jersey rose to move to the rear, he was mortally wounded by a sharpshooter's bullet that struck him in the breast, passed through his body, and struck a comrade in the thigh.[21]

By this time Sedgwick was sitting on a cracker box about a hundred feet behind the line, watching some of Ricketts's troops file into the works. The men then lay prone, with the troops on the left of the line overlapping the position of the right artillery piece. Sedgwick advised his chief of staff, Martin T. McMahon, of this discrepancy, and both officers strolled forward toward the piece to correct the alignment. As the soldiers moved farther to the right, an occasional minie ball whistled past, causing some of them to duck and dodge. Sedgwick chided his men good-naturedly, closing with the comment that the Confederates "couldn't hit an elephant at this distance."[22] Moments later a soldier moving directly in front of Sedgwick dodged as a bullet passed. The general chided this man also and repeated the elephant phrase. The infantryman saluted his commander and explained that he believed in dodging, because he was positive that dodging had once saved his life. Sedgwick smilingly bade the soldier to keep moving. Suddenly, the men heard the sickening sound of a bullet striking bone, and Sedgwick turned and collapsed in McMahon's arms, pulling both men to the ground. Col. Charles H. Tompkins, corps chief of artillery, summoned a doctor, but he was too late.[23]

Members of the Sixth Corps and many others in the Army of the Potomac were heartsick upon hearing of Sedgwick's death. Grant was visibly affected by the news. He said that Sedgwick's loss to the army was greater than the loss of an entire division. Oliver Edwards remembered that several Sixth Corps officers wept bitterly. The enlisted men were stunned into numb silence.[24] Uncle John's overall competence as a corps commander during his Civil War service was questioned in some postwar writings, but he was solid, dependable, and loyal, respected and admired by his troops.

Ricketts, who was now the ranking officer of the corps, informed McMahon that he declined to assume command because Sedgwick had wanted Wright to succeed him. Thus, Russell replaced Wright in division command, and Eustis, now apparently sober, was transferred from the Second Division to the command of Russell's brigade. The order from army headquarters assigning Wright to the command of the Sixth Corps was sent at 10:00 A.M.[25]

There was a delay in the operations of the corps while the changes in command were being executed and staffs reorganized. Soon, however, pickets from the three divisions were again gingerly feeling their way forward, where they discovered Kershaw's division and the Confederate Second Corps.

Confederate Second Corps

The left end of Ewell's line met the right of Kershaw's line about two hundred fifty yards west-northwest of the Harrison house, Ewell's corps headquarters. Rodes's division extended the line north-northeast for approximately one-half mile. The probable order of alignment by brigades from left to right was Ramseur, Daniel, and Doles, with Battle in reserve. The line lay in woods for the most part, and Rodes's men constructed earth and log works with some abatis in front. The northern portion of this part of the line, perhaps one-quarter mile in length, was occupied by the right regiments of Daniel's brigade and all of Doles's brigade. An open field about two hundred yards across lay in front of them. From Doles's position, where a narrow road crossed the field and entered the wood to the west, the line swung to the northeast for a little more than one-half mile.[26] Here lay the four brigades of Edward Johnson's division in the following order: Walker, Hays (whose Louisiana brigade had been transferred from Early's to Johnson's division and had been merged with Stafford's brigade, all under Hays, Stafford having been killed in the Wilderness), Jones (now commanded by Col. William Witcher), and Steuart. The Second Virginia Regiment of Walker's Stonewall Brigade, which connected with Doles's right, and the Thirty-third Virginia on the right of the Second were both in the open field, while the three remaining regiments of the brigade, the Twenty-seventh, Fifth, and Fourth, were in the edge of an oak wood with the field in front. The remaining brigades of the division also lay along the edge of these woods to the right. At the point where the line entered the woods between the Thirty-third and Twenty-seventh regiments, a narrow lane crossed the works and led south to the McCoull farm approximately one-quarter mile to the rear,[27] where Johnson established his headquarters.[28]

At daylight Johnson's men began to entrench, using primarily bayonets and tin cups as tools. A South Carolinian, who fought three days later in the

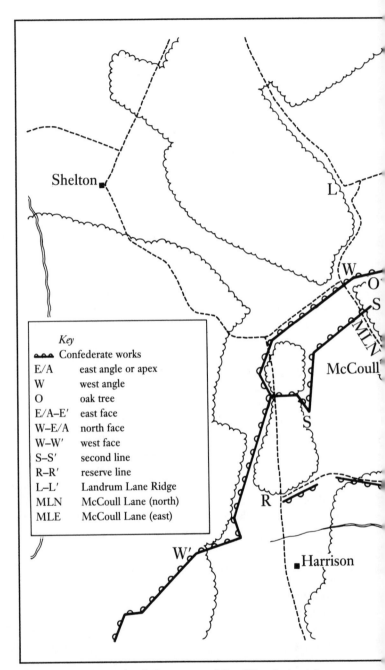

MAP 7-2. Confederate Works in the Salient, 9–11 May. The designations given for major features on this base map will be used exclusively in the remainder of the narrative.

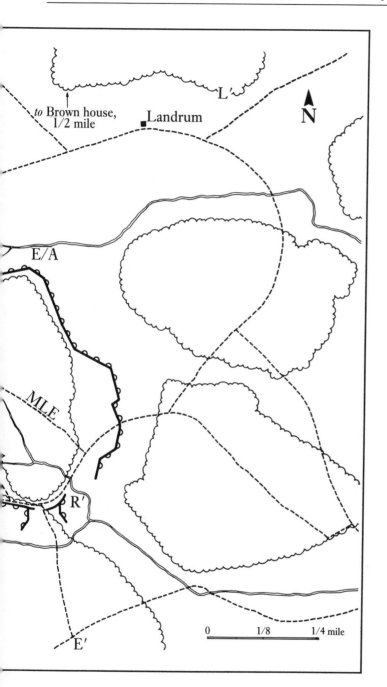

L'

to Brown house,
1/2 mile

Landrum

N

E/A

MLE

R'

E'

0   1/8   1/4 mile

works erected by Walker's Virginians, remembered that they had been constructed by driving a double row of stakes into the ground and filling the interval between with logs and dirt until they were three or four feet thick and breast high.[29]

Steuart's men on the extreme right of the line had half completed their works to the right and rear of Witcher's brigade when engineering officers appeared and ordered them to level their handiwork and to construct new works that would connect with Witcher's right nearly at a right angle to the main line and would face east-northeast. The disgruntled infantrymen began anew. At daylight, Union Sixth Corps batteries commenced firing upon Johnson's men as they constructed their works. This fire enfiladed the line from the left, so the Southerners constructed log traverses intermittently from Doles's position around to Steuart's, where the troops erected logs across their rear as well. A second line of works was begun approximately one hundred yards to the rear of the part of the line extending from Daniel's position to a little beyond the northern leg of the McCoull farm lane.[30]

The division now commanded by Gordon was retained as a reserve. In the morning it began to construct another reserve line of entrenchments, to extend due east from behind the left center of Rodes's line and to lie approximately midway between the McCoull and Harrison houses.[31]

Confederate First Corps

Richard H. Anderson spent the morning of 9 May sorting out the various brigades of his corps. He positioned those of Kershaw's division east of the Brock Road and those of Field's to the west. Kershaw's order by brigades from right to left was Humphreys (who joined Rodes's left), Henegan, Bryan, and Wofford. Wofford's left rested on the intersection of the Brock and Block House roads. The four guns of Parker's battery were stationed to Wofford's left and rear along the Block House Road. The artillerymen continued to improve the defensive strength of their position as best they could.[32]

West of the Block House Road the brigade alignment of Field's division from right to left was Bratton, DuBose, Law, G. T. Anderson, and Gregg. Bratton's three right regiments lay in the northern edge of a wood looking north across the fields of the Spindle farm. The remaining two regiments to the left were in the wood.[33] DuBose's four Georgia regiments continued the line west-northwest in the woods. Next were Law's Alabamians. At about the middle of their position, the line turned to the southwest. G. T. Anderson's brigade was next, with the right regiments in the wood and the remainder in the open. Gregg's brigade of three Texas regiments and the Third Arkansas occupied the left of the line extending nearly to the Po River. In front of the

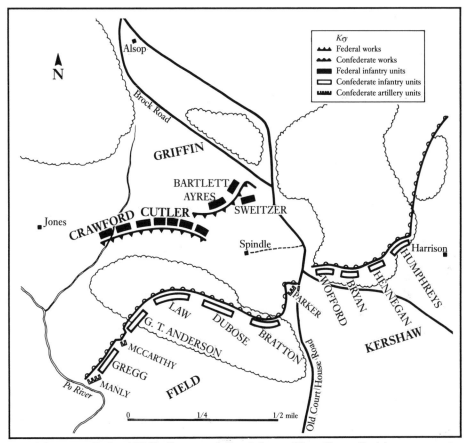

MAP 7-3. Federal Fifth Corps and Confederate First Corps Positions on 9 May

Texans the open ground sloped down to a small stream and ascended the opposite bank to the top of a hill where stood the W. W. Jones house, about three-quarters of a mile away.

B. C. Manly's four-gun battery was positioned near the left of the line.[34] Two Napoleons of McCarthy's Richmond Howitzers battery were also placed on the line with the infantrymen. Other pieces of Cabell's artillery battalion were positioned to the rear on more elevated ground, where their gunners would enjoy a more distant view and wider arcs of fire than their comrades in front.[35]

The infantrymen of the Confederate First Corps spent the morning constructing protective fieldworks. Most of them used bayonets to dig, not having spades and picks. Gregg's troops and those of G. T. Anderson, who were positioned in the open on the left, found some fence rails which they used to strengthen their works. For the most part, however, these Southerners had to rely primarily upon earthen works for their protection.

Union Fifth Corps

Across the Spindle fields facing Field's men lay Warren's Fifth Corps, which had sustained between thirteen hundred and fourteen hundred casualties on the previous day, mostly in the assaults against Laurel Hill.[36] The men spent the morning of the ninth in perfecting their alignment and in strengthening their fieldworks. This corps received orders, similar to those received by the Sixth, to advance pickets close to the enemy's works and to retain them there if at all possible.[37] The divisional alignment from left to right was Griffin, just southwest of the Brock Road, Cutler, and Crawford. The Maryland brigade of the defunct Second Division remained back at Warren's headquarters near the Alsop buildings. On the left of the line Griffin installed Bartlett's men and most of Ayres's brigade behind the fieldworks southwest of the Brock Road intersection. Sweitzer's troops advanced to the first low rise in front to function as a strong picket force.[38] The order of alignment within Cutler's division is not known, except for the position of the new addition, Lyle's brigade, which finally took its station on the extreme right of the division line after having built three different sets of earthworks during the day.[39] Cutler's left was located on the same rise occupied by Sweitzer's troops to the left, and the division extended west-northwest.[40] Crawford's two Third Division brigades and Coulter's brigade, which was added that day, spent most of the morning changing positions until finally they were placed where they extended the line to the west from Cutler's right across a small run that flowed southwest into the Po River. They skirmished lightly with some Confederate scouts while approaching their final position. Upon arrival they immediately entrenched.[41]

At about 11:00 A.M. some Confederate cavalrymen were sighted in the open fields to the right of the line in the area of the Pritchett house. The Maryland brigade, sent from Warren's headquarters, drove them off then erected a line of works there.[42]

At daylight Capt. Charles E. Mink's and Lt. Lester I. Richardson's batteries (H and D, First New York Light Artillery) assumed their position behind Griffin's works. Under his direction, they fired toward Laurel Hill in an unsuccessful attempt to discourage the activities of Confederate sharpshooters in advance of the Rebel position.[43]

At 9:30 A.M. Warren composed a confidential letter to Meade, the text of which illustrated Warren's unique style. He opened by reporting that a continuous Confederate wagon train was moving toward Shady Grove on the road from Parker's Store, and he offered his opinion that this fact should relieve all apprehension about the right of the army. He then offered Meade some advice. First, he suggested that, when an army movement similar to the one made on the night of the seventh was conducted, assigned points of concentration or other destinations should not be changed because of some minor consideration. Warren maintained that if the Sixth Corps had been permitted to adhere to its originally assigned schedule, it could have joined the Fifth Corps and whipped Anderson's corps and the portion of Ewell's which had arrived. (In retrospect, it is not at all certain that this would have occurred, but it appears that the Federals' advantage would have certainly been enhanced had Neill's division arrived at Alsop's at perhaps noon rather than at 3:00 P.M.)[44] Warren also suggested that Meade should accompany the column moving to the critical objective, so that an overall commander would be present should it become necessary to combine the operations of two or more corps. Warren said that whether or not he had Meade's confidence, he doubted the capabilities of both Sedgwick, who did nothing unless ordered, and Hancock, who had performed poorly in the Wilderness fighting.[45]

Warren did not forward this letter, because he must have been informed of Sedgwick's death while in the act of writing it. Ironically, if army headquarters had received Warren's letter and heeded its second point three days later, the 1864 campaign in Northern Virginia might have developed quite differently.

Confederate Third Corps and Union Second Corps

Early in the morning of the ninth, a courier from Wade Hampton delivered to Jubal Early at Shady Grove an order from Robert E. Lee to move the Third Corps along the Shady Grove Church Road toward Spotsylvania Court House. The troops were in motion by six o'clock and arrived in the vicinity of the Block House, where they were ordered to continue through the village and to assume a position just east of it, where they would entrench. They arrived at Spotsylvania at about noon.[46]

At Todd's Tavern, Hancock sent scouting parties to the west of his position soon after daylight. They reported finding no trace of the Confederate infantry force that had been engaged the previous afternoon. At 6:00 A.M. Hancock forwarded these reports to army headquarters and stated his belief that the enemy had left his front. A few minutes later, however, he reported that he expected to be attacked on the front of Birney's division, which was positioned across the Catharpin Road. The reason for this alarm is not known. In response, Meade sent Gibbon's division from near army head-quarters back up the Brock Road approximately one mile with orders to connect with Birney's left. The two large regiments of the Artillery Reserve functioning as infantry were sent from Piney Branch Church to Todd's Tavern. The alarm, however, proved to be false, and Gibbon soon was recalled.[47]

At noon Hancock received an order from Meade to move three of his divisions down the Brock Road and to connect to Warren's right. He was to leave one division at Todd's Tavern with a suitable amount of artillery. The final sentence of the order read, "All information here leads to the belief that they are passing to our left and you will be needed here."[48]

Grant Formulates a Plan

This order reflects a misapprehension on Grant's part which had begun to form at about 10:00 A.M., when he received from Burnside copies of Will-cox's reports of having sighted the enemy at 7:15 A.M. within half a mile of the Gayle house. The actual distance from Spotsylvania Court House to the Ni River crossing of the Fredericksburg Road is slightly more than 1½ miles. The map available to the Federal commanders indicated this distance as being closer to 3½ miles. Moreover, on the Federal map the position of the fictitious "Gate" coincided closely with the actual position of the Gayle house. It appears possible that Willcox, after learning that the house was named Gayle's, assumed that the spelling on the map was incorrect.[49]

When Grant was informed at 10:00 A.M. that Willcox had sighted Confederate cavalry and perhaps infantry four (actually less than two) miles east of Spotsylvania in the direction of Fredericksburg, he must have been somewhat surprised. He soon received Hancock's initial reports that the Confederate force opposite his position at Todd's Tavern had moved away. From these indications Grant began to suspect that Lee was shifting his army from west to east with the intention of positioning it between the Federal force and Fredericksburg.[50] At 10:15 he forwarded Willcox's reports to Meade and ordered him to send out scouts from the left of the Sixth Corps's position to the Fredericksburg Road. If any sizeable enemy force was moving in that direction, Meade would need to recall the army trains from their route of march southeast of Chancellorsville. Grant also said he would need to put strong pressure on the enemy's left flank.[51]

At 12:45 P.M. Burnside forwarded to Grant Willcox's message of 11:45 A.M. stating that he was heavily engaged by superior numbers. Grant reacted immediately with instructions. He informed Burnside that the enemy had disappeared from the right and was moving in the direction of Willcox's

Ulysses S. Grant
(National Archives)

position. He ordered Burnside to direct Willcox to hold his position to the last extremity and to expect the enemy force moving against him to be attacked from the west by the Army of the Potomac. At the same time Meade was advised that if the suspected Confederate move was actually occurring, his army must follow and attack vigorously.[52]

George G. Meade
(National Archives)

Thus evolved a Federal plan based upon erroneous suppositions. One reason for some of these errors was the Federals' failure to use cavalry for reconnaissance. Wilson and his Third Division troopers, who were familiar with the Fredericksburg Road, were riding south with Sheridan at this time. The three cavalry regiments that were retained with the Army of the Potomac

Winfield S. Hancock
(National Archives)

were working out of Chancellorsville that morning, picketing the roads north to the Rapidan River. These regiments, the Second Ohio, Third New Jersey, and Fifth New York, were formed into a provisional brigade, commanded by Colonel Hammond, and were assigned for duty with the Fourth Division of the Ninth Corps under Ferrero. Burnside had the Thirteenth Pennsylvania Cavalry Regiment assigned to him, but he apparently did not use it for reconnaissance at this time.[53]

Gouverneur K. Warren
(Mass. MOLLUS Collection, MHI)

John Sedgwick
(Mass. MOLLUS Collection, MHI)

Horatio G. Wright
(Mass. MOLLUS Collection, MHI)

Ambrose E. Burnside
(Mass. MOLLUS Collection, MHI)

Philip H. Sheridan
(Mass. MOLLUS Collection, MHI)

Robert E. Lee
(National Archives)

Richard H. Anderson
(Mass. MOLLUS Collection, MHI)

Richard S. Ewell
(Mass. MOLLUS Collection, MHI)

Jubal A. Early
(Mass. MOLLUS Collection, MHI)

J. E. B. Stuart
(Mass. MOLLUS Collection, MHI)

8

If You Can Hold Your Position, Do So

9 May

Union Second Corps

At noon the troops of Barlow's division retired from their works at Todd's Tavern and started down the Brock Road, followed in about an hour by Birney's division (for the geography of this area, see Map 5-1). Mott's division, together with the Artillery Reserve infantrymen, was retained at the tavern. Hancock's orders required him to march his First and Third divisions to the right flank of Gibbon's Second Division, which, after returning to army headquarters from Birney's left, had been advanced to the southeast toward the Po River.[1]

Gibbon's new position was to the front and slightly to the east of the T. Hart house, which faced the Po River, flowing roughly west to east one-half to three-quarters of a mile away. Barlow, followed by Birney, turned off the Brock Road, probably onto the road to Talley's, but perhaps onto the one to Hart's, and, moving forward and then left, assumed his position to the right of Gibbon's line, with Barlow in the center and Birney on the right. The brigade alignment from left to right was: in Gibbon's division, Col. Samuel S. Carroll, Brig. Gen. Joshua T. Owen, and Brig. Gen. Alexander S. Webb; in Barlow's division, Colonel Miles, Col. John R. Brooke, Col. Paul Frank, and Colonel Smyth; in Birney's division, Brig. Gen. J. H. Hobart Ward and Colonel Crocker.[2]

The Federals looked out across open fields to the valley of the Po and could see as far as the Shady Grove Church Road. At approximately 3:00 P.M. Grant and Meade visited Gibbon's position. They saw a Confederate wagon train moving along the road in the direction of Spotsylvania. A staff officer suggested to Meade that a battery could easily reach the train. Meade replied that that would merely frighten a few teamsters and mules. The three-inch rifles of Capt. Frederick M. Edgell's First New Hampshire Battery and perhaps others were brought forward, however, and their fire hastened the wagons along their way.[3]

Meanwhile, the Federals had begun to reconnoiter at least as far forward as the river. The only Confederate force in front of Hancock's men was a portion of Young's cavalry brigade of Hampton's division, primarily the Cobb and Jeff Davis legions, accompanied by two pieces of Capt. James. W. Thomson's horse artillery battery. At about 4:30 P.M., the Federal high command decided to force a crossing. Half an hour later, Barlow ordered Brooke's brigade to cross and to take possession of the closest part of Shady Grove Church Road. At 6:00 P.M. Brooke reported that his mission had been accomplished against light opposition. Hancock immediately ordered the remaining brigades of the First Division across the river, which Brooke reported to be 2½ feet deep at that point. The division assembled along the Shady Grove Church Road just north of Waite's Shop then marched east toward the Block House Bridge over the Po, the next objective. Miles's brigade led the movement in battle formation, followed by the remaining three brigades in column of march.[4]

Birney was ordered to take his division across at 6:00 P.M. His troops crossed at Tinder's Mill, where Hampton's troopers apparently offered stiffer opposition than they had at Brooke's crossing site. However, Birney's men soon drove the Confederates back and reached the Shady Grove Church Road. The Southern horsemen retired to Talley's Mill on Gladys Run approximately one-half mile south of Waite's Shop. Birney marched his troops east along the road to the Waite intersection.[5]

Gibbon's division crossed unopposed downstream from Barlow at the Pritchett house. After crossing, Gibbon apparently moved his men in battle formation, which greatly reduced their speed. At 7:00 P.M. Hancock ordered Gibbon to permit Barlow precedence on the Shady Grove Church Road, if the Second Division were not ready. An hour later, Barlow's column had passed Gibbon's.[6] At dark, Barlow arrived just to the west of the bridge, where the water was found to be too deep to ford. There were thick woods near the banks of the river, and advancing skirmishers would have to cross on the bridge. Hancock reported the situation to Meade at 10:00 P.M. and received instructions at midnight to continue the movement at first light.[7]

When Barlow's advance arrived near the bridge, the closest Confederates were those occupying the left of Gregg's Texas brigade's line, about half a mile northeast. They were unaware of the Federal presence on their left flank. The way was open to the rear of this line, but the Federal high command opted to wait until daylight before proceeding further. When Hampton first observed Union infantrymen advancing to cross the Po, he notified Gen. Robert E. Lee. Thus, the situation at the bridge at daylight was to be considerably different from the situation at 10:00 P.M. and at midnight.[8]

Union Fifth Corps

The troops of the Fifth Corps remained relatively inactive until late in the afternoon, when orders were issued to advance the skirmish lines. On the left of the corps line, the advanced picket force, the Ninth and Thirty-second Massachusetts regiments of Sweitzer's brigade, moved forward and drove the Confederate skirmishers from the rise on which stood the burned Spindle house and orchard. The Yankees continued forward a short distance and then hugged the ground while pioneers crawled forward to dig rifle pits. Some troops from Ayres's brigade also advanced as far as the Spindle house.[9] The remainder of Ayres's troops moved forward to the first rise in front of the original line of works. Here they joined the Twenty-second Massachusetts, Fourth Michigan, and Sixty-second Pennsylvania regiments of Sweitzer's command. Bartlett's troops remained in reserve.[10]

Sometime after dark the pioneers withdrew, and more infantrymen advanced to bolster the picket line near the orchard. At about midnight a sizeable force of Bratton's men suddenly charged from their works in the edge of the trees, driving the Federals from the orchard to their main line in their rear. Bratton reestablished a picket force on the orchard line.[11]

The operations of Cutler's division to the right of Griffin's are difficult to ascertain from the available evidence. Cutler reported that, under orders, he assaulted the enemy's position during the afternoon and was repulsed. Field's men opposite reported only minor skirmishing throughout the day. On the right of Cutler, the pickets of the Iron Brigade were driven in at dark, but they soon regained their position.[12] Also to the right of Cutler, Crawford's two brigades of Pennsylvania Reserves and Coulter's brigade spent the afternoon and evening in light skirmishing. They apparently gained some ground but relinquished the advanced positions after dark. The Maryland brigade remained in line to the rear of the W. W. Jones house on Crawford's right. At 3:00 P.M. Lt. George Breck's Battery L, First New York Light Artillery, was sent to Gibbon's position near the Pritchett house, where it relieved Edgell's Second Corps battery and where it suffered two casualties: one man was mortally wounded, and the battery commander received a minor wound. Capt. James H. Cooper's Battery B, First Pennsylvania Light Artillery, was dispatched to the same area and fired forty rounds at Confederates across the Po. Both batteries returned to the vicinity of the Alsop house after dark.[13]

At midnight Warren ordered his division commanders to have their troops prepared to drive in the enemy's pickets at first light. The goal was to find the Confederate main line of battle.[14]

Union Sixth Corps

Ricketts's two brigades that were on the right of the Sixth Corps line adjacent to the Brock Road advanced skirmish lines against the center and right-center of Kershaw's line in response to an order issued late in the afternoon.[15] The troops from the Second Brigade, on the right, moved forward approximately six hundred yards across swampy ground, and when they received a volley of musket fire from their right front, they retired. The First Brigade skirmishers to the left claimed to have advanced one thousand yards before they were fired upon by enemy troops entrenched two hundred yards in front, whereupon they also retired.

Neill's Second Division skirmishers had advanced over one-quarter mile when they encountered a Southern battle line to their right front and consequently retired a short distance. The right of Neill's skirmish line had met the right of Kershaw's line and left of Rodes's line, while the skirmishers on the left had received long range fire from Southerners manning the right of Rodes's line. Russell's First Division skirmishers had attempted to maintain alignment on Neill's left during the advance. They encountered no opposition because they were moving due east toward the Landrum house, three-quarters of a mile ahead.[16]

Two regiments of the New Jersey brigade of Russell's division were sent on an independent reconnaissance mission in the afternoon. The First and Fifteenth regiments were directed to advance as far as the "Block House and Alsop Road," if possible. This nonexistent thoroughfare was depicted on the Federal planning map. This reconnaissance was probably the result of Grant's order to Meade at 10:15 A.M. to investigate the area between the left flank of the Army of the Potomac and the advanced position of the Ninth Corps along the Fredericksburg Road. From the accounts available, it is difficult to ascertain the route of the two New Jersey regiments. They spent the night in the vicinity of Captain Brown's house, about three-quarters of a mile north of the northern tip of Ewell's line. The Jerseymen did not rejoin their brigade until the following night.[17]

On the left of the corps, the First Division formed in two lines with Upton's and Eustis's brigades in front and Col. Henry W. Brown's New Jersey brigade and Cross's brigade in the rear. On their right the order of Neill's brigades was Grant, Wheaton, Edwards, and Bidwell.[18] Artillery was placed at intervals along the line behind the infantry. Two and perhaps three batteries extended from the left of Ricketts's division to Wright's, at the left end of the line.[19]

Confederate Second Corps

The Union Sixth Corps batteries duelled periodically throughout the afternoon with Confederate guns from Braxton's battalion, positioned along Rodes's line, and from Maj. Richard C. M. Page's battalion, along Johnson's line.[20] This Union fire compelled Johnson's and some of Rodes's infantrymen to add traverses to their works. Harry Hays, commanding the combined Louisiana brigade, was wounded severely that day, possibly by this artillery fire. Col. William Monaghan of the Sixth Louisiana Regiment assumed command of Hays's old brigade and Col. Zebulon York assumed command of the five Louisiana regiments formerly commanded by Stafford.[21] Members of the Stonewall Brigade placed head logs atop their works for increased protection.[22]

Late in the afternoon troops of the Twenty-first Virginia Regiment of Witcher's brigade, which was located at the tip of the salient, finished their traverses. They were preparing to enter them and to savor their handiwork when the regiment was ordered to report to Gen. George Steuart, who was commanding the brigade on their right. The Virginians protested this order, as they did not wish to lose the opportunity to fight from behind such well-constructed works. Steuart sent them out three-quarters of a mile or more to the northeast, where they established an advanced picket line. One-third of the regiment manned the forward line, and the remainder assumed a position a few hundred yards to the rear in reserve. Their precise location cannot be determined, but in light of their adventures on the morning of 12 May, it would appear that they were about half a mile east-southeast of the Landrum house. In the evening Yankee skirmishers, probably from the First and Fifteenth New Jersey regiments, approached to within firing range of the left front of the Virginians' advanced line. The opposing pickets skirmished until dark, when the firing in this area ceased.[23]

Union Ninth Corps and Confederate Third Corps

When the van of Stevenson's division of the Ninth Corps arrived at the Ni River crossing on the Fredericksburg Road at noon, Willcox ordered Hartranft to take the remainder of his brigade across, with the exception of one regiment. Since the regiments of the two brigades of the Third Division were intermingled along the line, Hartranft was placed in temporary command of those regiments on the west of the road. He extended the line to the right three hundred yards or so in order to secure the safety of the river bank behind. Cutcheon positioned a company of sharpshooters from his Twentieth Michigan Regiment in advance at a deserted house.[24]

Shortly after midday Willcox began to report enemy sightings in the area around Spotsylvania Court House. From the top of the Gayle house he reported seeing Confederate cavalry, infantry, and wagons moving to both left and right. The cavalrymen were probably Stuart's troopers departing in pursuit of Sheridan's column. The infantry was the van of Cadmus Wilcox's division of Early's Third Corps arriving at the courthouse. These foot soldiers took a position a few hundred yards east of the village and formed a line to the north of the Fredericksburg Road. The wagons were observed moving south, and Willcox's artillerymen fired at them from the crest north of the river crossing.[25]

Grant heard this artillery firing and ordered Burnside to move to the front and to assume command there. However, by 4:20 P.M. Burnside was still back as far as the Orange Plank Road, and by 10:30 P.M. he had advanced only as far as J. Alsop's, where he apparently spent the night.[26]

In midafternoon Stevenson's division crossed the Ni. One brigade strengthened the Third Division's line near the crest, and the other spread out along the south bank of the stream to protect the crossing and nearby fords.[27] During the rest of the afternoon intermittent skirmishing occurred in this area as more of Early's corps arrived and as scouts were sent forward to locate and probe the Yankee position.

Potter's Second Division was ordered forward to J. Alsop's, where it arrived in the evening and joined Col. Elisha G. Marshall's Provisional Brigade. At 10:30 P.M. Burnside sent Grant a message that partially clarified the confusion about the geography of the Fredericksburg Road. He explained that Willcox's position was at Gayle's house, within 1½ miles of Spotsylvania, and that there was no such place as "Gate." This explanation, however useful, did not correct the erroneous position of the Ni River on the maps.[28]

The van of Cadmus Wilcox's Confederate Third Corps division, the brigade of Brig. Gen. James H. Lane, had arrived at the village at noon and assumed its position just to the north of the Fredericksburg Road, three or four hundred yards to the east.[29] Wilcox's remaining three brigades took a position to Lane's right. The division line extended south of the road. Scouts from Brig. Gen. Samuel McGowan's brigade reconnoitered to within sight of the Beverley house east of the road and observed Orlando Willcox's Federal troops there. When Heth's and Mahone's divisions arrived, they halted near the village.[30]

Thus Lee, in addition to frustrating the Federal attempt to occupy Spotsylvania Court House, now had successfully reunited the three infantry corps of his army following the march from the Wilderness. The period of consolidation, however, was to be short.

Sometime during the night, Lee ordered Early to send one of his divisions back along the Shady Grove Church Road and to assume a defensive position covering the Block House Bridge. In effect, this would extend the left flank of the army across the Po. Mahone's division was selected for this assignment, and it soon began marching back over the road on which it had arrived early in the afternoon. Lee also ordered Early to lead another of his divisions by way of the rear and left to drive back the Yankee column that had taken possession of the Shady Grove Church Road west of the bridge. Lee and Early may not have realized that they faced three divisions of Hancock's Second Corps. Early selected Heth's division for the task.[31] This left behind only Wilcox's troops, astride the Fredericksburg Road just east of the village, to face two divisions of the Union Ninth Corps. Moreover, there was a gap of more than a mile through the woods from Lane's left to Steuart's brigade on the right of Ewell's line. The Federals had been presented with a tremendous opportunity, but they were unaware of it because of faulty maps and because of their failure to use mounted reconnaissance troops. Sometime before dawn of 10 May, Burnside received the following message from Grant:

HEADQUARTERS ARMIES OF THE UNITED STATES
In the Field, May 10, 1864—1.30 A.M.

Major-General BURNSIDE:
Your note of 10.30 last evening just received. A division of Hancock's corps has been ordered to take position to-night between you and the present left of General Meade's army. If you should need its aid make no hesitation in ordering it to your assistance. If you can hold your position at Mr. Gayle's do so; if you ascertain that you cannot hold it quietly withdraw to the head of the column near Alsop's.

By command of Lieutenant-General Grant:

JNO. A. RAWLINS
Brigadier-General and Chief of Staff.[32]

Grant's pugnaciousness had apparently subsided with the sun.

It Is Ordered That We Attack 10 May

Federal Second Corps and Confederate Third Corps

From Spotsylvania, Mahone's division marched west by way of the Brock and Shady Grove Church roads and arrived immediately east of the Block House Bridge before first light. Lt. Col. David G. McIntosh's battalion of artillery accompanied the division.[1] Upon arrival, the infantrymen began to entrench on a rise of ground about three hundred yards east of the bridge. When completed, this line of works ran from the north side of the road about two hundred yards toward the left end of Field's line. South of the road, the works extended for approximately one-third mile, paralleling the course of the river.

Farther up the Po, Hancock had ordered that three bridges be constructed during the night for use in case the Federals needed to cross rapidly. One bridge was placed where Brooke's brigade had crossed on the previous afternoon, the second downstream where Gibbon had crossed, and the third bridge was a short distance downstream from Gibbon's crossing.[2] An artilleryman who used the center bridge remembered that it was a pontoon bridge whose boats were covered with canvas, the first such bridge he had seen.[3]

At first light Hancock ordered Miles to reconnoiter the area around the Block House Bridge to determine the practicality of attempting to force a passage. The officer commanding the reconnaissance reported that opposite the bridge, the Confederates were in strong force in entrenchments that commanded the crossing.[4]

Then Miles was ordered to send a regiment downstream to find a site where troops could cross unopposed. He selected his own Sixty-first New York Regiment, and at 6:00 A.M., accompanied by the indefatigable Lieutenant Robertson of Miles's staff, the men moved down the west bank of the stream for nearly a mile until they discovered a log lying across the water. Twenty men were sent across to reconnoiter. They were soon fired on, and

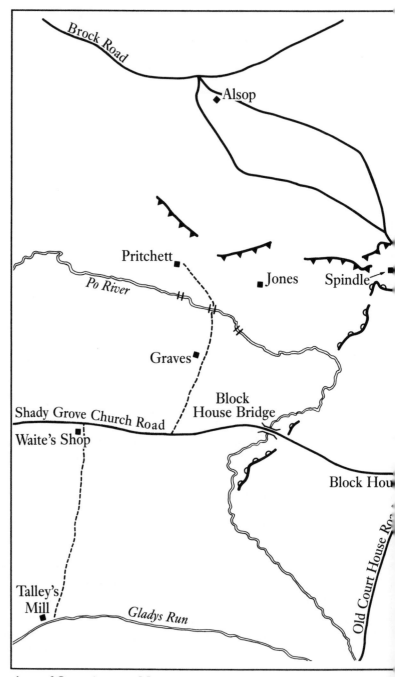

MAP 9-1. Area of Operations, 10 May

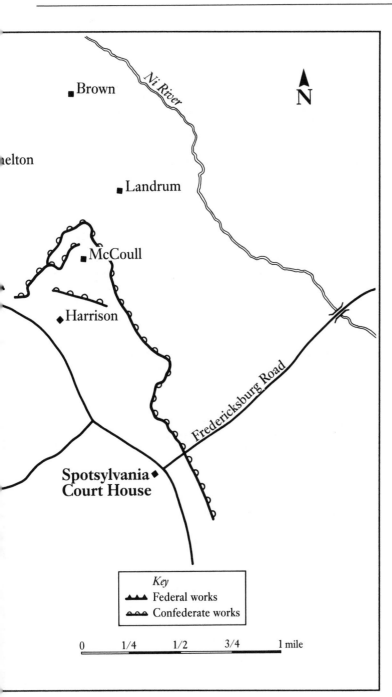

Brown

Ni River

N

ielton

Landrum

McCoull

Harrison

Fredericksburg Road

Spotsylvania ◆
Court House

Key
▲▲▲ Federal works
⌒⌒⌒ Confederate works

0   1/4   1/2   3/4   1 mile

five of them were wounded. They were immediately recalled and came back bringing their wounded comrades with them.[5]

Lieutenant Robertson then visited a house a few hundred yards west of the crossing point. There he was informed that the Po could be crossed farther downstream by first crossing Gladys Run at a mill dam. With twenty men Robertson went south to the mill, where another local resident told him that a large force of Confederates was moving west up the opposite side of Gladys Run. Robertson did not believe him and rode across the dam to see for himself. Arriving at the edge of a wood, he discovered that his informant had been telling the truth. Heth's Division, led by Jubal Early himself, was moving to drive back any Yankees along the Shady Grove Church Road west of the Block House Bridge.[6] They had left Spotsylvania early in the morning and had marched west to the Block House. There they had turned south, passing the Old Court House, and crossed the Po, after which they had turned west onto a road south of Gladys Run that paralleled the creek. Lt. Col. Charles Richardson's battalion of artillery along with the battery of Capt. Thomas Ellett accompanied the infantrymen.[7]

Meanwhile, Brooke's brigade of Barlow's division had also been ordered to locate a crossing site below the bridge. Arriving at a point approximately one-half mile below the bridge, Brooke sent his Sixty-sixth New York Regiment across. The New Yorkers advanced far enough to observe the works of Mahone's division. Word of their discovery was forwarded to Barlow, who ordered Brooke to retire his brigade to the Shady Grove Church Road and to establish a defensive position there.[8]

Simultaneously with the orders for Brooke's reconnaissance came orders to Birney to send a few regiments south on the road past Waite's Shop. These troops advanced as far as Talley's Mill on Gladys Run, where they skirmished lightly with some of Hampton's dismounted troopers.[9]

During the first hours of daylight Hancock forwarded to army headquarters descriptions of the strength of Mahone's works east of the river. Some of these sightings were obtained from scouts in treetops. Barlow and Lt. Col. Cyrus Comstock of Grant's staff also reconnoitered the enemy position.[10] Information from these sources led Grant to cancel Hancock's flanking movement. Instead, he was to attempt a massive assault against Anderson's position on Laurel Hill opposite Warren and against Ewell's position opposite Wright. Grant apparently assumed that Lee, in order to counter Hancock's flanking movement, had weakened Anderson's line and perhaps Ewell's as well. At 10:00 A.M. Meade ordered Hancock to transfer two of his three divisions from south of the Po to the right of Warren's line and to prepare for a combined attack by the two corps, which he would command. He also sent orders to Warren and Wright at this time. The combined assault was scheduled for 5:00 P.M.[11]

Gibbon's division immediately recrossed the river and assumed a position behind Crawford's (see Map 7-3). Birney's troops later crossed by the center bridge and were positioned in reserve behind Gibbon. These retrograde movements were conducted through the noon hour.[12] Barlow's troops remained south of the Po with Capt. William A. Arnold's Battery A and Capt. T. Frederick Brown's Battery B, First Rhode Island Light Artillery.

Union Fifth Corps and Confederate First Corps

At 7:00 A.M. Warren notified army headquarters that Crawford's pickets had relinquished their advanced position during the night. The major general reported that he had ordered all of his pickets along his line to drive back the enemy's pickets opposite and to establish themselves as close as possible to the Confederate main line.[13]

At 10:00 A.M. the batteries of Lieutenant Breck and Lt. Benjamin F. Rittenhouse were sent to the right of Warren's line, about four hundred yards behind the W. W. Jones house in the edge of a wood. For the rest of the morning they fired at the left of Field's infantry line and at the guns of Cabell's battalion, to its rear near the J. Perry house. Members of Gregg's Third Arkansas Regiment remembered that, during this fire, the infantrymen lay flat in the ditches behind their earthworks and watched the dust fly, suffering no harm themselves. These Federal guns also fired at Mahone's infantry and artillery east of the Block House Bridge.[14] Maj. W. A. Roebling of Warren's staff visited the right of the corps line and noticed that some batteries with Gibbon's division across the river were firing to the northeast in an attempt to enfilade Field's line and the artillery to its rear. This firing was soon halted, because it was hitting some of Crawford's skirmishers.[15]

Meanwhile, on the left of the corps line immediately to the west of the Brock Road, Griffin requested two batteries and was sent Mink's and Richardson's. He ordered them to direct their fire across the Spindle clearing at the trees beyond, to provide cover for infantry skirmishers attempting to move forward.[16]

Griffin visited Sweitzer's brigade at approximately 9:30 A.M. to explain the morning plan of operations: first, to retake the rifle pits along the rise where the orchard and burned Spindle house stood, then to continue to the edge of the woods in front and stop there. Griffin promised artillery support.[17] Approximately 250 men were selected from the Twenty-second Massachusetts and Fourth Michigan regiments. They advanced from the main line to the rifle pits on the first rise ahead and mingled with the brigade pickets there. At 11:30 A.M. Maj. Mason W. Burt, acting commander of the Twenty-second Massachusetts, ordered the troops forward, and they advanced with muskets at the trail position with bayonets fixed. From the next rise, Bratton's pickets dropped a few of the advancing Federals, but as most of Burt's men approached the rise with muskets still loaded, the Confederates bolted for the trees to their rear. Sweitzer's men rested for about two minutes in the reoccupied rifle pits and then continued forward. Arriving within fifty to one hundred yards of the trees, they were blasted by a volley of musketry from Bratton's South Carolinians and some of DuBose's Georgians in the trees ahead. Capt. William W. Parker's guns shivered the Yankees with canister from immediately south of the intersection of Brock and Old Court House roads, probably helped by some of Wofford's and Bryan's troops, who were east of the junction.

Most of the Federals retreated to the rise where the ruined house and orchard were. Some of the men, however, remained lying in shallow pits within one hundred yards or so of Bratton's works. One company of the Twenty-second Massachusetts, finding insufficient room in nearby rifle pits, crossed the road to the east side. One piece of Parker's battery began to fire regularly up the road, thus isolating these Massachusetts troops from their comrades. They hugged the ground at the foot of a low hill. This was the same site where some of Lyle's Second Brigade troops under Lieutenant Colonel Peirson had sought refuge on the morning of 8 May.

The main body of Major Burt's men on the orchard hill had little cover and were forced to remain prone, without firing. They were relieved or augmented at 3:00 P.M. by five companies of the Thirty-second Massachusetts Regiment. The survivors of the group in the advanced rifle pits and the company east of the road crawled back to safety after dark. Approximately one-half of the 150 members of the Twenty-second Massachusetts who participated in the advance were either killed or wounded.[18]

To the west of this action, Ayres reported to Griffin at 11:30 A.M. that his skirmishers had reoccupied some rifle pits beyond the orchard and were being supported by a regiment of Regulars. He complained of an enfilade fire from his right.[19]

To Griffin's right Cutler's skirmishers, at times heavily supported, attempted to advance, with little success. The Eighty-fourth New York of Rice's brigade moved forward two hundred yards into an open area, where it immediately received heavy front and flanking fire. It marched by the right flank into some woods, where it fired blindly toward the enemy while suffering from infantry and especially artillery fire, until relieved in mid-afternoon.[20]

On the right of the corps line Crawford reported as early as 8:30 A.M. that his skirmish line was advancing steadily. At 9:30 he informed Warren that his right was fairly close to the enemy's works and that his left was steadily driving Confederate skirmishers back through heavy woods. He identified the Rebels as belonging to G. T. Anderson's brigade. During the morning Warren reiterated his orders to Cutler and Crawford to drive back the enemy's skirmishers to their main line and to establish a position as close to that line as possible. These operations appear to have been preparations for a coordinated assault scheduled for later in the day.[21]

Union Sixth Corps and Confederate Second Corps

Late on the evening of 9 May Grant decided to position a division on Wright's left to connect the Sixth and Ninth corps. Mott's command, which was at Todd's Tavern, was selected and was under way at 3:00 A.M. The two Artillery Reserve regiments serving as infantry were returned to Piney Branch Church at that time.[22]

At daylight, three batteries of the Sixth Corps were once again positioned behind the infantry line. One section of Capt. William H. McCartney's Napoleons was stationed on the right of the corps line near the spot where Sedgwick had been struck the previous morning. The alignment of batteries to the left of McCartney's section was Capt. William B. Rhodes's Battery E, First Rhode Island Light Artillery, the remaining two sections of McCartney's, and Capt. Andrew Cowan's First New York Battery.[23]

That morning two mortars were carried forward and were placed into position on the right of McCartney's two guns. The Army of the Potomac opened the campaign with eight of these 24-pounder Coehorns, which were assigned to the Artillery Reserve. On 9 May, the Fifteenth New York Heavy Artillery Regiment, which had moved from Piney Branch Church down to the Brock Road that morning, detailed Company E of the Second Battalion to take charge of the mortar battery. The arrival of two of these pieces on the battle line on the morning of 10 May appears to have been the first deployment of this type of weapon in a combat field battle.[24]

Wright reported that his skirmishers, moving forward at first light, spent the morning feeling for the main Confederate battle line. They gradually turned to the right as they approached the works occupied by Johnson's division, whose line faced more northerly than did that of Rodes to its left.[25]

There was constant musketry sharpshooting and artillery firing between Wright's men and the Confederate troops opposite. Along Ewell's line the Virginia batteries of Capt. Lorraine F. Jones and B. H. Smith, of Lt. Col. Robert A. Hardaway's battalion, were positioned to support Rodes's division with Capt. Willis J. Dance's battery to the rear of the line in reserve. The three batteries of Lt. Col. William Nelson's battalion supported Johnson's division.[26]

During the artillery firing, some shots from Rhodes's and McCartney's pieces landed among Gordon's division, which was lying in reserve behind the line of works it had begun to construct on the previous day. As a result, this division moved forward to the area immediately behind the junction of Kershaw's right and Rodes's left.[27]

The two brigades of Mott's Second Corps division arrived near the Brown house beyond the left of Wright's line at approximately 7:30–8:00 A.M. There they found the First and Fifteenth New Jersey regiments of the Sixth Corps, who had spent a lonely night in the vicinity. The New Jersey troops were placed temporarily under Mott, who was himself under Wright's command. Mott was ordered to advance a heavy line of skirmishers south from the Brown house to discover what lay in that direction. He was also directed to find the forward position of Burnside's force to his left and to move to its support should Burnside request assistance.[28]

A short time after Mott arrived at the new position, Theodore Lyman, of Meade's staff, arrived there to brief him on his assignment and to attempt to pinpoint his position relative to the rest of the army. Lyman recorded that Mott appeared stupid and listless and that he refused to do anything until his men, who had been marching for four hours or so, had some coffee. Lyman returned to headquarters.[29]

After an hour had passed, Mott sent forward one of Col. William R. Brewster's New York Excelsior regiments to relieve the skirmish line south from the Brown house. A witness recorded that Johnson's pickets waited until the exchange had begun in the rifle pits, then fired a volley and began to advance toward the Federals. Brewster's troops fled to the rear, and the New Jersey regiments got back into the pits and fought off the Southerners. At ten o'clock in the morning Mott attempted a reconnaissance in force with some of his Excelsior regiments and the First New Jersey. They might have advanced far enough to see Johnson's works near the tip of the salient. At the first Confederate volley, they retreated to the Brown house and were followed by the skirmish line of New Jersey troops. At 11:00 A.M., shortly after the close of this operation, Oliver Wendell Holmes, Jr., now an aide-de-camp to Wright, arrived and urged Mott to push the Confederates toward Mott's right or Russell's left. Holmes thought Mott seemed stupid and flustered.[30]

At 8:55 A.M. a staff officer of Burnside's had gotten through to Mott and reported Burnside's position as being at J. Alsop's, about 2½ miles to the left and rear of Mott's position. This information was passed on to Wright and by him to Meade. Grant and Meade, however, were already aware of this. On the previous day Grant had strongly suggested that Burnside move his headquarters to his front line near the Ni River, but Burnside had opted instead to remain at Alsop's. What Grant and Meade wanted to learn was the location of the right of Burnside's battle line, so they could connect it with the Army of the Potomac.[31]

Meade's order to Wright for the planned combined assault at 5:00 P.M. included the provision that Mott's division was to be included in the attacking force. Wright notified his division commanders of the intended attack and directed them to examine carefully the terrain over which each would be advancing. Then they were to report personally at corps headquarters to explain their findings. Skirmish parties edged forward once again as midday passed.[32]

Union Ninth Corps

During the morning, Brig. Gen. Thomas G. Stevenson, the commander of the First Division, Ninth Corps, was killed by a chance shot. The general and members of his staff had established temporary headquarters directly in the rear of a bank of earth. A short distance to the rear stood a tree, and since the heat of the morning sun was already strong, the headquarters party moved back to the shade of the tree. They ate their breakfasts and were lying under the tree smoking and discussing their intention of relocating division headquarters to a site that would provide both more shade and safety when picket firing began in front. A minie ball from the Confederate skirmish line struck the general in the back of the head, fatally wounding him. Col. Daniel Leasure, commander of the Second Brigade, was placed in temporary command of the division.[33]

At 8:30 A.M. Willcox reported to Burnside that his pickets on the right had seen at least two regiments of Confederates moving from Willcox's left to right. These were the North Carolinians of Lane's brigade, who repositioned themselves during the morning to a site approximately three-quarters of a mile north of Spotsylvania.[34]

When Grant determined that a combined assault was to be delivered at 5:00 P.M., he sent Col. Horace Porter of his staff to Burnside with both oral and written instructions for the cooperation of the Ninth Corps in the enterprise. He ordered Burnside to reconnoiter during the day and to attempt to locate the right of Lee's line. At 5:00 P.M. his force was to be especially active in an attempt to discourage Lee from withdrawing troops from that section in order to reinforce the Confederate center and left. Moreover, if an opportunity for attacking Lee's right presented itself, Burnside was to assault with all of his available forces.[35]

Burnside informed Willcox of the Federal plan, saying that "it is ordered that we attack at 5 o'clock this p.m."[36] He also said that corps headquarters was in communication with Mott, who was approximately "2 miles in front of us, and his pickets extend over to the Second Michigan."[37] Actually, Mott was located approximately two miles to the right of the Ninth Corps line, not in front. Burnside was still back at the J. Alsop house when he sent this message, the time of which is unknown. It appears that he was capable of describing a location only in relation to his own position at the time. The message also indicated that a connection of sorts had finally been accomplished with the left of the Army of the Potomac. The commander of the Second Michigan stated that, shortly after midday, two regiments of Regulars, the Fourth and Tenth from the First Division, reported to him and that he immediately spread them out along the Ni River bank from the right of his regiment to a ford 1½ miles upstream, where they contacted Mott's pickets at 3:00 P.M.[38]

Willcox informed Colonel Leasure of the intention to attack at 5:00 P.M. and ordered him to notify his command, to issue orders for the proper preparation, and then to report to Willcox's headquarters in person. In the absence of specific guidance from Burnside, the two division commanders probably were going to compare notes and to attempt to come up with a plan of action.[39]

10

The First Gun Ever Lost by the Second Corps

10 May

Federal Second Corps and Confederate Third Corps South of the Po River

In midmorning Birney sent four regiments (the Fourth and Seventh Maine and Fifty-seventh and 141st Pennsylvania) south past Waite's Shop as far as Talley's Mill as a cover for Brooke's reconnaissance across the Po to the east. At approximately noon, Confederate opposition near the mill stiffened, and soon the Federals were being pushed back by infantrymen and cavalry in the van of Heth's division. The remainder of Birney's division had recrossed the Po by this time, and the advanced Union troops were left essentially to their own devices, with no orders. They sustained fairly heavy casualties as they retired across the river, and many of the survivors did not find their units until late in the afternoon.[1]

To the east of this action the members of Barlow's brigades became involved in a combat that made up for their lack of activity in the Wilderness fighting. Instructions from Second Corps headquarters required Barlow to dispose his force so that it continued to threaten the Confederates' left flank, but so that it also could be withdrawn promptly.[2]

Barlow realigned his force to face the approach of Heth's troops from the southwest. Brooke's and Frank's brigades were stationed a short distance to the south of the Shady Grove Church Road, facing south, with Brooke's left regiment perhaps three to four hundred yards west of the Block House Bridge. These troops hurriedly constructed crude fieldworks. Miles's and Smyth's brigades were positioned north of the road to the rear and slightly to the left of Brooke and Frank. Miles's troops on the left of Smyth's were due north of the bridge on a sharp hillcrest. The Twenty-sixth Michigan and Eighty-first Pennsylvania remained near the bridge to sound the alarm in case Mahone's troops attempted to cross the stream near the bridge.[3]

When Meade was informed that a substantial body of enemy infantry had appeared opposite Birney's former position and was now approaching and

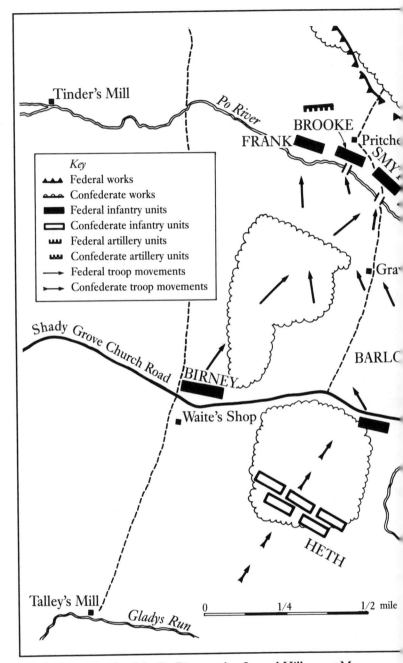

MAP 10-1. Operations South of the Po River and at Laurel Hill on 10 May, Noon to 8:00 P.M. The Federal attack of 7:00 P.M. is shown at Laurel Hill.

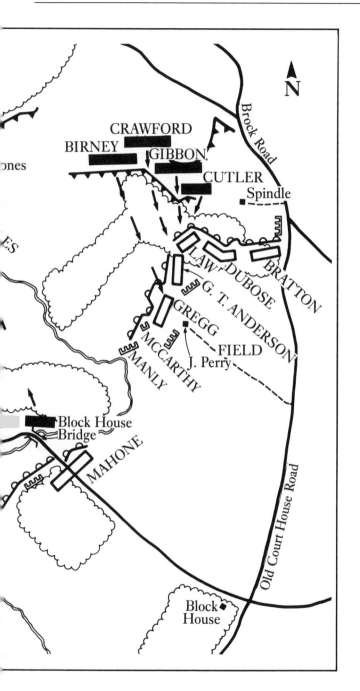

engaging Barlow's skirmishers, he ordered Hancock, who had been attempting to reconnoiter the area of the intended attack against Laurel Hill, to return to the south side of the Po River and personally supervise the withdrawal of Barlow's division to the north side. Hancock recrossed to the south side and ordered Barlow to pull back. The movement commenced at approximately 2:00 P.M.[4] Barlow withdrew the brigades of Brooke and Frank to their right and rear and placed them in a position which Hancock reported as being "on the right of Miles' and Smyth's brigades on a wooded crest in rear of the Block house road, about 100 paces in rear of the line of breastworks."[5] Most of Brooke's troops were in the body of trees northwest of the bridge. The alignment of Brooke's regiments is unknown, except that the 148th Pennsylvania manned the right of the line and that it was partially or completely in the open field immediately west of the wood. The Sixty-fourth New York and Second Delaware regiments were together somewhere in the trees.[6] It is difficult to define the precise line of Frank's brigade. It was to the right of and probably on a line with that of Brooke. An historian for the 125th New York Regiment wrote that the regimental line was in the edge of some woods looking out across the open field. If that wood was the one west of the Graves house, then a gap of at least three hundred yards existed between the two Federal brigades. This may have been the case, as an historian for the 148th Pennsylvania, which was on the right of Brooke's line, reported that members of his unit saw nothing of Frank's troops from the new position.[7] When Brooke's and Frank's men had reached their new positions, Barlow withdrew Miles's and Smyth's brigades two hundred yards south of the Po to the crest that overlooked the two lower bridges, where he intended to cross.[8]

Meanwhile, the advance skirmishers of Heth's division approached the Shady Grove Church Road from the south. They occupied the crude works south of the road from which Brooke's men had but recently departed. The Confederates who emerged from the trees along the road opposite Frank's position immediately lay down along the edge of the trees and began firing across the field.[9]

Soon the main body of Heth's division arrived, and portions of the division mounted an assault against the line occupied by Brooke's and Frank's troops. The Confederates received heavy fire and soon retired.[10] Sometime during this action a delegation of officers from the Third Brigade reported to Barlow and requested that he relieve Frank because he was drunk and unfit to exercise command. They recommended that a junior officer be placed in command of the brigade and offered to waive their rank if this were done. Barlow considered the request but declined to act immediately, telling the officers that they would have to get along as best they could for the present. Later in the day Frank was relieved and placed under arrest. Col. Hiram L. Brown, commander of the 145th Pennsylvania of Brooke's brigade, was placed in command of Frank's troops, who will hereafter be referred to as Brown's brigade.[11]

By this time all of the artillery batteries of the Second Corps, with the exception of Arnold's and Brown's, which were with Barlow south of the river, were deployed on the crest north of the Pritchett house, where they could cover Barlow's withdrawal. These guns could also reach Mahone's artillery south of the Block House Bridge and Cabell's guns on the J. Perry farm. Two Fifth Corps batteries were positioned on the left of this artillery line north of the Jones house.[12]

At 3:00 P.M. Birney's division was sent back to the heights above the bridges to cover Barlow's withdrawal. Here they suffered from Confederate artillery fire. The Eighty-sixth New York was in a particularly hot spot. A fragment from an exploding shell struck and immediately killed a captain. When the dying officer involuntarily straightened his legs, one foot nudged the hammer of a cocked musket lying nearby, which discharged and inflicted a severe wound upon the colonel. These two men were the most respected officers in the regiment. Unfortunate as this incident was, however, the unit was to endure a more trying ordeal later in the day.[13]

Heth's troops conducted two more vigorous assaults, both of which were unsuccessful and costly. Brig. Gen. Henry H. Walker, commanding a brigade of Virginians, received a serious wound in one foot, which had to be amputated. During these attacks the trees to the west of the Graves house were set afire. The fire spread quickly and began to approach the men of Brown's brigade from their rear. The trees at Brooke's position were also engulfed in flames.[14] Finally, an order was sent forward directing Brooke and Brown to retire their brigades across the river. (It does not appear that Miles's and Smyth's men were engaged to any extent during these Confederate attacks.)

It is not possible to present a clear description of these movements or to supply an accurate time when the movements began. Two of Brooke's regiments, the Sixty-fourth New York and 148th Pennsylvania, and very likely a third, the Second Delaware, never received the orders to retire. The troops of the Sixty-fourth New York could tell from the sound of the firing to their right that the Confederates were getting onto their flank and into their rear. They informed their regimental commander, Maj. Leman W. Bradley, that if he did not lead them out of the position, they were going to get out of it by themselves. Bradley reconnoitered to the right and confirmed the men's suspicions that the Rebels had advanced beyond the right flank of the line. The major announced that it was every man for himself and recommended that the troops bear to their left (east) when moving out. Forming into small groups, the New Yorkers moved toward the river and safety. One group skirted the river for a short distance and was fired upon from across the stream by Mahone's troops. Continuing upstream, they emerged into the open and discovered that they were immediately behind the final line of Barlow's troops, probably Miles's brigade, who were about to cross the river. There the New Yorkers found the rest of their regiment and recrossed to the north side.[15]

During this action the 148th Pennsylvania experienced an equally harrowing and costly ordeal. After being engaged for an hour or longer with no orders, the unit's commander, Col. James A. Beaver, became concerned about conditions to the right of his regiment, where Brown's brigade was supposed to be. He sent a reliable scout, who quickly returned with the information that enemy troops were there. By this time most of the Pennsylvanians had exhausted their ammunition, and Beaver decided to retire the regiment immediately. The right companies swung to their rear, and the men then moved down a shallow ravine toward the river. The last few companies were obliged to halt occasionally and to fire at pursuing Confederates. Beaver did not know of the existence of the bridges, so his men scrambled across the Po where they happened to strike it, probably a short distance downstream from the lower bridge. After collapsing from exhaustion on the northern bank and nearly strangling on a drink of whiskey which a sympathetic artilleryman offered him, Beaver learned that the remainder of the brigade had already crossed the river. He complained to Brooke about being left in the lurch but was informed that a staff officer had attempted several times to reach the regiment's position but had been stopped by the burning trees. The Pennsylvanians sustained casualties of 18 killed, 138 wounded, and 12 missing in this action.[16]

The rest of Brooke's regiments crossed the Po on the pontoon bridge opposite the Pritchett house. They suffered from enemy musketry and artillery fire between the north edge of the trees and the river.[17] Brown's troops were obliged to pass through burning woods all of the way from their battle line back to the river, sustaining casualties during the withdrawal. They crossed upstream from the middle bridge where Brooke's troops had crossed.[18]

When Brooke's and Brown's men fell back from the final position, Heth's troops followed them and entered the open fields north of the Shady Grove Church Road. They were fired on immediately by the Federal artillery on the crest north of the Po. Coincidentally, Lee's chief of artillery, General Pendleton, was visiting Cabell's battalion behind the left brigades of Field's division near the J. Perry house. Pendleton ordered Cabell's gunners to switch their fire from Barlow's retiring infantrymen to the Union guns north of the river in order to draw their fire from Heth's troops. Federal batteries were positioned north of the Jones house to counter this fire, and Edgell's battery succeeded in exploding a Confederate limber or caisson. Mahone's artillery was probably also engaged against Barlow's troops and against the Federal guns north of the Po at this time.[19]

Confederate accounts reflect the accuracy of this Union artillery fire, which might have been even more effective had not Birney personally interfered with the placement of the guns. On the right of the line, he advanced one battery in front of three others to a position which masked their fire. Then he pushed two of the front battery's pieces farther still, to where they effectively obstructed all of the guns. Col. John C. Tidball, Second Corps chief of artillery, corrected the alignment, but Birney immediately reinstated it. Later Birney and Barlow changed the positions of two of Brown's Napoleons on the far right and ordered them to fire at Confederate artillery positions in the vicinity of Mahone's infantry, which was out of effective range far to the left. The first round landed among the Federal batteries near the Jones house. Hunt and Tidball angrily demanded the cause of this firing and were told by Brown that he was complying with the express and peremptory orders of the two infantry generals. He said, however, that he would try to decrease the danger by firing only solid shot at high elevation to ensure overshooting the Federal positions.[20]

Amid the confused conditions caused by all of this artillery firing, the final phase of the withdrawal of Brooke's and Brown's troops occurred. Arnold's battery had been positioned near Brooke's final line when the withdrawal began. The captain decided to keep the two guns of the left section as an unsupported rear guard while the remaining four pieces pulled back. As the four guns disappeared to the rear, Arnold, who had remained with the left section, ordered the two three-inch rifles to be loaded with canister and the gun crews to lie down. Suddenly, he ordered his gunners to fire at Confederate infantry and artillery that had appeared before them. After a few rounds Arnold ordered the section to retire, as Heth's men swarmed toward the position. The battery horses were in the woods to the rear, and the Federals dragged the two pieces back by hand, quickly limbered up, and began to pick their way through the trees toward the river. The number six piece retired safely, but the horses drawing the number five gun became terrified and unmanageable because of the flames and the firing. When the animals wedged the gun firmly between two trees, most of the crew members, who reportedly were new men, headed for safety, leaving behind Arnold, the section commander, a sergeant and private from the crew, and a few drivers. The members of this party had no axes with them. With the assistance of some passing infantrymen, they frantically tried to free the gun, but failed. Finally, they reluctantly cut the horses loose and barely escaped capture. According to Hancock, "this was the first gun ever lost by the Second Corps" in action to the enemy in the war.[21]

When Barlow estimated that most of Brooke's and Brown's men had recrossed the river, he ordered Smyth to take his brigade across on the pontoon bridge and to form a line to cover the crossing of Miles's troops. Some of Heth's men attempted to rush the bridge at this time but were repulsed by Miles's and Smyth's infantrymen and the artillery. Barlow became concerned that Mahone might try to cross the Block House Bridge and ordered some artillery to fire on it. When reminded by Lieutenant Robertson and probably Colonel Miles that two of Miles's regiments were still monitoring the bridge, Barlow sent Robertson and another officer to withdraw the two units, which they did. Miles's brigade finally recrossed the Po. Aided by engineers, they dismantled the canvas pontoon bridge and destroyed the lower bridge. A detail had already destroyed the upper bridge.[22]

Sometime late in the action, after a courier from Heth or Early brought word that the Shady Grove Church Road was clear, Mahone crossed the Block House Bridge with his division and dug in north of the road. Early decided not to advance farther because of approaching darkness and because he had completed the assignment that Lee had given him. Heth, with Lee's approval, issued a congratulatory order to his troops that Hancock derided in his postwar report of the action, claiming that, if Barlow's division had not received imperative orders to withdraw, Heth would have had no cause for congratulations. At any rate, the men of Barlow's division had conducted themselves courageously and as competently as could be expected in a hectic and desperate situation. Hancock returned to Warren's front at 5:30 P.M. and discovered a portion of the Fifth Corps and his own Second Division under Gibbon engaged in an assault upon Field's position at Laurel Hill.[23]

Federal Fifth and Second Corps and Confederate First Corps at Laurel Hill

The train of events which led to Warren's attack is unclear. The Fifth Corps skirmishers spent the morning pushing as close to Field's main line as possible. They sustained fairly heavy casualties in these probes, which some of Field's troops regarded as organized assaults.[24]

Cutler's skirmishers had advanced toward Law's position in the trees and Crawford's toward G. T. Anderson's and Gregg's lines. Here they were severely punished by canister fire from two Napoleons of the First Company of Richmond Howitzers, which were posted along Gregg's infantry line. Sometime after 11:00 A.M. Webb's and Carroll's brigades of Gibbon's Second Corps division moved forward to a position between Cutler and Crawford, opposite the right of G. T. Anderson in the Confederate line. At 1:45 P.M. Crawford informed Warren that his troops had advanced about as far as possible and that they were suffering casualties.[25]

Sometime early in the afternoon Warren notified Meade that he believed that he could break the Confederate line in his front. At 3:30 P.M. Meade informed Hancock, who was south of the Po River, that the opportunity for attack was so favorable that he had ordered Warren to attack at once, using Gibbon's troops for support. In addition, he had ordered Wright to be prepared to attack right away or to send support to Warren if necessary. Meade directed Hancock to return Birney's division to the support of the Fifth Corps as soon as Barlow's troops were safely back north of the Po.[26]

Warren's attack began at 4:00–4:30 P.M. Ayres's and Bartlett's brigades on the left of the corps line were alerted for the assault and were directed to move slightly forward prior to the attack. A member of the 155th Pennsylvania on the advanced skirmish line remembered seeing a soldier rolling the body of a dead comrade in front of him for protection as the skirmishers advanced. The attack orders for Griffin's division, however, were either countermanded or never issued. They did not participate.[27] To their right Cutler's Fourth Division moved against Law's brigade, which had constructed strong breastworks from logs and fence rails packed with dirt. This was the first time that these Southerners had enjoyed such stout defenses, and they felt confident of success. They had retrieved some extra muskets from dead and wounded Federals lying in front of their position, and they had ample supplies of ammunition. They were ready for Cutler's men, even though they manned no picket line during daylight because the opposing lines were so close at this point.[28]

The Fourth Division brigades of Rice and Robinson had also spent the morning and early afternoon attempting to push up close enough to the Confederate line to discover its precise location and characteristics. They had sustained a considerable number of casualties in this unpleasant task. Cutler's other two brigades, Bragg's and Lyle's, had spent the morning in reserve along their works opposite Law's men. There they suffered from the random firing of Parker's three guns, which faced west, immediately south of the intersection of the Brock and Old Court House roads. These Virginia gunners, when not firing at Griffin's infantrymen in the Spindle farm clearing, fired blindly across the fronts of Bratton's and DuBose's troops and greatly interfered with the skirmishers of Rice and Robinson. Many of Parker's shells landed among Bragg's and Lyle's troops, who hugged the ground and wondered how any artillery fire could be so accurate. Some of the Federals were struck by parts of trees shattered by the fire.[29] One of Parker's shells bounded along the top of a low trench and hit the ground a short distance to the left of the 150th Pennsylvania Regiment. It struck a captain lightly in the left arm and came to rest about ten feet behind a line of prone soldiers. A sergeant remembered: "I took one glance at the grim messenger of death which rested so near; then flattening myself to mother earth, awaited the issue. My next sensation was that of sudden changes from hot to cold, accompanied by the wish that the ground would open and let me down. After enduring this unpleasant feeling for several minutes, which seemed like so many hours, and no explosion having taken place, I began to feel more comfortable, and finally ventured to raise my head high enough to take a peep at the shell. There it lay, as dangerous-looking as ever, but with no sign of a burning fuse about it."[30] Such harrowing experiences demoralized the Yankees.

The alignment of units within Cutler's division during the attack is not known precisely, and the description which follows is partly conjectural. Apparently Robinson's and Rice's brigades composed the front line and Bragg's troops the second behind Robinson on the left. Lyle's troops initially remained in reserve.

The wooded area between the opposing lines was dense and filled with a growth of cedar trees, whose sharp branches pointed in every direction.[31] As the three Federal brigades moved forward through these woods in the general direction of the apex of Law's line, they came under fire from some of Cabell's and Haskell's guns positioned on the hill behind Field's infantry line. Parker's three guns enfiladed the advancing Yankees from left to right. This fire and the difficult terrain so disrupted Federal alignment that Cutler's attack force appeared loose and disorganized by the time it came in view of Law's infantrymen, who halted it with a few volleys.[32] General Rice had apparently been near the front of his brigade during the initial advance. He then moved to the rear to summon Bragg's and Lyle's troops forward. Returning to the front, he was shot in the leg. (He died later in the afternoon, following its amputation.) Some of Bragg's troops moved forward and tried to remain, but soon all of the Yankees who were able returned to their starting points. It appears that Lyle's brigade provided little if any support. Law's men had expended a considerable amount of ammunition during the Federal advance and retirement. They again went out in front of their works and retrieved more muskets and cartridge pouches, which gave some of them four or five muskets apiece.[33]

Immediately to the west of this action two brigades of Gibbon's division also stormed Field's line. Carroll's troops were positioned to the right of Cutler's, and Alexander S. Webb's were to Carroll's right. Owen's brigade remained in reserve. These troops fared no better than their Fifth Corps comrades. Webb reported that, while hugging the ground in early afternoon, his men had studied the terrain ahead. By the time of the attack they had already convinced themselves of failure and were unenthusiastic. Carroll reported that a few of his men gained the Confederate works, but that the enemy's fire was too strong. The Federals retired.[34]

To the right of Gibbon's men, Crawford's division moved forward against Gregg's Texas brigade. Because of the open field in front of Gregg's works, the Yankees were exposed to enemy fire for a longer time than their comrades to the left. They suffered severely from the Texans' musketry and from canister fired by the two Napoleons of the Richmond Howitzers and from

Manly's battery near the left of Field's line. The Yankees soon withdrew to the relative safety of the trees to their rear.[35]

Field's men, however, did not escape unscathed. Federal artillery behind the Jones house supported Crawford's advance, but the Confederate artillerymen in line with their infantry ignored this Federal fire to save their ammunition for the Yankee infantry. Within their works, Gregg's infantrymen just had to take the fire. These works were approximately four feet high and three to five feet thick, with no obstruction in front. At some time during the action J. Mark Smither, of the Fifth Texas Regiment, was sitting, with no musket of his own, behind a comrade named Samuel Bailey. Smither was loading muskets and passing them to Bailey, who was firing at Crawford's advancing men. Immediately behind Smither sat a resting picket, who had retired into the works as the Pennsylvanians started across the field. Smither was in the act of handing Bailey a loaded musket when a shell struck the outside of the earthwork and bored through it, driving dirt and rocks before it. Four or five men, including Smither, were knocked down by the debris. The shell decapitated Bailey, knocked Smither senseless, and passed through the picket's body, taking the musket barrel with it.[36]

This unsuccessful attack by Warren was probably in its final stage when Hancock returned from south of the Po River and assumed command. Meade ordered him to attack the same segment of Field's line at 6:30 P.M. He had nearly completed his preliminary arrangements when a member of Meade's staff directed him to delay the attack and to send a strong force to the right of Barlow's position to counter a heavy force of Confederates that reportedly had crossed the Po River and was threatening the right flank of the army. Barlow's troops had taken a position along the crest that lay generally west from the Jones house. Miles's brigade on the right of the line was thrown back almost perpendicular to the remainder of the line and faced to the west. Advanced pickets from Miles's Twenty-sixth Michigan Regiment were posted near the Hart house, back up the Brock Road toward Todd's Tavern. Immediately before dark, Confederates were reported approaching that area.[37] They were probably a strong scouting party that Early or Heth had sent north across the river at Tinder's Mill or the crossing opposite Waite's Shop to seek out the Yankees. Reporting this situation to Barlow, Miles suggested that army headquarters, which was still located near the intersection of the Brock and Piney Branch Church roads, should be on the lookout. Some members of Grant's and Meade's staffs became frightened by this warning and ordered the headquarters wagons loaded for a rapid movement. Theodore Lyman arrived at headquarters at about this time and noticed the worried looks on the faces of some of the officers. A visiting congressman, Elihu B. Washburne of Illinois, Grant's original sponsor and patron, appeared thoroughly frightened. Some infantry and cavalry forces from Patrick's provost guard were sent out to stand in the approaching darkness.

Because of this alarm, army headquarters was moved southeast along the Brock Road to the intersection at the Alsop farm and then a short distance northeast out the Gordon Road.[38]

Miles's report of the sighting was forwarded to Meade at 6:15 or 6:30 P.M. At 6:00 P.M. Meade had sent a message to Barlow directly, Hancock apparently being out of immediate contact. His instructions were: If a Confederate force crossed the Po below Barlow's position to threaten the right flank of the impending Federal assault, Barlow should attack the enemy force vigorously without delaying to report the crossing or to request further orders. This order may have passed Miles's report enroute. The immediate response to Miles's report was that the Napoleons of Capt. Nelson Ames's Battery G, First New York Light Artillery, and the Third Battalion of Fourth New York Heavy Artillery, functioning as infantry, were sent to his position. Meanwhile, Hancock had ordered a part of his command, possibly Birney's division, to proceed to Barlow's support. Just as these troops were preparing to move, Meade cancelled the order to support Barlow, having apparently decided that the Confederate reconnaissance posed no threat. He ordered Hancock to get on with his assault against Laurel Hill.[39]

The units that participated in the final Federal attack against the Laurel Hill position were, from left to right, Robinson's and Lyle's brigades of Cutler's division, Webb's and Owen's brigades of Gibbon's division, Crawford's two brigades of Pennsylvania Reserves, and Ward's brigade of Birney's division. They began moving forward at approximately 7:00 P.M.

As Lyle's men and the troops of the Iron Brigade advanced, their lines were once again enfiladed from the left by Parker's battery and were also struck by canister from Haskell's guns. After struggling through the cedars and emerging into the area of sparser tree growth, they were blasted by musket fire from Law's brigade directly in front. Law's infantrymen fired and tossed their weapons to the rear, where company officers reloaded them. An officer bit the cartridge, inserted it in the muzzle, and then rapped the butt of the weapon sharply on the ground or a rock to seat the cartridge. Then he tossed the musket back to the infantryman, who by this time had another ready for reloading.[40]

Some of Lyle's troops approached fairly close to the works. A color-bearer of the Thirty-ninth Massachusetts was wounded in the face by bird shot. A member of the color guard of the Sixteenth Maine was wounded by a shot, which also cut two feet off the end of the staff of the national colors that he had been carrying. When Corp. Luther Bradford of the Sixteenth, who was carrying the state colors, received the order to retire, he realized that he was the sole unwounded member of the color guard. With the help of another member of the regiment, Bradford somehow made his way unscathed back down the slope and through the cedar growth while carrying both stands of colors.[41]

The participation of the Thirteenth Massachusetts in the assault was a private soldier's dream. One-half of the regiment's enlisted men were supporting Rittenhouse's battery near the Jones house, and the remainder were detailed to carry ammunition up to the line from the rear. So when the attack order came, the officers of the regiment went in alone.[42]

Sometime during the action the woods connecting the opposing lines at this point caught afire. The bodies of some Federal dead and wounded were consumed by the flames.[43]

The troops of Webb's and Owen's brigades, posted west of this action, contributed little. They apparently realized the hopelessness of their assignment. A member of Owen's brigade reported disgustedly after the war that no officer higher in rank than brigadier general had taken the trouble to examine the approaches to the enemy's works along this part of the line. He reported that the troops advanced a short distance, halted, opened fire briefly, and then retired rapidly. Some of them retreated in confusion beyond their starting point. After the attack Webb could find only three of his eight regiments together. He placed Maj. Patrick J. Downing of the Forty-second New York under arrest for misconduct. Staff officers found the scattered troops in the rear gathered about their regimental colors, preparing coffee.[44]

To Gibbon's right, the Pennsylvania Reserves moved forward against G. T. Anderson's brigade of Georgians. Details of the Reserves' participation are scanty. One account claims that some of them reached the enemy's breastworks. Colonel Wainwright, however, wrote that night in his journal that after the attack, he saw the Reserves reforming to the rear of Griffin's division nearly as far back as the south fork of the road through the Alsop farm. He also recorded the prevailing rumor that the Pennsylvanians had behaved poorly during the action. At any rate, they sustained additional casualties and apparently accomplished little.[45]

On the right end of the Federal line, a portion of Ward's brigade of Birney's division achieved a temporary, if costly, success. Crocker's Second Brigade remained in reserve and was not engaged. Ward's regiments were massed in column from front to rear in the following order: Eighty-sixth New York, Third Maine, 124th New York, Ninety-ninth Pennsylvania, 141st Pennsylvania, Twentieth Indiana, 110th Pennsylvania, and Fortieth New York. There was no appreciable space between the regiments, and the formation was almost a solid mass. While the troops were awaiting the order to move forward, General Crawford of the Fifth Corps came walking past with members of his staff. The men could hear the general express his misgivings about the proposed attack. He thought that the entire idea was madness and that it would end in disaster. His pessimism did nothing to enhance the enthusiasm of Birney's men. As dusk was approaching and as they had begun to hope that operations would be suspended for the day, the order to advance arrived.[46]

The Federals moved forward through the trees into the thinner growth of cedars. Here their tight formation began to loosen, and they began to receive artillery fire from Haskell's guns ahead. The head of the column came into the open field at about two hundred yards from the Confederate works. Then the lead regiments broke into a run.

After Warren's attack of 4:00 or 4:30 P.M. had subsided, the men of Gregg's brigade had gradually relaxed, and soon many of them were asleep behind their works. The commanding officer of the Third Arkansas withdrew a portion of the regiment from the line, so that the men could prepare a supper of sorts with food gathered from dead and wounded Yankees lying out in front. The crew members of the two Napoleons of the Richmond Howitzers section under the command of Lt. Meriwether Anderson had moved a short distance to the left of their pieces to observe a movement of troops, possibly Mahone's, on the far side of the Po River. One of the gunners happened to glance back and spotted Ward's men running across the field.[47]

The lead Yankee regiment was now only one hundred yards from the part of the works occupied by the Third Arkansas and First Texas regiments of Gregg's brigade and the left regiment, either the Seventh or Eighth Georgia, of G. T. Anderson's. The Virginia artillerymen sprang to their pieces and swung the gun nearest the Federals to the right, firing whatever load happened to be in the tube to blow away a light traverse obstructing their view to the right front. One or two rounds of canister were fired from this piece at the two lead Yankee regiments, the Eighty-sixth New York and Third Maine.[48]

The men in the third regiment in the Federal column, the 124th New York, were ordered to lie prone, perhaps fifty to one hundred yards from the works, immediately after the first artillery round was fired. The remaining five regiments apparently advanced only a short way into the field before they were struck by shell and canister fire from Manly's guns near the left end of Gregg's infantry line. The Federals soon broke formation and fell back in confusion into the trees to their left rear. Eventually, they were collected by members of Hancock's and Birney's staffs. Soon the 124th New York also retired, having had only four men wounded.[49]

As the troops of the Eighty-sixth New York and Third Maine approached the Confederate works, a few members of the First Texas fired a round or two, but they could not stop the two Yankee regiments. The Northerners clambered over the earthworks and bayoneted a color-bearer and a few other members of the unit who were either still asleep or just awakening. The attackers swept through the few Arkansas troops in the works and drastically disrupted the evening repasts being prepared a few yards behind the line. Here a brief hand-to-hand melee ensued until the Arkansas and First Texas men broke to the rear. Col. Robert S. Taylor, commanding the Arkansas regiment, was seen shouting excitedly and swinging a frying pan around his head, showering hot grease in all directions.[50]

Some of the Confederates retired down the slope directly behind the works, and others ran to their left past the two Napoleons. By this time, the men from New York and Maine were in a confused mass immediately behind the earthworks. A large group of them began to move down the back side of the works toward the two artillery pieces.

Lieutenant Anderson ordered his two guns rolled back a few yards and swung to the right, where they could fire down the rear of the abandoned earthwork. The wheels were chocked to prevent any movement caused by recoil, and the Virginians opened fire with double charges and, in a few cases, triple charges of canister. The Yankees gamely continued their confused advance into this fire, each round of which swept away some of the men in the front rank. Nevertheless, they reportedly advanced to within thirty yards of the Napoleons before starting to waver and slow down. Some of them probably began to wonder where the remaining regiments of the brigade were. Suddenly, the rallied First Texas and Third Arkansas regiments came swarming back to the works. This reportedly was the first instance of the war where any of this brigade had been driven from an assigned, fortified, defensive position, and the Southern infantrymen were furious. The Fourth Texas, near the Napoleons, and some of G. T. Anderson's troops at the opposite end of the area of breakthrough put strong pressure on the Yankees, who retreated over the works and across the field.[51] The Federals continued to suffer losses until they reached the comparative safety of the trees. They had behaved nobly indeed but had accomplished little. A tabulation of Federal casualties sustained during the Battle of Spotsylvania lists losses of 125 for the Eighty-sixth New York and 74 for the Third Maine. Most of these occurred during this action at Laurel Hill. One officer of the Eighty-sixth entered in his diary that night that his regiment went into the attack with 200 men and lost 115 killed, wounded, and missing.[52] Until that day the Texans had disdained to carry bayonets, feeling that they were a useless encumbrance to an infantryman. They carried them from then on.[53]

On the Confederate side Gregg came around and shook the hand of each member of both gun crews and profusely thanked them for holding the line until his men could be rallied. Field dashed up on horseback and dismounted to shake hands with all of the gunners. He had watched the action from a hilltop and had been sure that the position was lost until he saw the Virginians shatter the Federal formation with canister fire. He told them that at the time he had had no reserves to send to that part of the line.[54] Actually, the breakthrough was not a serious threat because the Union regiments had not been supported.

Ward's troops had been massed in a solid formation for their attack, at least in its initial stages. East of there, along a part of the Union Sixth Corps's line, another Union attack used a similar formation.

11

One of the Classic Infantry Attacks

10 May

Federal Sixth Corps and Confederate Second Corps

Early in the afternoon Russell reported to Wright that a position had been found in front of the First Division's line from which a successful assault might be launched. In the wooded area of pine trees to the south of the Shelton house, Sixth Corps skirmishers, assisted by artillery fire including possibly mortars, had succeeded in gradually forcing the Southern pickets first to fall back to the edge of the trees and then to retire across the field into their works. These works were occupied primarily by the three Georgia regiments of Doles's brigade, which were flanked on their left by Daniel's brigade and on the right by Walker's Stonewall Brigade.[1]

Lt. Ranald S. Mackenzie of the U.S. Corps of Engineers had been reconnoitering the open fields around the Shelton house. He had followed a path to the southeast which entered the pines and arrived at the edge of a field across which, at a distance of two hundred yards or more, he saw Doles's line of works. He had asked General Russell to join him, and they had examined the enemy position from the edge of the trees. Russell had calculated that, if an attack force could be massed there unseen, it should be able to reach and to enter the enemy works in front without sustaining too many casualties, even though parts of those works appeared to be quite formidable, containing head logs on top and traverses to the rear.[2]

Wright approved of the proposed site of attack. The generals decided to assault with twelve infantry regiments drawn from Neill's and Russell's divisions. The regiments selected were the Fifth Maine, Ninety-sixth Pennsylvania, and 121st New York from Upton's brigade; Fifth Wisconsin, Sixth Maine, Forty-ninth and 119th Pennsylvania from Eustis's (formerly Russell's) brigade; Forty-third and Seventy-seventh New York from Bidwell's brigade; and the Second, Fifth, and Sixth Vermont from Grant's brigade. Together these regiments would total between forty-five hundred and five

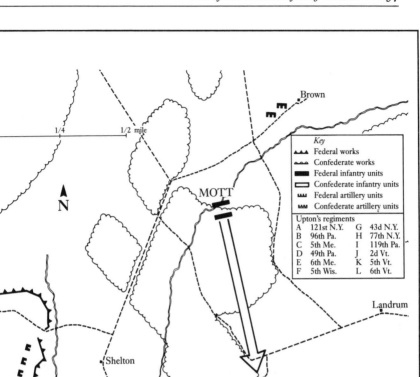

MAP 11-1. Mott's and Upton's Attacks on 10 May, 5:00–7:30 P.M.

thousand infantrymen. Immediate command of the assault force was entrusted to Col. Emory Upton, whose handling of his brigade in the successful offensive operation at Rappahannock Station the previous November had marked him as a fighter.[3]

The colonel ordered the twelve regimental commanders forward to the observation point to study both the intended route across the field and the Confederate works on the opposite side. He then told them the details of the attack. The formation would consist of four lines of three regiments each. The first line from right to left was to include the 121st New York, Ninety-sixth Pennsylvania, and Fifth Maine; the second line the Forty-ninth Pennsylvania, Sixth Maine, and Fifth Wisconsin; the third line the Forty-third New York, Seventy-seventh New York, and 119th Pennsylvania; and the fourth line the Second Vermont, Fifth Vermont, and Sixth Vermont. The four regiments on the right flank were to line up to the right of the path and the remaining eight regiments to the left. The first line was to load and cap its muskets, while the remaining three lines would just load them. They were to fix bayonets. The interval between the four separate lines was supposed to be only ten feet.[4]

Upton instructed the commanders of the 121st New York and Ninety-sixth Pennsylvania to turn by their right flank after crossing the first line of works and to charge a Confederate battery stationed one hundred yards or so down the line. This was B. H. Smith's four-piece battery, consisting of two Napoleons and two three-inch rifles and belonging to Lt. Col. Robert A. Hardaway's battalion. In the morning this battery had replaced Braxton's guns in support of Rodes's segment of the line. These pieces were protected by earthworks in front and traverses along the sides. The Fifth Maine on the left of the first Federal line was to turn in the opposite direction and to open an enfilading fire.[5]

The second line was to halt at the works and to fire to the front as necessary. The third line was to lie down behind the second line and to await orders. The fourth line was to advance only to the edge of trees, lie down, watch, and be ready for any assignment. Upton warned the commander of this final line, Col. Thomas O. Seaver of the Third Vermont, that he might have to form his three regiments obliquely to the left to cover the flank of the assault force. All officers were instructed to repeat the command "Forward" constantly from the beginning of the advance until the works were carried.[6]

After forming west of the Shelton house, each of the twelve regiments moved silently down the lane in column of fours, and, turning off to its right or left as required, faced front. The front rank of the first line was probably fifty yards or so from the edge of the field. The men were ordered to lie down and to maintain silence. Some of them were told that they would be supported from their left by Gershom Mott's two brigades, which totalled seventeen regiments.[7] Earlier, Meade had directed Mott to establish a connection with Burnside's troops to his left. He also had ordered that, should Burnside become engaged, Mott should move his entire division to the support of the Ninth Corps without waiting for orders. In preparation for the scheduled attack, however, Meade modified Mott's instructions slightly. He now said that if Burnside should be attacked before 5:00 P.M., Mott should immediately attack to the south with his two brigades from their positions near the Brown house, rather than rushing to Burnside's aid. If Burnside insisted upon reinforcements, Mott should send only a part of his division. Headquarters believed that in that situation, Mott could be most useful by attacking with his entire force from his present position. Ambiguous directions such as these did nothing to improve the dispositions of subordinate officers.[8]

Mott received these new instructions at 2:00 P.M., when he was informed that Capt. George H. Mendell of the Corps of Engineers would report to him and would explain Wright's plans for Mott's men in the attack. In addition, Mendell was to assist in selecting the actual point of attack and was to remain with Mott until the operation was completed.[9]

Mott immediately informed Wright that because he had needed such a large number of pickets to comply with the order to connect with Burnside's right, he now estimated that he would have only twelve hundred to fifteen hundred troops available for the attack. Moreover, he felt certain that he could not get the pickets back from the left by 5:00 P.M. and asked if he should recall them anyway. Wright advised him not to recall his pickets but to have them advance at 5:00 P.M. from wherever they happened to be. He also told Mott to attack vigorously with the rest of his division from his position southwest of the Brown house at the proper time. Wright urged Mott to use his artillery freely. This consisted of Capt. Edwin B. Dow's Sixth Maine Battery of six Napoleons.[10]

Mott's route during his advance was to be south through a body of trees occupied by Confederate pickets from Witcher's brigade, the Louisiana brigade, and perhaps the right-hand regiments of the Stonewall Brigade. When the Federals emerged from the southern edge of these trees, they would be approximately five to six hundred yards from Johnson's works. If they continued straight ahead, they would strike these works four to five hundred yards to the left of Upton's men.[11]

What Meade and Wright expected Mott to accomplish is difficult to determine. Perhaps they hoped that Mott and Upton could puncture the Confederate line and cause the Southerners to abandon the north face of the salient. More likely, Mott's troops were expected to pin down Johnson's regiments and to prevent them from going to the assistance of Rodes's men, who would be contending with Upton's force. It is even conceivable, in view of Upton's instructions to his second and third lines to remain at the point of break-through rather than continue forward, that Mott's two brigades were to pass through the Confederate works behind Upton and to exploit the initial success. Some regimental historians from units in Upton's force believed that this was the case. It appears more likely, however, that any follow-up would be by Wright's men, approaching from Upton's right rear. Wright was also under orders to provide reinforcements for Warren, should he request them during his attack against the Confederate position at Laurel Hill.[12]

Wright was confronted with the problem of attempting to coordinate the movements of two separate forces in an unmapped area. The few known features of the terrain had been discovered by active skirmishers and by couriers, who had spent much of the time in their travels to and from Mott's headquarters at the Brown house dodging the bullets of Confederate pickets. Upton's men would have to advance two hundred to two hundred and fifty yards to close with the enemy, while Mott's troops would have to travel at least five times that distance, with the beginning of their route being through a wooded area. Prospects for successful coordination do not appear to have been promising.

The Union plan for a combined attack all along the line at 5:00 P.M. began breaking down when Meade gave Warren permission, sometime after 3:00 P.M., to attack Laurel Hill immediately. At 3:45 P.M. Wright was ordered to attack with his own troops and Mott's, but he was not yet ready. Sometime during the confusion of Warren's initial attack and the withdrawal of Barlow's division to the north bank of the Po River, someone decided to postpone the combined assault from 5:00 to 6:00 P.M. A staff officer of Wright's remembered delivering the delay message to Russell, although he did not mention the time of delivery. Whether Mott too received the postponement order in time to comply is questionable. (Battery commander Andrew Cowan did not, and his position was closer to Sixth Corps headquarters than was Mott's.)[13] Mott likely conducted his attack at about 5:00 P.M. in compliance with his original instructions from Wright. The few official reports of Mott's subordinates reflect this.[14]

Mott's Attack

Mott positioned his force in two lines, with Col. Robert McAllister's First Brigade occupying the first line and the Second Brigade, apparently under the command of Col. William Blaisdell of the Eleventh Massachusetts, manning the second. The number of infantrymen in this attack force is not known. It was probably as low as the twelve hundred to fifteen hundred, as Mott had earlier warned Wright. This would represent four or five regiments at the most. The adjutant of the Fifteenth New Jersey, whose Sixth Corps regiment along with its sister unit, the First New Jersey, would march on the right of McAllister's line, maintained that only two regiments from the Second Corps were on their left. Apparently most of Mott's Second Brigade, the old Excelsior, had been assigned to locate Burnside's right. McAllister's Sixth New Jersey was detailed as the advanced skirmish line for the operation.[15]

At 5:00 P.M. Mott instructed McAllister to move his brigade forward from the northern portion of the woods. They began to pick their way through the trees, following the advancing skirmishers. Behind McAllister came the second line. Confederate pickets near the southern edge of the wood fired on the skirmishers, then immediately retired south to the relative safety of their breastworks in the salient. They alerted Confederate officers to the presence of the advancing Federals, and when Mott's men emerged into the field six hundred yards or so from the breastworks, the guns were ready for them. The artillerymen of Page's and Nelson's battalions waited until the Yankees reached the slight crest along which lay the Landrum lane before opening fire with canister. After receiving a few volleys, Mott's entire force broke and fled in confusion back to the safety of the trees, with most of the men returning all of the way to their starting point.[16]

The Eleventh New Jersey was on the left of the line. Its historian claimed that, when the line broke, the regimental commander, Col. John Schoonover, ordered the regiment to lie down. The men remained in this advanced position until Mott sent instructions for them to establish a picket line in the wood.[17]

McAllister, the commander of the Second Brigade units, and the commander of the two New Jersey regiments from the Sixth Corps held a small council of war. They decided that the only sensible thing to do was to permit the men to fall back to the starting point, which the men had already done without waiting for orders. Mott apparently stayed at the Brown house during the attack. Dow's battery covered the advance and suffered the loss of one crewman killed.[18]

Mott's attack thus failed. His troops maintained the poor reputation that they had earned in the Wilderness fighting. From the Federal point of view, all that had been accomplished was the expulsion of some Confederate pickets from the woods north of the salient and the establishment of Union pickets there.

Upton's Attack

The three Sixth Corps artillery batteries, Rhodes's, McCartney's, and Cowan's, that would support Upton's effort were ordered to open fire at 5:00 P.M.

on the targeted part of the Confederate line. They were to fire for ten minutes only. The end of their fire was to be the signal for Upton to move his men forward. The time for the attack, however, was postponed for one hour. Cowan, who was farthest north along the line, did not receive the order to delay and dutifully opened fire at 5:00 P.M. He was then ordered to continue to fire throughout the one hour period of delay. Smith's Confederate battery sporadically answered Cowan's fire during this period.[19]

General Ewell had been informed at 4:00 P.M. that Doles's skirmishers had been driven in earlier in the afternoon. Doles was ordered to regain his skirmish line and reportedly was preparing to do so when his line was struck by Upton's assault. A few Confederate skirmishers might have redeployed in shallow rifle pits in front of Doles's left and Daniel's right but only twenty or thirty yards in advance of the works.[20]

At approximately 6:00 P.M. Rhodes's and McCartney's batteries added their fire to Cowan's for ten minutes, and then all three ceased firing. The Federal infantrymen were ordered to move forward to the edge of the trees. From there, according to Upton, with a wild cheer and faces averted, the men in the front line led the rush for the Confederate works. Thus began what a British military historian writing in 1908 labelled "one of the classic infantry attacks of military history."[21]

It probably took the three regiments of the first line no longer than sixty to ninety seconds to reach Doles's works. The Georgians appear to have been somewhat surprised by the attack, firing at the approaching Yankees individually rather than by volley. The fire from the Second and Thirty-third Virginia regiments of the Stonewall Brigade to Doles's right was more troublesome to the Federals. A color-bearer of the Fifth Maine recalled that this fire was so severe that the regiment crowded approximately fifty yards to its right while crossing the field and intermingled slightly with the men of the Ninety-sixth Pennsylvania. He stated that most of the one hundred casualties sustained by his regiment in this action were from wounds to the left side of the body.[22]

When the first line of Federals reached the works, those who climbed on top were shot instantly by the Georgians. Others held their muskets at arms length and fired downward, while some hurled their weapons over the works. Soon a concerted effort was attempted, and the Federals went over en masse, overpowering Doles's troops by sheer weight of numbers. At some points along the line there was brief but bloody hand-to-hand combat.[23]

The color-bearer from Maine, W. E. H. Morse, went through at a depression in the works. There was a shallow swale at this point, and it appears that Smith's guns were sited so as to cover this weak spot in the line. When Morse passed through the line, he immediately noticed a full line of Confederates lying behind the works and assumed that he and his colors were about to be captured. Most of the Southerners, however, were holding empty muskets, and Morse's comrades, who followed him closely through this low section of the works, carried loaded ones. A few of the Federals fired at the helpless Georgians, but most of the Yankees began to shout at the Rebs to get across the field.[24]

Most of them scrambled over the works and raced across the field. The crew members of Smith's battery had been firing furiously since the action had begun. When they saw several hundred Georgians double-timing across the field, they assumed this to be a Confederate counterattack and leaped on top of their traverses, cheering wildly. They soon noticed, however, that the Southerners had no weapons and, realizing what had happened, the artillerymen jumped back down to their guns and resumed firing. Other Confederates farther up the line supposed that Doles's troops were retreating Federals and fired into them, inflicting casualties upon their comrades.[25]

Sorting out the precise roles of the four separate Federal lines after they penetrated the line of works has proved impossible. All twelve regiments fought along or beyond the Confederate works before the action stopped after dark. It appears that many Federals from the first and second lines continued forward and captured the lightly held second line of works, sixty or eighty yards behind the first. Some of the Yankees on the left of the attacking line continued ahead in the direction of the McCoull house. Their comrades turned to the right, moved down behind the second line of works, and began to fire into Smith's battery from its right and rear.

At the first breakthrough, Smith's guns had fired at the point of entry until their fire began to endanger some of Doles's troops and Daniel's right-hand regiments, who were retreating through the battery's position. Suddenly, a mass of Federals poured into the battery from the rear and soon captured three of the four guns, using bayonets, musket butts, and pistols. Smith and about twenty-six of his men were captured. The crew of the piece on the left continued to fire until Yankees overran the gun to their right and began moving behind them. The Confederate gunners then clambered over the works in front of their gun and ran to the left down the line for 50 to 250 yards before reentering their lines. The escaping gunners took enough implements with them to prevent the Federal infantrymen from working the guns.[26]

At the breakthrough, the 121st New York and Ninety-sixth Pennsylvania may have moved down the rear of the works toward Smith's position as ordered, although this is not certain. The right-hand regiment of Daniel's brigade was the Thirty-second North Carolina, which was probably posted near Smith as a support for the guns. A member of the regiment claimed that its position was taken from the rear and that 225 enlisted men and 6 officers from the unit were captured and hurried to the Federal rear.[27]

The Federal troops who had continued straight ahead past the second line of Confederate works were soon joined from the rear by comrades of the second and possibly the third attack lines. They turned to their left and fired into the left rear of the Second and Thirty-third Virginia regiments of the Stonewall Brigade, causing the Second to break in confusion and flee to its right into the trees, taking the Thirty-third with it. Their brigade commander, General Walker, halted and rallied them, turned them around, and eventually formed them into a line facing their overrun works. He then sent for his remaining three regiments, and soon the brigade was formed into line just inside the trees and was firing across the field at the Federals, who stood their ground and fired back.[28]

It would appear that at this critical phase of the attack a Federal force, Mott's division or some other, was to have crossed the Confederate line at the breakthrough point and to have exploited the initial success. Unfortunately for the Federal cause, none did.[29]

General Lee, who apparently was near the Harrison house when Upton's men penetrated Doles's line, immediately rode forward to rally the fugitives who had escaped to the rear and to organize a counterattack. Members of his staff pleaded with him not to expose himself to what appeared to be certain death, as had the officers and men of Gregg's Texas brigade four days earlier in the Wilderness. Lee finally consented to remain clear of the action but told the members of his staff that they must see to it that the line was restored. The staff members leaped upon their horses and galloped off in all directions.[30]

A few minutes after the Yankee breakthrough, a staff officer rode up to Witcher's brigade at the tip of the salient and ordered all or part of it to form a line of battle perpendicular to its present position and to move down the line behind the breastworks recently vacated by the regiments of the Stonewall Brigade. They soon became engaged with the left-hand regiments of Upton's force. The staff officer also reportedly ordered the artillery pieces near the tip of the salient to move to the rear immediately. If these pieces did in fact leave, they must have returned very quickly. Some of them reportedly fired over the works of the Stonewall Brigade at Upton's men, and others near the apex of the salient were positioned in advance of the works and fired down the front of the line.[31]

A staff officer arrived at Steuart's Brigade on the northeast face of the salient and ordered it to face to its rear and to move immediately to the threatened sector of the line. These Virginians and North Carolinians dashed in a ragged formation through the trees across the northern portion of the salient. One group of one hundred or so turned slightly to its right and arrived at the rear of the breastworks immediately east of a point where some Federal regiments, probably Vermonters, were maintaining a deadly fire across the field and up the line from the opposite side of the works. Steuart's force attempted to get at them, but it was unable to withstand their fire and the fire coming in from the opposite side of the breakthrough. Finally, the Carolinians simply lay on their side of the breastworks and watched for any further Federal advance. The remainder of Steuart's men arrived at the edge of the field and, advancing into the clearing, engaged the Federals there.[32]

Ewell's whereabouts when this began are unknown, but he soon appeared among the men of Daniel's brigade, who had retreated down the line of works. He helped to arrest this movement and promised that reinforcements would soon be on hand. Suddenly, Battle's brigade hurried past the point where Ewell was rallying Daniel's men and filed out into the McCoull field, forming a line of battle from which they opened fire on Upton's men. Daniel's brigade formed a line behind the works and perpendicular to them, and began to advance back in the direction of Smith's guns. Some of Ramseur's troops may have accompanied Daniel.[33]

The area near the guns was a scene of pandemonium. A group of Yankees from the Forty-ninth Pennsylvania and Sixth Maine had turned three of the pieces around and were trying unsuccessfully to fire them. A captain from the Forty-ninth appeared out of the smoke and asked if anyone had a file or nail to spike the guns. A veteran private growled that he thought that it was a hell of a place to be asking for a file. This response to the captain gave one of the Pennsylvanians the giggles. He was leaning against a cannon wheel at the time, and although he was thoroughly frightened by the bullets flying in all directions, he could not help laughing in the captain's face. Soon the laughing stopped as enemy infantry appeared from the Confederate rear. They forced the Federals to relinquish the guns and to retire to Doles's first line of works.[34] These Confederates were from Gordon's three brigades, which had been stationed in reserve northwest of the Harrison house, behind the junction of Kershaw's and Rodes's divisions. Evans's brigade had double-timed in columns of fours through the trees along the path that led north from the Harrison house. Suddenly, the acting brigade commander, Lt. Col. Thomas J. Berry of the Sixtieth Georgia, turned to the left and loudly announced to his men the presence of Yankees little more than one hundred yards away. The Southerners faced left and fired a volley, forcing the enemy to retire behind the earthworks. After bitter fighting at close quarters, the troops with Berry and some of those from Robert D. Johnston's brigade reoccupied Smith's battery.[35]

Johnston approached Ewell, who was excitedly pulling his moustache with both hands. Seeing Johnston, he shouted "charge them, General, damn'em, charge'em!" Johnston assured him that they would charge as soon as the men were in position. The North Carolinians double-quicked across the front of part of the broken line without firing, while under heavy fire themselves.

Johnston halted them, faced them to the front, and shouted the order to charge, which they did, driving Upton's men back.[36]

Some of Smith's gunners had been hiding among the traverses. They now sprang up and swung the pieces around. Others, still carrying the tools of their trade, returned with the infantry reinforcements. General Lee had sent reserve gunners forward to man the recaptured pieces in case the original crews were all gone. The replacements consisted of volunteers from A. W. Garber's battery, led by Maj. Wilfred E. Cutshaw himself. Colonel Hardaway and Maj. David Watson from artillery battalion headquarters helped to get two of the pieces firing canister again, and they continued to serve as gun crew members. By this time most, if not all, of Upton's men still on their feet were back behind Doles's two lines of works. They were not yet finished fighting. The Federals maintained a deadly musketry fire from their partially protected position behind the works and inside some of the traverses. This fire prevented Daniel's men from advancing beyond the offset between Doles's two lines of works immediately north of the artillery position, and their presence there hampered the efforts of the gunners (who by now included some men from Jones's battery) to fire at the Yankees to their right front.[37] A few infantrymen from the Forty-ninth Pennsylvania lay about sixty yards in front of the recaptured guns and harried the Southern artillerymen. Major Watson was mortally wounded during the action, possibly by this fire.[38]

At this stage of the action, Upton rode back to the edge of the trees to order up the three Vermont regiments. He discovered that they had already advanced to the earthworks and that they were firing furiously. The Sixty-fifth New York of Cross's brigade had also come across the field to join in. The Federal force remained at Doles's works firing at targets around an arc of 180 degrees. They stayed in this position for at least one hour. As darkness fell, Upton realized that his precarious position was untenable without support. He reported this to Russell. Instead of reinforcements, the Colonel received the order to withdraw. Written orders were sent forward, and the Federals fell back to their camps. Some of the Vermonters, including members of the Third Regiment who had been on picket and had gone in with the attack, did not receive the original withdrawal order and remained fighting in the works until later orders to retire reached them.[39]

Upton's attack had failed. Its initial phase, however, had been very successful indeed, in large part because no attacking Federal infantryman had discharged his weapon until the Confederate line had been breached (this was in contrast to the attack of the Maryland brigade against Laurel Hill two days earlier). Upton reported his casualties as approximately one thousand killed, wounded, or missing. The Forty-ninth Pennsylvania suffered the highest regimental loss, sustaining 216 casualties of 474 engaged. The regiment's commander, Col. Thomas M. Hulings, and an unidentified lieutenant colonel were among those killed. The commander of the Sixth Maine, Maj. George Fuller, was killed near Smith's guns. Upton himself had been slightly wounded.[40]

The number of Confederate casualties is uncertain. Ewell reported a total of 650, of whom 350 were prisoners. He wrote his report ten months after the event, and his figures, especially for prisoners, appear to be low. Upton reported that his men captured one thousand to twelve hundred Confederates, mostly from Doles's three regiments, the Thirty-second North Carolina of Daniel's brigade, and Smith's battery. The provost marshal, Gen. Marsena Patrick, whose information could be expected to be accurate, entered in his diary that 913 enlisted men and 37 officers had been captured by Upton's force. Col. John C. Higginbotham, commanding the Twenty-fifth Virginia of Witcher's brigade, was killed, along with Col. Edmund Brabble of the Thirty-second North Carolina. In addition, many Confederate field officers were wounded. Doles's three regiments, which had broken camp on 4 May with 1,567 troops, were down to approximately 550 men.[41]

At 8:15 P.M. Lee ordered Ewell to have his officers collect their men and to refresh them in anticipation of a possible renewal of the fighting at daylight. In addition, Ewell was to ensure that Rodes improved his section of the line with perhaps a ditch on the outside and abatis in front. In response, a party from the Thirty-third Virginia spent most of the night cutting down small pine trees that stood in front of the regiment's position and converting them into abatis.[42]

Grant, too, acted in response to the Sixth Corps's operations. Having been authorized by his government to confer field promotions upon officers for special acts of gallantry, he promoted Upton to the rank of brigadier general (an action later confirmed by the Senate). Doubtless, the ambitious Upton was pleased by this promotion, but he was not pleased by the manner in which the efforts of his troops had been supported. After their troops had returned to their own lines, both he and Russell reportedly uttered bitter reproaches about this lack of support. Later in the evening Wright reported to Meade that he did not want Mott's troops stationed on his left because they were of no support to him at all.[43] When Grant and Meade, who had spent most of the afternoon monitoring the actions of Hancock and Warren west of the Brock Road, returned to their headquarters sometime during the evening, they were approached by Wright and perhaps Russell and Upton, who described the mechanics and the fortunes of Upton's assault. As Grant listened, he may have begun to estimate the possible success of a similar attack executed on a much larger scale.

Federal Ninth Corps and Confederate Third Corps

When Burnside received the preliminary order for the advance to be conducted at 5:00 P.M., he discussed with Horace Porter, of Grant's staff, the advisability of bringing Potter's division forward and attacking with three divisions toward Spotsylvania or instead using the Second Division as a support for Mott's two brigades. Porter urged the former course, claiming it to be more in line with Grant's desires. Burnside could not decide, so at 2:15 P.M. he asked Grant what should be done. Grant did not receive the message until about 3:15 P.M. He responded that it was by then too late to accomplish anything useful with Potter's troops and that Burnside would have to decide for himself whether to send one of the two divisions south of the Ni River to Mott's support. Grant offered his opinion that Mott would be all right and that Burnside should attack promptly with his two divisions at the designated time.[44]

At approximately 3:30 or 4:00 P.M., Burnside ordered Potter to march his division to the front and to join in the advance. Burnside also informed Willcox of Potter's movement and said that he was leaving his headquarters to join Willcox at Gayle's house. He ordered Willcox to open fire with his artillery at 5:00 P.M. and to be prepared to follow up with his infantry at once.[45]

Precise details of the advance are few. Burnside considered the movement to be merely a reconnaissance rather than an attack and reported it as such. The advance probably did not begin until nearly 6:00 P.M. Potter's division arrived in time to support the movement with one brigade on each side of the Fredericksburg Road. Colonel Hartranft of Willcox's division, who commanded the Federal troops on the right of the road, reported that, after advancing a short distance, he received an order to halt his right regiment and to swing his line clockwise, so the troops on the left of the road could angle across the road. He complied with the order as best he could, but the troops across the road continued straight ahead, and Hartranft was forced to thin his advancing line considerably in order to maintain the connection. The skirmish lines, followed by the main body of troops, moved forward one-half mile or perhaps a little farther before halting at dark. Potter reported that, by about 10:00 P.M., some of his troops had advanced to within one-quarter mile of Spotsylvania, where they began to entrench.[46]

Burnside and Porter watched the movement from near the Gayle house. Although unable to see very much, Porter sent two messages to Grant describing the situation on Burnside's part of the front. The first courier was never heard from, and the second arrived at headquarters late at night. By this time Grant had obtained an idea of Burnside's position relative to that of the Army of the Potomac. At 11:00 P.M. he voiced to Meade his concern about the isolation of the Ninth Corps. He ordered Burnside to move up and connect on his right with the Sixth Corps by advancing Potter's division to the front, if it were not already there, and placing it to the right of Burnside's other two divisions.[47]

The Confederate force opposite Burnside's advancing troops was composed of the four brigades of Cadmus Wilcox's division, which were positioned along a line that crossed the Fredericksburg Road about one-eighth of a mile east of the hamlet. Along parts of McGowan's brigade's front, the Union advance drove in the Confederate skirmishers. Southern artillery opened fire, however, and the Yankees in turn were forced back. The Rebels then reestablished their picket line. Jubal Early, who was Wilcox's acting corps commander, in a postwar narrative referred to Burnside's effort as constituting only some artillery firing.[48]

Thus, the action of 10 May came to a close. The Federal commanders had tried to execute simultaneous attacks along parts of the line, but they had been unable to coordinate them. When Warren had been permitted to attack prior to 5:00 P.M., the entire plan for a Federal combined assault had collapsed. The Sixth Corps participation had consisted of only twelve regiments. Upton's men were initially successful, but there was no designated support force to exploit his breakthrough. On the left of the line the Ninth Corps was still too far from the Army of the Potomac to augment Meade's operations.

For the second consecutive day, the eastern access to Spotsylvania Court House had been protected successfully by a single Confederate division. That night Lee reported the results of the day's activities to Richmond and offered his thanks that the number of Confederate casualties had been small.

12

The Enemy   11 May
Are Preparing
to Retreat

Morning on the Federal Side

At 7:30 A.M. Meade dispatched a circular to his three
infantry corps commanders directing them to decide what force would be
sufficient to maintain their positions, and how many troops would thus be
available for an offensive movement or to extend the front of the army. If
stronger or additional fieldworks would permit more troops to be used for
offensive operations, construction was to begin immediately. The circular
also reported that Burnside had approached to within one-quarter mile of
Spotsylvania Court House against little opposition. The only extant response
to this circular is from Wright. He reported that he needed eight thousand
troops to man his works and picket line, leaving approximately six thousand
available for other operations. Wright also reported that Mott needed one
thousand troops for picketing, leaving sixteen hundred available for other
duty.[1]

On the previous morning, in a message to Halleck, Grant had submitted
his initial request for infantry reinforcements. He had suggested that ten
thousand men be forwarded from the defenses of Washington. He had also
requested resupply of forage, provisions, and musket ammunition.[2]

On the morning of the eleventh, Grant updated his appraisal of the military situation in northern Virginia, estimating twenty thousand Federal casualties, including eleven general officers. In this message Grant included his
famous statement that he proposed "to fight it out on this line if it takes all
summer,"[3] a phrase whose precise meaning will probably be debated as long
as the war is studied. Grant also forwarded to his government his opinion that
Lee's troops had become shaky from the intense fighting and that they were
being kept in line during Federal attacks only by the utmost exertions of their
officers.[4]

Meade and Burnside were ordered to issue two days' rations and enough
ammunition to refill the cartridge boxes of their troops and then send every

available wagon to Belle Plain for supplies. Burnside's Fourth Division of Colored Troops and some of the three remaining cavalry regiments were to escort the wagons. The requested reinforcements were to escort them from Belle Plain back to the army. In addition, Grant suggested that Meade send back all of the guns of the Artillery Reserve, but he left this decision to Meade.[5]

At dawn Mott's division, without its pickets, who still connected with those of Burnside, moved to its right and rear, behind the left of Wright's line, to replenish its ammunition supply. Later in the morning, Hancock was ordered to send Birney's division to the left of Wright's line and, in conjunction with Mott's troops, to establish a solid connection between Wright and Burnside. This movement, however, was subsequently cancelled. Portions of Russell's division then moved forward to occupy a line that lay in the woods northeast of the Shelton house and that connected with the line formerly occupied by Mott. At 5:15 A.M. Burnside ordered his Provisional Brigade to march from J. Alsop's and to join him as soon as possible near the Ni River crossing of the Fredericksburg Road. The artillerymen escorting the Artillery Reserve were ordered forward from Piney Branch Church to join Warren.[6]

At 11:15 A.M. Grant's headquarters received word that Confederate sharpshooters had worked their way behind Wright's line on the left and were firing at it from the rear. Grant ordered Meade to direct Wright to hunt down the Southern riflemen and kill them all, apparently regarding them as bushwhackers. By the time Meade's courier found Wright the Southern sharpshooters had disappeared.[7]

Immediately before noon Hancock was ordered to reconnoiter as far back as Todd's Tavern and also south of the Po River. Miles's brigade, stationed on the right of Barlow's position, closest to those points of interest, was selected for the assignment. These two scouting missions were to be a final check for any significant Confederate force threatening the right flank of the Union Army before its Second Corps left that section of the line after dark. These reconnaissances were reported to Lee, and he was obliged to evaluate their significance in relation to other reports received that day as he tried to fathom what the Yankees were planning to do next.[8]

Morning on the Confederate Side

In the morning Heth's division moved back from its position near the Shady Grove Church Road west of the Block House Bridge to the vicinity of Spotsylvania Court House, where it assumed a position extending from the village south-southeast for about half a mile, to the Massaponax Church

Road. Mahone's five brigades remained west of the bridge to protect the left flank of the army.[9]

Portions of Wilcox's division, which had been holding the courthouse area while Heth and Mahone were absent, were moved farther to their left. Brig. Gen. James H. Lane's brigade was positioned about one-half mile from the western edge of the Fredericksburg Road. After moving farther to the left, Lane was dissatisfied with his brigade's new position. Leaving his right regiment in place, he moved his four remaining units forward and formed them into a line which faced the northeast. Lane's left regiment, the Twenty-eighth North Carolina, was reportedly closed to the right of Steuart's brigade along the east face of the salient. Lane reported that Walker's brigade of Heth's division was on his right, indicating that the brigades of these two divisions were intermingled.[10]

On Ewell's front there had been a slight sidling to the right by front line units. The previous evening, when Steuart's and a portion of Witcher's brigades had been sent to aid in repulsing Upton's force, Witcher's remaining troops and the Louisiana brigade had moved slightly to their right in a rather spread-out attempt to cover the north face of the salient and its apex. When the detached forces returned, they discovered that two of Witcher's regiments were occupying the line from the apex south, down the eastern face. Steuart's men reoccupied the works to the right of these two regiments. Witcher's returning troops went into position just to the left of the apex, with the Louisiana brigade and Walker's Stonewall Brigade on their left.[11]

Farther to the left, along the line of Rodes's division, the shattered remnants of Doles's three regiments were withdrawn from the line and posted in reserve. Battle's Alabamians filled the void until 8:00 A.M., when they withdrew and took a position on the left of the division's line. Daniel's and later Ramseur's brigades moved to the right, so Daniel's men connected with the left of the Stonewall Brigade. The usefulness of Battle's troops was apparently still suspect as a result of rumors about their performance on the evening of 8 May. At 10:00 A.M. the five Louisiana regiments of Hays's old brigade, now commanded by Monaghan, were moved to the left of the Stonewall Brigade between Daniel and Walker.[12] The works were strengthened all along the lines, especially on the north face of the salient. The members of the Stonewall Brigade erected more traverses at intervals along their line.[13]

The survivors of Smith's battery were consolidated into an artillery section of two three-inch rifles. They silently and sadly buried their three fallen comrades near Spotsylvania that morning.[14]

To the west, the members of Gregg's brigade also buried their dead immediately behind their works. A member of the Fifth Texas recalled that the troops were obliged to scoop out the dirt for the shallow graves while lying prone because of the fire of Yankee pickets.[15]

Afternoon Operations

For his reconnaissance missions Miles divided his brigade into two parts. He sent the Twenty-sixth Michigan, Eighty-first Pennsylvania, and 183d Pennsylvania across the Po and the Sixty-first New York and 140th Pennsylvania to Todd's Tavern. The first group crossed the river at Tinder's Mill and advanced against Confederate cavalry skirmishers southeast toward the intersection immediately north of Waite's Shop. Near there, the Yankees came upon more of Hampton's troopers behind fieldworks. The Federals soon retired to their former position north of the river. The two regiments that marched to Todd's Tavern discovered no trace of Confederates and returned at dark.[16]

Hampton's horsemen reported these Federal reconnaissance missions to their commander, who passed the information on to Early, and he in turn transmitted it to Lee, who was obliged to consider the possibility that Grant was preparing for a movement around the left flank of the Army of Northern Virginia by way of Shady Grove. He ordered Early to have Mahone's division at Shady Grove by daylight and early in the afternoon sent Thomas's and Scales's brigades from Wilcox's division west from their positions near Spotsylvania to augment Mahone's force. These two brigades proceeded along the Shady Grove Church Road as far as the Po River crossing. There they prepared to pitch camp in the rain, which had begun to fall early in the afternoon. Suddenly, they were ordered to fall in, and soon they were marching back toward Spotsylvania in the muddy darkness. Lee had canceled the missions to Shady Grove.[17]

Lee was also watching his right flank. He sent a Second Corps topographer, Jedediah Hotchkiss, to reconnoiter this area. Hotchkiss reported that he had discovered the Federals in three lines of battle, vulnerable to a flank attack. Lee sent him west after Early, whom he wanted to lead Heth's and Wilcox's divisions in an attack against Burnside's men. Hotchkiss could not find Early, who was probably investigating Miles's sorties beyond the Confederate left.[18]

In midafternoon, Rooney Lee, whose troopers were operating beyond the army's right flank, sent his father a report that indicated that the Federal force east of Spotsylvania appeared to be pulling back across the Ni River. A wagon train behind the Federal line had disappeared and infantry pickets on the Union far left were falling back. At 4:30 P.M. the cavalryman passed on to army headquarters the information that Federal trains were moving back in the direction of Fredericksburg and that their infantry was definitely in motion to the rear.[19]

This movement by Burnside's troops is one of the more puzzling features of the operations conducted that day. Grant's last order, on the night of the tenth of May, had said Burnside must advance Potter's division if he had not already done so (he had) and place it to the right of his corps line, so that it formed a connection with the left of the Sixth Corps. In his report, which was written in November 1864, Burnside stated that the entire Ninth Corps was ordered sometime on 11 May to withdraw to the north side of the Ni River and to assume a position which would cross the Fredericksburg Road approximately one mile from the river. This new line was to extend from across the road northwest past the Harris house, cross the river, and connect with Mott's left near the Landrum house. A road was to be cut through intervening woods and a bridge constructed across the river.[20]

With little hard evidence on the subject, it is logical to assume that the idea for this withdrawal was Grant's and that the order for execution came from his headquarters. The authors of a Ninth Corps regimental history claimed that Burnside protested the movement earnestly. However, Lt. Col. Cyrus Comstock of Grant's staff recorded in his journal that night that, when he arrived at Burnside's headquarters late in the afternoon, he was surprised to discover that Burnside had withdrawn all of his corps across the river. The lieutenant colonel wrote that Burnside was able to reoccupy the abandoned position south of the river with little difficulty, but that he grumbled at having to do so. This conveys the impression that perhaps the corps commander was the instigator of the move. Until more evidence is uncovered, this episode will remain a mystery.[21]

The movement to the rear began at approximately 4:00 P.M. The Ninth Corps infantrymen destroyed the bridges across the Ni after all troops had crossed to the north side. The Yankees marched back from the river for about one mile, where they were halted in the road. They stood there for an hour in a heavy thunderstorm and were drenched by the time they were told to recross the river. Now the Ni was swollen, and the foot soldiers were obliged to scramble back across on loose fence rails which had been laid on the stringers of the former bridges. The works were reoccupied with no interference from the Confederates. The Second Division reentered the works near the deserted Beverley house north of the road. Potter reported that all of his men were back in the line by 10:00 P.M. In the evening Maj. Gen. Thomas L. Crittenden arrived to assume command of the First Division, and Colonel Leasure returned to the command of his brigade.[22]

General Lee's Dilemma

Sometime during the afternoon Lee ordered that, if any segment of the salient line were attacked, Gordon should immediately move his division from its position in reserve to the threatened point, without waiting for orders from anyone. Lee recognized the weaknesses inherent in the salient, especially after the initial success of Upton's attack on the previous evening, so he ordered a third defensive line to be built across the base of the rough triangle formed by the salient. Work began on this line during the day.[23]

Late in the afternoon Lee rode to the Harrison house to confer with Ewell and his chief of artillery, Armistead Long. Lee was trying to correlate the various and confusing intelligence reports that he had received of Federal reconnaissance missions beyond the army's left across the Po and to Todd's Tavern, and, on the right, the apparent withdrawal toward Fredericksburg. Ewell was unable to supply any helpful information. The early morning withdrawal of Mott's troops from the Brown lane might also have been observed and reported by Confederate pickets stationed along or in advance of the Landrum lane. In the afternoon, skirmishers from Mott's Eleventh New Jersey and the entire Twenty-sixth Pennsylvania Regiment had advanced in the general direction of the Landrum house, apparently hoping to gain a position from which to observe the northern approaches to the salient. This Federal attempt to advance the skirmish line was unsuccessful. If the action was reported to Lee, he probably attached no special significance to it. It was, however, the one operation conducted before dark that day that offered a reliable clue as to Federal intentions.[24]

In the evening Lee arrived at Heth's headquarters in the church immediately south of the courthouse. He had reached a decision. Regarding Miles's moves on the left as mere feints or, in fact, reconnaissances, Lee told Heth that "the enemy are preparing to retreat tonight to Fredericksburg." He directed Heth to prepare his troops for immediate movement at a moment's notice. Heth was not to disturb his artillery, however, until orders for the move were issued.[25]

Lee was determined to attack the Federals if, for whatever reason, they retired from their present position and moved toward Fredericksburg. He was concerned about the time required to withdraw the front line artillery pieces if a movement by the army became necessary during the night. Ewell's guns in the salient and, to a lesser extent, Anderson's on Laurel Hill especially worried him. He directed Pendleton to issue orders to the corps chiefs of artillery requiring them to withdraw before dark those guns that would be difficult to move rapidly after nightfall.[26]

Alexander did not withdraw any of his guns. The roads to his rear generally were unobstructed, and he made provisions to ensure that they would remain so throughout the night. He ordered his ammunition chests mounted and positioned his carriages for rapid movement, but the guns remained in place.[27]

Lee apparently returned to Ewell's headquarters at the Harrison house before Pendleton's written order had arrived. He briefed Ewell and General Long on the need to withdraw the guns before dark and to have everything

McCoull house—Edward Johnson's headquarters
(Mass. MOLLUS Collection, MHI)

prepared to move during the night, since Lee believed that the Federals were withdrawing from the army's front. The narrow path which led from the northeast portion of the salient to the Confederate rear lay mostly in dense woods. Long ordered the withdrawal of the guns that were east of the northern leg of the McCoull farm lane, which included the seven batteries of Lt. Col. William Nelson's and Maj. Richard C. M. Page's battalions plus one battery of Cutshaw's. The guns rumbled to the rear immediately before sunset and went into park near Spotsylvania. No one had thought to inform Edward Johnson, whose infantry these guns had been supporting, about the decision to withdraw them. He first learned about it when he saw them moving out. He asked someone what was going on and was told that the movement was in obedience to orders and that a general movement of the army was being contemplated.[28]

The men of Maryland Steuart's brigade, along the east face of the salient, were similarly surprised when the six or eight artillery pieces located near the

Harrison house and outbuildings—Ewell's headquarters
(Mass. MOLLUS Collection, MHI)

apex and the two pieces farther south along their line were limbered up and moved to the rear. They queried an artillery officer, who replied that he did not know why the move was being made, only that the guns and crews had been ordered back to camp. Steuart's people felt uneasy, but they assumed that other batteries soon would replace the ones removed.[29]

The eight guns of the batteries of Maj. James M. Carrington and Capt. W. A. Tanner remained in position, Carrington's near the west angle and Tanner's farther west, just beyond the left flank of the Stonewall Brigade. The two batteries supporting Rodes's troops on the left face of the salient were also kept in position.[30]

Three Confederate accounts suggest that Lee originally intended to withdraw the infantrymen of Johnson's division simultaneously with the artillery pieces. Campbell Brown (of Ewell's staff) said that Lee had directed Ewell to withdraw the infantrymen from the front line and Long to withdraw the artillery. Ewell suggested that the foot soldiers would rest better where they were because their shelters could protect them somewhat from the rain that had begun to fall. Lee agreed but ordered the artillery to move back.[31]

Lt. Col. Hardaway maintained that he received notification that General Long had ordered all of the guns withdrawn at dark. He notified Ramseur and then sought out Long to find out what was being planned. He met

Confederate defensive works at Spotsylvania
(Mass. MOLLUS Collection, MHI)

General Lee, who said that he did not intend for the guns to move back until the infantry did so. Hardaway immediately sent orders to his battery commanders to remain in position until the infantry retired. The orders to battalion commanders Nelson and Page were not changed and their batteries withdrew at dark.[32]

Major Cutshaw confirmed these statements. He recalled that General Long directed him to send for his horses and to be ready to move out when General Johnson's division retired, but not to move until the infantrymen did.[33]

In his formal report Long merely stated that his orders were "to have all the artillery which was difficult of access removed from the lines before dark. . . ."[34] He ordered all of the batteries on Johnson's front to withdraw

Confederate abatis
(Mass. MOLLUS Collection, MHI)

except Carrington's and Tanner's, which had access to the northern part of the McCoull lane. The corps batteries farther southwest could move to the rear on the path that led south past the Harrison house.

As darkness settled over the field, the Confederate Second Corps pickets shivered occasionally as the damp air grew chilly. They listened to their empty stomachs rumble and peered into the wet darkness. Approximately two miles west of the salient, the cavalry vedettes of Wade Hampton's division and Billy Mahone's infantry pickets prepared to spend an equally miserable night in the rain. If these pickets were alert shortly after dark, they may have detected the sounds of movement coming from the Yankee position opposite them, north of the Po River.

III Thunder in the Morning 12 May

13 General, 11–12 May the Line Is Broken

Grant Decides on Another Combined Assault

At 3:00 P.M. Grant directed Meade to move after dark the three Second Corps divisions that were on the right of the army's line. They were to march behind Warren and Wright to a position between Wright and Burnside, in the area of the Brown house. Hancock's Fourth Division, under Mott, had already been there for two days. From this area Hancock and Burnside would attack the Confederates at four o'clock the following morning. During the assault, Warren and Wright were to press close to the enemy's works before them and to attack if a favorable opportunity arose to do so. Grant closed his orders by saying that Upton's attack on the previous evening would have been entirely successful if Mott and Burnside had supported it adequately and if the attack had been executed at 5:00 P.M. as originally intended.[1]

At 4:00 P.M. Burnside received notification of the proposed operation, with instructions to prepare his troops quietly, so as not to alert the Confederates. He was to attack vigorously at 4:00 A.M. Staff officers from Grant's headquarters were to be sent to assist both Burnside and Hancock. Apparently one of the staff officers who would be sent to Burnside, Lieutenant Colonel Comstock, was to provide guidance and perhaps an occasional prod, should that become necessary (Grant intimated as much to Meade in his 3:00 P.M. message).[2]

Grant had elected to use a large force to attack a seemingly vulnerable section of the Confederate line, the northern portion of the salient, which was manned by Johnson's division of Ewell's corps. Whether the Federals knew the precise location of the tip, or apex, of the salient is uncertain. In his memoirs, Grant stated that the reconnaissance conducted by Mott's troops during the afternoon had discovered the existence of the salient. From analyzing the directions in which the lines of Wright, Mott, and Burnside faced, the Federal high command should have been aware that a large bulge in Lee's line existed somewhere between the Brock and Fredericksburg roads. The operations of Upton and, to a lesser degree, those of Mott on the tenth and of Mott again on the eleventh had established the position of the Confederate line along the north face of the salient. Nothing, however, was known about the continuation of this line to the east.[3]

Meade sent his order to Hancock at 4:00 P.M. directing him to withdraw only Birney's and Barlow's divisions and to move them to the position between Wright and Burnside. Since Gibbon's troops were posted on the line among Fifth Corps units, Meade feared that their immediate removal would alert the enemy. He promised Hancock that Gibbon's division would be withdrawn before daylight and sent to join in the attack if at all possible.[4]

Meade called his three corps commanders to his headquarters and discussed the proposed assault with them. Among other things, Hancock wanted to know the point to be attacked and the approaches thereto, only to discover that no one at headquarters had any appreciable knowledge of these factors. Comstock, who had been to the area of the Brown house that morning, was sent to reconnoiter the area of the proposed advance with Lt. Col. Charles H. Morgan, Hancock's chief of staff, and Maj. William G. Mitchell, an aide-de-camp. In the rain Comstock missed a turn and the three Federals ended up in Burnside's lines, where Comstock learned of the Ninth Corps's withdrawal to the north side of the Ni River. The members of the party retraced their steps and arrived at the Brown house immediately before dark. The only assistance which Mott was able to offer was to point in the general direction of the Confederate position. The three officers crept forward to the picket line, where they discovered that their view was blocked by a ridge. They decided to recommend that the front of the Second Corps assault column be formed in the area of Mott's picket line. Then they returned in the dark to their assigned stations, Morgan and Mitchell to report to Hancock and Comstock to spend the night with Burnside.[5]

In the Sixth Corps, Wright issued instructions at 5:00 P.M. to his division commanders that required Russell and Neill to withdraw their commands from the front line. Russell was to occupy a position directly to his rear and Neill a position near the Alsop house, which was Warren's headquarters. The rifle pits of the corps were to be manned by Ricketts's division and by Mott's troops until Mott moved them into position for the assault.[6]

Instructions for the Fifth Corps were sent at 6:30 P.M. Meade ordered Warren to move his troops to the part of the line on their right presently held by Hancock's men. He said he would station a division of the Sixth Corps near Warren's headquarters for support in case he were attacked or outflanked during the main assault the following morning. Meade also said he was moving army headquarters early in the morning to the vicinity of the Hicks house, about half a mile north of the Brown house. Warren ordered

Griffin to have Bartlett's brigade report to corps headquarters at 3:00 A.M. for deployment on the right of the line and alerted Crawford to extend his troops to the left after Gibbon's Second Corps division pulled out of the line.[7]

Meanwhile, Hancock had summoned his three division commanders to his headquarters at 7:00 P.M. to explain what he knew of the proposed attack. His information was sparse. Barlow, whose division was to lead the movement and the assault itself, remembered that no information was available about the enemy's strength and dispositions, cooperating friendly forces, plan of attack, or even the purpose of the attack. The officers were told that the intended operation was a very important one and that the gratitude of the nation would be due them if the operation were successful. Hancock ordered Barlow to report with his division to corps headquarters at 10:00 P.M., where staff and engineering officers would lead his men to the proper location for the attack and would furnish him with all necessary information.[8]

After dark, details from Barlow's and Birney's divisions crept forward and lit large fires in an attempt to deceive the Confederates opposite.[9] Barlow reported to corps headquarters at the proper time and was joined at the head of his division by Lieutenant Colonel Morgan and Major Mendell of the engineers. During the day, Mendell and Wright had explored the area around the Brown farm and the roads leading to it from the north. They had discovered a shorter route than the one intended for Hancock's column. At the corps commanders' meeting, Wright had suggested that Mendell accompany the head of Hancock's column.[10]

From the scanty evidence available it is not possible to determine the exact route of Hancock's First and Third divisions, which were followed later by Gibbon's troops. The distance by known roads was less than three miles. Capt. William H. Paine of the engineers led the guns of the corps artillery on a road farther to the north than that which the infantry used. Hancock did not ride at the head of the column. His position during the movement is not known. He reportedly stopped at Wright's headquarters tents during the night to ask directions.[11]

Rain, mud, and darkness made the march miserable. The tired infantrymen of Barlow's and Birney's divisions plodded along in silence for the most part. They managed to maintain a relatively close formation despite their exhaustion and the conditions of the march. Pioneers carrying axes accompanied the column.[12]

From the standpoints of military history and human interest, it is a pity there was no voice-recording instrument at the head of the marching column. Barlow asked Morgan and Mendell for additional information on the impending attack and was told that they had little or nothing to offer. Hancock's chief of staff then began to express in a loud voice his indignation at the absurdity of the situation in which he was ordered to conduct a movement to prepare for an important attack, with no available information on the position or strength of the enemy. Morgan was probably the second most proficient swearer in the Federal Second Corps, ranking directly below his mentor Hancock. The colonel profanely abused his superiors' methods of conducting operations, especially those of the present evening. Captain Mendell also interjected his professional opinions on these subjects from time to time.[13]

Barlow, too, was angry at the situation, but because he did not have any heavy responsibilities during the march, he gradually relaxed. As he listened to the two other officers voice their displeasure, he began to laugh. Soon he had to grasp his saddle's pommel with both hands to keep from falling off his horse. He jokingly told Morgan that, when they arrived at their destination, he hoped that the troops would be faced in the proper direction, so that they would not march away from the Confederates and have to circle the earth and come up in the enemy's rear. This probably did nothing to improve Morgan's frame of mind. Miles and Brooke were riding with the head of the column and adding their complaints about the absurdity of the situation. Miles became so incensed and loud that Barlow finally ordered him to be quiet. Thus, the mounted officers and the infantrymen plodded, each in his own manner, through the mud, rain, and darkness toward the most famous attack of their army's history.[14]

Shortly after midnight on the fateful day of 12 May, the head of the column arrived in the vicinity of the Brown house. Mott's troops had returned to the area and were trying to catch some sleep in the rain. Barlow instructed his brigade commanders to permit their men to rest on their arms and then entered the house looking for anyone who could supply him with some useful information. He found Mott indoors, but he learned no more from him than had Morgan earlier in the evening.

Barlow eventually found an officer, Lt. Col. Waldo Merriam, who gave him a small amount of information about the terrain over which the advance would be conducted. Merriam, who was the commander of the Sixteenth Massachusetts Regiment, had been Mott's field officer of the day on the eleventh. He had participated in the unsuccessful reconnaissance advance on that day as well as in the attacks on the tenth. During these operations, he had glimpsed fleeting views of the area between the Brown house and the Confederate works along the northern face of the salient. He drew a sketch for Barlow on a wall of one of the rooms in the house. From this Merriam explained that a treeless corridor about three to four hundred yards wide extended from below the Brown house south for close to five hundred yards, until it joined the open fields of the Landrum farm. The Federals guessed that, if an advancing column marched down this corridor and kept going straight across the fields, it would eventually strike the Confederate works at the desired point.

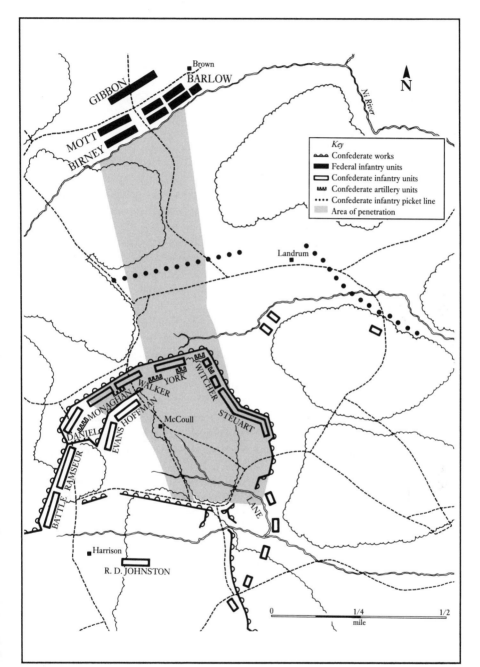

MAP 13-1. Federal Second Corps Assault on 12 May, 4:45–5:15 A.M. Area
of farthest penetration is indicated.

In 1879 Barlow claimed that the information derived from this rough sketch was his basis for selecting the disposition of his division for the advance. Moreover, he claimed that he did not see Hancock from the division commanders' meeting at 7:00 P.M. on the eleventh until 1½ to 2 hours after the opening of the attack, and then only because he went to the rear looking for his corps commander.[15] Barlow's version of this phase of the preparations for the assault conflicts, however, with other accounts. One of his aides, Lt. John D. Black, claimed in 1896 that Hancock called another meeting of his division commanders late at night at the Brown house. During this session Barlow reportedly again asked about the terrain to be crossed by the advancing column and the nature of the enemy defenses. The only information offered was that the distance to the enemy's works was something less than a mile. Barlow then facetiously asked whether there was a chasm one thousand feet deep between his starting point and the enemy's works. When no one could honestly deny that there was, the exasperated general announced that, under these circumstances, he was assuming the right to form his division as he pleased, choosing two lines of masses. Others reminded him that on the tenth Mott had reportedly been repulsed almost exclusively by artillery fire, and they questioned the wisdom of offering so large a target to such artillery. Barlow replied that he would have enough troops together when crossing the works to capture any artillery that might be deployed in the vicinity. After a discussion of this point, Barlow received permission to form his division as he desired.[16]

Black's account does not reflect the manner in which one would expect Hancock to conduct a council of war. It is possible, however, that the corps commander silently agreed with Barlow's contention that, with the utter lack of intelligence concerning the target area and the enemy's dispositions therein, it was best to go in with a heavy mass of troops to cope effectively with any situation.

Hancock officially reported that the precise direction of advance "was ascertained by a line determined by a compass on the map from the Brown house toward a large white house known to be inside the enemy's works, near the point we wished to strike."[17] This was the McCoull house, which had been discovered by Upton's troops in their attack on the tenth when they had advanced into the McCoull clearing. Meade had reportedly furnished Hancock with the approximate location of the house just before the two generals parted on the eleventh. In his statement made in 1879, Barlow mentioned neither the use of a compass nor of a compass bearing.[18]

Thus, however the details for the preparation of the attack were worked out, the troops were placed in their assigned positions as they arrived at the clearing on the Brown farm during the early morning hours. Birney's troops probably arrived after 2:00 A.M. and Gibbon's, who did not leave their works opposite Laurel Hill until 1:00 A.M., arrived at 3:00 A.M. or later. The Twenty-sixth Michigan of Miles's brigade was not relieved from the picket line until 11:00 P.M. After marching alone for most of the rest of the night, it reached the front in time to join its brigade in the advance without halting.[19]

Barlow's division was formed across the northern end of the treeless corridor immediately north of a small run whose course lay across the intended line of advance. Brooke's and Miles's brigades occupied the front line, with Smyth's and Brown's directly behind and closed up tightly. The individual regiments were doubled on the center, that is, in column alignment two companies wide. There were five-pace intervals between regiments and ten paces between brigades. The resulting formation was a nearly solid mass 275 to 300 men across and 20 deep. The Second Delaware of Brooke's brigade was positioned to the left of the formation as protection against any enemy force from that direction.[20] On the right of Barlow's troops, Birney's division formed two deployed lines. The ground in front of it was marshy and covered by a dense forest of low pines. This had been the route of Mott's unsuccessful assault on the tenth. Mott's two brigades were deployed to the rear of Birney's troops. Gibbon's men, when they arrived, were placed farther to the rear in reserve.[21] Barlow's and Birney's divisions, which together would compose the first line of assault, totalled about eleven thousand troops. The entire Second Corps attack force numbered nearly nineteen thousand.

The corps artillery arrived in the darkness at the edge of a field five hundred yards south of the Couse house, about one mile out Gordon Road northeast from Alsop's. This area was the site of the Fifth Corps's field hospitals. The gunners went into park just north of the Gordon Road near some deserted buildings and awaited orders.[22]

As the Federal infantrymen arrived at their prescribed positions for the attack, they promptly lay down and tried to get some sleep. The cool rain continued to fall intermittently on the relatively warm ground, and, as the air temperature dropped during the night, a ground fog began to form that soon restricted visibility to less than fifty yards.

Confederate Apprehensions

Shortly after midnight, when Barlow's division began to arrive in the vicinity of the Brown house, Confederate pickets from Steuart's division who were posted out from the apex of the salient near the Landrum house heard and reported what they described as a steady rumbling sound. As a result, two of Steuart's aides visited those pickets and subsequently stood for one-half hour on top of the breastworks listening to what sounded to them like a subdued roar of far-off falling water. The two officers concluded that the sounds indicated either a flanking movement or the massing of large numbers of Federals for an attack against the salient near its apex. They awakened Steuart and warned him. He sent a message to Johnson at the McCoull house, stating his belief that his position would be attacked at daylight and requesting the return of the artillery.[23]

Johnson immediately sent a staff officer to Ewell's headquarters at the Harrison house to report that the enemy were probably massing opposite his division for an attack and to request the immediate return of the guns. Ewell received this information at about 1:00 A.M. Accounts of the immediately ensuing sequence of events vary. According to one version, Ewell told Johnson's staff officer why the artillery had been withdrawn from the front line and did not appear to be overly concerned about the suspected buildup in front of Johnson's position. The staff officer then returned to Johnson and persuaded him to ride in person to Ewell. He did so and convinced Ewell to order the return of the guns.[24] A more plausible version contends that, when his courier did not return after a reasonable amount of time, Johnson dispatched another and soon was informed by Ewell that the artillery had been ordered back and would be in position by 2:00 A.M.[25]

Ewell endorsed Johnson's message and, without notifying Lee, forwarded it by courier to his chief of artillery, Armistead Long. Whether this courier was assigned to Ewell's headquarters or was one of the two which Johnson had dispatched originally is not known. He might very well have been Johnson's, because he did not find Long's headquarters tent near Spotsylvania with the order for the return of the guns until 3:30 A.M. The fog was probably partly to blame for the delay of this important message, which was to cost the Confederates dearly.[26]

Col. Thomas H. Carter, who commanded the artillery battalions of Page and Cutshaw, was awakened and ordered to have his guns in position by daybreak. The colonel endorsed on the order that the time was then twenty minutes before daybreak, that the men were all asleep, and that he would have the guns in place as soon as possible. Page remembered being awakened at 3:40 A.M. The horses had been unhitched and unharnessed, and, as the men worked furiously in the wet darkness, Page and Carter consulted and decided where to position the batteries upon their arrival. Soon Page's four batteries, followed by Cutshaw's two, were pounding up the Brock Road. They had to cover about two miles, much of it over narrow, muddy roads and trails. Cutshaw's third battery, Garber's, was still in position behind Rodes's line on the west face of the salient. The fog remained thick.[27]

About three-fourths of a mile from the village, Page turned to the right off the Brock Road on to a woods road and led the cavalcade north and then northeast in the darkness. He and Carter had decided to place the four-gun battery, which was commanded by the colonel's brother, Capt. William P. Carter, at the apex of the salient. The four guns that had been Page's battery, now commanded by Lt. Charles R. Montgomery, were to be placed immediately to the left of Carter's position. The two-gun section of Capt. Charles W. Fry's battery under Lt. W. A. Deas was to be posted about one hundred yards to Carter's right along the east face of the salient. (Fry was absent on detached duty with his other two guns.) The four pieces of Capt. William J. Reese's Alabama battery were to take a position to the right of Lieutenant Deas's two guns, farther down the east face. While ascending a hill at a point about halfway up the salient, one of Montgomery's pieces had some kind of accident, which kept it from going on with the rest of the battery.

The march continued along the narrow open space behind the works occupied by Steuart's brigade along the east face of the salient. Page recalled that he heard some scattered musket fire at this time, but he could see very little in the heavy fog and faintly dawning light. Arriving immediately behind the apex, Page explained to William Carter that this was to be his position and hurriedly showed Montgomery his assigned spot to the left. He then rode back and showed Deas and Reese their positions behind Steuart's line. Some of Captain Carter's men unlimbered the first piece and pushed it forward to the apex. They suddenly began to shout for ammunition. The Yankees were attacking![28]

The Federal Attack against the Salient—Initial Phase

The scheduled time for the attack was 4:00 A.M. At 3:45 A.M. Hancock informed Meade that, because of the poor visibility, he would begin a short time after four o'clock. He estimated that by that time all of his infantry would be in order. He also said that none of his artillery was where he wanted it, but he assumed that his corps chief of artillery had placed it somewhere.[29]

At 4:30 A.M. Hancock decided that it had become light enough to advance and ordered the move forward at 4:35 A.M. A little earlier, Birney had reportedly informed Hancock that he doubted whether his men could force their way through the swampy terrain. Hancock had replied that Birney must get them through.[30]

Hancock's troops stepped off promptly at quick time with arms at right shoulder shift and bayonets fixed. Brooke's Sixty-sixth New York Regiment, detailed as advanced skirmishers, marched at intervals of one to two paces thirty yards ahead of the brigade. Brigade pioneers carrying axes marched at intervals along the front. Miles's brigade and the front rank of Birney's division to the right were probably preceded by similar contingents.[31]

The front rank of the advancing mass of troops led the way across the run and ascended the hill opposite. At the top they captured a thin advanced line of Confederate pickets who were overrun before they could fire or escape to the rear. The Yankees continued south over the crest of the hill, where they were heard by the members of the advanced picket line of the Twenty-first Virginia Regiment, located to the southeast. The left end of the Virginians' line was probably on the high ground immediately northeast of the Landrum house. Some of these Southerners fired at the Second Delaware as it moved past in the gloom, and they killed Lt. Col. David L. Stricker. At this time, Hancock ordered Gibbon to advance his troops as support on the left of Barlow's division. Gibbon immediately dispatched Owen's and Carroll's brigades. The Eighth Ohio and First Delaware regiments were detached to deal with the Confederates near the Landrum house but discovered that most of them had departed.[32]

Picket officers reported to the commander of the Twenty-first Virginia, Col. William Witcher, who also commanded the remainder of Jones's former brigade back at the apex, that a gigantic Federal force had run right over the regiment's pickets on the left without even slowing down. Witcher gathered the members of his regiment together and soon realized that the direct route back to his position in the line was or soon would be cut off. He led his men southeast in an attempt to regain the Confederate line farther south, along the east face of the salient.[33]

Meanwhile, the leading troops of Barlow's and Birney's divisions had descended a slope and had begun to climb another, the Landrum lane ridge, on which was stationed the main Confederate picket line, troops from the Stonewall and the two Louisiana brigades. When the mass of Federal infantry emerged from the fog in front of these Southerners, some of the Confederates fired one round and then all of them took to their heels. The Federals had been briefed to maintain silence until they were close to the enemy works and then to double-quick forward with a yell. When the Confederate pickets fired from the dark hill ahead, many of the Yankees assumed that they were approaching the main line of enemy works and someone raised a cheer. Responsibility for this noise might be traced to the nervousness of rookies, the inherently mercurial temperaments of Smyth's Irish Brigade, or Col. Edwin R. Biles of the Ninety-ninth Pennsylvania, of Birney's division, who, at the first round of Confederate fire, reportedly let out a yell loud enough to be heard back in Washington.[34]

The cheer was taken up by hundreds of voices, and Barlow's and Birney's men dashed forward to the top of the rise. Here they discovered no defensive line but an open field descending gently, if brokenly, ahead for at least the two hundred yards or so that they could now see through the dissipating fog. By this time the intervals between regiments and brigades in Barlow's division had nearly disappeared, and the formation was one solid mass. To the right,

Birney's men had managed to keep pace despite the swampy woodland. Mott's two brigades brought up the rear. Continuing a short distance farther, the men in the front rank suddenly noticed a change in the color of the ground out at the limit of their vision. The veterans knew that this discoloration was caused by excavated dirt—earthworks. They had a little over two hundred yards yet to go.[35]

Confederate Stirrings in the Salient

Sometime in the early morning hours, after Johnson had become concerned about a possible attack against his position, he reported his misgivings to Gordon, who offered him Pegram's old brigade of Virginia regiments, now commanded by Col. John S. Hoffman of the Thirty-first Virginia. Johnson planned to place these troops in the second line of works behind Walker's brigade and to the right of Gordon's old brigade of Georgians, now commanded by Col. Clement A. Evans. Evans's troops were located immediately to the right and rear of the point where Smith's battery had been overrun on the tenth. Gordon retained his third brigade, Robert D. Johnston's, to the rear near the Harrison house.[36]

Edward Johnson alerted his brigade commanders to the threat and ordered them to have the men prepared to resist a probable assault at daylight. In Steuart's brigade, a circular was sent to the regimental commanders ordering them to have their men in battle positions in the works by one-half hour before daylight. Because of the dampness, a captain of the Third North Carolina had his men unload and clean their weapons in the darkness. At about 4:00 A.M., Johnson directed the field officer of the day of Witcher's brigade, Maj. D. W. Anderson of the Forty-fourth Virginia, to have the regimental commanders waken the men, get them into position, and ensure that their weapons were in working order. Similar instructions were issued to the Stonewall and Louisiana brigades.[37]

Witcher's brigade of six Virginia regiments had sustained heavy losses in the Wilderness fighting. General Jones had been killed, and practically the entire Twenty-fifth Virginia Regiment had been captured. The Twenty-first Virginia was posted one-half to three-quarters of a mile out in front, to the northeast of the apex. The Forty-second Virginia was on picket during the night, probably three to four hundred yards in front of the apex and extending around to the right for a short distance. At daybreak the Forty-eighth regiment marched out of the works to relieve the Forty-second for the day. The exchange along the picket line had just begun when the Virginians heard the cheering of Hancock's troops. The sound seemed to be close, but the Southerners could see very little in the fog. Both regiments headed east to try to regain their lines, as did their sister regiment, the Twenty-first, from farther to the front. This left only two of Witcher's regiments manning the works from immediately below the apex southeast to the point where they connected with Steuart's left.[38]

The number of Confederate infantrymen who were occupying the works of Johnson's division at the time when Hancock's attack struck can only be estimated. A figure of thirty-eight hundred to four thousand appears to be close, assuming the following strengths: Monaghan's Louisiana brigade, 750; Walker's brigade, 1000; York's Louisiana brigade, 750; Witcher's brigade, 400; and Steuart's brigade, 1000. Most of these troops were at their posts when the vans of Barlow's and Birney's divisions emerged from the fog approximately two hundred yards in front.[39]

Federal Breakthrough of the Salient Line

When the infantrymen of Barlow's division saw the extent and alignment of the Confederate line ahead, they altered their direction slightly to the left, to strike the enemy line head on rather than at an angle. This adjustment also ensured that Brooke's men on the left of the division line would overlap the east angle.[40] This slight swerve to the left caused a gap between Barlow's and Birney's formations, and McAllister's brigade from Mott's trailing division accelerated forward into it.[41]

The Federals continued to within one hundred to one hundred fifty yards of the works. Here, in a slight depression between two slopes, they encountered abatis constructed mostly from small pine trees. The pioneers hacked furiously at the obstacles with axes, and the front line infantrymen tore them away with their bare hands. During this delay in the advance, the remaining interval between forward and rear echelons disappeared, as the second line troops of Barlow's and Birney's formations continued to press forward.[42]

At the time when the Yankees arrived at the abatis and began to clear them away, the Confederate infantrymen were given the order to fire. Walker's brigade did not fire, because it was too far to the left for its members to see Birney's approaching troops. York's Louisiana brigade took aim at the mass of Yankees in front and squeezed their triggers, with very little effect. The damp night air had done its work, and the powder charges would not ignite. They hurriedly inserted new caps, but these produced only the same popping sounds as the originals.

By this time the lead Federals had broken through the abatis and were charging up the slope, yelling as they came. Not one Yankee musket had yet been fired. York's brigade could offer little effective resistance after the Federals reached the works except brief hand-to-hand combat. They were soon overpowered. Some of them escaped to the rear, but many were captured. In the Second Louisiana regiment, an order to fall back was given before the Yankees arrived at the works. Those who heard the order escaped, while those who did not became prisoners. Miles remembered seeing bayonet wounds for the first time in the war.[43]

At the apex, when Capt. William Carter's gun crew shouted for ammunition, a round was hurried forward and fired out into the Landrum field. Carter ran forward and was helping to reload the gun when an authoritative voice behind him barked the order to stop firing. Turning around, Carter was flabbergasted to see a large number of Federals a few yards away, with muskets leveled. He shouted at the Yankees not to shoot his men.[44]

If, at this time, the Confederate captain looked to his right down the part of the line occupied by York's brigade, his heart must have sunk. Hundreds, perhaps thousands, of Yankee infantrymen were pouring over the works. Some of them soon began to herd Confederate prisoners over the front of the works and across the fields to the north. Others emerged in the rear from between the traverses and began to move in force behind the Southern works in both directions. Still others continued straight ahead down the middle of the salient. This segment of Johnson's line had ceased to exist.

Thus, the breakthrough of the Confederate line occurred between the east angle and a point approximately three hundred yards west. The Federals who crossed here were, from right to left, troops from Birney's two brigades, those from Miles's, and the extreme right elements of Brooke's brigade of Barlow's division. The right of Brooke's brigade crossed the works approximately forty yards to the west of the east angle. It was probably these troops and some of Miles's left elements who captured Captain Carter and his battery. Smyth's men piled in directly behind Brooke's, and Brown's followed Miles's. A member of Smyth's 116th Pennsylvania, possibly a former millhand, jumped down between two traverses shouting exuberantly, "Look out, throw down your arms, we run this machine now."[45] Most of Brooke's troops passed immediately to the east of the east angle, where they appeared in front of Witcher's two regiments and Steuart's brigade.[46] These Confederates had kept their powder dry and were able to offer brief resistance.

Immediately before the Federal breakthrough, a group of Federals had appeared opposite the center of Steuart's line. They might have been from the Second Delaware Regiment or from portions of Owen's and Carroll's brigades. The Confederates had fired at them, and they had immediately disappeared in the trees.[47]

At the time of the breakthrough, the Forty-fourth and Fiftieth Virginia regiments of Witcher's brigade and the First and Third North Carolina, on the left of Steuart's, had stopped Brooke's men from coming over the works, only to hear demands of surrender from their rear as Barlow's troops moved down behind the line in force. Steuart's men had constructed protective walls across the rear of their traverses, and now they were trapped in these pens. There was brief hand-to-hand combat, but the Southerners were heavily outnumbered and had little chance. In a few instances Confederates were killed by excited Federals after they had surrendered. Steuart reportedly turned the southern half of his line to the left rear, where they briefly resisted the Federals inside the salient line, until Yankees from outside of the line climbed over the works and took them from the rear. The two artillery pieces commanded by Lieutenant Deas got off a round or two before being overrun.[48]

Farther south along the line, Reese's Alabama gunners were able to fire twenty-five rounds or so of case shot and canister before being silenced. John Purifoy, a member of the battery (who would later become secretary of state for Alabama), remembered that, as the four guns went into position nearby, infantrymen were lounging quietly behind their works confident that their pickets were on watch. Suddenly, the gunners of the left section spotted a column of Yankees emerge from the trees to their left front, and they clamored for permission to fire. The corporals ordered canister loaded, and both guns fired. Steuart immediately ordered that the firing cease. He feared for the safety of his pickets. Reese echoed Steuart's concern. However, the gunners remonstrated that there were no Confederate pickets in sight, only plenty of Yankees. They continued firing, despite the orders to cease fire. Soon they saw Barlow's troops moving down behind the line of works. They swung the two three-inch rifles of Reese's right section around to the northwest and opened fire on the Yankees with double charges of canister. This fire temporarily halted the enemy advance. Page rode up and ordered the right section to retire. The right gun was taken off successfully, but the other was captured, as were the two pieces of the left section. Reese and the only other commissioned officer present with the battery, Lt. Dwight E. Bates, were taken prisoner, along with three sergeants, two corporals, and twenty-eight privates. Four privates lost their lives in the action.[49]

Back near the east angle, Carter's four guns and Montgomery's three had been overrun by the first Federals over the works. Thus, in the initial stage of the action, twelve of the fourteen pieces which Major Page had led back to the line had been captured, along with most of their crew members.[50]

As the troops of Brooke's, Owen's, and Carroll's brigades continued to advance south behind the works of Steuart's brigade, their numbers and the impetus of their assault decreased. Some dropped off to escort prisoners to the rear or to search for booty. The remainder continued on, a disorganized mass intermingled without regard for unit integrity. Following behind the line of works as the direction changed to the south and then to the southwest, these Federals were able to get in the rear of Lane's two left regiments, the

Twenty-eighth and Eighteenth North Carolina, many of whom were captured before Lane was able to extricate them. Fifty or sixty members of the Eighteenth Regiment who had escaped made a reckless charge against the advancing mass of Yankees, stopping its forward movement and causing many of the enemy to break to the rear. Soon Lane's five regiments were positioned in line behind a segment of abandoned works which faced generally north. From there they were able to halt this portion of the Yankee advance.[51]

Nearly all the men of Steuart's brigade were captured, including its commander. Steuart surrendered formally to Col. James A. Beaver of the 148th Pennsylvania of Brooke's brigade. When Steuart identified himself, Beaver assumed that Jeb Stuart had been captured, although the Confederate officer standing before him did not fit the description of the famous cavalry commander. The problem of identity soon was straightened out, however, and Beaver detailed a most grateful corporal from Smyth's Irish Brigade to escort the Confederate brigadier to the rear.

Maj. Gen. Edward ("Allegheny") Johnson was also captured, but where or by whom is not certain. He reportedly was nearly shot for ignoring repeated demands to surrender, as he belabored his men with his walking cane to continue fighting and swung at armed Yankees in his anger and frustration.[52]

Back at the Brown house, Hancock received Johnson courteously and soon sent him on to headquarters, where he arrived at 6:30 A.M. Grant and Meade both shook his hand and tried to make the mortified Confederate feel comfortable. Finally, Seth Williams, of Meade's staff, took him to breakfast, which might have improved his disposition somewhat, considering what he had been through.

Steuart would have received comparable courtesy, but for his surliness over being captured. He refused to accept Hancock's offered handshake and was sent immediately to the provost marshal with the other prisoners. Patrick later provided Johnson with an ambulance but not Steuart.[53]

Birney's Troops Capture Most of the Stonewall Brigade

To the right of the area where Barlow broke through, the men of Birney's division, followed almost immediately by McAllister's brigade, crossed the works, capturing most of York's Louisianians there and the two four-gun batteries of Carrington and Tanner. Thus, twenty artillery pieces were overrun in the initial assault, as the Federals later claimed.[54]

In Birney's formation, Crocker's brigade was to the right of Ward's. The right regiments of the division probably crossed the works at, or immediately east of, the west angle. Some of the Federals looked after the Louisiana prisoners or searched for trophies while the rest continued forward in the general direction of the McCoull house. Most of these soon turned to their right and moved down behind the works of the Stonewall Brigade. The Virginians became aware of musket fire from their right rear, but they were unable to see very far in that direction because of the persistent fog and powder smoke. Suddenly, a horde of Yankees swarmed upon the Fourth Regiment on the right of the brigade line and overpowered them by sheer numbers. The exuberant Federals fought their way down Walker's line both inside and in front of the works and captured most of the members of the Fourth, Twenty-seventh, Fifth, and Thirty-third Virginia regiments after bitter hand-to-hand combat. Most of the Second Regiment, on the left of the line, escaped. Walker was severely wounded early in the action. Thirty-eight of the Louisianians to the left of the Stonewall Brigade were also captured. The rest of Monaghan's men moved one hundred yards or so to their left and mingled with Daniel's troops.[55]

A color-bearer of the Eighty-sixth New York, Stephen P. Chase, recalled that, when Ward's brigade went over the works, the regiments were already confusingly intermingled. A short time thereafter the regiment's colonel ordered Chase to take the colors to a certain knoll and to gather as many members of the regiment there as possible. The colonel planned to collect the remainder and to bring them to the knoll. The sergeant proceeded as ordered and arrived with four or five companions from his unit. Soon, Hancock and some of his staff appeared from the direction of the Landrum house. A lieutenant left the entourage and rode up to Chase and his party. After swinging his sword around his head a few times, the lieutenant profanely ordered the group back up to the works. Chase patiently explained his orders then, showing perhaps the combat infantryman's disdain for a certain type of staff officer, maintained that it would require more competent authority than the lieutenant to order him to leave his assigned position. The officer brandished his sword and threatened to cut the color-bearer down if he did not move at once. At this time, Hancock rode up to see what the trouble was. After saluting the colors, the general listened to Chase's explanation and immediately told the lieutenant that he was in the wrong. Bidding Chase a good day, Hancock again saluted the colors and rode away. The sergeant returned the salute with the flag. After a short distance, the staff officer looked back, and Chase saluted the lieutenant in the most profane way he could think of.[56]

While some of Ward's men were regrouping, Alexander Webb's brigade of Gibbon's division also participated in Birney's action. Why Webb reinforced the Third Division instead of following the rest of the Second Division against Steuart's line is not known, but he saw his share of action, nonetheless. One of his regimental commanders, Maj. James W. Welch of the Nineteenth Maine, captured a Confederate flag, that of the Thirty-third Virginia. Welch was severely wounded that day, and Webb himself was shot from his horse in front of the second line of works.[57]

To the left of Walker's brigade, Junius Daniel's Carolinians had manned their works at the first firing. The Federals who had captured the members of the Stonewall Brigade halted their movement down the line in order to round up their prisoners. This gave Daniel time to swing back his right regiment, the Forty-fifth, to a position perpendicular to the works, and from there they opened fire on the Yankees ahead. After a round or two, Daniel moved the Forty-fifth farther to the right, probably as far as the second line of works, and placed another of his regiments to the left between the Forty-fifth and the original line. These Carolinians soon dropped to the ground to fire, because farther south along the line Garber's and Jones's batteries, which had been withdrawn from their positions immediately behind the works, had swung around facing north on a low hill about fifty yards behind Daniel's men and were firing over them with canister.[58]

By then it must have been between 5:00 and 5:15 A.M. The Yankees had overrun approximately three-fourths of a mile of Ewell's front and had captured much of Johnson's division along with twenty pieces of artillery. This was unquestionably a brilliant achievement. At 5:15 A.M. Grant and Meade received Hancock's initial report that his troops had taken the enemy's first line with hundreds of prisoners. Some of the junior members of both staffs became ecstatic at the news. They may have actually believed that the Army of Northern Virginia had finally been defeated and that its superb commander would submit to the apparently disastrous consequences of the situation and attempt to save his army by withdrawing farther south. If so, they were to be disappointed on both counts.[59]

Initial Confederate Reaction to the Breakthrough

General Lee arose as usual at 3:00 A.M. and ate a meager breakfast. On this fateful morning he was unaware that Johnson had misgivings concerning a possible Federal attack and that the artillery that had been withdrawn the evening before had been called back. He finished his breakfast, mounted Traveller, and as was his custom, started forward to visit the front lines. He apparently had not ridden very far before he heard the opening shots of Hancock's assault. Hurrying forward, Lee soon encountered infantrymen of Johnson's division running to the rear. He shouted for them to stop and regroup. Some, with doubtful countenances, stopped running, but many paid little attention to their commander's orders and continued to the rear. Lee was probably near the reserve line of works that lay partially across the salient at its midpoint. Soon Maj. Robert W. Hunter of Johnson's staff galloped out of the woods on an artillery horse and announced that Johnson's line had been broken. Lee ordered Hunter to accompany him to General Gordon.[60]

Gordon's orders from the previous day were to support either Rodes's or Johnson's division as required, without waiting for specific instructions. When he heard the first firing from the direction of the apex, Gordon ordered R. D. Johnston to advance his brigade toward the sound of the firing. Johnston led his four regiments of North Carolinians at a rapid pace across the empty works of the reserve line and into the trees east of the McCoull house. Visibility in this wooded area was still restricted to perhaps only ten to twenty yards. Continuing toward the apex, the Confederates were unexpectedly confronted by a mass of Federals moving south, who immediately opened fire. The outnumbered Confederates were overpowered and reeled to the rear with heavy losses. Col. Thomas M. Garrett, commanding the Fifth North Carolina, was killed, and Robert Johnston was severely wounded.

Gordon now knew the situation was serious. He sent a courier to Evans, ordering him to hurry his brigade from its position on the left to the vicinity of the McCoull house. Gordon also dispatched a staff officer to locate Hoffman's brigade and to withdraw it if possible to the same point. From the sound of the firing, he could tell that the Yankees were moving down the east side of the salient behind Steuart's works. When Evans arrived near the McCoull house, he was ordered to send three of his six regiments into the woods to the east to locate the head of the Federal advance and to delay its forward progress as long as possible, so Gordon could form a line of troops to the rear. These three units, one of which was the Thirty-first Georgia, obeyed their instructions and fought desperately until nearly surrounded. Then they retired to the rear, each man on his own hook. Many were forced to surrender. Then as the Federals approached the McCoull house from the northeast, Gordon ordered Evans to withdraw his remaining three regiments south, probably as far as the works of the reserve line.[61]

As his old brigade pulled back, Gordon grew increasingly concerned about Hoffman's brigade. These Virginia troops had just arrived at their position along the right of the second line of works across the northern part of the McCoull farm lane when they heard the first firing of the Federal assault. The Virginians were unaware at first that the line had broken. As they were becoming accustomed to their new surroundings, members of the Thirteenth Virginia on the left of the brigade line noticed the crew of an artillery battery to their left suddenly swing their guns around and begin to fire down the line obliquely to the rear of the Virginians. The infantrymen shouted to the gunners that they were firing into their own men, but the artillerymen paid no attention and continued to fire. The battery soon ceased firing, and the infantrymen were ordered into line and hurried to the rear.

On the right of the brigade line, the commander of the Forty-ninth Regiment, Col. Jonathan C. Gibson, was taking a nap when he was awakened by one of Gordon's couriers, who whispered the news that the enemy had broken through Johnson's line and had captured most of his division. The colonel could not believe the report, because there had been so little firing, but the courier convinced him that it was true and urged him to move the brigade against the captured works. Gibson suggested that the messenger give these instructions to Colonel Hoffman, who was the ranking officer of the brigade, but the courier insisted that there just was not enough time for such niceties of protocol.

Before long Gordon's staff officer appeared and led the brigade east toward the break in the line. The head of the column soon received fire. They turned around when they saw the vast number of Yankees behind Johnson's works. After moving back into the McCoull field, the guide showed Gibson the Harrison house, about six hundred yards to the south, and the Virginians marched there swiftly. There they discovered three of Evans's regiments and a solitary figure on horseback, the commander of the army, Gen. Robert E. Lee.[62]

At the time when Hoffman's brigade arrived and began to take its position to the left of Evans's regiments, Gordon was returning from the woods to the east. He had been attempting to rally and to reform the remnants of Evans's other three regiments, which had been fighting to delay the Federal advance in that direction. As he rode toward the left of Evans's line, he spotted Lee and immediately spurred forward to report. He requested instructions and, without waiting for them, hurriedly informed the general that he intended to attack up the salient with Evans's and Hoffman's brigades. By this time an occasional bullet had begun to whistle in from the north. Lee listened to Gordon's briefing, gave his approval, and told the brigadier to proceed.

As Gordon turned away, Lee, instead of moving out of the way to the flank or rear of the infantrymen, nudged his mount forward in front of the junction of the two brigades. With hat in hand he stared impassively ahead in the direction of the Federal breakthrough. Undoubtedly Gordon was aware of Lee's attempt to accompany Gregg's brigade in its counterattack north of the Orange Plank Road on 6 May and of his reckless disregard for his personal safety while attempting to rally the survivors of Doles's brigade following Upton's breakthrough on the tenth, so he rode out and remonstrated with Lee. Lee apparently did not even look at him. Gordon then shouted to his troops to help him. When the foot soldiers realized what was happening, they began to shout imploringly to their beloved commander not to endanger himself, telling him that they would retake the broken line. Lee remained immobile as his troops behind him pleaded with him to move back. Gordon reached across and grasped Traveller's bridle, but he was jostled away by the crowding horses of other staff officers. Finally, a sergeant from one of the Virginia regiments strode forward, grasped the horse's bridle, and led the commander to the rear. Lee offered no resistance or complaint.[63]

The situation preceding this "Lee to the rear" incident, as it was often labelled, was different from that along the Orange Plank Road in the Wilderness on the morning of 6 May. That day, a portion of the army was being routed, and Lee, in the midst of the retreating troops and the confusion of incoming musketry and artillery fire, was unable to halt the movement. Suddenly, the van of Longstreet's eagerly awaited corps appeared, double-timing up the road. As Lee realized that the situation could now probably be retrieved, he discarded his appearance of calm and reserve. Waving his hat back and forth, he loudly cheered the tough Texans of Gregg's brigade as they moved into position. Fired with the excitement of battle, he rode beside these troops, continuing to cheer them and urging them forward.

Near the Harrison house on the morning of 12 May conditions were different. A disaster of unknown magnitude had occurred along a part of the army's line. The only reserve force immediately available was preparing to advance against the unknown danger. There was no excitement, no appreciable danger from enemy fire, only a sense of urgency. In this situation Lee did not speak; there was no word of encouragement to men or officers. He merely sat and stared in the direction from which "those people" were expected to appear.

Gordon's Counterattack

Gordon shouted the order to advance and the two brigades, perhaps three thousand to four thousand strong, stepped off east-northeast, with Hoffman's Virginians on the left and Evans's Georgians on the right.[64] The Southerners soon entered an area of pine trees, then splashed across a small branch, and approached the reserve line of works. A considerable number of Yankees had reached these works in the trees and, with colors planted, awaited the advance of the two Confederate brigades. When the Rebels became visible in the fog, the Federals opened fire.[65]

The Virginians on the left fired a volley in return and unleashed their frightening battle yell as they dashed forward. Hancock's men stood their ground at the reserve line of works for approximately one minute in bitter hand-to-hand combat and then broke for the rear, pursued by the Confederates. Continuing forward, the Forty-ninth Virginia, on the right of the brigade line, struck Steuart's original works from the right rear a short distance below the point where they crossed an extension of the eastern part of the McCoull lane. This regiment and the Thirty-first Virginia pursued the

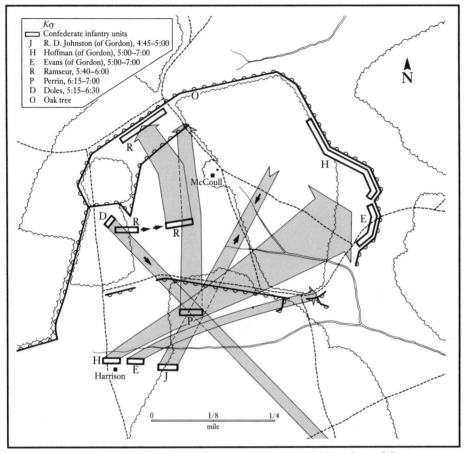

MAP 13-2. Initial Confederate Reaction to the Breakthrough, 12 May, 4:45–7:00 A.M.

Federals across the works for a short distance, until the Yankees disappeared into a pine thicket. The Southerners then returned and occupied the recaptured works.

The Thirteenth and Fifty-second regiments on the left of the advancing line struck Steuart's works perhaps three hundred yards or so south of the east angle, where a group of Federals offered temporary resistance and then retired. The members of the Thirteenth Regiment continued to advance up the line behind the traverses, as the Yankees ahead of them leaped out of these pens and ran to their rear. The Virginians reached a point about one hundred fifty yards from the east angle, where they were hit by fire from enemy troops in traversed enclosures along the west face of the angle. There the Confederates halted.

Thus, as a result of hard fighting against disorganized Federal troops, Hoffman's men had regained most of Steuart's line. In addition, they had recaptured four artillery pieces. They had, however, become scattered and disorganized for the same reasons as had Hancock's attacking Federals. Because of this, they moved to their right to form a more solid line that would connect with the left of Evans's Georgia regiments. This move placed the Thirteenth Virginia on the left of the brigade line, reportedly one hundred fifty yards south of the east angle. In this action, captured colors of the Third North Carolina and Tenth Virginia regiments were retrieved from dead Federals. Col. Hiram L. Brown, who commanded Barlow's Third Brigade, was captured sometime during the action.[66]

At Gordon's command to advance, the three regiments of Evans's brigade moved off promptly on the right of Hoffman's Virginians. After entering the trees, the Georgians apparently veered slightly to the right in a more easterly direction than Hoffman's troops. The Sixty-first Georgia, on the left of the brigade line, struck the works of the reserve line near its eastern end. With no support on its left, the regiment soon was overpowered by larger numbers of Yankees. Sixty-five officers and men and the unit's tattered battle flag were captured. The survivors fled to the rear in the fog and eventually reorganized under Lee's personal direction near the west end of the reserve line, where they remained for the rest of the day.

The remaining Georgia regiments occupied the works due east of the reserve line, and after the Yankees withdrew up the salient, the Confederates sidled to their left up the line of works as far as the extension of the eastern McCoull lane. There Colonel Gibson of the Forty-ninth Virginia discovered them to his right. A Georgia sergeant informed Gibson that only two regiments and a small portion of the third were in line there, that Evans was not with them, and that he did not know who was in command. Evans's troops had been roughly handled, but they did complete the reoccupation of the Confederate line along the eastern face of the salient.[67]

Rodes's Response

While Gordon fought to regain the eastern face, a staff officer from corps headquarters (Maj. Campbell Brown, Ewell's stepson) sought reinforcements for him. After vainly searching through the fog for Ewell and Rodes, Brown took it on himself to order Doles's shattered command across the salient. The major next asked General Kershaw, who was nearby, if he would send some troops to the right. Kershaw declined but did offer to sidle Wofford's and Humphreys's brigades right to occupy Battle's and Ramseur's sectors respectively, an offer which was gratefully accepted. Battle was eager for action, and his Alabamians later reinforced Ramseur in counter-attacking.[68]

By then Ramseur was already heavily engaged, but not off to the east, where Brown had intended. Instead, at about 5:30 A.M., Rodes had sent him to help Daniel secure and regain the western side of the salient, where Daniel had already blunted the Union drive down the western works.

Before daylight, Ramseur had ordered his four regiments of North Carolinians under arms. At the first indication of the Federal breakthrough, he had positioned his reserve Second Regiment perpendicular to his line, as had Daniel with his Forty-fifth Regiment. Now that he had orders to reinforce Daniel, Ramseur withdrew his regiments from behind their works, forming them in a line which faced north and which extended a short distance out into the McCoull field. From their new position the Carolinians fired north at Yankees, who by this time occupied the north side of the second line of works. Daniel's men were hard pressed and were beginning to waver when Ramseur was ordered to attack and to retake the segment of the line originally occupied by Daniel's right regiments, Monaghan's Louisianians, and the left regiments of the Stonewall Brigade.[69]

Ramseur moved his brigade out into the McCoull field and formed his regiments in a line, with the Fourteenth on the left, then the Fourth, Second, and Thirtieth. The Carolinians suffered heavily as they assumed their position in the open. Their line faced generally northwest and was nearly parallel with the upper leg of the second line, behind which Birney's and Mott's troops were pouring a withering fire into the Southerners. Still the Confederates maintained their rank and moved forward. As Ramseur shouted the command to charge, they dashed ahead with a yell and wheeled slightly to their left to strike the second line of works head-on. As the Southerners approached, the Federals fired another volley and then fell back behind the first line of works.[70]

Ramseur received a painful arm wound just before arriving at the second line. There was a pause in the movement until Col. Bryan Grimes of the Fourth North Carolina realized that Ramseur was temporarily out of action and assumed command of the brigade. Grimes ordered the four regiments to continue the assault, and the Confederates clambered over the second line of works and dashed for the original line. Birney's and Mott's troops stood their ground on the north side of these original works, and when the Southerners closed with them, there was bitter and bloody personal combat. Finally, the Federals broke for their rear across the clearing and disappeared into the trees. Ramseur's men reoccupied the works. The Thirtieth Regiment on the right flank of the brigade extended the line nearly as far as the McCoull farm lane.[71]

Perrin's Alabamians

Four of the five brigades of Mahone's division had spent most of the night near the Po River crossing of the Shady Grove Church Road. They had been recalled and had arrived at the courthouse a few minutes after Hancock's troops had entered the Confederate works of the salient.[72] Perrin's brigade was immediately ordered to proceed into the salient. It probably marched northwest along the Brock Road and turned onto a path which led to the Harrison house. One of Perrin's soldiers, Alfred L. Scott of the Ninth Alabama, remembered that the brigade deployed into battle formation and after proceeding an indeterminate distance north into the salient, was ordered to halt. This halt probably occurred between the Harrison house and the reserve line of works. The men were ordered to lie down.

Scott noticed a group of mounted general officers near them. The group consisted of Ewell, Rodes, a member of Lee's staff, and Perrin. These officers looked very excited. Gordon was talking rapidly. Perrin was turning from one general to the next as if begging to be told what he should do. Ewell glanced down and noticed the members of the Ninth Alabama lying almost under his horse's hooves. He deemed it appropriate at this time to remind the prostrate infantrymen that it did not look good for soldiers to be lying down in the presence of the enemy. Scott leaped to his feet and reported that the men had been ordered to lie down, whereupon Ewell told him that in that case it was permissible to be prone. Suddenly, Gordon told Perrin that he was willing to assume the responsibility for ordering the Alabamians to charge. Perrin shouted his brigade to attention and spurred his horse to the front, and the members of his five regiments dashed forward with a yell.[73] It had been about half an hour since Ramseur's counterattack.

Soon after the advance began, Perrin was shot from his horse, mortally wounded. Reportedly, he was in the act of leaping his mount over some captured works, possibly the reserve line of works, although the incident could have occurred at the second line of pits immediately behind the west angle. His troops advanced past the McCoull house, where three bearers of the Ninth Regiment's colors were shot in the course of just seventy-five yards. The Eighth and Tenth regiments, on the left of the brigade line, advanced at least as far as the second line of works near the point where it crossed the McCoull lane.

Alfred Scott, near the right of the line, claimed that his brigade had just about cleared the McCoull field of Yankees when the Southerners were raked by a volley from the trees to their right. The regiment turned that direction and advanced into the woods, driving some Federals before them. Suddenly, the Alabamians again came under a heavy fire, now from the south. They assumed that they were mistakenly being fired upon by other

Confederates from what had been their rear. When the color-bearer waved the flag on high, however, the volume of incoming fire increased, and the Southerners realized it was Yankee fire. The Southerners fired back, whereupon the Unionists, who were probably retiring before the advance of Hoffman's Virginia regiments, disappeared from view.

The subsequent operations of Perrin's brigade are unknown. Some members of the Ninth Regiment spent the rest of the morning and most of the afternoon with the Thirteenth Virginia of Hoffman's brigade among some traverses along Steuart's recaptured works, along the eastern face of the salient.[74]

Thus, by approximately 6:00 A.M. all of the Federals west of the northern extension of the McCoull farm lane had been driven back out of the salient proper. The counterattacks of Gordon's division and Perrin's brigade, which ended one hour or so later, were to drive out the remaining Yankees. Though the salient itself had been cleared, no Confederates manned the part of the line from Ramseur's right to and slightly south of the east angle. Hancock's men occupied the outer side of most of this part of the works. Yankees were still inside the traverses formerly occupied by York's Louisiana brigade and the right regiments of the Stonewall, from which they could fire upon Ramseur's right regiments.[75]

At 5:55 A.M., as a result of Ramseur's counterattack, Hancock asked that Meade order Wright to attack with his Sixth Corps on the right of the Second. Shortly thereafter Hancock received messages from army headquarters welcoming the news of his success and informing him that Wright had been ordered to attack immediately. Meade urged Hancock to hold the captured area and, if possible, to press on and take more territory. He also was informed that Burnside's Ninth Corps to his left had initiated its attack on schedule.[76]

14

If You Will Promise Me, I Will Go Back

12 May

Neill's Second Division of the Federal Sixth Corps

Wright had been ordered to withdraw his First and Second divisions from their positions in the line and to hold them in the rear as a reserve force. The time when these movements were executed is not known, although Getty reported that the Second Division moved back on the afternoon of the eleventh. Both divisions were apparently standing by for assignment by 4:00 A.M. Immediately after Hancock's breakthrough, Russell's division moved toward the right flank of the army. The precise destination of this march is not known. They marched until 7:00 A.M., when they were ordered to retrace their steps to their starting point. A chaplain of the New Jersey Brigade offered the explanation that the division was intended as a support for the right flank of the army in case the Confederates attacked there, thinking that Federal troops had been removed from this flank to participate in the assault on the center. They had, in fact, been removed, but Lee was too busy at the time coping with the breakthrough and the subsequent advance into the salient to think about a flank attack.[1]

Meantime, Neill's Second Division was ordered to the left at approximately 4:00 A.M. and arrived at 4:30 A.M. in a field to the northwest of the Brown house to await assignment. Shortly after 6:00 A.M. Wright was ordered to move Neill's and Ricketts's divisions forward to Hancock's right. A staff officer soon rode up to the Second Division and, noticing Col. Oliver Edwards's brigade ready to move, ordered it forward. That day the brigade consisted of three regiments, the Tenth and Thirty-seventh Massachusetts and the Second Rhode Island. The Seventh Massachusetts had been retained on picket duty back in the corps's rifle pits. Edwards led his three regiments south, generally following the route which Birney's troops had taken earlier through the woods southwest of the Brown house. Emerging from the cover of the trees, they crossed the Landrum lane ridge and arrived at an area along the captured Confederate works afterwards known as the "Bloody Angle"—an appropriate designation indeed.[2]

This segment of the line contained two slight bends which were approximately fifty yards apart. The east bend of approximately ten degrees was slightly more than three hundred yards west of the apex of the salient. An oak tree, measuring about twenty inches in diameter five or six feet from the ground, stood immediately behind the works there. About fifty-five yards further west along the line was another bend of perhaps twenty degrees. This bend was designated the west angle. From here the topography of the line of works sloped downhill to where the McCoull lane crossed the line.

North of the works was a small valley in the Landrum field. Opposite the oak tree, this valley was about thirty yards from the works, but it angled northeast to nearly one hundred yards from the works. From there the valley curved south nearly to the works about seventy yards up the line from the oak. The edge of the valley opposite the Confederate works will hereafter be called the crest.[3]

Fighting in this area began a short time after the arrival of Edwards's three regiments at 6:30 A.M. Except for one brief respite, the fighting was to continue uninterrupted for more than twenty hours.

The alignment of Edwards's three regiments, which totalled nine hundred men, was the Thirty-seventh Massachusetts on the left, then the Second Rhode Island, and the Tenth Massachusetts. The right company of the Second lay at the tip of the west angle, with the rest of the regiment and the Thirty-seventh extending the line to the left along the outside of the works. The Tenth Regiment lay along the right face of the angle and connected on its right with some troops of Brewster's Excelsior Brigade of Mott's division, some of whom had retired inside the works as Ramseur's and Perrin's counterattacks drove the Federals out of the McCoull field further to the west. When Edwards's men arrived at the works, there were no Confederates opposite, although Mott's troops might have been firing obliquely to their right at Ramseur's and vice versa. Suddenly, two lines of yelling Confederates, probably some of Perrin's men, assaulted Edwards's line from the woods to the south.[4] This attack was repulsed by the three New England regiments assisted by oblique fire from Mott's men.

After a short time Bidwell's and Wheaton's brigades followed Edwards's onto the field. Bidwell was ordered to support Edwards and deployed his men in the edge of the trees one hundred yards or so to the rear of the three New England regiments. Wheaton moved obliquely to his right behind Bidwell's line and took a position in the trees opposite the point where the McCoull lane crossed the works.[5]

As a result of Gordon's counterattack, Hancock called on both Meade and Burnside for support. In response, Meade sent Col. Lewis A. Grant's Vermont brigade of Neill's division to the left to relieve Barlow's division from the front line, instead of accompanying its sister brigades south to a position opposite the west angle. As the Vermonters marched toward their assigned position near the east angle, they were hit by Confederate artillery fire. Arriving near the captured works, Colonel Grant discovered Barlow's command in some disorder after its retirement to the Federal side of the works. Grant replaced Barlow's skirmishers south of the captured line and formed his brigade in two lines to the north of these works. Some of Gibbon's and Birney's men were fighting off an enemy assault to Grant's right, which was probably conducted by some more of Perrin's Alabamians.

Meanwhile, the remaining units of the Second Corps were attempting to shape themselves with Neill's men into some sort of order on the north side of the captured works. The eventual Union alignment, from right to left, was Brewster's brigade (Mott), Edwards's three regiments (Neill), McAllister's brigade (Mott), Birney's division, Gibbon's division including Webb's brigade, and Grant's brigade (Neill), with Barlow's troops to the rear of Gibbon and Grant and with Neill's other brigades behind Edwards. Later in the day Barlow's infantrymen would construct and occupy a line of works that would extend generally eastward from the east angle. This line would subsequently be extended by other Federals to the northeast and eventually north all the way to the vicinity of the Landrum house.[6]

The long-range artillery fire that had hit among Grant's troops was from Confederate Second Corps guns that had been hurried from the rear, positioned behind the reserve line, and aimed northward and northeast against the Landrum field and the woods north of it. Additional artillery support came from four First Corps guns positioned behind Humphreys's Mississippians to Daniel's left and from two Third Corps guns operating from behind the east face of the salient. Shortly after 6:00 A.M., during this shelling, an aide-de-camp of Hancock's was showing Wright where to position his troops when a shell exploded nearby, painfully wounding but not disabling Wright. He established his field headquarters in a wooded ravine located about six hundred yards north of the west angle. Incoming artillery fire caused him to move one hundred yards or so to another location, which proved to be even more dangerous. By early afternoon, Wright joined Hancock at the Landrum house.[7]

Meanwhile, back at the west angle, Edwards's New Englanders were adapting to the novelty of manning the forward side of a defensive work. The front troops rested against the wall of excavated dirt in front and peered under the head logs. The rain, which continued to fall intermittently, was very heavy at times, so that by now these Yankees presented a most bedraggled and unmilitary appearance. To Edwards's right, the members of the Excelsior Brigade, some of whom were in the log compartments on the

Confederate side, continued to fire obliquely down the line at Ramseur's North Carolinians and inflicted some casualties there. This pressure caused Rodes to request support for the right flank of his line, and Lee responded.

At approximately 7:30 A.M. the Federal infantrymen of the Excelsior Brigade noticed a body of Confederates marching in column toward them along the northern segment of the McCoull farm lane. These Rebs appeared to be passing through a veritable shower of artillery fire. The Excelsiors and possibly the members of the Tenth Massachusetts to their left ceased firing at Ramseur's men and prepared to direct their attention to these approaching newcomers.[8]

Arrival of Harris's Mississippians, 7:30–8:00 A.M.

The reinforcements were Harris's brigade, Perrin's comrades from Mahone's division. As they marched from the vicinity of the Block House Bridge toward Spotsylvania, they had apparently halted for a short rest at the Brock Road intersection. There Col. Charles S. Venable of Lee's staff had discovered them and directed Harris to lead his men into the salient.

As the brigade, approximately eight hundred strong, passed up the clearing of the Harrison house, some Federal artillery shells struck nearby, fired by Yankee Second Corps gunners deployed by Hancock along the Landrum lane ridge. With the poor visibility, they were probably firing by ear at the McCoull clearing. Near the Harrison house, Lee joined Harris and Venable at the head of the column. The general's horse was excited by the firing and became difficult to control. At one point it reared just as a bouncing solid shot passed under its belly, narrowly missing one of Lee's stirrups. This was one of the closest encounters with death or injury from enemy fire that Lee had experienced since the Mexican War, and it caused the Mississippians to plead with their commander to take cover, just as Gordon's troops had done a little more than two hours before. Lee replied, "If you will promise me to drive those people from our works, I will go back!" They promised with loud shouts. Lee then ordered Venable to guide the brigade to Rodes.[9]

The Mississippians went forward in the general direction of the McCoull house. The order of regiments from front to rear was the Sixteenth, Nineteenth, Twelfth, and Forty-eighth. Venable discovered Rodes near the McCoull spring, just northeast of the house. The column halted, and as Venable and Rodes conversed, a courier arrived from Ramseur's brigade with word that they could hold on for only a few more minutes unless reinforced, because of enfilading fire on their flank. Rodes immediately detailed a staff officer to lead Harris and his men forward and to position them to the right of Ramseur's line.

The Mississippians passed immediately to the west of the house and reached the lane. It was probably at this time that the Federals ahead saw them. The Yankees fired an initial volley at Harris when he was fifty to seventy-five yards south of the second line of works. This unexpected fire caused his brigade, which was still in column formation, to halt. Then Rodes's staff officer disappeared to the rear. One of Harris's couriers galloped after the guide but was unable to catch up with him.

Harris was in an unenviable situation, with his troops massed in the open under enemy fire from directly in front. He apparently had not been briefed as to the precise location of the line of works ahead or about which troops were there. Soon a private soldier from the Tenth Alabama of Perrin's brigade appeared out of the smoky mist. He told Harris the approximate locations of the right flank of Ramseur's brigade and of the enemy's troops. Harris decided to file his four regiments to the east of the lane far enough for the last regiment to clear the pathway and then to face them to the north and to advance them to the breastworks. The Sixteenth and Nineteenth regiments had left the lane and were moving east through the trees when they were spotted by the Federals of the Excelsior Brigade and by Edwards's troops, who opened a deadly fire upon them. Harris realized that, under this fire, he would be unable to deploy his four regiments as he had planned without prohibitive losses. He ordered the Sixteenth and Nineteenth regiments to face to their left and to charge the works. This they did, suffering severe casualties in the process. Both unit commanders, Col. Samuel E. Baker of the Sixteenth, and Col. Thomas J. Hardin of the Nineteenth, were killed. Harris reported two hundred to three hundred Yankees captured in this advance, probably behind the second line of works and in the traverses.

The Twelfth Mississippi moved forward and deployed behind the works with its right along the lane. The Forty-eighth assumed a position to the left of the Twelfth, connecting on its left with Ramseur's troops. Thus, Harris's infantrymen occupied the front line from a point to the west of the northern McCoull lane east nearly to the west angle. They had kept their promise to General Lee. They were to maintain this position unsupported under more or less continual fire for longer than nineteen hours.[10]

Harris's troops secured their grip on the works only after hand-to-hand combat with Federals of the Excelsior Brigade, some of McAllister's men, and the right companies of Edwards's Tenth Massachusetts. Finally, Mott's troops retired from the works and regrouped to Edwards's left rear. The Tenth, however, maintained its position along the line for approximately fifty yards southwest from the west angle. A short time later some of Ramseur's and perhaps some of Perrin's troops crossed the breastworks and entered the trees one hundred yards or so in front. From there they opened a deadly enfilading fire upon the right of the Tenth Massachusetts, which threw it into confusion and drove it from the works. These Federals regrouped on the crest of a slight knoll to the rear of Edwards's Second Rhode Island. The right companies of this regiment swung back also to the left of the Tenth. These Federals now faced southwest, and their direction of fire was nearly parallel with the line of works.[11]

A member of Company C of the Tenth Massachusetts recalled that by 9:00 A.M. he and many of his comrades had fired all of their ammunition. They lay on the knoll, slightly exposed to the Confederate fire. Some of them decided to return to the outside of the breastworks, where they assumed they would be safer. There they were immune from fire from directly in front but not from the right. One man's Enfield rifle was struck twice by musket fire in a short period of time. He and two comrades crouching outside of the works had been bunkmates during the previous winter at Brandy Station. One of them decided that it was safer back with the rest of the regiment on the knoll. He broke for the rear and was immediately shot and killed. Another was shot through the heart at the works and died instantly. A short time later, a mass of Confederates swarmed over the works and captured the remainder of the Yankees who were crouching there.[12]

As a result of this action Wright requested assistance from Hancock. At approximately 7:00 A.M. Barlow had ordered Brooke to withdraw his troops from the confused mass of Second Corps infantrymen who were attempting to reform north of the captured works near the east angle. Brooke had managed to collect about one thousand of his men near the Landrum house and had replenished their supply of ammunition by 8:00 A.M., when Hancock rode up and ordered him to move his troops to the right and to report to General Wright of the Sixth Corps. Hancock directed Brooke not to become engaged except as a last resort. Brooke led his men west along the Landrum lane ridge and entered the trees, then turned south and arrived at approximately 9:00 A.M. in the rear of Wheaton's brigade. The troops of this Sixth Corps unit were deployed in two lines and were lying prone under the trees. A heavy skirmish line was engaged to the front. Brooke's men lay down to the rear of Wheaton's.[13]

Arrival of McGowan's South Carolinians, 9:30–10:00 A.M.

On the eleventh of May, McGowan's brigade had been relocated from a position south of the Fredericksburg Road to one just north of it. Soon after the sounds of Hancock's assault were heard on the twelfth, the South Carolinians were moved farther left behind the line, to a sharp angle in the works. Here some of Burnside's gunners fired on them. Greater danger and greater duty awaited them elsewhere that morning, for at approximately 9:00 A.M.

Wilcox ordered McGowan to march his brigade to Ewell's relief.[14] The precise route by which McGowan led his men into the salient is uncertain. He probably moved southwest across fields to the Brock Road and then followed Harris's route up the path to the Harrison house. McGowan reported to Ewell, who directed Rodes to send the fresh brigade northward in support of Harris's brigade. The Carolinians continued their advance in column until arriving near the McCoull house. Here McGowan formed the regiments into line of battle, with the Twelfth on the right, then the First Provisional Army, the Thirteenth, Orr's Rifles, and the Fourteenth. Enemy bullets whistled in among the Southerners from the trees to their right front.[15]

The advance continued to within fifty yards of the second line of works, where McGowan was disabled by a severe arm wound. Soon thereafter the next ranking officer in the brigade, Col. Benjamin T. Brockman of the Thirteenth Regiment, fell mortally wounded. Col. Joseph N. Brown, who was with his Fourteenth Regiment on the left of the brigade line, inherited command of the brigade. When McGowan was wounded, the regiments of the brigade, except the Twelfth on the right, halted near the second line of works. One of these men remembered that there was some confusion as to whether they should continue straight ahead or turn toward the right. The Twelfth entered the trees and, passing around the right end of the second line of works, advanced to the first line.[16]

Back behind the second line, Lt. Col. Isaac F. Hunt, who had assumed command of the Thirteenth Regiment, could see Confederates ahead behind the main line of works. He noticed Gordon passing in the smoke and rain and asked him for permission to move his regiment farther to the right. Gordon told him to take it to the area where the fighting was the heaviest.[17]

Hunt moved along the rear of the second line until he met Lt. Col. Washington P. Shooter, commander of the First Regiment. The two colonels climbed atop the second line of works in order to see forward over the smoke. They saw many Yankees out in front of the first line, and Hunt, not knowing whether Colonel Brown of the Fourteenth Regiment was alive or dead, ordered the entire brigade to move forward to the first line. The four regiments dashed forward through the mud and came up behind Harris's men, who were fighting desperately to repulse some Yankees who were advancing on their position. Some of the Mississippians shouted to the Carolinians to move farther to the right. The Carolinians faced in that direction and moved east behind the works, suffering severe casualties that included the death of Colonel Shooter. The First Regiment led the way until it came to the left of the Twelfth, where its members faced left and entered the trench behind the breastworks. The trench was ankle deep in water. On the right, the members of the Twelfth had their hands full firing from between the traverses at Yankees in front and enduring musket and artillery fire from their right.[18]

Hunt took in the situation and soon realized that no other Confederates were positioned to the right of the brigade and that Yankees occupied the opposite side of the works to the east as far as he could see through the rain and smoke. Soon, Yankees were observed crossing the works to the Confederate right. Hunt detached some infantrymen and placed them in a caisson lunette to the right rear, where their fire checked the movement of the Federals.[19]

Thus, the men of McGowan's brigade, by now approximately one thousand strong, had arrived at the position designated by Ewell in the works to the right of Harris's brigade. At the beginning of their stay there, the Fourteenth Regiment, on the left of the brigade, was behind the right regiment of Mississippians. Next, to the right, Orr's Rifles and the Thirteenth Regiment were crowded together several lines deep. The First Regiment extended the line in front of the oak tree, and the Twelfth completed the formation with an extended line to the right. The right of the brigade, which was the right flank of the Twelfth Regiment, rested approximately 235 yards west of the east angle, or apex, of the salient.

No Confederates occupied the southern side of the stretch of works between the Twelfth's right and the apex, while the northern side of that sector was more or less continually occupied by Federals. The greatest test for these South Carolinians was to be posed by enemy troops from directly in their front.[20]

More Federal Reinforcements at the West Angle

A short time after L. A. Grant's brigade (of Neill's division) replaced some of Barlow's disorganized troops near the east angle, Hancock informed Colonel Grant that the right of the Sixth Corps needed assistance and directed him to move his second line of troops to that area. Hancock promised to forward the remainder after he found some of his own troops to replace them. Grant moved right to the north of the west angle, where he was ordered farther to the right to the support of Wheaton's brigade of his own division. He discovered Wheaton's men attempting to advance through an area of small trees and thick underbrush under heavy fire from Confederate works ahead. Grant formed his troops behind Wheaton's and sent his Fourth Vermont Regiment to the right of Wheaton's line, where its members reportedly advanced to and briefly held a small part of the Confederate works. Wheaton's advance was soon abandoned. Grant left his Fourth Regiment under Wheaton's command and led the rest of his troops back to the vicinity of the west angle, where the other half of his brigade soon arrived from the left.[21]

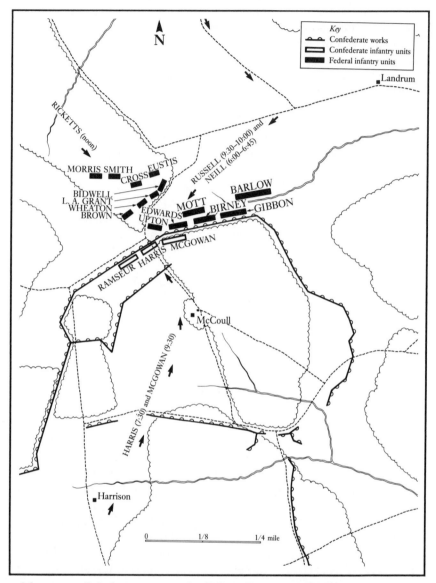

MAP 14-1. Reinforcements to the Salient Front, 12 May, 6:30 A.M. to
Noon. Noon positions are indicated for units engaged in the fighting near
the west angle. Barlow and Gibbon were not heavily engaged after 9:00 A.M.

Arrival of Russell's Division, 9:30–10:00 A.M.

Between 9:00 and 9:30 A.M. the First Division of the Federal Sixth Corps arrived from its trek to the right of the army. Russell immediately sent Upton's brigade forward with orders to support the right flank of the Second Corps. Upton rode ahead of his troops and arrived at the slight crest immediately to the north of the west angle. There he claimed to have observed Federal troops extending along the outside of the works as far as the point where his attack on the tenth of May had broken through. These troops consisted of Edwards's Tenth Massachusetts, some of Wheaton's men, and the Fourth Vermont of Grant's brigade. Upton galloped back to the lead regiment of his marching column, the Ninety-fifth Pennsylvania, and ordered it to hurry forward. Upton's intent was to pass over the crest and to place his regiments on the right of Edwards's line. When he arrived back at the crest, he saw that all of the Federals beyond the west angle had been driven from the works. Wheaton's men were not visible, and the Tenth Massachusetts was behind the crest, facing southwest. These withdrawals had been caused by the rigorous fighting of Harris's Mississippians and by the advance of McGowan's Carolinians to the works.

When Upton's Ninety-fifth Pennsylvania topped the crest, it received blistering fire from these Confederates. The Pennsylvanians halted and filed to their right behind the crest. The crest there extended west from the west angle at an angle of approximately thirty degrees to the main line of Confederate works. Upton soon halted the regiment and ordered the men to lie down. The left of the unit rested near the works, and the right, which was refused, lay behind the crest. The Pennsylvanians were hard-pressed to maintain this position in the face of heavy musket fire from the nearby Confederate works. Soon, however, the remaining regiments of the brigade arrived, and Upton placed them in support of the Ninety-fifth and to its right behind the crest. The brigade was to remain there fighting for seven hours.[22]

In the account cited above, Upton did not mention Edwards's three regiments at all. Lt. Col. Joseph B. Parsons, commanding the Tenth Massachusetts, remembered when Upton arrived on the field. Parsons claimed that at about 10:00 A.M. he was standing behind the crest in the pouring rain when a mounted officer rode up from the rear through a slight ravine, dismounted, and asked for the commander of the regiment. Parsons identified himself and was ordered to advance his regiment across the crest and to occupy the outside of the Confederate works. Parsons began to explain that the small area between his regiment and the works in front was subject to heavy enemy frontal and flanking fire. The newcomer, however, curtly interrupted Parsons, saying he was not interested in explanations. He identified himself as General Upton and ordered the colonel to move his regiment forward immediately. Parsons refused to obey the order and was prepared to surrender his sword to Upton rather than to order his men into a position where he thought they would be slaughtered. Upton threatened Parsons with a court martial and stalked away. He returned shortly and asked Parsons the name of his brigade commander. Parsons named Colonel Edwards, who was probably on the left of the brigade line with his own Thirty-seventh Massachusetts. Upton returned in thirty minutes with Edwards, who advised Parsons to obey the order, as Upton outranked them both. Parsons still balked and advised Edwards to answer Upton as he had. While this conference was going on, a column of Federal troops appeared in the ravine. Upton told the two officers that he would demonstrate with these troops how the works in front could be taken and held. He formed the newcomers in the ravine to the right of the Tenth Massachusetts in column of regiments and ordered the first regiment to charge over the slope to the enemy works. As this unit appeared on the crest, it received a murderous fire from both front and flank and was driven back in confusion with heavy losses. Upton ordered the next regiment to advance, with a similar result. The new general then informed Edwards that troops could not survive beyond the crest and that he had ordered the third regiment of these new troops to report to Edwards. He also advised the colonel to extend the line from the right of the Tenth Massachusetts around the knoll.[23]

Thus, Upton's regiments assumed a position behind the slight crest which led northwest from the west angle. The advance of McGowan's South Carolina regiments to the works had forced the Second Rhode Island from its position astride the angle along the outside of the works. Most of these New Englanders retired beyond a small knoll which lay to the northeast of the oak tree. The remainder moved to their left and mingled with the right companies of the Thirty-seventh Massachusetts, which now occupied a position near the outside of the works from the oak tree east for perhaps 125 yards.[24]

The area near the west angle and the ground immediately to the north and northeast of it, a rectangular area slightly larger than two acres, now became the storm center of a battle whose prolonged intensity probably had not been approached in land warfare up to that time. All eight brigades of the Sixth Corps's First and Second divisions, as well as other Union troops, would be drawn into the cauldron. The Confederates would be represented only by McGowan's and Harris's infantrymen. They would prove sufficient.

While it is impossible to present a comprehensive account of all of the action there that morning, some fragments are available. When the Tenth Massachusetts and most of the Second Rhode Island were driven from the outside of the works at the west angle at approximately 10:00 A.M., Wheaton sent his Ninety-third Pennsylvania forward to the crest as support. He then ordered Colonel Brooke to move his Second Corps brigade forward to relieve his first line. Brooke reported, "I repeated the orders of General Hancock; notwithstanding which, and the fact that two lines of his own corps were then lying in my front and between my command and the enemy, he peremptorily ordered me in. I obeyed, passing over two lines of the Sixth Corps, which were lying on their bellies in my front, and reaching the front line relieved it."[25]

Brooke's troops exhausted their supply of ammunition after an hour of firing. Shortly thereafter, the colonel noticed some of his sergeants crawling back with blankets and caps to borrow ammunition from the Sixth Corps infantrymen to their rear. The incensed Brooke ordered his noncoms to remain where they were. He stormed up to Wheaton and reported that his men had exhausted their ammunition supply and that other troops were necessary to hold the line. Wheaton relieved the Second Corps troops with some of his own. Brooke led his brigade back to the left, where he reported these facts to Hancock in person.[26]

From approximately one hundred yards behind Edwards's line, Bidwell sent his Forty-ninth and Seventy-seventh New York regiments forward to the works at the angle, but they were driven back to the crest. The remaining three regiments of this brigade deployed to the right in support of Upton. Later the Forty-ninth and Seventy-seventh were relieved at the crest, but the units which relieved them were soon driven back by intense musketry. The New Yorkers, with the assistance of some Vermonters of Grant's brigade, advanced and reestablished the position along the crest.[27]

Brown's First New Jersey Brigade followed Upton's to the front. It arrived opposite the west angle just before 10:00 A.M. and discovered Bidwell's and Wheaton's troops already there. The Jerseymen were moved to their right by the flank through an area of scraggly pine trees, then halted opposite the segment of works occupied by the left of Harris's brigade and the right of Ramseur's. The Yankees' formation for their charge consisted of a front line with the Fifteenth, Fourth, and First regiments from right to left, and a second line composed of the Third on the right with four companies of the Second to their left.[28]

As soon as the five regiments emerged from the cover of the trees, they received a volley from Confederates behind the works ahead. The direction of the advance turned obliquely left toward the west angle and oak tree. As the Yankees dashed across the clearing, they presented an inviting target to Ramseur's men farther down the line, who seized the opportunity. The adjutant of the Fifteenth New Jersey remembered that the first enemy volley from that flank seemed to sweep away the entire right wing of the regiment. The brigade sustained nearly two hundred casualties crossing the clearing. The advance continued, however, and some Federals, including most of the left wing of the Fifteenth Regiment, actually entered the works briefly before retiring. The Fifteenth brought back a captured battle flag and some prisoners. In this action, which lasted for about thirty minutes, this unit sustained approximately 150 casualties, including all of the color guard save one and seven line officers. The survivors of the brigade were rallied behind their starting point and placed in reserve. They were through fighting for the day.[29]

Immediately in front of the works, James Mangan of the Fifteenth Regiment was struck by two bullets, one in his right forearm and one through a shoulder. He lay in a trench outside of the works next to Capt. James Walker, acting commander of the regiment, who had been killed there. Nearby lay a man with a broken leg, who was still full of fight. He was able to load his musket but could not get at his caps. Mangan capped his comrade's rifle, and that persistent Yankee fired at any Confederate who showed his head over the top of the works scarcely five feet distant. After a time the soldier was killed by a shot to the head, and Mangan was taken prisoner. Later his arm was amputated, and after the surgery, he lay on the ground for ten days and nights without shelter. As soon as he began to regain some strength, he buried his amputated arm in a grave with a dead soldier. Mangan was exchanged in September.[30]

Federal Artillery Action

The artillery batteries of the Sixth Corps had remained in position behind that corps's rifle pits, which were nearly one-half mile to the west and northwest of the west angle. After Hancock's troops had been pushed back behind the first line of captured works, these gunners were ordered to fire blindly over the trees into the salient. As a result, when Wright moved his Second and First infantry divisions forward to the area of the west angle, he had no guns available to accompany the foot soldiers.[31] Col. Charles H. Tompkins, Wright's artillery chief, requested the loan of a battery from the Second Corps. Col. John C. Tidball dispatched Battery C of the Fifth United States Artillery under command of 1st Lt. James Gilliss. By this time, Tidball had batteries operating from the Landrum lane ridge, firing over the captured works into the salient. Lieutenant Gilliss reported to Tompkins and asked for the services of a staff officer to show him the battery's intended position. The artillery colonel could provide only an orderly who, Gilliss soon discovered, knew nothing about the intended position. The lieutenant assumed a position which partially answered Tompkins's description of the desired spot. His six Napoleons opened fire blindly over the trees with solid shot to hit at one thousand yards, as ordered by Tompkins. The position was probably to the rear of the western end of the Landrum lane in the edge of the woods. Gilliss considered this mode of operation to be a complete waste of ammunition, since he was unable to determine the effects of his fire. However, he was only a first lieutenant, and he continued to obey orders.[32]

Soon a staff officer rode up to Gilliss from the direction of the front and informed him that General Upton requested that he advance one of his sections three hundred yards, to a position to the right of Upton's brigade. Gilliss demurred, and the officer rode away but soon returned repeating the request. Gilliss again refused, and, as the officer disappeared a second time, the lieutenant began to consider that since he was supposed to be supporting the Sixth Corps perhaps he would be justified in complying with Upton's request. At any rate, when the staff officer returned again, perhaps accompanied by higher authority (one account claims Wright himself), Gilliss acquiesced and ordered the section commanded by 2d Lt. Richard Metcalf to follow Upton's officer forward. The section was manned by Metcalf and twenty-three enlisted men, including Sgt. William E. Lines, who commanded one gun crew while the lieutenant commanded the other. During the movement forward the staff officer was shot from his horse. Some of the battery horses were also shot and were dragged along by the rest. The bodies of some wounded and dead Federals were crushed by the wheels of the guns during the dash forward in the driving rain. Metcalf established his two pieces to the right of Upton's troops, a reported three hundred yards from the Confederate works.

The two guns had fired a round or two when suddenly a group of Harris's Mississippians climbed over their breastworks, making a desperate charge against Upton's line on the crest and Metcalf's guns. The Union artillerymen shivered these Confederates with double charges of canister, and the attack was repulsed, although some of the Southerners penetrated Upton's line. Metcalf now switched to spherical case shot and shell set at one second timing and aimed just over the top of the breastworks. It would appear that sometime during the action, the two pieces were pushed forward and were operated much closer to the works than three hundred yards. Because they were in the open, the artillerymen began to be hit. Sergeant Lines remembered that Metcalf's piece fired only nine rounds, while his own was able to fire fourteen times. The sergeant's crew was assisted by two infantry officers, both of whom were soon shot. After eleven men had been wounded, Metcalf decided to retire, but as the limbers were being drawn forward, most of the horses were immediately shot down. Later in the day, some nearby infantrymen helped to drag the two guns by hand back to safety. The limbers, riddled with bullets, were not retrieved until the following day. Thirty-nine bullet holes were counted in the sponge bucket under Sergeant Lines's piece.[33] Metcalf reported one man killed and nine wounded, with nine horses killed and five wounded. These figures may represent only the casualties in his own crew, because Sergeant Lines claimed after the war that all of the gunners of both crews, except for himself and his lieutenant, were hit.

In addition to the two officers mentioned, at least one other infantryman assisted the gunners. A twenty-year-old private of the Fourth New Jersey named John P. Breech, who stood only five feet four inches tall, ran out from his regiment's position in the trees and helped to carry ammunition forward to the men who were operating the pieces. When the gunners retired from the guns, Breech rejoined his regiment. Thirty years later he received a Medal of Honor for conspicuous gallantry in volunteering to help serve the battery.[34]

The volume of musketry which produced such effective results was soon being maintained by all units, Federal and Confederate, near the west angle. This continual fire aimed at the top of the breastwork or the crest was maintained to discourage surprise attacks such as the one attempted by the Mississippians.

15

See That Your Orders Are Executed

12 May

Ninth Corps Operations, 4:00 A.M. to Noon

Burnside initially interpreted his orders for the attack to mean an assault directly along the Fredericksburg Road against the courthouse itself. However, consulting with Comstock after dark on the eleventh, he learned that his corps was to attack farther to its right against the eastern face of the salient. His objective was to establish and maintain at all hazards a connection with the left of Hancock's Second Corps. An attack against the village appeared to be promising, because the Federals knew that some portion of the Confederate Third Corps had been located more than three miles west of the village on the tenth and eleventh. However, by sunrise of the twelfth, these troops of Mahone's division had all returned to the vicinity of the village, except for Brig. Gen. Ambrose R. Wright's brigade of Georgians, who had been left behind to cover the Block House Bridge crossing on the Shady Grove Church Road.[1]

Burnside's plan called for Potter's division to lead the advance, followed by Crittenden's. Willcox's division was to remain in reserve, and Marshall's Provisional Brigade, consisting of one regiment of dismounted cavalry and two of heavy artillery, was to remain in the works astride the Fredericksburg Road, which were generally between the two Beverley houses, and in advance of that line. Potter's troops started at 4:00 A.M.[2] With the Second Brigade in advance, they left their bivouac near the abandoned Beverley house and marched in the wet darkness northwest along a wagon path. After a short distance the lead brigade sidled to its right to permit the First to come up beside it on the left. The division continued the advance in a two-brigade front.[3]

Because of sketchy accounts, an accurate description of the operations of the Ninth Corps against the eastern face of the salient during the morning is impossible. Potter reported that his troops took two lines of detached rifle pits and some prisoners. Then they assaulted the Confederate main line, and the right brigade carried a segment of it, including two artillery pieces.[4] On the right of the Second Division line, the Ninth New Hampshire, five hundred strong, emerged from some trees to cheers from hard-pressed Second Corps troops. Soon an officer from one of Hancock's brigades rode up and begged the commander of the New Hampshire regiment to change front to the left and fire at some advancing Confederates. Immediately after making this request the officer was shot from his horse. The Ninth Corps regiment wheeled to its left, advanced a short distance, halted, and opened fire. Many of the muskets misfired because of damp powder. Suddenly, a force of Southerners appeared out of the fog scarcely fifty yards to the left front. The Hampshiremen had become separated from the remaining regiments of their brigade. As volleys were exchanged at close range, some Confederates began to work around the Federal unit's flank. The New Englanders, carrying their wounded commander in a blanket, retired into the woods to the east, where they located and rejoined the remainder of their brigade. The regiment sustained over two hundred casualties in this brief action. The Second Corps troops had disappeared to the north. Thus, the initial connection between Burnside's and Hancock's corps was short-lived.[5]

From Burnside's headquarters, Comstock telegraphed Grant at 7:00 A.M. that Potter's connection with Hancock was reportedly broken. The time of this message suggests that the Confederates involved in this action were Hoffman's Virginia regiments of Gordon's division.[6]

Farther to the left on Potter's line, at the junction of the two Federal brigades, the members of the Seventeenth Vermont occupied a knoll. They had arrived there at 5:00 A.M. and later spotted some Confederates about 150 yards ahead in a swampy ravine. For more than an hour the Vermonters fired at the exposed Southerners, whose only route of withdrawal lay across open terrain. Just as they had expended their last cartridges, the New Englanders were relieved at 7:00 A.M. by the Forty-eighth Pennsylvania of the First Brigade. The Pennsylvanians' commander, Lt. Col. Henry Pleasants, decided to move his unit around the right of the knoll and assume a position closer to the enemy troops. While the two Federal regiments were exchanging positions, approximately fifty Confederates raced up to the top of the knoll and surrendered. They belonged to the Twenty-sixth Georgia of Evans's brigade.[7]

When the Pennsylvanians had advanced to within seventy-five yards of the ravine, they opened fire. The Southerners returned the fire. More Southerners joined those in the ravine, and Pleasants was notified that these Confederates wanted to surrender. He ordered his men to continue firing. Finally, the Southerners threw down their muskets, ran up the knoll in a body, and surrendered. There were approximately two hundred of them from the Twenty-sixth and Thirteenth Georgia regiments.[8]

The Thirty-sixth Massachusetts occupied the left of Potter's line. While crossing an open space east of the woods in which Lane's line was located, these Federals received a volley of musketry from some Confederates in the edge of the woods ahead. As the Yankees continued forward and entered the woods, the Southerners retired and moved south as if to get on the left flank and rear of the Federal regiment. The three left companies of the Thirty-sixth were deployed facing the left to cover that flank when the Confederates again retired from sight. The New Englanders stood in the dark woods and wondered about their left flank. Crittenden's troops were supposed to connect there but had not yet made an appearance. The Massachusetts men were aware that their brigade connected on its right with Simon G. Griffin's, who in turn supposedly had joined Hancock's left. The skirmish line somewhere in front was firing continually. Soon the main body received instructions to prepare for an assault straight ahead against the enemy's main line.

As the New Englanders got ready to execute this order, word came from the right of the line telling of Hancock's success in capturing four thousand prisoners and forty artillery pieces. Suddenly, a large force of Confederates appeared in front of the skirmish line, moving from the Federals' right to left. The Yankee skirmishers fired a volley at these Southerners, who ignored the fire and kept marching. There were shouts to cease firing, and word soon came from the right of the division that these were Hancock's prisoners, who were moving to the rear. Before the New Englanders had time to digest this strange bit of intelligence, news came from the companies on the left that these Confederates were deploying across the regiment's left flank, apparently standing at order arms. The Federal captain in command of the left wing of the regiment walked toward the Rebels along a woods road waving his sword and advising them to surrender. He shouted that they would not be harmed if they did, and he asked them to move into the Federal line. The captain had come very close to their front rank when suddenly they shouldered their muskets and let fly with a volley. Miraculously the captain was not hit. He returned to his skirmish line and ordered the companies under his command to open fire. The Confederates then assaulted the line of the Thirty-sixth Massachusetts and were repulsed with difficulty. Suddenly, an order arrived directing the entire brigade to charge. As the men of the Thirty-sixth rose to their feet and started forward, they were joined on their left by the Twenty-first Massachusetts Regiment from the First Division. The two regiments advanced together and reportedly drove the opposing Confederates back to their main line of entrenchments. At about this time, Gordon's counterattack cleared the works on the eastern face of the salient, and Potter's men retired and threw up rifle pits. Later in the morning, Potter's and some of Crittenden's troops attempted additional assaults, which were unsuccessful.[9] These later assaults were executed in response to urgent messages from both Grant and Hancock. At or immediately before 6:00 A.M., when Hancock's right was forced back beyond the Federal works, Hancock began to urge Burnside to advance rapidly. After Gordon's counterattack forced Hancock's left back, his pleas for support on his left increased in both number and earnestness.[10]

Lt. Col. Cyrus B. Comstock was Grant's liaison with Burnside during the morning. He telegraphed progress reports to Grant independently of Burnside. As Hancock's requests for support came in to Ninth Corps headquarters, Comstock undoubtedly urged speed and possibly offered some tactical suggestions. At one point Burnside snapped that he would command his own divisions. Ten minutes later the general apologized to Comstock for the outburst and asked his advice. From this Comstock concluded that Burnside was rather weak and not fit to be corps commander.[11]

Grant had also been urging Burnside to act more vigorously. At 8:00 A.M. he suggested to Burnside that the best way to connect with Hancock was to push the enemy with all of his might. Burnside reported at approximately 9:30 A.M. that he had established solid contact with Hancock. At 10:00 A.M. Grant asked Comstock how things were progressing on the left, ordering him to tell Burnside to push hard with everything he had, including his Provisional Brigade. Comstock's reply is not extant, but at 10:20 A.M. Grant brusquely ordered Burnside to move one division to the right to Hancock's assistance and to attack with the remainder of his force. He advised Burnside that Warren and Wright had been attacking vigorously all day, and he ended the message with the admonishment to "see that your orders are executed." Upon receiving this censure, Burnside accused Comstock of complaining to Grant that he was slow. Comstock denied this, claiming that his information to Grant contained only what Burnside was actually doing.[12]

Thus, Burnside's performance during the morning appears to have been lackluster at best. The troops of his Second and First divisions who became engaged fought tolerably well, however, considering the fact that neither they nor any of their officers had any prior knowledge whatever of the terrain where the actions occurred. The Federals might have fared better if Potter's and Crittenden's troops had been already near their starting points, which would have entailed moving the exhausted men during the darkness into an uncharted area. Apparently, neither Burnside nor anyone else in the Federal high command ever considered this action. The use of scouts in this area any time after 9 May would also have been helpful. Grant had ordered this, but it was not done.[13]

Operations of the Union Fifth Corps, 3:00 A.M. to Noon

At 3:00 A.M. Bartlett's brigade was withdrawn from behind the rest of Griffin's division immediately west of the Brock Road and was sent to the right to occupy the segment of the line formerly held by the Second Corps, connecting with the right of Crawford's division of Pennsylvania Reserves. At the same time Warren's aide-de-camp, Colonel Roebling, led Kitching's brigade of heavy artillery troops forward and positioned them to Bartlett's right, leaving space between into which the Maryland brigade was soon inserted. As visibility increased, Cabell's gunners spotted these Federals, who had moved to the right of the line and were establishing advanced skirmish lines there. A few of these batteries opened fire at the newcomers with little or no effect.[14]

At 5:00 A.M. Warren notified Crawford of Hancock's initial success and advised him to have his command ready to advance and to press his skirmishers up to the enemy's entrenchments, which Warren believed would soon be evacuated. At 6:00 A.M. Meade informed Warren that Wright was being ordered in and that Warren must be prepared also to attack immediately, when ordered to do so. Warren replied that he was "firing from five batteries on the enemy's position, and ordered my skirmishers to push their line forward wherever it is possible." At 6:30 A.M. he sent a circular to his division commanders informing them that the corps could receive an order to advance at any moment. When the order came, they were to precede their main lines of battle with a strong line of skirmishers to draw an initial volley from the enemy. After this their main lines were to charge.[15]

At approximately 7:30 A.M. Meade dispatched a message to Warren stating that the right of the Sixth Corps was being attacked heavily and that Wright desired support. Meade believed that Warren's imminent attack would relieve the pressure upon Wright to some extent, but that Fifth Corps troops should still be sent to their left lest that flank be turned in the event of a reverse to Wright. At the same time, Warren received a message directly from Wright that asked for troops to support the right of the Sixth Corps and to extend it. In response Warren withdrew Bartlett's brigade, except for the First Michigan and 118th Pennsylvania regiments, who were skirmishing in advance of the line near the Po River. He sent the remainder of Bartlett's regiments to the left. Kitching's two large regiments of heavy artillery troops also were ordered to Wright's support from Warren's line at this time.[16]

These messages of Wright's and Meade's require clarification. The only pressure which the Sixth Corps had experienced up to this time was Perrin's attack, which had been repulsed by Edwards's three regiments and Mott's troops to their right. However, by 7:15 A.M. the approach of Harris's brigade across the McCoull field may have been reported to Wright, prompting his request for support. By his right, the Sixth Corps commander meant the area to the west-northwest of the west angle, in the general direction of the Shelton house. He knew that any Confederate force that advanced in that direction would have to face only Ricketts's two attenuated brigades, and he had a healthy respect for the common Confederate practice of counter-attacking. Wright might have expressed this concern in his message to Meade.

By this time Meade had moved his headquarters farther from the action, to the Armstrong house east of the Ni River. Probably Meade merely passed Wright's request for support to Warren, hinting strongly that some Fifth Corps troops be moved to the left. As a result, Bartlett's regiments were dispatched. Actually, Wheaton's brigade soon assumed its position in the area that concerned Wright.

Finally, at 8:00 A.M., Grant sent an order through Meade to Warren to attack immediately with as much of his force as possible and to be prepared to follow up any success with the rest of his troops. This attack was intended primarily to occupy Anderson's attention and to discourage him from sending reinforcements to Ewell. Warren replied that he had issued the attack orders. He complained, however, that those orders had not given him time to attack first two key points from which he expected trouble: the enemy works opposite Crawford's division toward the right of his line and Kershaw's troops immediately east of the Brock Road, who could enfilade any Union advance across the Spindle farm clearing. At daylight Wofford's brigade had moved to Rodes's support from immediately east of the Brock Road, but Warren was unaware of this move.[17]

Meade probably received Warren's reply simultaneously with the news that a force of Southerners (Harris's brigade) had driven Mott's Excelsior Brigade away from the outside of the works along the west face of the west angle and had occupied the inside of these works in force. Meade's anger against Warren undoubtedly began to simmer. Warren was justified in fearing the fire from Kershaw's troops opposite the right end of the Sixth Corps line, but this was an unfortunate time to complain about it to army headquarters. At any rate, Meade believed that Warren's troops were advancing to the assault as ordered. At eight o'clock he notified Hancock that Warren was initiating his attack.[18]

Warren recorded that his attack was begun at 8:15 A.M. Roebling recalled that since this would be the fourth or fifth time that the troops had attempted this segment of the Confederate line, which appeared no weaker than before, the infantrymen exhibited little enthusiasm for the operation.[19] From Griffin's division on the left of the line, Sweitzer sent forward three of his regiments to the attack, the Ninth and Thirty-second Massachusetts and the Sixty-second Pennsylvania. They dashed forward, drove the Confederate pickets from the rise where the burned Spindle house stood, and continued toward the line of trees ahead. Bratton's men waited until the advancing Yankees were fifty yards away before opening fire. There the Union advance faltered, and most of the Yankees lay down. Soon, one of the regiments broke for the rear. The remaining two followed shortly and suffered heavy losses in the process. The Thirty-second Massachusetts sustained nearly one hundred casualties in thirty minutes of work. Some of Ayres's regiments may have shared in the action.[20]

To the right of Griffin's troops, the men of Cutler's division inched forward through the trees and apparently did not make contact with the enemy until later in the morning. As the Iron Brigade moved forward for the fourth time against the same position, it was one regiment short. On the previous day the Second Wisconsin reported fewer than one hundred men present for duty and listed its two field officers as wounded and captured. From Henry Hill on the plains of Manassas to Laurel Hill in Spotsylvania this unit had fought in most of the great battles of the East. Now the survivors were withdrawn from the rifle pits and detailed as division provost guard for the remainder of their enlistment. It had been a fighting regiment indeed.[21]

To Cutler's right the Pennsylvania Reserves and Coulter's brigade advanced a heavy skirmish line toward Gregg's and G. T. Anderson's works in the clearing on the left of Field's line. They also would not make contact until later in the morning.[22]

Warren Antagonizes Meade

At 9:10 A.M. Warren informed Meade that Griffin was anxious to have Bartlett's brigade back and requested that it be returned. He closed the message with the news that he could not advance his Fifth Corps troops any farther at the present time. He was informed curtly that Bartlett's troops would be retained until army headquarters determined where they were needed most.[23] At the same time, Warren dispatched another message to the Armstrong house, which, in retrospect, can be seen as a factor in determining Meade's, and eventually Grant's, appraisal of Warren's qualities as a commander. The message read, "My left cannot advance without a most destructive enfilade fire until the Sixth Corps has cleared its front. My right is close up to the enemy's works, and ordered to assault. The enemy's line here appears to be strongly held. It is his point-d'appui if he throws back his right." Meade was furious. This dispatch contradicted Warren's message shortly after 8:00 A.M. that the order to attack immediately had been given to the troops of the Fifth Corps. The later message indicated to Meade not only that no attack had been executed but also that the corps commander seemed averse to making it at all.[24]

Meade informed Warren through Humphreys that the order to attack immediately at all hazards with his entire force was peremptory. Humphreys had previously spent some time reconnoitering the area of the Fifth Corps's operations and appreciated the problems of Warren's troops at Laurel Hill. At 9:30 A.M. he sent Warren a sympathetic message, "Dear Warren, Don't hesitate to attack with the bayonet. Meade has assumed the responsibility and will take the consequences. Your friend, A. A. Humphreys." The chief of staff also informed Warren that Bartlett's brigade would be returned to Griffin, that both Hancock and Wright reported being hard pressed, and that from this Meade believed that the enemy could not be very strong in Warren's front.[25]

At 9:40 A.M. Warren reported that his "lines nearest the salient of the enemy are reported constantly advancing up to the enemy's works. My orders are to attack with the bayonet without regard to consequences that may result unfavorably." At 10:05 A.M. Humphreys told Warren that Meade inferred from the tenor of Warren's dispatches that the corps commander did not expect his attack to be successful. If the attack should fail, Warren was to make dispositions to withdraw his troops and to send them as rapidly as possible to the support of Wright and Hancock. The Federal high command apparently reasoned that, if the troops of the Fifth Corps were not going to accomplish anything beneficial along their assigned segment of the army's line, they might as well be used where some good might be achieved. This same mode of operation had been applied to the corps's activities in the Wilderness fighting.[26]

Upon receiving Meade's peremptory order to attack, Warren reiterated at 9:30 A.M. the order to his three division commanders to charge the enemy's entrenchments with their entire force regardless of the consequences. In his message to Griffin and Crawford, Warren used the words "do it," suggesting that these two officers had been authorized the same discretion concerning the obedience of orders which Warren insisted upon in his own relationship with army headquarters. The Fifth Corps infantrymen moved forward.[27]

On the left of the line, Griffin sent portions of Sweitzer's and Ayres's brigades forward. John Bratton, commanding the Confederate brigade immediately to the west of the Brock Road, reported that the Yankees came across the clearing beautifully, in two lines of battle. The initial volleys from the Southern infantrymen and from Parker's battery on the road pulverized the Federal ranks, however, and soon the surviving Northerners ran back.[28] Many of them took shelter behind shallow hills in the undulating ground of the clearing. A group of Federals were rallied behind such a crest in the woods in front of Bratton's two left regiments, the First and Fifth South Carolina. Confederate artillerymen fired indirectly into this pocket of troops, doubtless inflicting casualties, but the gunners had been ordered to conserve ammunition whenever possible and soon ceased to fire. Bratton's troops on the left of the brigade line continued to hear heavy musket fire from behind the crest in front, but no bullets came in their direction from these invisible Yankees. After a period of time, Bratton ordered skirmishers forward from his First and Fifth regiments. They crept up to the rim of the crest and reportedly discovered the Federals on the opposite side firing at unknown targets. The Carolinians jumped to their feet with a yell and charged. Approximately forty of the surprised Federals surrendered outright, and the remainder fled back to their lines. As they crossed the clearing, more were hit by the fire of Bratton's troops and Parker's guns.[29]

After the repulse, Sweitzer advanced his Twenty-second Massachusetts and Fourth Michigan regiments to the forward rifle pits in case the Confederates counterattacked. They did not. To Sweitzer's right Ayres advanced his entire brigade except for the 140th and 146th New York regiments. The Yankees came up against the Georgians of DuBose's brigade and were driven back in confusion with heavy losses.[30]

To Griffin's right Cutler formed his division in three double lines, from front to rear, the Iron Brigade, Bragg's brigade of Pennsylvania regiments, and Lyle's brigade. The position of Rice's brigade in the formation is unknown. All of the action was to occur in the wooded area which lay between the works of Law's Alabamians and those of Cutler's division. The Seventh Indiana Regiment was positioned on the right of the Iron Brigade's line. One of its members remembered that, when the order for the attack came, the Pennsylvania Reserves regiments to the right refused to move forward.[31]

The Iron Brigade moved down a slope into a shallow ravine and started up the opposite slope, soon coming to a belt of thick abatis, where it halted. Law's troops and the artillery to their rear opened a deadly fire, but the Iron Brigade stood its ground and fired back. Bragg's men pressed forward and intermingled with the front brigade, with all of the troops firing as fast as possible. Officers of both Federal brigades attempted to get the men to move forward. Cutler notified Warren of the halt, and at 10:40 A.M., Warren asked Cutler to report in writing if he thought that the troops could not carry the position in their front. Five minutes later Cutler responded that his brigade commanders reported that they could not carry the works and that they were losing heavily. Cutler admitted that he could not get the men to advance farther up the hill. The order to retire was given, and the Yankees returned to their works. Lyle's brigade did not become engaged, although it sustained casualties from artillery fire.[32]

It appears that the troops of Crawford's division, including Coulter's brigade, did not advance beyond the line of trees across the clearing from the works manned by G. T. Anderson's and Gregg's brigades. Perhaps individual regiments attempted to advance toward these works, but there was no concerted effort at the brigade level. Field recalled that these Federal attacks against his division's position extended from the Brock Road left as far as Law's brigade. At 10:30 A.M. Warren told Crawford that, if he could not assault, he should withdraw Coulter's brigade from the line and send it to Warren, holding the division line with the Pennsylvania Reserves. Warren informed Crawford that Cutler had reported that the right of his advancing line had passed over Crawford's troops. Crawford offered the excuse that, at the time when Cutler's men first advanced, his own troops had already been repulsed.[33]

At 10:30 A.M. Bartlett's brigade had returned from the left, and Warren ordered Griffin to place these troops in the Sixth Corps's works to the east of the Brock Road. They were to replace Ricketts's men, who had been sent farther to the left.[34] Warren apparently decided then that his belated attacks had failed. He began to issue directives for the withdrawal of his troops from their lines, in preparation for service elsewhere. This decision underlay his message to Crawford, cited above, to forward Coulter's brigade to corps headquarters. By this time, however, Meade had concluded that, in this critical phase of the army's operation, the Fifth Corps required direct supervision and perhaps a new commander.

Shortly after 10:00 A.M., Meade informed Grant that Warren seemed reluctant to attack, that army headquarters had ordered him to attack at all hazards, and that if his assault should be repulsed, he was to draw in his right flank and forward his troops as rapidly as possible to Wright and Hancock. At 10:30 A.M. Meade ordered Humphreys to attend to the shortening of the Fifth Corps's line and to the forwarding of the reinforcing troops to the left. This order could be considered as being tantamount to the replacement of Warren by Humphreys in corps command.[35]

Warren had been closer to Meade than any other corps commander in the army, but in this instance Meade believed that drastic measures were necessary. The Federal high command realized that the capture of Johnson's line had presented a tremendous opportunity, and they meant to exploit it.

Indeed, at 10:40 A.M. Grant sent the following to Meade: "If Warren fails to attack promptly, send Humphreys to command his corps, and relieve him. I have ordered Burnside to push on vigorously and to send a division to Hancock." In fact, Warren was not officially relieved of command, and Humphreys apparently exercised sufficient tact in this delicate situation that no delay in execution occurred because of any discomfiture of Warren's. It is possible that Warren directed the extraction of his troops from their works and their initial movement to the left, while Humphreys observed from a discreet distance. At any rate, by nightfall the original chain of command had been reinstated.[36]

In the meantime Meade had decided to visit Hancock, whose headquarters by now were at the Landrum house. He arrived at approximately 11:25

A.M. From there he could see the intense fighting at the west angle half a mile away. He asked Humphreys about the situation on the right. Humphreys replied that Crawford was moving to Wright, but this was untrue. At the same time, Warren informed Cutler that his troops would be replaced in the line by the First Division, but he was to retain his skirmishers in their advanced positions. At about noon Warren told Meade that Cutler's troops were nearly clear of the line and were beginning to march toward the left. At 1:00 P.M. he reported that all of Cutler's men were on their way and asked whether he should bring the remainder of the corps also. He said that Humphreys had gone to learn more definite information about what was being planned.[37]

At 1:30 P.M. Meade told both Humphreys and Warren that he wanted two divisions of the Fifth Corps. Cutler was to report to Wright and Griffin to Hancock. Also he noted that a headquarters engineering officer was conferring with Wright to locate the Sixth Corps's flank and to discover how best to cover it. The engineer was to report later to the two officers. Meade instructed his chief of staff to make the best disposition possible of Crawford's division, the Maryland brigade, and the rest of the corps artillery, but to be prepared to forward all of these troops if so ordered. Thus, by noon Federal operations on the right flank of the army's line had been abandoned in favor of strengthening the center, where the major effort was being attempted.[38]

Afternoon and Evening Operations: Federal Ninth Corps and Confederate Third Corps

During the morning operations of the Ninth Corps, Orlando B. Willcox's Third Division had been designated a reserve force. As the other two divisions moved off to their right toward the assigned positions for their assaults, this unit followed slowly. It was the left flank of the army's attacking line, and Willcox was concerned about protecting that flank as it advanced. No cavalry was available to him.[39]

The First and Second divisions did not take their four assigned artillery batteries with them, so these guns were available for use on the left of the corps. Burnside ordered Capt. Joseph W. B. Wright's Fourteenth Massachusetts Battery to deploy at a point along the Fredericksburg Road. The Second Michigan Infantry Regiment of Hartranft's brigade was detailed to support this battery until further notice. After one hour the battery was moved approximately one-half mile to the right, and it assumed a position on a low ridge that lay perpendicular to the corps's line of battle. The Michigan infantrymen, about two hundred strong, moved into a shallow ravine on the side of the ridge. As the morning wore on and no action developed along the Fredericksburg Road, more guns were moved close to Wright's battery.

These included two sections of Capt. Adelbert B. Twitchell's Seventh Maine Battery and two sections of Capt. Edward W. Rogers's Nineteenth New York.[40]

In the initial morning advance of Willcox's infantry, Hartranft's brigade had preceded Christ's. Christ was too ill for duty that morning, and his brigade was eventually to be commanded by Col. William Humphrey of the Second Michigan. After Hartranft's men had followed Crittenden's division a short way toward the right, some Confederate batteries near the courthouse opened an enfilading fire upon the marching column. Willcox ordered Hartranft to change front to the left. After the artillery firing ceased, Hartranft sent forward six companies from his Fifty-first Pennsylvania as skirmishers. They drove in some Confederate pickets and secured an advanced position on a slight crest in woods. The Second Brigade established itself to Hartranft's left, and its skirmishers advanced into the woods ahead.[41] That morning Christ's brigade had only three complete regiments, the First Michigan Sharpshooters, the Twentieth Michigan, and the Fiftieth Pennsylvania. The inexperienced Sixtieth Ohio had been detached to Marshall's Provisional Brigade, which remained in position across the Fredericksburg Road. The men of the Seventy-ninth New York who had not reenlisted as a unit had been withdrawn from the line in preparation for returning home, as their term of service had expired. (This was one of the first of many Union regiments to arrive at this pleasant situation during the late spring and early summer months.)[42]

Hartranft was preparing to advance his skirmishers again when he suddenly received orders to withdraw his brigade except for the skirmishers and to march to his right to the Second Corps's position. This order was in response to Grant's directive to Burnside at 10:20 A.M., which had ordered him to forward one of his divisions to Hancock's relief. Hartranft withdrew his troops and started them in the prescribed direction. His lead regiment had moved one-half mile when the order was countermanded. He returned to his former position and discovered that, in his absence, his skirmishers had been driven in. He ordered them forward. He also discovered that the Second Brigade had retired a short distance, although its skirmishers still were deployed in the woods in front. Hartranft sidled his regiments to their left in order to cover part of the position formerly occupied by the Second Brigade. By then the time was close to 1:00 P.M.[43]

At 2:00 P.M. Hartranft and Humphrey received orders to attack the Confederate position to their front. Sometime earlier, Burnside had sent Willcox the order to attack on the left of Crittenden's division. Willcox had responded that he expected the enemy to attack and to attempt to turn his left flank, but the order to attack at once was reiterated. Willcox spent some time positioning his two brigades of infantry and his two artillery batteries for the advance.

The division chief of artillery, Lt. Samuel N. Benjamin, was ordered to post additional batteries to the left and rear of the infantry. Finally, all was ready, and at 2:00 P.M. Willcox ordered Hartranft to move forward. The Pennsylvanian's five regiments stepped off in an alignment from right to left of the Eighth Michigan, 109th New York, Twenty-seventh Michigan, Fifty-first Pennsylvania, and Seventeenth Michigan.[44]

Confederate Dispositions Southeast of the Salient in the Morning

The Confederate infantrymen, who were manning the line from the southeast corner of the salient south to Spotsylvania, were from Wilcox's and Heth's divisions of Early's Third Corps. At the time when Hancock's troops struck Edward Johnson's works, about 5:00 A.M. on the twelfth, the brigades of Scales and Thomas were reporting back to their division commander Cadmus Wilcox near the village, having returned from their march west out the Shady Grove Church Road. From the muffled sound of the firing, Wilcox could not determine whether the action was occurring at Lane's position or farther north. He sent the two returning brigades north with orders to assume a position to the rear of Lane as support for that part of the line. They arrived just after Lane had established his five regiments facing north behind the abandoned line of works that ran east to west. The Federals were retiring from Lane's immediate front.

Simultaneously with the arrival of Scales and Thomas, some troops from the remnant of Doles's brigade arrived from the opposite side of the salient. Portions of these four Confederate brigades pursued the retiring Yankees for three or four hundred yards before being recalled by Wilcox. Lane's men moved a short distance to the rear to rest.[45] Scales's and Thomas's troops then were positioned facing east behind the line of works that led south from the southeast corner of the salient. This line of works descended for three hundred yards or so to a small stream, south of which the ground rose again, and the line of works ran southeast for three hundred more yards. There the line emerged from woods into open fields and the direction changed to due south for sixty yards. The line then swung back to the southwest for 650 yards until it again swung left to a southeasterly direction and eventually crossed the Fredericksburg Road three hundred yards or so east of the village. This bulge in the line, which began at the right flank of Thomas's brigade, was to be known as Heth's salient.[46]

The brigade alignment to the right of Thomas is uncertain. Davis's Mississippians and Archer's Tennessee brigade were probably here, extending to the point where the line entered the field and changed direction to the south.

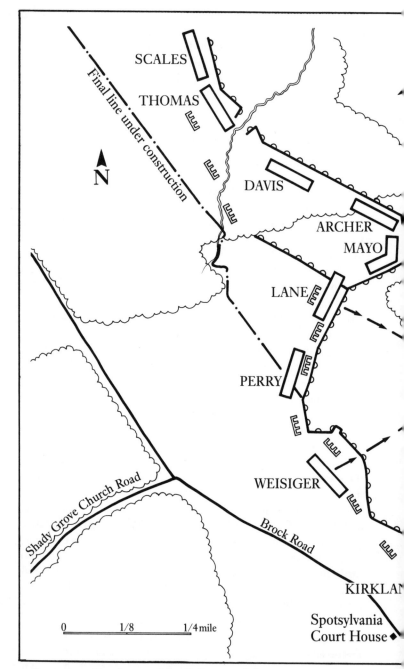

MAP 15-1. Operations Southeast of the Salient, 12 May, 2:00–4:00 P.M.

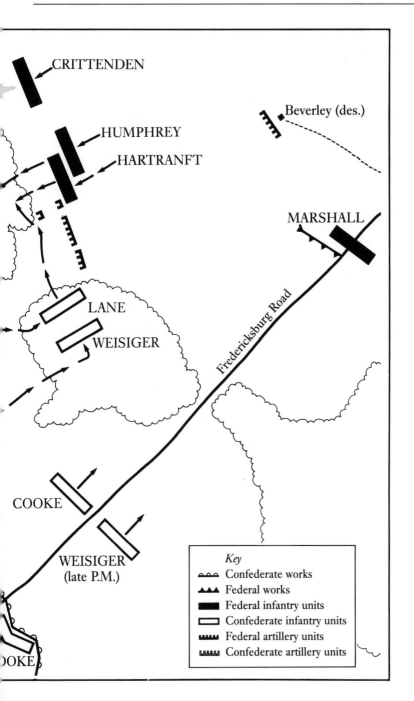

CRITTENDEN

Beverley (des.)

HUMPHREY

HARTRANFT

MARSHALL

Fredericksburg Road

LANE

WEISIGER

COOKE

WEISIGER
(late P.M.)

OOKE

Key
Confederate works
Federal works
Federal infantry units
Confederate infantry units
Federal artillery units
Confederate artillery units

Walker's brigade, commanded since the tenth of May by Col. Robert M. Mayo, occupied the eastern face of Heth's salient and extended most of the distance down its right side. McGowan's South Carolinians had been on Mayo's right until ordered away to Ewell's relief at 9:00 A.M. After this, Lane's regiments were brought down and inserted into the line along the right face of the salient. The relative positions of the remaining four available brigades, Weisiger's and Perry's of Mahone's division and Kirkland's and Cooke's of Heth's, are uncertain. Kirkland's troops were reported to be directly in front of the village and Cooke's in the courthouse yard. The twenty guns of Poague's and Pegram's battalions were positioned behind the line of works extending from the courthouse north to Heth's salient. Farther to the left the three batteries (thirteen guns) of Nelson's battalion of Ewell's corps were stationed.[47]

The crucial point of the Confederate defense appeared to be at the west angle, but Lee and Ewell were doubtless aware that the entire eastern face of the salient was likewise important and vulnerable, as Burnside's attack had shown. The Confederates manned a line extending from 150 yards or so south of the east angle for perhaps one-half mile. They enjoyed little, if any, artillery support, and their regiments were intermingled without regard for brigade integrity. For the most part, they lay behind the works under heavy musket fire and awaited Federal assaults.[48]

Shortly after McGowan's brigade moved off at 9:00 A.M., Lane was ordered to place his troops in this newly vacated segment of the line along the right face of Heth's salient. The North Carolinians moved in behind the works and began to accustom themselves to their new surroundings. Soon the brigade's battalion of sharpshooters, commanded by Capt. W. T. Nicholson, was ordered to reconnoiter the area directly to the east of the salient, where he discovered Federal troops in line facing the Confederate left of the salient. The eastern end of this Federal line appeared to rest in the woods directly in front of the eastern face at a distance of four or five hundred yards. These Yankees were the infantrymen of Orlando Willcox's two brigades.

Soon Lane ordered his Seventh and Thirty-third regiments, under the command of Lt. Col. Robert V. Cowan of the Thirty-third, to reconnoiter the oak wood which lay opposite the right face of the salient to see if the Federals also had a line of battle in that direction. Cowan deployed four companies from two regiments to precede the advance as skirmishers. They engaged some Federal skirmishers and drove them back to their main line. The commander of the Confederate skirmishers reported this to Cowan, who, in the meantime, had received instructions to attack the enemy as soon as their position was ascertained. He was in the process of forming his two regiments for an attack when he was joined by Lane and the remaining three regiments of the brigade.[49]

Lane's Advance

Lane's orders from Early and Wilcox were to move his regiments into the woods out from the right face of the salient and to align them parallel with the works along the face. He was then to move his column forward northeast until it overlapped the left of the Federal line. At that point the troops would face to their left and charge up the Yankee line. Weisiger's brigade of Mahone's division was to support the attack. Mahone introduced Weisiger to Lane and then rode back to the Fredericksburg Road. Wilcox watched Lane's regiments file into the woods and then rode to Heth's position at the salient.

Shortly after 2:00 P.M. Lane moved his regiments as directed and faced them to the northwest in the following order from right to left: the Seventh, Thirty-third, Thirty-seventh, Eighteenth, and Twenty-eighth. Weisiger formed his troops one hundred yards to the rear. Suddenly, a courier from Wilcox delivered an order to Lane to advance rapidly at once. He swung his Seventh Regiment to the right to guard against an attack from that direction. Lane notified Weisiger of his order to move and requested that he follow in supporting distance. Then Lane issued the order to advance, and his troops moved forward through the trees.[50]

The Confederates kicked up a few enemy skirmishers in their initial advance. Emerging from the wooded area into a clearing, they spotted some Federal artillery pieces to their right front, scarcely more than one hundred yards away. Lane had been told to try to silence these guns, which had been enfilading the right face of Heth's salient, but his primary mission was to strike the left flank of Burnside's line. His men turned slightly to the right and headed for the guns, which consisted of Wright's battery, two sections of Twitchell's, and two sections of Rogers's. Wright and Twitchell were on a slight ridge, with Hartranft's Second Michigan Infantry Regiment in support in a shallow ravine immediately to the north. Just to the right of these Michigan troops, Rogers had placed his two sections on a low rise, with two guns advanced to within fifty yards or so of the oak trees in front.[51]

The Southerners, with some company officers of Lane's Thirty-seventh Regiment in the lead, headed for Rogers's four pieces. All of the cannoneers of the advanced section were quickly disabled by musket fire. Rogers ordered his drivers forward to work the guns. Some infantrymen, including the acting regimental commander, Capt. James Farrand, ran forward to help. Wright's and Twitchell's gunners from the left fired canister at the Confederates in the clearing. Other Federal batteries in the rear of the abandoned Beverley house also fired. Some Carolinians had approached to within twenty or thirty yards of the muzzles of the two advanced pieces when the rest of the Second Michigan rushed out of the ravine and charged. The Southerners retired into the trees in front of Rogers's position. Captain Farrand was killed while operating one of the pieces. The Yankee artillerymen had ten fatalities and six wounded, most of whom were in the advanced section. The Second Michigan suffered two killed and ten wounded in the action.[52]

Burnside observed the action from the rear. At one point he forwarded instructions to Wright and Twitchell to prepare to spike their guns, which appeared to be in danger. However, this action proved unnecessary.[53]

After reentering the wooded area, Lane's troops continued their rapid advance to the northwest in a disorganized mass. They suddenly and unexpectedly collided with a battle line of Federals from Hartranft's brigade, who were advancing across the Southerners' line of march from right to left. A wild melee ensued.[54]

The Advance of Orlando Willcox's Division

The troops of Hartranft's brigade had moved forward shortly after 2:00 P.M., followed by the three regiments of the Second Brigade, under Colonel Humphrey: the First Michigan Sharpshooters, Twentieth Michigan, and Fiftieth Pennsylvania, from right to left. The Federals soon came under artillery fire. Willcox ordered Hartranft to alter his direction of march slightly to the left.[55] Suddenly, Lane's troops piled into the left of Hartranft's line in the dark, wet woods. The Carolinians already had been involved in two bloody engagements that day, and they might have been more alert to danger than were Hartranft's men. At any rate, they appear to have enjoyed the initial advantage in the sudden encounter. On the left of the Federal line, Col. Constant Luce, commanding the Seventeenth Michigan, was near the left of his regiment, urging his men to maintain their proper alignment with the regiment to their right. A private soldier of the Fiftieth Pennsylvania Regiment, following the Seventeenth, tapped Luce on the arm and told him that enemy troops were on his immediate left flank and advancing. Suddenly, a Federal shell exploded nearby, killed the Pennsylvanian, and hurled his body against Luce, knocking the colonel to the ground. A line of Confederates rushed across the prostrate Federals, surrounding and capturing nearly the entire Seventeenth Michigan Regiment. In the melee, forty-eight of the Yankees, including their colonel, managed to escape. Moreover, they brought out fifty or so captured Confederates with them, including the commander of the Thirty-seventh North Carolina, Col. William M. Barbour.[56]

The Carolinians continued forward and routed the Fifty-first Pennsylvania. They captured both stands of colors from this regiment and one stand from the Seventeenth Michigan. Lane's men also struck the Fiftieth Pennsylvania of the following brigade. About one hundred of these Yankees were captured. The remainder fought their way to the rear in bloody hand-to-hand combat.[57]

The members of the Twentieth Michigan Regiment advanced across a small clearing. They were ordered to halt and to lie down just before Lane's men struck. The Confederates who swept over the Fiftieth Pennsylvania to the left of the Twentieth began to work in behind its left flank. The commander of the Twentieth, Maj. George C. Barnes, decided that it was time to go. He faced his men to their left and advanced the regiment in column into the woods. There he halted his troops and faced them again to their left when he discovered disorganized groups of Lane's men between his position and safety. He ordered a charge, and the Michiganders lunged forward. They fought their way through and brought off their colors safely, with a few prisoners as well, although thirty of them were captured by the Confederates.[58]

On the right of the second line, the First Michigan Sharpshooters advanced across an area of small bushy trees that briefly concealed their presence from the Confederates in front. They reached a hastily constructed breastwork of rails, which Confederate skirmishers had been using as cover, reportedly fifty yards from the main line of works. Here the Sharpshooters discovered the Twenty-seventh Michigan Regiment of Hartranft's brigade.[59]

The two Federal regiments remained pinned down in this position for one hour. When the Twentieth Michigan moved to the rear, Mayo's Virginians along the east face of the salient became free to concentrate their efforts on the sharpshooters and on the Twenty-seventh by firing obliquely to their left and enfilading the left of the two Yankee regiments. To the right of the Twenty-seventh, a flanking regiment, perhaps the Eighth Michigan or 109th New York, was withdrawn unexpectedly, after which an enfilading fire began to harass the Michiganders from that direction. Both ends of the Yankees' line were refused. After repeated requests for permission to retire, they finally received the order to fall back. Both Union regiments had exhausted nearly all of their ammunition supply. Although the force of Lane's advance had not carried as far as their positions, the Twenty-seventh sustained 187 casualties and the First Sharpshooters, 155.[60]

To the right of Willcox's division, a portion of Crittenden's command advanced at approximately the same time as Willcox's. The 100th Pennsylvania and Twenty-first Massachusetts of Leasure's brigade pushed to within fifty yards of the Confederate works to their front. There they lay on the ground and fired at any Southerner who showed above the top of the works. They withdrew, however, when they received the report of what had happened to Willcox's men on their left.[61]

In Lane's battle there were many strange and deadly encounters in the woods. A few soldiers were captured and escaped, only to be recaptured. At least one of these escaped a second time. In a letter to a brother, Sgt. J. H. Levan of the Fiftieth Pennsylvania described his ordeal. "I was taken prisoner twice before I got out of the woods. The first I knew of our being surrounded was when I heard someone say, 'Surrender you d— Yankee, it is all up with you.' I looked up and saw a terrible big officer swinging his sword over my head. My blood ran cold. I thought of the horrors of Libby Prison, and then I thought of home. The last thought gave me courage and strength. So I jumped for him and took him in the pit of the stomach. I then gave a yell and started on the run. I thought I was free, when another greasy Johnny presented his gun in my front, which caused me to halt. 'Drop that gun, its all up with you.' he said, when some one took him alongside of the head, which caused him to drop mighty sudden, and away went I, and if I did not do some tall running there is no snakes. . . . I am the only sergeant out of five left. The whole eight corporals are killed or wounded. The Regiment is very small. Our loss is 333."[62]

One Confederate remembered that "everyone was trying to fight his way back to our works." Lane's life was saved by Pvt. P. A. Parker of the Thirty-seventh Regiment, who shot and killed a Yankee who had leveled his musket at Lane ten paces from the brigadier and was preparing to fire. After his troops became engaged, Lane sent a request to Weisiger to move up on his right. Together they would swing back to their line, a move which could garner many more prisoners. After a time Lane spotted what he said were two lines of enemy troops moving down from the direction of Ewell's front. Having received no indication that Weisiger intended to comply with his request, Lane moved his troops back to the works.[63]

The extent to which Weisiger's five Virginia regiments participated in the action cannot be determined. Lane claimed that they did not move out of the oak wood in which they were standing when his North Carolinians initially moved forward. He also claimed that, some time after the action began, Weisiger's troops fired into the back of his men. Two of Lane's lieutenant colonels hurried back to ask the Virginians to stop. Mahone rode up to one of these colonels and said that he would derive great pleasure from reporting the colonel to General Lee for leaving Mahone's men alone in the woods to do all of the fighting. Lane said that, as his troops were retiring, Capt. E. J. Hale, Jr., of his staff, met Weisiger and, at the Colonel's request, the captain guided the brigade out of the oak wood.[64]

Another cause of contention between these two Confederate brigades was the matter of captured flags. The Federals lost three stands of infantry colors, two from the Fifty-first Pennsylvania and one from the Seventeenth Michigan. They lost also the guidon from Rogers's battery. Lane claimed for his troops the capture of the flag of the Seventeenth Michigan, one of the Fifty-first Pennsylvania's, and the artillery guidon. On the thirteenth of May, Lane received acknowledgment from Lee's headquarters of the receipt of these prizes and assurance that credit for them would be forwarded to the secretary of war along with the names of the captors. Nearly one week later Mahone officially claimed that one of his privates had captured the flag of the Seventeenth Michigan and that his troops had captured some of the three hundred or so Federals that Lane claimed for his brigade. In these controversies, the evidence appears to favor Lane. In his postwar writings, Early credited Lane's men with the captures and maintained that Mahone's brigade did not become seriously engaged.[65]

About this time Lee decided to attempt another flank movement from farther to his right, to be executed by Weisiger's brigade and Cooke's of Heth's division and followed by other units of Early's corps. Lieutenant Nicholson and his sharpshooters were sent east up the Fredericksburg Road to reconnoiter. They discovered the terrain on both sides of the road to be very rough, with rugged ravines covered with pine trees and undergrowth. There was at least one line of Yankee entrenchments across the road, and possibly more. As a result of this information, Lee decided not to proceed with the movement. However, Weisiger's and Cooke's brigades, apparently at Early's urging, were sent up both sides of the road. They crossed two sets of unoccupied breastworks and discovered a stronger main line of works farther on. They retired after suffering some casualties, primarily from artillery fire. In response, Brig. Gen. Orlando Willcox sent two regiments to the road to buttress the Provisional Brigade there, but these infantrymen did not become engaged. This marked the end of operations at this end of the lines for the day.[66]

Later in the afternoon Marshall's Provisional Brigade lost its unattached status. It was assigned permanently to Crittenden's First Division.[67]

16

If It Should Be My Luck to Come Home

12 May

Lee Decides to Abandon the Salient

Sometime in the forenoon, Lee realized that his embattled soldiers would be unable to drive the Federals from their positions opposite the works along the north face of the salient. Therefore, he decided to abandon the salient line and to establish a new one approximately twelve hundred yards to the rear. A segment of this new line had already been begun by engineers on the previous day.

It would be too dangerous to abandon the lines during daylight because of the heavy pressure being exerted by the enemy along the northern face. The advanced position would have to be maintained until the rear line was completed and ready for occupancy after nightfall. As it happened, it was to be many hours after dark before these works were ready. The troops who would construct them were engineers and the survivors of Allegheny Johnson's division, augmented perhaps by some artillerymen. These soldiers began their labors in earnest under continual urging from higher authority for more speed.

The Confederates who were to bear the burden of maintaining the forward line were the infantrymen of Harris's and McGowan's brigades. When the South Carolinians joined the Mississippians in the works at 10:00 A.M., the total number of fighting men in the two brigades was approximately sixteen hundred. This number began to decrease immediately.[1]

At the beginning of the action, Col. Joseph Brown stayed at the left of the brigade line with his Fourteenth Regiment, probably unaware that he was the ranking officer remaining and was therefore in command. Lt. Col. Isaac Hunt of the Thirteenth Regiment was near the right of the brigade line. He refused this end of the line somewhat to prevent Federals from entering the salient farther east with impunity. After a time Hunt informed Brown that he should assume command of the brigade. Brown did so, then joined Hunt near the west angle. Brown soon surmised that the line occupied by his troops from that point east must be held at all hazards to avert disaster. There the Yankees lay closest to the works, behind the slight crest and knoll. Constant musket fire had to be maintained to prevent them from mounting a coordinated rush over the works. A steady stream of Federal bullets poured just over the top of the works and under the head logs, occasionally striking an unwary Confederate.[2]

Brown decided that an officer with authority had to be stationed near the left of the brigade to shift troops to the right as replacements for those who were killed and wounded. He designated Colonel Hunt for this assignment. Hunt was also to be responsible for ensuring that a constant supply of ammunition was available to these troops. Brown decided to remain near the right of the line, prepared to react to the emergencies that he felt sure would arise there. Thus, the parameters for the operation, command, and control of the brigade were established. They would remain in effect for seventeen hours.[3]

Meade Plans Another Massive Assault

By midday the two brigades of Ricketts's Sixth Corps division had been brought over and positioned in the woods which lay northwest of the west angle and east of the Shelton house. Thus, the entire infantry force of this corps was deployed against the Confederate position at the west angle.[4]

By midmorning Meade had given up hope that Warren would achieve any beneficial results against the Laurel Hill position. He had ordered Warren to withdraw most of his troops from their part of the line and to send them left to positions opposite the north face of the salient. Shortly after noon, Humphreys asked Wright if he saw a point of attack that might promise success if the entire Fifth Corps were used. Wright believed that a large force could carry the enemy line at the west angle, but that he could not accomplish this with his own troops alone. At this time Cutler was leading his division from its position opposite the Spindle farm, with orders to report to Wright.[5]

Meanwhile, the intense musket fire continued in the area of the west angle and northeast of it. Near the east angle, the men of Miles's brigade, along with those of Brooke's who had returned from the right, began to construct a line of works which would be a prolongation of the line along the north face of the salient to the east. This new line was to extend generally east from the apex for approximately two hundred yards. Hancock, unsure of what, if anything, Burnside was accomplishing to his left, prepared to defend his left flank with his own troops if necessary.[6]

Saga of the Twenty-sixth Michigan Regiment

Most of Barlow's troops spent the late morning hours reforming and constructing the line of works east from the apex. As of noon Capt. Nathan Church, acting commander of the Twenty-sixth Michigan of Miles's brigade, had managed to collect only about one hundred men from the regiment. At midday he was ordered to withdraw his men from the construction work and to move, with some additional troops from the Sixty-first New York, to the vicinity of the west angle. Who selected these troops and why they were chosen is not known. The Twenty-sixth appears to have been a better than average regiment and was occasionally used for special operational assignments.[7] These Federals crawled along the outside of the works in front of Gibbon's, Birney's, and Edwards's men. They halted just before reaching the point opposite to the oak tree. There, still unobserved by any Confederates, their small column overlapped the right of Brown's line by about one-half the length of a regiment. Suddenly, the Yankees leaped to their feet and fired a volley over the top of the works. Some of them clambered over the top and dropped in among the Southerners, jabbing and swinging their muskets. From farther along the line Confederates charged in and drove them back over the works. They now commenced to fight across the works at point blank range. To make matters worse, a Union battery from near the Landrum house was attempting to lay shells just over the top of the works at this point, a fire which endangered friend and foe alike.[8]

Surrender! Who Surrender?

At approximately 2:00 P.M. an episode occurred which had its humorous side, despite the horrible environment and a tragic ending. Captain Church noticed a handkerchief being held aloft on a musket rammer from within a traversed enclosure near the east end of the Confederate line. Shortly thereafter he spotted one or two more tokens of surrender a short distance farther along the enemy works. With much difficulty Church managed to persuade his men to cease firing.[9] Some of the Federals stood up and held their muskets pointing downward. Seeing this Brown called to them to lay down their arms and to come into the Confederate line. A Federal officer answered that he was awaiting the surrender of Brown's troops; the Confederates had raised a white flag, and therefore his men had ceased firing. Brown replied that he was in command of this portion of the line and that if any flag had been raised, it had been without authority. Moreover, unless the Federal officer came in, the Confederates would resume firing immediately. The Northerner asked Brown for a conference, and permission was granted.[10]

During this somewhat acrimonious parley, another Yankee officer climbed on top of the works manned by the Twelfth South Carolina. Here, with sword in hand, he shouted to the Southerners that they had been surrendered by an unnamed Mississippi colonel. At this announcement Col. Thomas F. Clyburn of the Twelfth Regiment began to shout, "Shoot, men, shoot!" But at his side Capt. Cadwallader Jones echoed each shout with one of his own, "Don't shoot! don't shoot!" Carrying a flag of truce of some sort, a subordinate Federal officer then approached Brown and informed him that a white flag was being displayed on the right of Brown's line. The Carolinian angrily informed the Federal that, unless his commander surrendered, firing would be resumed. The junior officer started to return to his line, but, failing to hold his flag high enough to be seen at a distance, he was shot midway between the two lines, which at this point were only twenty yards apart. The lines of troops immediately reopened fire.[11]

A similar incident occurred near the left of the South Carolina brigade line. The Confederates noticed a light-colored flag, possibly a state color, being waved from the mass of Yankees opposite their front. The Southerners and subsequently the Yankees opposite ceased firing, and much shouting ensued. Southerners asked Northerners whether they wished a truce. Northerners replied by asking if the Southerners wished to surrender. Confederate officers, ignoring the flag, ordered their men to resume firing, but the men implored their superiors to hold up in case the Yankees wished to surrender. During this confusing period, a Federal lieutenant walked across to Lt. John N. Carlisle of the Thirteenth South Carolina and demanded his surrender. When Carlisle refused, the Yankee then requested permission to return to his line, since he obviously had crossed under a mistaken impression. Carlisle admired his pluck and let him go, but the Yankee was shot after taking a few steps and crawled into the Confederate line a prisoner.[12]

Farther to the Confederate left, a Federal captain reportedly walked over to the Sixteenth Mississippi regiment and asked the men of that unit whether they had surrendered. When informed that they had not, he asked to speak to the regimental commander. The acting commander, Maj. E. C. Councell, advised the Yankee that, since the regiment had not surrendered, the Federal officer was now himself a prisoner. The Northerner refused to accept this situation and began to return to his line. He was shot.[13]

After the firing resumed, Captain Church and his little band maintained their front until 2:20–3:00 P.M., when they were relieved from their perilous position. They rejoined their brigade on the left of the line. The Twenty-sixth Michigan sustained 139 casualties that day. The commander, Maj. Lemuel Saviers, was hit four times. Seven of the nine members of the regimental color guard had been struck. Further to its credit, the regiment claimed the honor of being the first to plant its colors on the enemy works in the initial assault, which had occurred so long ago, at 4:50 A.M.[14]

Fighting at the Bloody Angle—Federal Operations

The rain which had fallen steadily all morning eased somewhat at noon. Through the afternoon, showers occurred intermittently and were heavy at times. Out in front of the west angle, four Federal brigades—Edwards's, Upton's, Grant's and McAllister's—lay in the mud along the north side of the slight crest and knoll. To the rear of these troops at distances which varied from fifty to one hundred yards, were the brigades of Wheaton, Bidwell, Eustis, and the Excelsior of Mott's division. The front rank of the four advanced brigades maintained a steady stream of fire aimed at the top of the segment of Confederate works, which extended from the south face of the angle northeast to about eighty yards east of the oak tree. This was the point where Brown's line terminated inside the works. Opposite this point the Thirty-seventh Massachusetts Regiment of Edwards's small brigade held a position with a brigade of the Second Corps—McAllister's, the Excelsior, or perhaps Ward's—to its rear in support. The Second Rhode Island lay to the right and rear of the Thirty-seventh and slightly refused. At times some of the Thirty-seventh were firing under the head logs simultaneously with the South Carolinians from the opposite side. Men were bayoneted through these openings. Soldiers on both sides of the works occasionally reached their muskets over the top, pointed them downward, and fired. Sometimes they lost their weapons to enemy soldiers who wrenched them from their hands. Rifles were not all that was pulled over the works. In a few cases a soldier reached over the top of the logs and manhandled an enemy soldier into captivity, or worse if he resisted.

Many Yankee musket barrels became so hot that they could no longer be used safely, and a few of them burst. Edwards refused to attempt relieving his men with regiments from the rear. He feared the possibility that, during the exchange and accompanying cessation of Federal fire, the Confederates opposite would be able to deliver deadly volleys into the unprotected Yankees, who would be in the open. He ordered the troops of one of the Second Corps regiments in his rear to crawl forward, so that they could pass their serviceable rifles to his men and could take the fouled ones back to clean them. This operation was performed more than once during the action.[15]

To the right of Edwards's position, Bidwell's and Eustis's brigades moved forward in close support of Upton's, and soon these brigades became intermingled. Just prior to this, Upton again presumed to command Edwards's troops as he passed through this part of the line to confer with Birney to the left. Edwards paid no attention but kept his men at their work. When Eustis, who outranked Upton, arrived at the front line, Upton's supremacy, real or imagined, ended.

Edwards asked Eustis to bring his own brigade, Upton's, and Bidwell's forward and to attempt to reoccupy the outside of the works along the right face of the west angle. This area had been held by the Tenth Massachusetts that morning. Edwards believed that, from this position, by firing to their left oblique, the three brigades would relieve some of the pressure which Brown's right regiments were maintaining on Edwards's men. Edwards accompanied Upton and Bidwell among the troops of the three brigades in an attempt to get them to move forward, but in the confusion of the intense firing, the attempt was unsuccessful. These Federals remained massed behind the crest, firing at the enemy works ahead from the left of the oak tree west along the right face of the angle, which was manned primarily by Harris's Mississippians.[16]

The left end of Upton's brigade line at times rested close to the Confederate works. A member of the Fifth Maine positioned there remembered at one time seeing twenty-four different stands of Federal colors near this point of contention. Although regiments and brigades were mingled confusedly, groups of men periodically surged forward to the works in an attempt to hold the position gained there. In these situations, a Yankee occasionally leaped on top of the works and fired down into the Confederates, using his own musket and others which comrades would toss up to him. Some of these desperate soldiers got off three or four shots before their lifeless bodies tumbled down on one side of the works or the other. Invariably these advance groups of Federals were forced back from the works by intense enemy fire, which had been shifted to their position from other nearby points along the line.[17]

Many Federal regimental accounts claim that their members fired three to four hundred rounds each that day. It appears that the Yankees were able to maintain an adequate supply of ammunition for these front line troops during daylight. Ammunition cases were dragged to the rear of the masses of troops. Company officers broke them open, and the ammunition was passed forward to the front line by infantrymen who in some places lay in lines ten deep.[18]

Federal Artillery Action

Some of Hancock's corps artillery was firing from positions along the Landrum lane ridge. The adventures of Gilliss's battery and especially Metcalf's section have been explained. At one time Hancock's chief of artillery, Col. John C. Tidball, sent sections of Ames's and Brown's batteries forward to positions immediately in front of the east angle and farther right in the abatis. They fired at Brown's infantrymen to their right front, exhausting all of their canister ammunition supply. They continued to fire shot and shell until ordered back from their unprotected positions to a line immediately in front of the Landrum house.[19]

After the initial success of Hancock's infantrymen in the morning, these foot soldiers turned around some of the captured Confederate guns and attempted to fire them. Volunteers from Ames's battery ran forward with lanyards and friction primers to help the infantrymen with the guns. Ames's men retrieved nine guns. Farther to the right, some of McAllister's New Jersey troops manhandled four captured guns back to the Federal side of the works. They fired these pieces for a short time before the guns were hauled back by artillerymen from Dow's battery. Sixteen of the twenty pieces which had been overrun in the morning were secured by nightfall.[20]

When Hancock's men were pushed back to the first line of works in the morning, the Sixth Corps batteries were ordered to fire, blindly for the most part, into the salient for the remainder of the day. Capt. George W. Adams's Battery G, First Rhode Island Light Artillery of three-inch rifles, fired 873 rounds that day.[21]

Tompkins's batteries did not fire with impunity, for Brown's and Harris's troops delivered a heavy volume of musket fire into the open area north and northeast of the west angle. Lt. Col. Thomas W. Hyde, a member of Wright's staff, was ordered to direct a section of artillery forward to assist the infantry with canister fire. He watched the gunners gallop forward over a slight rise little more than one hundred yards north-northeast from the oak tree in the works. Seeing from the top of the rise how close they were to the battle line, the artillerymen had begun to initiate a turn into battery position when they were struck by a volley of musketry. Every man and horse was killed instantly. The men sitting on the caissons remained there, frozen in death.[22] At dawn on the following morning, a major from Cutler's division reached up and touched one of these artillerymen to convince himself that he was really dead. During the night Colonel Hyde recalled that he had not heard the guns open fire after they had disappeared over the rise. On the next morning he walked forward to investigate a scene that looked like a posed museum display. A member of Ricketts's division remembered that the body of a dead Federal lay across the trail of one of the guns. Because the Confederates had maintained a fire on this point to prevent any Yankees from manning or retrieving the two guns, the dead Federal's body had been struck so many times that it was actually shot in two. Suddenly, the legs separated from the torso, and both sections dropped into the mud. The intense firing continued.[23]

Horatio G. Wright and the Responsibilities of Command

The twelfth of May marked only the fourth day of Wright's command of the Sixth Corps during the campaign. On previous occasions he had been placed in temporary command in Sedgwick's absence, but those experiences had done little to prepare him for such intense fighting. He had been wounded slightly early in the action. From his headquarters, at first in the trees six hundred yards north of the west angle and later at the Landrum house, he could not see the firing line and had to rely for information on messages from his division commanders.

It is not known what precise information Russell and Neill forwarded to Wright, but in his communications with army headquarters, he frequently said that his front line troops were hard-pressed to maintain their positions. If he meant that his infantrymen were experiencing difficulty, for whatever reason, in holding their positions while lying along the reverse side of the crest and while attempting to maintain a steady volume of fire against Confederates who were firing just as steadily at close range from behind breastworks, his choice of words was adequate. However, if he meant that his troops were fighting off concerted Confederate attacks along the crest, he was wrong.

Yet it was on such information that Meade and Grant were obliged to base their decisions, for they were entirely dependent on situation reports from their corps commanders. They had established their headquarters sites more than 1½ miles from the scene of the action. The front line commanders, moreover, controlled not only the flow of information but also the implementation of their superiors' plans. The fate of the Fifth Corps is a good case in point. Meade had transferred it to the center in hopes of spearheading a renewed assault, but Wright, apprehensive for the security of his sector, used these reinforcements to bolster his front and to stand ready to meet possible counterattacks.

The first Fifth Corps force to reach Wright was Cutler, with three brigades, who reported at 2:00–2:30 P.M. His Fourth Brigade, Lyle's, from the defunct Second Division of the Fifth Corps, had been sent to the old Sixth Corps works immediately to the east of the Brock Road to reinforce Bartlett's brigade, which was already there. Wright immediately ordered Cutler to relieve Wheaton's brigade, whose regiments were located at different points along the crest, generally northwest from the angle. Cutler chose Bragg's brigade of Pennsylvania regiments for this assignment, and it succeeded in getting into position at 3:00 P.M. Shortly thereafter a portion of Robinson's Iron Brigade was sent into the front line farther to the east, near Edwards's position. Since Cutler's troops were intended to form part of an assault force rather than to serve as relief for the Sixth Corps troops in the front line, Wright's actions, in this instance, ensured the failure of Meade's and Grant's attempt to mount an assault against the northwest face of the salient.[24]

As early as 1:00 P.M. Wright suggested to Humphreys that his troops fighting opposite the west angle be relieved because they had been engaged there all day. Later Wright said he felt confident that an assaulting column composed of the remaining two divisions (Griffin's and Crawford's) of the Fifth Corps and the few Sixth Corps troops available could carry the enemy's line at the west angle. Wright was given discretion, apparently subject only to Hancock's advice, to decide whether the assault should be executed.[25]

As the afternoon progressed, Wright's confidence in the enterprise began to wane. He learned that Griffin's and Crawford's divisions together would total only five thousand men. He estimated that he would be able to furnish no more than one thousand infantrymen from the Sixth Corps for the assault and informed Humphreys that he doubted that these totals were sufficient to ensure success. He was fearful of a Confederate counterattack in the event the Federal attack failed. With this possibility in mind, both Wright and Hancock put some of their men to work constructing entrenchments to the rear of their forward positions.[26]

Finally, at 5:15 P.M. Wright notified headquarters that he had decided against the attack. The reason for his decision was "not that it might not succeed, but in view of the disaster which would possibly follow a failure."[27] It would be interesting to learn Meade's outward and Grant's inner reactions to this strange explanation. Wright also reiterated his concern that the number of troops available was not sufficient to ensure a reasonable prospect for success. He claimed that Hancock fully concurred in his views. At 6:15 P.M. Meade approved Wright's decision against making the assault.

Oliver Edwards and the Responsibilities of Command

At approximately 4:00 P.M., the Confederate fire on Edwards's position slackened somewhat, and he decided to relieve his three regiments with units of the Second Corps brigade to his rear. The switch was made successfully, although Edwards permitted his men to retire only twenty-five or thirty yards, to replenish their supply of ammunition. At about this time Edwards received an order to report to his division commander, General Neill. Edwards recorded that, since the situation on his front was fairly stable, he decided to report as ordered, implying that had the situation been critical, he would have remained at his post despite orders to the contrary.[28]

He reported to Neill and requested that his exhausted men be relieved. He was informed that this would not be possible and that he must remain in command of his segment of the line all night. Edwards readily agreed to remain in command but argued that his troops were becoming too exhausted to stand, load, and fire for very much longer. Neill replied that the orders from corps headquarters were for Edwards's men to hold both his own part of the line and Upton's, to his right, because Upton's and Bidwell's brigades were to be withdrawn as soon as it was dark. The colonel saluted and returned to the line feeling that his brigade was being imposed upon quite heavily.[29]

General Russell, commanding the First Division, accompanied Edwards and commiserated with him. When Russell saw the numbers of troops which were to be removed from Edwards's right flank, he told the colonel that he would send forward the Tenth New Jersey Regiment of his First Brigade to help man the position there. This regiment had become separated from its brigade on the evening of 8 May and apparently had not yet rejoined. Russell also promised that, if Edwards and his troops had not been relieved by daylight, he would conduct a part of his division forward and would relieve the troops himself. The commander of the Tenth New Jersey reported to Edwards sometime after 5:00 P.M. Colonel Parsons, of the Tenth Massachusetts, was detailed to lead the fresh regiment into position. Parsons reportedly led the Jerseymen up out of the ravine and across the open slope, which was littered with the bodies of dead Federals, to the breastworks in front of Upton's position on the crest.[30]

Edwards ordered the newcomers to commence file firing to their left oblique, and this relieved some of the pressure against his own front. At about 6:00 P.M. the Second Corps regiments manning Edwards's front line used the last of their ammunition, and the colonel replaced them with his Tenth Massachusetts, Second Rhode Island, and one wing of the Thirty-seventh Massachusetts. Soon thereafter a regiment to the left of Edwards's position withdrew from the line with the excuse that its members were out of ammunition. Edwards awakened the troops of the wing of the Thirty-seventh Massachusetts in reserve and ordered them to advance and to fill the vacancy in the line. They did, but with empty muskets, having passed their recently acquired ammunition resupply forward to the front line troops.[31]

As if Edwards were not experiencing enough difficulty, the commander of the supporting Second Corps brigade immediately to the rear attempted at this time to withdraw his command, stating that his troops had neither ammunition nor rations. Edwards called over a file of his own troops, and while they stood with their muskets aimed at the officer, Edwards made it clear to him that neither he nor any of his men were going anywhere unless properly relieved by higher authority. They stayed.[32]

Upton's brigade retired from the crest at approximately 5:00 P.M. One of the regiments that replaced Upton's men was the First Massachusetts of McAllister's brigade, under the command of Col. Napoleon B. McLaughlen. This unit's term of service had nearly expired and it had been assigned to picket duty in the rear. At 2:00 P.M. Colonel McLaughlen had volunteered to help out up front and had been granted permission to do so. His men moved into Upton's former position on the crest and maintained a heavy volume of fire until long after dark. Lt. Col. Waldo Merriam, of the Sixteenth Massachusetts, who had drawn the map for Barlow on the wall of the Brown house early that day, was killed there along the crest. The troops of Mott's division were regarded by some as the weak link in the chain of the Federal Second Corps, but many of them fought very well indeed that day.[33]

During the afternoon some of the Coehorn mortars were put into operation. Unfortunately, the precise locations of these weapons and their targets cannot be determined. It appears reasonable to assume that they would have been firing at Brown's and Harris's troops behind the works in the vicinity of the west angle. This is the first recorded use of these weapons in field combat in the war.[34]

Warren's Command Fragmented

At some time between 3:00 and 5:00 P.M. Griffin led Ayres's brigade and most of Sweitzer's from their positions west of the Brock Road to report to Hancock. They were joined by the five regiments of Bartlett's brigade, who had been relieved from their position behind the old Sixth Corps works east of the road. Crawford's Pennsylvania Reserves plus Coulter's brigade replaced Griffin's troops west of the Brock Road. The Maryland Brigade was also dispatched toward the left at this time. Griffin's troops probably marched on the Gordon Road, which lay northeast from the Alsop farm. While these troops were en route, Wright made his decision not to conduct the planned assault but apparently did not notify Griffin, who arrived with his troops north of the Landrum house at dark. There they assumed a position in support of the Second Corps.

After marching a relatively short distance, the Maryland brigade halted somewhere to the rear of the Sixth Corps to function as a support element. None of these troops became engaged with the enemy. As a result of these movements, the only Union troops remaining west of the Brock Road were the three brigades of Crawford's division, a battalion of heavy artillery troops, and a cavalry detachment from army headquarters that was on watch farther to the west. These troops would not be disturbed during the night.[35]

On the South Side of the Works near the West Angle

The infantrymen of Brown's and Harris's brigades enjoyed some measure of protection behind their log works, whereas their opponents were exposed in the open, especially when firing. The Southerners' situation was not to be envied, however. They were jammed into the enclosures several lines deep. There were no head logs atop the side walls of these pens, and any Rebel who attempted to fire obliquely over the walls was likely to be struck, since sheets of bullets were continually passing by. As a result, some Confederates merely sat in the mud against the traverse walls and waited to repel any Yankees who might succeed in getting over the front wall.[36]

The Twelfth South Carolina Regiment on the right of Brown's brigade occupied the most critical and dangerous position. It was stretched thinner than any of its sister regiments. It was the target of constant Federal musketry from the front, right front, and right flank. Oliver Edwards's troops and Birney's to their left maintained a steady volume of fire against this part of the works. Farther to the east along the line, some of Birney's and perhaps Gibbon's troops occupied a few of the log enclosures captured from York's Louisiana brigade. From there the Yankees maintained an annoying fire down the line at the right of the Confederate position. Brown had to be alert for any Federal assault from that direction; however, none was attempted.

The heaviest Federal fire came against the Confederate line from Brown's right flank west to the west angle. During the afternoon the Yankees there were able to maintain firing lines for extended periods of time within ten to twenty yards of the breastworks. This is where the firing and grappling over the top of the works occurred. The Federals involved came from the Twenty-sixth Michigan and from Upton's, L.A. Grant's, and Bidwell's brigades.

As a result, the greatest number of Confederate casualties occurred within the right half of Brown's line. As Brown called for replacements for these casualties, infantrymen from farther to the left ran up behind the line and took their places in the enclosures to the right of the oak tree. This process of replacement began before noon and continued into the night. In the afternoon, Colonel Hunt, on the left of Brown's line, found it necessary to request that infantrymen from Harris's brigade sidle to their right to maintain a continuous line. He did not ask in vain. By late afternoon Hunt was sending and leading to the right almost as many Mississippians as South Carolinians, and by nightfall all of the pens occupied by Brown's troops contained Mississippians as well.[37]

Both the Carolinians and Mississippians were short of line officers due to casualties in the Wilderness fighting. Many of the enclosures, which were fifteen to twenty feet wide, were manned exclusively by enlisted men, who would move instinctively to an endangered part of the line without orders. Thus, when a Yankee surge of perhaps fifty to one hundred men carried over the head logs and into a pen or two, temporarily overpowering the Southerners, nearby comrades immediately climbed over the adjacent traverses to get at them. Others from elsewhere along the line stormed into the rear of the enclosures firing, swinging, and stabbing until the intruders had been driven out, killed, wounded, or captured.[38]

Thus, conditions inside the log compartments, which had been bad in the morning, rapidly worsened as the day progressed. The shallow trenches immediately behind the forward walls of the enclosures partially filled with rain water. Soon, the entire ground surface inside of the pens had become a muddy, bloody mess. The bodies of dead and wounded Confederates lay in this muck and were sometimes stepped on by comrades fighting desperately to hold the position. Late in the afternoon, during the infrequent lulls in the fighting, exhausted Southern infantrymen dragged bodies to the rear of the enclosures in order to provide more room for the men still on their feet. There was no time to tend to the wounded.[39]

The trees immediately behind Brown's position and the right part of Harris's suffered severely from the constant Federal fire, which was usually aimed at the head logs atop the front of the works. Just before sunset, a tree approximately eight inches in diameter near the large oak east of the west angle was struck by an artillery shell twenty feet from the ground. Its trunk was severed, and the top portion fell a short distance, lodging in the branches of another tree. Nearby Confederates paid little attention to this but continued firing.[40]

The Southerners managed somehow to maintain an adequate supply of ammunition for the troops on the firing line. Some of Harris's men apparently carried or dragged the containers forward along the northern part of the McCoull lane. Many of these Mississippians were hit while performing this hazardous duty. Volunteers from among Brown's troops also dragged ammunition boxes forward. In some instances piles of loose cartridges were tossed upon tent flies and then manhandled to the front line.[41]

Just before sunset, R. H. Anderson was ordered to send two First Corps brigades to their right as a reserve for the troops battling in the area of the west angle. Warren's men had not attacked Field's troops since late morning. Lee apparently assumed that it was now safe to weaken the left of his line to ensure the survival of the all-important center. He chose Humphreys's and Bratton's brigades for this assignment. As Bratton moved off, DuBose's Georgians extended their right into the edge of the Spindle field as far as the Brock Road. Humphreys's and Bratton's men filed into position behind the reserve line of works, which lay across the salient approximately midway between the McCoull and Harrison houses. It seems that they were ordered not to leave this line of works unless the troops fighting in front were driven back, in which case appropriate orders would be forthcoming. As darkness arrived, the Mississippians and South Carolinians lay behind the line of entrenchments. They could hear the roar of musketry from six hundred yards in front, where their comrades continued fighting desperately to hold the line.[42]

Darkness Brings No Relief

At dark Colonel Edwards ordered his regiments to slacken their fire gradually, to see whether the Confederates had ceased to fire. He discovered that the Southerners were still maintaining a heavy fire against his brigade front and ordered his troops to resume firing. Since they had been firing at the same general area all day long, they were able to continue in complete darkness. The muzzle flashes from Confederate muskets doubtless provided targets.[43]

Shortly after dark, the Sixth Wisconsin and Twenty-fourth Michigan regiments of the Iron Brigade were ordered up to the crest to relieve the Seventh Wisconsin. These two regiments slogged through the ravine, which was cluttered with wounded men and discarded weapons. They took their position along the crest, standing in mud halfway to their knees, with bodies all around them. From there, they fired at the top of the Confederate works until they were numb with fatigue. Some of them sank down into the bloody mud and fell asleep under fire. Their officers, who were just as tired as the men, moved among the prostrate forms, shaking them and shouting at them to resume their places on the firing line. In many cases the officers were exhorting dead men, but they were too numb with exhaustion to know it.[44]

Behind the Federal Front

Immediately after approving Wright's decision not to attack, Grant and Meade sent directives to consolidate for the night the advanced positions that had been gained in the morning. At 8:00 P.M. Hancock was ordered to strengthen his line as much as possible and to maintain a reserve force, which was to be available for any segment of his own or the army's front that the Confederates might attack. The Federal high command's fear of an enemy assault reflects the effects of Wright's and Hancock's claims throughout the day that their troops were continually hard-pressed. At 5:45 P.M. Hancock informed Burnside that their corps still were not joined and asked whether he intended to complete the connection soon. Hancock then expressed his fear that the enemy might break through at that point.[45]

It is difficult to know why Hancock feared a Confederate attack against any part of his line. The most recent Confederate assault against a Second Corps position had been between 8:00 and 8:30 that morning, when a part of Perrin's brigade had attacked the captured segment of the works manned by Gibbon's and some of Birney's troops.

On the eastern face of the salient, Hoffman's Virginia regiments lay behind Steuart's old works, with the left regiment beginning 150 to 200 yards south from the apex. They were operating only defensively. Other troops of Gordon's division might have been posted in the woodland east of the McCoull house, but they certainly did not constitute a threat to either Hancock or Burnside. Perhaps the mental and physical strains imposed by marching most of the night and fighting all of the day were beginning to affect everyone.[46]

Wright intended to extend his advanced line west in the trees from the west angle to a swampy area lying southwest of the Shelton house and just short of his old north-south line of works. After dark he pleaded with army headquarters for Cutler's and even Griffin's troops to relieve his men fighting at the west angle. Finally, at 11:00 P.M., Meade sent Wright a terse message that Warren had been under fire all day also and that the two divisions had been sent to form a column of attack, not to relieve the Sixth Corps troops in their battle lines. Warren's troops were needed on the right of the Sixth Corps to guard its flank.[47]

Meade asked if Wright could shorten his line at all and was told to reply quickly, as Warren was waiting at army headquarters for the answer. Wright replied that he could not shorten his line, because Hancock could not extend his right. This meant that Wright would have to maintain the position at the west angle with his own exhausted troops, who were still under incessant fire. Wright claimed that he could not maintain the connection with Hancock's troops to his left without the services of Cutler's men and asked that they be left with him until he could readjust his lines after daylight. This request was granted.[48]

Meade ordered Griffin's division back to Warren, at the right of the line. He ordered Warren, apparently again in full command of his Fifth Corps, to establish an entrenched line extending from Wright's proposed right flank across the Brock Road toward Fifth Corps headquarters at Alsop's.[49] Meade told his three corps commanders that no offensive operations were planned for the following day (the thirteenth), but that each of them should remain alert for possible Confederate attacks. At 6:10 P.M. Grant ordered Burnside to strengthen his position, to permit his men to rest whenever possible, and to plan to harass the Southerners opposite his position with artillery fire on the next day. Later, at 9:00 P.M., Grant advised Burnside to ensure that his troops were awake and under arms by 3:30 A.M., as headquarters suspected that Lee would attempt to retrieve the initiative at daylight and that the Ninth Corps was the most likely target.[50]

As these calculations were made by commanding officers at headquarters in the rear, their exhausted enlisted men at the front kept to their work. They stood or lay in the mud and continued to fire at the top of the log works.

After Dark on the South Side

As darkness fell with no noticeable cessation of the firing, Colonel Brown sought some relief for his exhausted Carolinians. He sent Colonel Hunt to the left across the McCoull lane to Ramseur's position. The officers whom Hunt met there said that their orders required them to keep the troops in their present positions, even though they were not under attack and were receiving only an occasional cross fire from their right front. Hunt returned and reported to Brown, who later ordered him to find General Harris or anyone else in authority who could provide some relief. Hunt wandered down the McCoull field in the darkness and stumbled upon Bratton's brigade behind the reserve line of works. Bratton told Hunt that, according to his orders, his troops could not leave their position. Once again Hunt returned to his brigade, this time by walking toward the loudest firing. He reported his lack of success to Brown, who placed him in command of the brigade and went himself to search for Harris.

Brown moved to the left of Harris's line, where he found an officer who told him Harris was somewhere in the rear. Brown finally found Harris, and they conferred in the rain. Harris sent a courier farther to the rear for instructions. Soon an order from Rodes arrived directing the two brigades to withdraw at 4:00 A.M., when the new line in the rear was to be completed. Brown returned to his men, and the instructions were passed down the line of traverses.[51]

Man's Inhumanity to Nature

The trees behind the Confederate position were struck constantly by the Federal fire and were to bear the scars of this battle as long as they stood. Sometime between midnight and 2:00 A.M. the large oak tree east of the west angle crashed to the ground. Its trunk had been cut in two by Federal musket balls. The oak fell to its right front, and its top branches landed in the adjoining enclosure, which at the time was manned primarily by members of the First South Carolina Regiment. The tree scratched some of them, and knocked one unconscious briefly. The end of the tree did not end the shooting. All the while, the firing continued.[52] (See Appendix C.)

Confederate Withdrawal from the Salient

From midnight on, the volume of musketry at the west angle gradually diminished, because everyone was exhausted, and because Upton's and Bidwell's troops withdrew from the firing line. Finally, at 4:00 A.M., immediately before daybreak, word came down the Confederate line of traverses to fall back quietly. The exhausted infantrymen of Brown's and Harris's brigades stumbled through the mud to the rear and assembled in a field behind Early's line of works, one-half mile northwest of the courthouse. Their losses were cruel. Approximately one-half of Harris's eight hundred troops had become casualties, including two regimental commanders killed. The majority of these casualties had occurred during the movement forward to the works. Of McGowan's one thousand to eleven hundred Carolinians, 451 were struck. Two regimental commanders were dead, one of whom had a son who was also killed. Colonel Brown's younger brother was mortally wounded.[53]

These Southerners had exhibited devotion to duty and physical endurance that almost defy belief. Doubtless, some had leapt the works and had surrendered during the day, and after dark a few might have slipped to the rear without orders to do so. But the vast majority had stuck it out, the South Carolinians for over eighteen hours and the Mississippians for nearly twenty. During this time they had defended their position, unsupported, without food, their only water that scooped from puddles in the mud. No Confederate line or staff officer of division level or higher had seen fit to visit them after they had established their position at the works. They had fought their fight alone.

The Federals did not significantly interfere with these two Confederate brigades as they withdrew. Colonel Edwards remembered that Confederate firing had all but ceased by 3:00 A.M. A short time later he sent some skirmishers over the parapet, who discovered that the Southerners were retiring. A member of the First Carolina said that, when he and his comrades withdrew, there were no Yankees in sight along the crest.[54]

To the left of Harris's position, Ramseur's troops reportedly retired at 3:90 A.M. To Ramseur's left, Kershaw's units probably remained in position until all withdrawing friendly forces had passed south of the reserve line. Then Kershaw's men dropped back to their assigned position in the new line south and southwest of the Harrison house. On the east side of the salient, Hoffman's Virginians and the troops from Battle's, Perrin's, Doles's, and R. D. Johnston's brigades withdrew sometime after 3:00 A.M., leaving a skirmish line behind. Those Confederates who manned the line farther south might also have retired at this time, but this is not certain. At daylight Bratton's and Humphreys's troops withdrew from the reserve line to the new line in their rear. This new line, much of which lay along a crest, paralleled the Brock Road from three to five hundred yards away.[55]

James A. Beaver, commander of the 148th Pennsylvania Regiment. He accepted the personal surrender of Brig. Gen. George H. Steuart.

(Mass. MOLLUS Collection, MHI)

Edward ("Allegheny") Johnson. Most of his division was captured.
(Mass. MOLLUS Collection, MHI)

Nathaniel Church, Twenty-sixth Michigan Regiment. He led a special mission.
(Photograph collection of William M. Horton, now in the possession of Christopher M. Calkins)

Man's Inhumanity to Man

After daylight, some Yankees crept forward to examine the interior of the Confederate works that lay to the east of the west angle. While crossing the open space between the crest and works, they made their first grim discovery. Many of their comrades had been hit in this area, especially on the small plateau extending from the oak tree northeast to the front of the right flank of Brown's former position. The bodies of the Federal infantrymen had been literally shot to pieces. Later, members of the burial details collected the pitiable remains in blankets. Most of these fallen Yankees were interred in that saddest of marked graves, the one labelled "Unknown."[56]

Capt. Fred Sanborn of the Fifth Maine was acting assistant adjutant general for Upton on the twelfth. Sometime on that morning he had been ordered to lead his parent regiment forward to the crest. While Sanborn waited for the men to form, an acquaintance, Capt. Frank L. Lemont,

Joseph N. Brown, Fourteenth South Carolina Regiment, acting commander of McGowan's brigade
(Varina D. Brown, *A Colonel at Gettysburg and Spotsylvania*, p. ii)

Oliver Edwards, Thirty-seventh Massachusetts Regiment, acting commander of the Fourth Brigade, Second Division, Sixth Corps
(Mass. MOLLUS Collection, MHI)

approached and told him that they were the only two captains of the regiment still with the army. Six had fallen in the attack on the tenth, and Lemont wondered whose turn was next. Later Sanborn discovered his colleague's body near the works. He recalled that there was no space larger than four inches on the body which had not been struck. He counted eleven bullet holes through the soles of the shoes.[57]

A former schoolmate and intimate friend of Captain Church, who was also in the Twenty-sixth Michigan, had been shot and had fallen across the top of the works. On the morning of the thirteenth, Church asked members of the regiment about his friend and was told by some who had seen him fall the approximate location of the body. An officer who accompanied the captain remembered that what they discovered at the site no longer resembled a human being but appeared more like a sponge. Church was able to identify his friend only by the color of his beard and the pieces of a letter.[58]

Colonel Parsons of the Tenth Massachusetts remembered that his major's horse had fallen approximately ten yards in front of the Confederate line and had been reduced to mincemeat. The colonel recalled that only a few Confederates were lying outside the works near the west angle, but that he could hear sounds from behind the log walls.[59]

Most of the Yankees who climbed on top of these works near the west angle and gazed down into the enclosures behind were veterans of several hard-fought engagements, but they were not prepared for what they found here. In places the Confederates lay three and four deep in the mud. Some had been trampled completely out of sight. Wounded Southerners lay helplessly pinned down by the bodies of two or three dead comrades. Thirty dead were counted in one pen. Colonel Edwards noticed a hand move in the midst of a heap of bodies, and when the dead were removed, a Confederate colonel with a broken leg was recovered. Some survivors of the New Jersey brigade crossed the field where they had charged on the previous morning. When they looked down into the pens, many of them became ill. Responding to the moans and cries of wounded Confederates, however, they dropped into the bloody muck and dragged them to drier ground and safety.[60]

A diarist in the Twentieth Indiana Regiment recorded on the thirteenth: "We, for the first time, had a chance to breathe and eat. The trench on the Rebel side of the works was filled with their dead piled together in every way with their wounded. The sight was terrible and ghastly. We helped off their wounded as well we could, and searched for our own wounded in front. Captain Corey was killed and never found. Captain Thomas was found with twelve bullet wounds. He had fallen and then been shot to pieces, possibly by his friends. The horses of the regular battery were so shot that each was not over ten or twelve inches thick."[61]

After the war most of these Federals were to remember with pride the part that each had played in the fighting against the west angle. Many, doubtless, refought the battle often at veterans' reunions. The first letters which many of them wrote home after the twelfth of May, however, reflected a sense of repulsion and awe toward the fighting on that day. Many men were unable to describe with any degree of clarity their own experiences there. A letter by a sergeant in the 149th Pennsylvania was typical, "I cannot describe to you what I have seen so I will not try. If it should be my luck to come home, I can tell it you but I cannot write it. . . . Kiss the boys, tell them that I think of them often and hope they may never see what I have."[62] A few recorded that they wished that some of the politicians and fire-eaters at home could enjoy the experience of viewing such scenes.

In a letter written on 14 May, Charles E. Wheldon, a color-bearer in the First South Carolina, said that during the action, Col. Charles H. McCreary of his regiment had fallen wounded almost in his arms and that the top of the flag had been shot away. Furthermore, a bullet had torn open his shirt and inflicted a slight shoulder wound, but he was all right. He complained that the men in the ranks knew very little of how matters stood in the campaign because they were continually moving from one location to another. In this regard, John J. Dillard of Evans's Twenty-sixth Georgia Regiment wrote to a friend on 20 May asking him to write because the only things that he was hearing were rumors and guns. Dillard, who had received two slight wounds, said that the Confederate troops were as badly worn out as he had ever seen them but that their morale remained high.[63]

Concerning morale, a gunner in Graham's Virginia battery of Ewell's corps was optimistic in a letter home, "all of our men seem to be in the best of spirits and they want Old Grant to fight us again so we can slauter the drunken scoundrels again. there is hundreds and thousands of thir dead a laying in front of our breastworks yet unberried."[64]

Thus, the fighting which opened at approximately 4:30 A.M. continued for nearly twenty-three hours before sputtering to a close. The number of Federal losses incurred that day was approximately seven thousand, including Major General Wright, who was slightly wounded, and Brigadier Generals Carroll and Webb, who were seriously wounded. Confederate casualties are estimated to have been five thousand to six thousand, which includes three thousand captured from Johnson's division. In addition, eighteen to twenty Southern artillery pieces were lost. Lee was deprived of the services of one major general and seven brigadier generals: Daniel and Perrin were killed or mortally wounded; McGowan, Ramseur, R. D. Johnston, and Walker were severely wounded; and Allegheny Johnson and Steuart were captured. It had been one of the most trying days of Lee's military career.[65]

Sometime during the action a courier delivered to Lee the catastrophic news that his chief of cavalry, J. E. B. Stuart, had died from a wound received in action with Sheridan's cavalry at Yellow Tavern, immediately north of Richmond. Lee quietly informed the members of his staff and, after a pause, said emotionally that Stuart had never brought him a piece of false information. The Army of Northern Virginia and its brilliant commander could ill afford many more days like the twelfth of May.[66]

IV North-South Becomes East-West

13–21 May

17 Difficult Things Are Being Attempted   13–15 May

In his formal report Grant explained the Federal operations of 12 May in three sentences. In closing he complimented, unintentionally perhaps, the Army of Northern Virginia by stating that the resistance offered by its soldiers on that day "was so obstinate that the advantage gained did not prove decisive." He then said that "the 13th, 14th, 15th, 16th, 17th and 18th were consumed in maneuvering and awaiting the arrival of re-enforcements from Washington."[1] This extremely general description of events was to mean, of course, different things to different people.

For example, Colonel Edwards's three regiments were relieved as promised by General Russell in person, at the head of one of his brigades, at 6:30 A.M. Edwards led his New Englanders back to the vicinity of the Landrum house, where they stacked their arms and, to a man, lay down. They immediately fell asleep without even thinking about making coffee or eating. Their colonel recorded that they lay motionless in the mud and rain into the early afternoon, looking like lines of dead men awaiting burial. As the afternoon progressed, small groups would arise, boil coffee, drink it, and immediately return to their beds of mud. Not until just before dark did they pitch their tents in preparation for a night of more sleep, protected from the rain. They had occupied their position in front of the works to the east of the west angle for nearly twenty-four hours and had been exposed to enemy fire for three-quarters of the time. They had earned their rest and their thirteen dollars pay for the month.[2]

In a letter written home, a member of the Sixth Corps's New Jersey brigade used a phrase that was perhaps representative of the feelings of disappointment and the grudging admiration they felt for their counterparts in the Army of Northern Virginia during this phase of the campaign. After describing the role that his regiment, the First New Jersey, played in the operations of 12 May, during which the unit lost 175 enlisted men and all but three of its officers, he offered his opinion that, "I think the enemy has got the worst off the Bargain but they seam to stick to us yet."[3]

Shortly after daylight Grant and Meade were anxious to learn whether Lee's men were "sticking" in the general area of Spotsylvania Court House or retiring to a position farther to the south. At 5:30 A.M. Wright sent army headquarters news that his Sixth Corps troops occupied the works at the west angle and that the Confederates appeared to have abandoned that segment of their line. He was ordered to send a large reconnaissance force forward. At the same time, Hancock reported that his sharpshooters had advanced approximately one-half mile into the salient without finding any enemy troops. He was directed to continue to advance cautiously. Warren reported no change in the enemy's dispositions opposite his position. Confederates were reported to be still in place in front of Burnside on the Federal left.[4]

At approximately 7:30 A.M. Barlow sent word that his skirmishers, proceeding down the eastern face of the salient, had been stopped by a strong Confederate skirmish line. These were probably some of Gordon's troops stationed behind the eastern segment of the reserve line of entrenchments. Hancock reported this collision to army headquarters at 8:00 A.M. and said that, at that time, Gibbon was advancing his division to locate the new Confederate position.[5]

Actually this reconnaissance in force was executed only by Gibbon's Second Brigade, normally commanded by Brig. Gen. Joshua T. Owen, but led on this mission by Col. Samuel S. Carroll of the Third Brigade. Carroll had been wounded in the right arm during the Wilderness fighting but had refused to leave his post. Early in this advance he was struck by a bullet, which shattered his left arm, and he was carried from the field. The brigade entered the salient at, or just south of, the east angle and, proceeding southsouthwest, drove the Confederate pickets from the reserve line. Continuing forward, they sighted the main enemy line, whereupon they retired.[6]

Simply sighting that line did not mean the Yankees really understood where it ran. The reconnaissance, indeed, misled Hancock into drawing a very inaccurate map of the new enemy position. At 10:15 A.M., however, he forwarded to headquarters his fairly accurate appraisal that the Confederates had abandoned the salient and had formed a line that was a relatively straight eastward extension of their line opposite Warren's corps.[7]

During the morning, the troops of Miles's and Brooke's brigades of Barlow's division were busy moving dirt. Along the northern part of the eastern face of the salient, they strengthened and reversed Steuart's old works for their own use on the east side. Farther south, near the point where the eastern lane from the McCoull house crossed the former Confederate line of works, they constructed a two-hundred-yard stretch of entrenchments that faced nearly due south, with its eastern end near the right flank of the Ninth Corps. The Yankees in these works were at least half a mile from the Confederates' final line.[8]

Well after the Second Corps reconnoitered the center and eastern part of the salient, Wright selected Ricketts's division to perform a similar mission down the western side. Few details of this operation, which began at approximately 10:30 A.M., are known. The Yankees might have advanced as far as the reserve line of Confederate entrenchments north of the Harrison house before being recalled. They discovered an entrenched picket line of Confederates in front of a main line of works with artillery.[9]

To the wounded men lying inside the salient, these Federal reconnaissance missions on 13 May appeared as instruments of either salvation or terror, depending on which uniform the stricken soldier wore. Edwin Emery, a color-bearer of the Seventeenth Maine Regiment of Birney's division, had advanced on the morning of the twelfth with a handful of comrades almost as far as the McCoull house, where they were driven back by Hoffman's Virginians. While retiring, Emery was struck in the thigh by a bullet. He managed to hand the color to a comrade before falling to the ground, but he lay in the woods south of the part of the works later occupied by McGowan's South Carolinians. A short time after he fell, a line of Southerners passed over him and soon passed him again on the way to the rear. Later a stray bullet struck Emery in the neck. He lay for the rest of the day and through the night with bullets and artillery shells striking near him from both directions. He and another wounded comrade lay on their backs and attempted to catch falling drops of rain on their lips. Finally, sometime after first light a line of Yankee skirmishers approached and called for the two wounded infantrymen to come in. They both crawled to safety.[10]

J. W. Bone, a member of the Thirtieth North Carolina of Ramseur's brigade, had an even more harrowing ordeal. During his brigade's counterattack across the McCoull field, Bone was struck by a bullet that entered his body at the right breast, passed through his lung, went out near his backbone, and lodged in some clothing that he was packing on his back. He kept the bullet long after the war. As he lay and listened to the fierce sounds made by the members of his brigade fighting their way across two lines of works, he became sick, with shortness of breath and increasing pain. As the fury of the fighting along the works increased, he decided to try to get to the rear and safety. He stood up and stumbled a short distance before he sank weakly to the ground. Shortly thereafter, a stray bullet struck him. After resting for a few minutes, he tried again but was soon forced to stop by exhaustion. Once again he started up a slight hill to get behind a large tree, but he was struck a third time. He managed to reach the tree, crawl behind it, and collapse while bullets and artillery shells struck all around him. Later, he again tried to move farther to the rear but had to give up. He lay there for the rest of the day, and, as darkness approached, he unrolled his blanket and spread it around him as best he could. He dozed intermittently throughout the night. Any Confederates who noticed him as they fell back to their new line probably assumed that he was dead. In the morning he awoke to see Ricketts's skirmish line approaching his position. The Yankees halted in line about a hundred yards from where he lay and opened fire at the Confederate line behind him. He lay in this exposed position all through the day and night of the thirteenth. Just before dawn of the fourteenth he stumbled and crawled with the aid of a stick farther to the rear. After collapsing again from exhaustion, Bone managed to wave a white handkerchief, and finally some Confederate pickets came out to where he lay and dragged him into the safety of their position. One wonders what men such as Bone and Emery must have felt years later when they read in accounts of the battle statements such as "nothing of significance occurred on the thirteenth of May."[11]

Before the results of these reconnaissances were known, Grant informed Meade at 8:40 A.M. that he believed that any Confederates who were encountered in a defensive position were merely the covering force for the withdrawal of Lee's army from the Spotsylvania area. He suspected that Lee was moving out and did not want the Southern force to get away undetected. He ordered Meade to push forward at least three divisions to ascertain whether the Confederate army was still in front in force. Meade issued the necessary orders to Hancock, Wright, and Warren at 9:30 A.M.[12]

These orders were not followed explicitly, but from information received in the late morning and early afternoon, Grant and Meade were able to guess the location of the new Confederate line fairly accurately. When the corps commanders appeared unsure as to how far the feeling operations should be pushed, Meade and Grant informed them that it was not the intent to bring on a battle against the Confederates in their new position but merely to discover the precise location and strength of that position. On an endorsement to one of these explanatory messages, Grant stated his belief that it was necessary to "get by the right flank of the enemy for the next fight." At 4:35 P.M. Meade ordered Warren and Wright to prepare their commands for movement after dark and to report to army headquarters for instruction.[13]

Allegheny Johnson's Division Reduced to Two Brigades

In special orders dated 14 May, Lee announced his decision to consolidate the survivors of the Stonewall Brigade, Witcher's brigade, and the three Virginia regiments of Steuart's brigade into a single brigade of Virginia regiments, which, until further notice, would be assigned to Gordon's division. The newly formed unit was to be commanded by the surviving ranking officer in the fourteen regiments. His identity was apparently still not known on the fourteenth. The ten Louisiana regiments were to be reunited again as a brigade and also to be assigned to Gordon's command. Thus, Gordon, whom Lee recommended for promotion to major general for his services in the Wilderness on 6 May and in the salient on 12 May, assumed command of five brigades.

This arrangement was to remain in effect until A. P. Hill's health improved enough for him to resume command of the Third Corps. At that time Early was to return to his division in the Second Corps. When this occurred, on 21 May, Early's two brigades, Hoffman's and R. D. Johnston's, reverted to his direction. Gordon then retained command of Evans's brigade, the consolidated brigade of Virginia regiments, and the Louisiana brigade. Meantime, the First and Third North Carolina regiments of Steuart's brigade were transferred temporarily to Ramseur's brigade.[14]

This juggling of brigades that had been imposed upon Lee by the events of 12 May overshadowed another sinister development—the serious losses in infantry regimental colonels and lieutenant colonels within the army. Since the opening of the campaign on 5 May, the number of these casualties had grown to at least seventy, with thirty of them being fatalities. These officers had molded the characters of their units and were the superior officers whom the infantrymen obeyed instinctively in desperate combat situations. Their replacements would need time to justify their promotions and gain the confidence of their men. Much of this initiation would have to be accomplished while under fire.[15]

Also at this time Lee was obliged to choose either Fitz Lee or Wade Hampton to be successor to Stuart as commander of the Cavalry Corps. For the time being he directed that the three division commanders of horsemen report to him separately.

Federal Recommendations for Promotion and Demotion

In a message to Meade dated 12 May Stanton extended the gratitude of the War Department to the army commander and his troops for their achievements to date in the campaign. Mentioning the Federal casualties among officers, the secretary requested that Meade forward the names of officers whom he desired to be appointed to the rank of brigadier general of Volunteers. Meade asked his three corps commanders for recommendations and received the names of Carroll, McCandless, and Upton. In his request to Warren, Meade suggested without much subtlety that the Fifth Corps's nominee be from Meade's old command, the Pennsylvania Reserves. In addition, he requested immediate promotion of Wright and Gibbon to the rank of major general of Volunteers and asked that Wright be assigned permanently as commander of the Sixth Corps. He also urged the speedy confirmation of Humphreys's previously submitted nomination to the rank of major general.[16]

Similarly, Grant asked Burnside to recommend an officer for promotion. Burnside suggested Col. Simon G. Griffin, who was commanding Potter's Second Brigade. The general in chief approved Meade's requests, added Hancock's name for promotion to brigadier general in the Regular Army, and forwarded all the names to Washington. In addition, he asked that Meade be promoted to the rank of major general in the Regular Army. Grant reported that Meade had more than met his expectations and that Meade and Sherman were the most qualified officers for large commands that he had encountered. He earnestly requested that Sherman be promoted simultaneously with Meade, saying that he did not wish to see one of these officers promoted at that time without the other.[17]

Some of Grant's military family did not share their commander's views of Meade's attributes. During the day, these staff officers apparently complained of, or at least questioned, the necessity of Meade's position with the Army of the Potomac. They claimed that, since Grant had to pass orders through Meade to corps commanders, there was the danger that the spirit and force of the orders could be altered by Meade's or Humphreys's choice of words. They also complained that Meade's position as army commander was false, because he was given little operational responsibility beyond implementing Grant's tactical decisions. If he failed, responsibility for the failure would not be attributed to him, and if he succeeded, he would not receive ample credit for his efforts. Moreover, his violent temper made him difficult to deal with.

Grant listened to his subordinate officers and then explained that, while he was well aware that embarrassments had arisen from the present organization, he would not change it. He was responsible for all of the armies of the United States and could not afford to become bogged down in the myriad duties of an army commander. Furthermore, Meade was very capable and perfectly subordinate. Finally, Grant stated that he would always award to Meade full credit for his accomplishments.[18]

While Grant recognized the services of Meade and other officers, he and Meade also dealt with subordinates who were not measuring up. Nowhere was this greater than in the Federal Second Corps. For all the laurels that it had won for its temporary success and its captures on the morning of the twelfth, Hancock was experiencing difficulties with a few of his officers. Colonel Frank had been relieved and placed under arrest for drunkenness on the tenth.[19] Barlow issued orders assigning Colonel Beaver to the command of his Third Brigade and directed Beaver to report to division headquarters. Beaver, who felt a sense of parental responsibility for every man in his regiment, reported to Barlow as ordered but requested permission to decline the advancement, claiming that he could do more with his own regiment than he could do with the brigade. This was the second or third time that he had refused, and Barlow asked sharply when Beaver would be willing to accept the command of a brigade. Beaver replied that, when attrition left him the ranking officer of the brigade in which his 148th Pennsylvania was assigned, he would accept command.[20]

On the twelfth, after Birney's troops had retired to the outside of the captured Confederate works, Brig. Gen. J. H. Hobart Ward, commanding the First Brigade, had been sent to the rear in arrest. Hancock had noticed him acting strangely and had discovered that he was drunk. Col. Thomas W. Egan of the Fortieth New York had assumed command of the brigade.[21]

In an even more substantial shift, which went beyond subordinates and affected structure, at 7:00 A.M. Hancock requested and received permission to consolidate his Third and Fourth divisions, the whole to be under Birney's command. Mott resumed command of his brigade (formerly McAllister's), which became the Third of the Third Division, and Brewster's brigade became the Fourth of that division. In his request, Hancock stated his belief that, if the Fourth Division continued alone, it would soon become useless because its commanders seemed incapable of controlling their troops.[22]

On a more positive note, the Federals could see two artillery pieces standing in the woods approximately four hundred yards to the south of the east angle. They had been recaptured on the morning of the twelfth by the troops of the Thirteenth Virginia as they drove Barlow's men back out of the salient. The Virginians had dragged the two pieces back to a run immediately northeast of the McCoull house. Later in the day a detail of Confederates was directed to retrieve these weapons but failed to do so. On the afternoon of the thirteenth, one hundred volunteers from Miles's brigade crept forward with ropes, under a covering artillery fire, and succeeded in dragging the pieces back into the Landrum field. The spokes of the wheels had been heavily damaged by musketry, and one of the carriages collapsed as it was being manhandled over the works. A number of splintered limbers and caissons were also captured at this time.[23]

Another Federal Night March

While the Yankees thus gathered their spoils and reassigned their officers, Grant planned new operations, which would test some of those officers and perhaps win new laurels. He decided that during the hours of darkness, the Fifth and Sixth corps should march to the left behind the Second and Ninth to positions at and beyond the Fredericksburg Road. At 4:00 A.M. Warren's troops were to attack down the road toward the village, and Wright's men, to

Warren's left, were to advance along the Massaponax Church Road to the same objective. Burnside was directed to support the Fifth Corps attack with infantry and artillery if so ordered. Hancock was to maintain a threatening attitude on his front and to be prepared to attack there immediately if ordered.[24]

The route of march for the infantry was to be by way of the Shelton house, the Landrum house, and then east to a ford on the Ni River. Next the troops were to move northeast toward the Harris house by a track cut through the woods. The final stretch would be to cross large open fields to the Fredericksburg Road, a little less than one mile from the Ni River. Warren was instructed that, if the Ni were unfordable east of Landrum's, his infantry should move down the right bank behind the Ninth Corps's position. The distance to be traveled was six to seven miles. Warren instructed Colonel Wainwright to have his guns on the Fredericksburg Road opposite the Beverley house by first light. The route for the artillery was to be northeast up the Gordon Road from Alsop's to army headquarters near the Armstrong house, from which a guide was to conduct the gunners the rest of the way.[25]

Grant believed that the Confederate force that held the right flank of the line south of the village was weak. This maneuver was an attempt to occupy that area. He expected the move to require Lee to react with Anderson's corps and to enable the Federals to engage some of the enemy in the open field. Grant was correct about the strength of the Confederates who were manning the right of their army's line. Only two to four infantry brigades and some of Rooney Lee's horsemen occupied this general area, although they were supported by numerous artillery pieces immediately north of the village. If Warren and Wright could bring their troops to the designated jump-off points and initiate their assaults en masse and on time, the prospects for Federal success appeared to be good.

These were large "ifs." Rain had been falling intermittently for more than forty-eight hours. Roads and paths that had been used to any extent were now quagmires of sticky mud. Moreover, the infantrymen who would be marching on these paths were approaching physical exhaustion. For nine straight days, they had been fighting, fortifying, or marching. Friday had proved no different. They had spent much of the daylight on the thirteenth digging new entrenchments or strengthening old ones. Now they were marching again. Guides with flaring, sputtering torches along the intended route of march would help the columns find their way.

At 8:10 P.M. Warren issued a circular directing his troops to move off immediately. Griffin's division led, followed by Cutler's, Crawford's, the Maryland brigade, the heavy artillery troops, and the artillery brigade, in that order. At 9:00 P.M. Warren issued another circular in which he explained the purpose of the move and described the terrain on which the assault would be executed: generally open country favorable for a rapid advance. He reported that the enemy's force in the target area was expected to be light and positioned in rifle pits. The ground would allow the enemy's use of artillery, but its effects would probably be slight in the poor visibility of early dawn. Hence, the imperative necessity for initiating the attack on time. Griffin's division was to lead the assault, supported closely by Cutler's, with Crawford following the Fourth Division.[26]

The lead brigade of Griffin's division did not step off until 10:00 P.M. At 11:45 P.M. Warren informed Meade that the rear of his Fifth Corps column had just begun to move. He apologized for the late start and hinted that there would be more delays during the march. Supplies from the Fifth Corps train park at Salem Church had been en route to the front on the thirteenth. Because of the relatively short notice given for the movement, there had not been time to unload and issue the needed supplies, and these wagons were now standing, many of them stuck in the mud, on the road from Alsop's east to army headquarters and beyond. Warren pinpointed the problem accurately when he closed this message with the promise to do his best, then added, "but very difficult things are being attempted on these night movements over such roads."[27]

Operations of 14 May

The exhausted troops straggled from the beginning of the march, despite the efforts of officers to prevent it. The Ni posed little problem, for it was only knee deep at the ford east of Landrum's. Beyond it many of the troops fell asleep in the mud during temporary halts and were left when their comrades moved on. At 1:15 A.M. Warren wrote Meade from Wright's headquarters, four hundred yards or so east-northeast of the Shelton house, that his three infantry divisions had passed that point, leaving the Maryland brigade and the artillery still to come. He reported that at that time he was departing to join the head of his column.[28]

Somewhere along his route, Warren came upon some members of the Thirteenth Massachusetts of Lyle's brigade. They were sitting out a delay when Warren and two or three aides approached. The foot soldiers roundly cursed the officers and refused to move out of the way. Warren apologized to his troops for the condition of affairs, identified himself, and explained that he must be permitted to go through. At this the soldiers quickly moved aside and permitted their commander to pass. Just before 3:00 A.M. Wright reported to Meade that the rear of Warren's column had just passed his headquarters and that it would be impossible for him to have his own troops in position to attack at 4:00 A.M.[29]

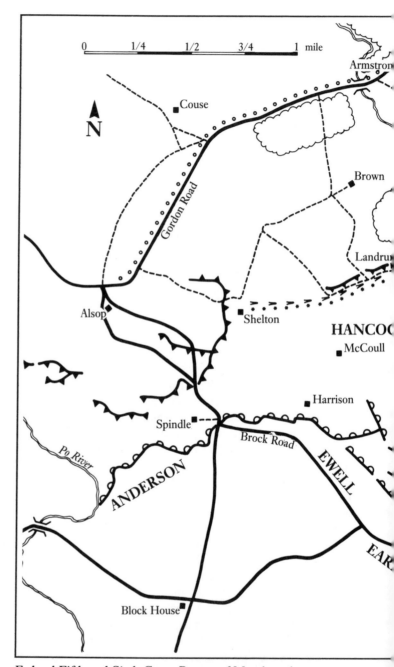

MAP 17-1. Federal Fifth and Sixth Corps Routes of March to the Fredericksburg Road on the Night of 13–14 May

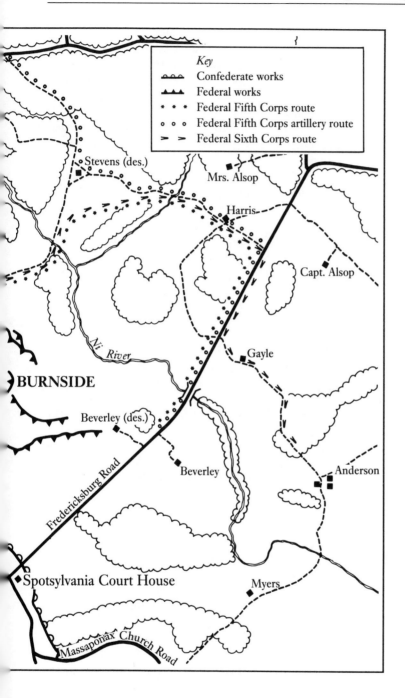

Major Roebling of Warren's staff rode ahead at about 2:00 A.M. to find Burnside and to attempt to locate the destination of march. After thirty minutes of searching he found Burnside and his chief of staff, Maj. Gen. John G. Parke. Neither of these officers could supply him with any useful information. They sent for Colonel Marshall, commanding Burnside's Provisional Brigade, and he conducted Roebling down the Fredericksburg Road, across the Ni, and past a column of Griffin's troops, to the point where the head of this column had halted opposite the Beverley house, about 1¼ miles from the courthouse. By then the time was 4:00 A.M., the hour at which the joint assault was to have been initiated. Only one thousand to twelve hundred of Griffin's exhausted infantrymen were in place.[30]

At this time Warren sent Meade a situation report that the troops who were on hand were too weary to be of immediate service. He reported that many of his men had become lost, despite the precautions taken, and that he must await their arrival before attempting any assault.[31]

Colonel Wainwright had another harrowing night. At 10:00 P.M. he started leading a column of 120 wheeled vehicles, including guns. He forced his way through the mass of supply wagons that jammed the road northeast from Alsop's and, in some cases, had his men push wagons onto their sides in order to clear a path. Arriving at the bridge over the Ni River about one-quarter mile west of the Armstrong house, he discovered an upset wagon in the middle of the span. The bridge timbers had given away, and the vehicle had fallen part way through the flooring. After this damage had been cleared, he led his closed-up column forward a short distance, then he encountered another traffic jam. He shunted the stalled vehicles to the side of the road and continued nearly to army headquarters at Armstrong's.

From there the road passed through a narrow defile in which it would be impossible to pass or to overturn wagons. His guide reported at army headquarters, and Wainwright sent him ahead with members of his staff to see whether the road could be cleared farther on. He himself rode ahead for nearly a mile, discovering an unbroken string of wagons, and he realized that his column would just have to wait until the supply column moved on. At headquarters everyone was asleep except Major Duane, who offered Wainwright a welcome drink. Wainwright paced back and forth in the rain as he watched the supply wagons crawl along.

At approximately 1:30 A.M. the guide told Wainwright that he had found someone who could lead the column by a shortcut through the woods. Wainwright immediately accepted the offer of assistance. The ensuing march was a nerve-wracking movement, conducted single file over narrow paths in the darkness, rain, and accumulating ground fog. Wainwright followed the guide, who rode a white horse. Each lead driver kept his horse's nose pressed close to the back of the vehicle ahead. The rear of the column emerged onto open ground at first light. A relieved Wainwright galloped ahead and struck the Fredericksburg Road near Burnside's headquarters. When he reached the Ni River bridge, he noticed that the head of Cutler's division had just arrived there.[32]

At 6:30 A.M. Warren informed Meade that the prospects for a successful assault appeared to be remote because of the physical condition of the troops. Warren suggested that perhaps his assault should be called off. Meade told him to make dispositions for his attack and to report when his forces were all in place. At 7:30 A.M. Warren reported that approximately twenty-five hundred troops were present from Griffin's division and about thirteen hundred from Cutler's. All of his artillery had arrived, but Crawford's infantrymen and Kitching's heavy artillery troops had not yet appeared. At this time, Warren also reported that Griffin was sending out a small force to occupy a hill, a mile or so southeast of the Beverley house, that commanded the Federal position there and appeared to be occupied by a small force of Confederates with artillery.[33]

Operations on the Myers Farm

A house stood on this hill, which was a part of the Myers farm.[34] The Confederates there consisted of a picket force from Chambliss's cavalry brigade and William M. McGregor's battery. They had been picketing the area south of the village since 10 May. On the night of the twelfth, the entire brigade had reconnoitered toward Fredericksburg on the Telegraph Road to see whether the Federals were moving in that direction. On the thirteenth, the artillerymen had been engaged off and on throughout the day and three men had been killed. Now, on the morning of the fourteenth, the battery was still in position near the Myers house, supported by some dismounted troopers. The rest of the brigade was stationed more than half a mile southwest.[35]

Griffin directed Ayres to send a force from his brigade to occupy the hill. Ayres selected the 140th New York and Ninety-first Pennsylvania regiments. Lt. Col. Ewell S. Otis of the 140th commanded the force, which numbered three hundred to four hundred infantrymen. As they moved out, Wainwright placed Cooper's and Breck's batteries, twelve guns, in position near the Beverley house.[36] These Federal guns soon fired on the Myers house, and McGregor's battery responded. When the Southerners spotted the advancing Yankees, they sent a courier with the news to the rest of Chambliss's troops, along the Massaponax Church Road. A member of the Ninth Virginia recalled that the brigade bugler sounded "To Horse" and that soon the troopers were galloping forward. They entered a wood about half a mile from the action and dismounted. After a short delay there, they double-timed forward along a woods road and entered an open field approximately 250 yards from the Myers house. Some Yankee infantrymen in this field immediately opened fire, but the Southerners formed a line of battle and charged. When they had advanced to within one hundred yards of some small outbuildings, they were subjected to severe musketry and the fire from Cooper's and Breck's guns. At this point, they wavered momentarily but then dashed forward to the outbuildings, only about forty yards from the main house. Colonel Otis's Federals had already arrived near the house and were occupying an adjacent orchard. Soon the heavier firepower of the Federal infantry and artillery began to take effect, and the Confederates were forced to retire, leaving their dead and severely wounded comrades on the field.[37]

In addition to being a good defensive position, the Myers farm provided the Yankees with an excellent view of the country to the west, toward the Confederate position, including their line south from the village. Meade determined to hold this point. He ordered Wright, whose column had arrived at the Fredericksburg Road at 9:00 A.M. or so, to send a force to occupy the newly captured position.[38]

Wright's troops had not begun their march until 3:00 A.M. because Warren's men were passing. Wright probably followed the route taken by Warren as far as the Fredericksburg Road. From there, instead of following Warren's troops down that road and across the Ni River bridge, his men entered a road to the left that passed the Gayle house. After nearly a mile, the head of the column arrived at a group of deserted buildings known as the Anderson plantation, which included a relatively large main house. The farm was north of the Ni, just under a mile east of the Beverley house and five-eighths of a mile north of the Myers house, which it overlooked. Upton's brigade had led the corps's order of march, and, upon arrival at the Anderson farm, was ordered to occupy the hill where the Myers house stood, south of the Ni.[39]

Upton led his four regiments, by now reduced to fewer than eight hundred infantrymen, down the slope to the Ni River, across the stream, and up the opposite bank to the Myers house. There he discovered Ayres's two regiments, whom he relieved. Before departing, Colonel Otis probably briefed Upton about the approximate location of Warren's left flank near the Beverley house. Upton understood that he was to establish a picket line extending from Myers hill to the Fifth Corps's left. He sent a dispatch to Wright stating that, if Myers hill was to be held, another brigade was necessary. Apparently all that could be spared were the Second and Tenth New Jersey regiments from Brown's First Brigade. Upton posted a lookout with a field glass on the roof of the main house, who reported Confederate cavalry watching the Federals from the southern end of the field. The Yankees threw up a breastwork of fence rails in front of the house and near the outbuildings.[40]

At 9:00 A.M. Meade informed Warren that the planned attack was suspended for the day. He told Warren to conceal the main body of his troops as much as possible but to send out skirmishers to learn the position and strength of the enemy in front. He also advised that Hancock had been directed to withdraw the Fifth and Sixth Corps's pickets remaining on the right and to send them around to the left of the army to rejoin their commands.[41]

From daylight Meade spent the morning of the fourteenth at the Gayle house. Sometime after midday he and Wright rode forward to the Myers hill to examine the position there. At about 4:00 P.M., the lookout on the Myers house roof spotted Confederate infantry skirmishers advancing across a hill about eight hundred yards southwest. Upton sent forward his Ninety-sixth Pennsylvania and two companies of the Second New Jersey to occupy the woods in that direction. Lt. Col. William H. Lessig, who was commanding the detachment, entered the edge of the wood and found two Confederate infantry brigades that were forming for an advance. Lessig hurriedly withdrew his troops across the field and informed Upton, who sent forward the Ninety-fifth Pennsylvania and Tenth New Jersey to the breastwork near the house.

The Southerners were Ambrose R. Wright's Georgia brigade and probably Harris's Mississippi brigade, which Early and Mahone had sent to discover what the Federals were up to. The Georgians advanced thirty yards or so out into the field, halted, and opened fire on the Yankees. Soon, Harris's troops joined them on their left. Suddenly both brigades yelled loudly and charged the Federal breastworks. Simultaneously, some of Chambliss's cavalrymen and McGregor's battery appeared opposite the left of Upton's line and opened a punishing flank fire. Upton's command fired a round or two and then broke for the rear down the slope to the river. They crossed the stream and climbed up the opposite slope to the vicinity of the Anderson buildings.

Meade had a close call. He was near the left end of the picket line when the Confederates who were advancing through the trees drove back the Federal skirmishers. He was temporarily cut off. Captain Michler, who was accompanying Meade at the time, knew of a ford across the Ni farther downstream where the Federal officers hurriedly crossed and escaped capture. Losses on each side totalled approximately one hundred, including Lt. Col. Charles Wiebecke, commander of the Second New Jersey, who was killed.[42]

Meade determined to retake the Myers farm immediately and ordered Wright to do so, using his entire infantry force if necessary. He ordered Warren to cooperate in the operation if requested by Wright. Wright formed Russell's division on his right front with Ricketts's on its left and Neill's in reserve behind Ricketts at the Anderson buildings. Ayres's Fifth Corps brigade was to retrace its route of the morning and to strike the Confederate position from the northwest. The twelve pieces of Capt. William A. Harn's and Capt. Richard Waterman's batteries were positioned near the Anderson house, where they fired on the target across the river just after 6:30 P.M. Harn fired 100 rounds, and Waterman 127.

At 7:00 P.M. Meade asked Warren what all of the cannonading meant. His subordinate, who had a good view of the Myers hill, informed him that the firing was from Wright's guns and that it might as well be halted because the Confederates appeared to have left the area. Warren then passed this information to Wright and stated that Ayres's troops would advance as soon as the guns ceased firing. The firing was halted and Russell's, Ricketts's, and Ayres's men moved forward. Ayres's troops arrived first and discovered that the Confederates had, in fact, departed. The Sixth Corps troops were delayed because they had to ford the river, which in some spots was waist deep. The members of the Sixth Maryland Regiment ruined all of their ammunition and most of their rations in the water. They eventually reached Myers hill, however, where they relieved Ayres's men.

Wright reported to Meade that his troops held the position and expressed his fear that the Confederates might have retired to the east, where they could threaten his left flank. He suggested that his men be permitted to withdraw north of the Ni. Meade ordered Wright to remain where he was, however, to have his men entrench, and to open roads to his rear and toward Warren's position. As this work was begun, another Confederate reconnaissance confirmed that the Yankees were indeed moving into position in force southeast of the Fredericksburg Road.[43]

Hancock on the Right

At 9:30 A.M. on the fourteenth, Hancock was ordered to relieve the pickets of the Fifth and Sixth corps, who were now located beyond the right flank of the army, and to send them to their parent commands. He was also enjoined to look to his right flank, which was now the right of the entire Union force. Col. James L. Bates, who was in command of these Fifth Corps pickets, received orders at 11:00 A.M. to withdraw, whereupon he proceeded to the right of the picket line and initiated the process of extraction.[44]

From west of the Brock Road, Charles Field's pickets advanced at about 3:00 P.M. and discovered that all of the Yankees were gone from their front. With some of Kershaw's pickets, they followed the retiring Federals and skirmished lightly with them. During the morning Edgell's Federal Second Corps battery, supported by the Third Battalion of the Fourth New York Heavy Artillery, had been maintaining an intermittent diversionary fire upon Field's division from a hill southwest of the Shelton house. The Federal artillerymen retired at 3:00 P.M. to the vicinity of the Landrum house.[45]

At 6:15 P.M. Hancock informed Meade that Confederate pickets were engaging his skirmishers along a creek approximately half a mile north of the Shelton house. He retained the Fifth and Sixth corps pickets for possible use and sent the men of the Fourth New York Heavy Artillery north with orders to construct works hurriedly along the path leading southwest from the Brown house. He also sent Crocker's brigade from Birney's division to help construct and occupy these works. In addition, he posted four batteries behind the works facing to the northwest. Hancock reported that Confederate cavalrymen had been spotted to the rear of the enemy's infantry skirmishers.[46]

Tom Rosser Visits a Hospital

When Wade Hampton learned that the Federals opposite the Confederate left had disappeared, he ordered Rosser to reconnoiter to the northeast and to attempt to locate the new right flank of the Union army. Rosser and his men crossed the Po River, probably at Tinder's Mill, rode north to the Brock Road, and then rode southeast until they arrived at the intersection northwest of Alsop's. There they took the Gordon Road northeast, over which Colonel Wainwright and his caravan had struggled on the previous evening. About a mile beyond the intersection, fields appeared on the left of the road. This cleared area was the property of the Couse family, whose main house stood one-quarter mile back from the road and had been the recent site of the Union Fifth and Second corps' hospitals.[47] These hospitals had been established on 9 May. When they received the order for the movement of the Fifth and Sixth corps for the night of the thirteenth, they made strenuous efforts to evacuate as many of the wounded as possible, since the area would be unprotected. All of the corps ambulances were tied up elsewhere, either picking up wounded from the field or making deliveries to Fredericksburg. Empty ammunition wagons and some quartermaster's vehicles were pressed into service, and all but 420 casualties from the Fifth Corps and 200 from the Second Corps were removed. Four medical officers and a number of medical attendants were left behind, with some medical supplies, tents, and three days' rations.[48]

When Rosser's troopers arrived on the fourteenth, they entered the Fifth Corps hospital area and removed approximately eighty Confederate wounded who were able to walk. They captured all of the medical attendants who were not displaying a medical badge on their uniforms. Rosser apparently received an oral promise from the commanding Federal medical officer that the wounded Yankees would be considered prisoners until exchanged. In a postwar report, Hampton complained that this promise was not honored. If not, one reason might have been that Rosser's men carried away most of the rations that had been left for the wounded. Katherine Couse said that the Southern horsemen spent their time there generally rummaging around and confiscating various items.[49]

The doctor in charge of the Second Corps hospital sent word to Hancock of the presence of Rosser's men, and Hancock sent the Twelfth New Jersey of Carroll's brigade to the scene. As they approached, the Confederates withdrew, after asking Federal medical personnel directions to the road to Fredericksburg. It was nearly dark when the Yankees arrived, and one of them, mistaking surgeon Thomas Jones of the Eighth Pennsylvania Reserves for a Confederate, shot and killed him. The infantrymen shared their rations with their wounded comrades.[50]

Meade Wants His Second Corps

At 8:40 P.M., in a message to Meade, Warren described the terrain within the triangle bounded by the Beverley house, the Myers house, and Spotsylvania Court House. He repeated Wright's assertion that the Confederates who had driven Upton's troops from Myers hill had approached on a road south of the village, and he stated that Confederates had been seen moving to the Union left. Meade passed this information to Grant and suggested that since he would like to unite the corps of his army, he be given permission to bring his Second Corps around to the left early in the morning. Grant acceded to this but stipulated that Hancock leave one division behind as support for Burnside's right flank until that flank was rendered properly secure by realignment. Birney's division of four brigades was selected for this assignment.[51] Movement orders trickled down from Second Corps headquarters during the night. Meanwhile, at Robert E. Lee's headquarters at Spotsylvania, other movement orders were being drawn up.

Lee Finally Reacts

At 3:30 P.M., R. H. Anderson informed General Lee that Warren's pickets and sharpshooters had withdrawn and that the enemy's main line of works opposite Laurel Hill was empty. Lee asked Ewell for information and learned that although the Federals still occupied the salient, their force was not known. Rooney Lee kept his father informed of the Federal buildup east of the Fredericksburg Road. Late in the afternoon, Anderson's chief of staff, Moxley Sorrel, directed E. P. Alexander to withdraw his artillery pieces from their forward positions in preparation for a possible move to the right. The movement order arrived after dark, and the men of Field's division trudged off through the mud to the Brock Road, where they turned southeast to the village. Their destination was to be near a church about a mile south of Spotsylvania. They arrived at the village an hour or so after midnight and waited for daylight before proceeding to their assigned position.[52]

Thus it appears that until 3:00 P.M. the Confederates were unaware of the fact that the Union Fifth and Sixth corps had abandoned their positions, a movement which had begun sixteen hours earlier. In retrospect Grant's plan for the day appears to have been sound. If, anytime during the morning hours, Meade had been able to mount a coordinated attack with Warren's and Wright's troops east of the Fredericksburg Road, he would have encountered little significant opposition. In what manner and with what forces Lee might have reacted to such an attack is a point of conjecture. It does not matter though, for Warren was correct: night marches conducted by weary troops over muddy roads were difficult undertakings, indeed.

Operations of 15 May

At 4:00 A.M. Gibbon's and Barlow's divisions of the Federal Second Corps, preceded by the corps artillery except for Birney's guns, took up the line of march for the Fredericksburg Road. The troops of Birney's division were expected to move left along the rifle pits as Gibbon's and Barlow's men departed. They were then to mass to the rear of Burnside's right flank and to remain until Burnside relieved them. At 5:30 A.M., in a response to a question from Birney, Hancock suggested that Birney, rather than follow the remainder of the Second Corps across the Ni River, should follow along the entrenchments around the east angle until he arrived behind Burnside's right flank. In addition, he should consult with Burnside as soon as possible.[53]

As Birney's troops prepared to sidle to their left along the entrenchments across the north face of the salient, Kershaw dispatched a strong reconnaissance party, accompanied by artillery, from the left of his position at the intersection of the Old Court House Road and the Brock Road. These Confederates moved north, passing the spot where John Sedgwick had been killed on 9 May. Along the way they picked up thirteen artillery caissons that had been abandoned by the Federals.[54] Their route is difficult to establish. Birney later informed Hancock that they followed his division as it moved to its left and that they fired on his retiring pickets, inflicting casualties. The pickets were Crocker's troops, northeast of the Shelton house, and Egan's, east and southeast of it. After waiting in mass in a wood east of the east angle, Mott's brigade moved forward at 10:00 A.M. into breastworks under a heavy fire from Confederate skirmishers. Mott moved because some Federal pickets had been driven in. These breastworks were probably the ones lying immediately to the northeast of the Landrum house.

The artillery that accompanied Kershaw's infantry was placed where its fire enfiladed Mott's line, causing two Federal regiments on the right of the line to retire in confusion between 11:30 A.M. and noon. Birney continued to withdraw his troops eastward across the Landrum farm. By 12:45 P.M., he told Hancock that he had established a solid line behind works from Burnside's right to the Landrum house. He had established picket lines between Landrum's and the river and between Landrum's and the Brown house. Two brigades were positioned to Burnside's right rear as a reserve.[55]

Thus, the Federal line now faced west and extended from the Landrum house south and southeast beyond Myers hill. Kershaw's reconnaissance party returned to its position immediately north of the Brock Road. In midafternoon Burnside, who was now in command of the right flank of the Federal line, notified Grant that an enemy force of unknown size was moving toward the Federal right.[56]

Rosser's Reconnaissance

At the Couse homestead, the Twelfth New Jersey Regiment departed before daylight under orders to rejoin its division as soon as possible. Mrs. Couse remembered that Rosser's men returned and were prowling around the hospital area after first light. After a time, they mounted and rode off to the northwest toward Piney Branch Church.[57]

The Federal Second Ohio Cavalry Regiment attached to General Ferrero's command was positioned in the vicinity of the church. Since the ninth of May, Ferrero had been attempting to monitor the rear of the army's position with detachments located at Todd's Tavern, the Furnaces, Dowdall's Tavern on the Orange Turnpike, Ely's Ford, United States Ford, Banks Ford, and the Orange Pike into Fredericksburg. In addition, he had maintained a mounted patrol six miles south from Fredericksburg on the Telegraph Road. To cover this vast area, he had the services of three cavalry regiments, the Fifth New York, Third New Jersey, and Second Ohio, and his own two brigades of untried black regiments of infantry.

On 13 May, Grant had given Ferrero permission to withdraw the outpost at Todd's Tavern to Piney Branch Church. The detachment at the tavern had retired to the vicinity of the church on the evening of 14 May. Later, when two other companies rejoined in the night from detached duty escorting ambulance trains to Belle Plain, the Ohio regiment was practically whole again. During the night the major portion of the regiment had camped on the Catharpin Road, east of the church, on a hill that overlooked a ford across a small stream to the west. One company had been on picket west of the church in the direction of Todd's Tavern.[58]

During the morning of the fourteenth, three troopers from the Ohio regiment had been dispatched separately to the field hospital at Couse's to check the condition of the wounded there. The first of these had been conversing with a doctor when Rosser's men appeared. The Federal cavalry-man had barely escaped capture, and, after eluding some pursuers, he had arrived by a roundabout route back at his unit, where he had reported to the regimental commander. His two comrades had been captured on their way south to Couse's.[59]

Rosser's men approached the intersection west of Piney Branch Church at about midday on the fifteenth. Most of Ferrero's men in camp to the east were sleeping, but a few were eating or cleaning weapons. Their horses were unsaddled. Suddenly, a shot rang out a short distance down the creek from the ford across the Catharpin Road. The drowsy Federals were puzzled because there had been no sign of enemy activity in the area for days. A minute later three or four more shots rang out, followed by the terrifying Rebel yell. The camp was in pandemonium.

Officers shouted conflicting instructions. One Federal company in camp was already mounted, having been scheduled to relieve the picket company west of the church. These horsemen dashed down the hill to the ford and engaged the Virginians, who were approaching along the road from the west. A few dismounted Federals also ran down to assist at the ford. The rest attempted to saddle the remaining horses. The picket company was attacked at this time but managed to escape by retreating around the northwest flank of the engagement occurring along the Catharpin Road. Most of Rosser's men fought dismounted. After a few minutes a large group of Virginians moved off the road to their right. They crossed the creek below the view of the combatants up near the road. Moving upstream they soon opened a flanking fire on the Yankees who were fighting at the ford, and the Yankees began to fall back. Some of the Confederates south of the road then moved up to it, and the remaining Yankees were forced to swing northwest of the road as they departed to avoid capture.[60]

Immediately after the attack began, Maj. A. Bayard Nettleton, who was in temporary command of the Ohio regiment, dispatched a warning to Ferrero at Chancellorsville that he would probably be forced north to the Orange Plank Road and requested assistance. The outnumbered Yankee cavalry fought a retiring action up the Catharpin Road against the pursuing dis-mounted Confederates. After passing a sharp bend in the road, three or four Federals would turn their horses around and when the Virginians appeared around the bend, the Yankees would rapidly empty their carbines at them before riding on.[61]

When the Federals arrived at the plank road near Alrich's, they took a position immediately to the east of the Catharpin Road, in a large field with the plank road at their rear. Rosser's men halted in the edge of the trees on the opposite side of the field about 350 yards from the Yankees and opened fire. The Federals replied to this fire, but Nettleton realized the disadvantages of being in the open and soon moved his troopers north across the plank road, behind a low ridge. The Confederates were now obliged to advance into the field to get within firing range. This they declined to do.

The beleaguered Federals realized the importance of holding this position on the Orange Plank Road and prepared for some severe fighting. Suddenly, they spotted a small group of Federal horsemen rapidly approaching along the road from Chancellorsville. One of the riders carried the flag of the Fourth Division, Ninth Corps. The group was General Ferrero and his staff.

A regiment of infantry followed the horsemen, marching at the double-quick with fixed bayonets. At the sight of the foot soldiers, the Ohio troopers cheered loudly. The infantrymen they greeted were members of the Twenty-third Regiment, United States Colored Troops, and they were the first blacks to participate in a directed combat action in the Northern Virginia theater of operations.

The infantrymen halted opposite the field and faced south. They then advanced across the field in a pouring rain. The dismounted Confederate horsemen skirmished briefly with them and then withdrew to their horses and rode back down the Catharpin Road.[62]

Thus, the first engagement of Federal black troops with a contingent of Lee's army could be considered a token success, even though it had not been much of a fight. The regiment had two men wounded. A section of Durell's Pennsylvania battery accompanied the Twenty-third Regiment but apparently did not fire a shot.[63]

Rosser had discovered that Yankee infantry was in the area. (Prisoners revealed that the force was the Ninth Corps.) He also learned that the Federal trains and cattle herds had been moved from the plank road toward Fredericksburg. He still wished to locate the right of the main Federal line. Arriving at the point where the Ni River crosses the Catharpin Road, he led his troopers down the stream.[64] They followed the Ni southeast to the vicinity of the Armstrong buildings. These had been Meade's headquarters from the twelfth through the early morning of the fourteenth of May, when Meade had relocated to a point near the Harris house, just off the Fredericksburg Road. Some of Rosser's stragglers swung back through the area of the Couse house and, according to the woman of the house, plundered the hospital camps yet again.[65]

At Armstrong's, Rosser sent a party up the road to the northeast in the general direction of the Orange Turnpike. With the main body of his brigade, he rode southeast on a road which the Federals had constructed on the night of 13 May. This nearly impassable thoroughfare led to the Stevens house and from there to the Fredericksburg Road near Harris's. Rosser's presence south of Armstrong's was reported to Burnside, who forwarded the information to Grant's headquarters at 2:40 P.M.[66]

Grant was concerned that the Confederates might be crossing the Ni north of Burnside's right flank in force. He directed Meade to alert Warren and Wright to be prepared to advance against the enemy should Burnside be assaulted. Meade issued the order to his two corps commanders at 3:30 P.M. At 4:40 P.M. Warren replied that he had just received the order. Ten minutes later, no doubt thinking of his troops' experiences on the Laurel Hill front, Warren asked Meade whether, if Confederates attacked the Ninth Corps, it would not be better for the Fifth to cross the Fredericksburg Road and reinforce Burnside against enemy troops who were in the open than to attack entrenchments directly in front. Warren was apparently unaware that Barlow's and Gibbon's divisions of the Second Corps were positioned behind Burnside. Meade's reply was somewhat curt: "Dispatch containing suggestions received. Your orders will be sent to you when Burnside is attacked. In the meantime they are unchanged."[67]

At Burnside's suggestion, Grant ordered Meade to dispatch a force to the Stevens house. Meade sent Gibbon's division. Before it could arrive, Rosser withdrew and returned to the Confederate lines. He reported the findings of his mission directly to Lee. These included the presence of Federal infantry along the Orange Plank Road and cavalry at Chancellorsville and at Zoan Church on the turnpike. He also reported that the right of the Union line was in the vicinity of the Brown house.[68]

Cavalry East of the Village

While Confederate cavalry probed the right of the Federal line, Union horsemen were engaged in similar activity beyond the Confederate right. At about noon Grant gave Meade his opinion that the next Federal attack should be made by Wright on the left of the line and that it should be supported by Hancock. Grant suggested that officers from Wright's and Hancock's staffs gather information concerning the approaches to the Confederate line from the front and left of the Sixth Corps's position.[69] In response, Meade sent the Fifth New York Cavalry to Wright at 1:00 P.M. with orders to investigate the roads and the terrain to his front and left. This regiment had been released from Ferrero's jurisdiction the previous evening and was now attached to the headquarters of the Army of the Potomac. The New Yorkers rode east to Massaponax Church on the Telegraph Road. From this point they drove a

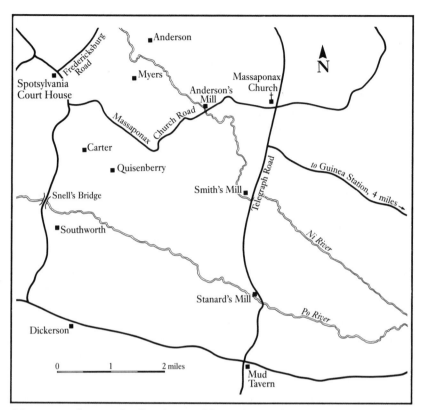

MAP 17-2. Area to the Southeast of Spotsylvania Court House

squad of Chambliss's troopers south across the Ni River at Smith's Mill. They established picket stations at Smith's Mill and along all of the roads leading from Massaponax Church. Wright informed Meade that he had extended his infantry pickets beyond Anderson's Mill as far as the church road. Under Burnside's command the Thirteenth Pennsylvania Cavalry Regiment was also operating on the Union left. Prior to the arrival of the New Yorkers, the Pennsylvanians reportedly drove a Confederate cavalry force south for one mile on the Telegraph Road. Their commanding officer reported that the Confederate horsemen were picketing the ford and that no enemy infantry was present north or south of the river.[70]

Remainder of Confederate First Corps
Is Moved to the Right of the Line

As the Federals constricted their line on the right and extended to their left, Lee's cavalry kept him informed. Rosser advised him that the right of the Federal line now rested near the Brown house and that Federal supply trains had been moved east toward Fredericksburg. In fact, the Artillery Reserve and its ammunition supply had also been moved to Fredericksburg. The facilities at Belle Plain, which was located seven miles to the east of Fredericksburg on the mouth of Potomac Creek, had become operational, and the Fredericksburg Road now became the main Union supply artery.[71]

The time Rosser's report arrived is not known. However, when Rooney Lee reported to his father that his pickets had been driven in at Smith's Mill at 2:30 P.M., Lee decided to move the remainder of his First Corps to the right of the line. He hoped for an opportunity to strike the Federals as they lengthened their line to the south. He warned Ewell, who was soon to command the left of the line, to be especially alert and asked him to attempt to discover whether the Federal rear was weak enough to warrant an attack.[72]

Meanwhile, the rest of Edward Johnson's force was brought up from the rear and reinserted in the line. One account claims that just six hundred men survived from an entire division. While in the rear, some members of the Twenty-first Virginia Regiment had camped in a field where they had discovered a rabbit's nest containing four little ones. The mother had been frightened away when the soldiers had entered the field. The hardened soldiers had vied with each other in their efforts to care for the baby animals. They had held oilcloths over the nest when it rained. Some had wanted to construct a house for the animals. When they moved to the front, they worried about the safety of their charges. Three days later these same men watched with intense satisfaction and cheered as the guns of their corps's artillery smashed the bodies of advancing Yankee infantrymen.[73]

R. H. Anderson received the order to move Corps headquarters and Kershaw's division to the right of the line at 10:00 P.M. The troops were under way by 11:00 P.M. and marched for three hours more through mud and water three to four inches deep. In the wet darkness they arrived approximately two miles south of Spotsylvania on the road to Snell's bridge and went into camp.[74]

18

The Army Is in the Best of Spirits

16–18 May

Federals Gain a Few and Lose a Few

The day of 16 May was to see little fighting. At 8:00 A.M. Grant sent the following message to General Halleck in Washington:

> We have had five days' almost constant rain without any prospect yet of its clearing up. The roads have now become so impassable that ambulances with wounded can no longer run between here and Fredericksburg. All offensive operations necessarily cease until we can have twenty-four hours of dry weather. The army is in the best of spirits and feel the greatest confidence in ultimate success. The promptness with which you have forwarded reenforcements will contribute greatly to diminishing our mortality list in insuring a complete victory. You can assure the President and Secretary of War that the elements alone have suspended hostilities and that it is in no manner due to weakness or exhaustion on our part.[1]

This interesting message requires some analysis. In truth, the major roads were literally mud filled. In the afternoon Meade reported that his medical director had informed him that there were six thousand wounded at Fredericksburg who could not be moved because of the condition of the roads to Belle Plain. Meade said general hospitals would have to be established unless the Rappahannock River could be opened to navigation as far as Fredericksburg. If the river were usable, the casualties could be evacuated to Washington by that route. Meade also suggested that should the Federal force be detained for any considerable time in the present location, it would be well to repair the railroad from Fredericksburg south to Hamilton's Crossing. According to the army's chief quartermaster, this task could take ten to twelve days. Meade closed by saying, "if the enemy dispute the passage of the Pamunkey or either of the Annas this road would be useful." This statement indicates that the two generals had already been discussing additional moves south toward Richmond.[2]

It would be enlightening to learn what Grant's criteria were in determining that the army was in the best of spirits at this time. When he was recognized, he was usually cheered by behind-the-line troops and occasionally by front-line troops who were serving on details to resupply ammunition or rations. The majority of the infantrymen who were doing the marching, fighting, and sleeping in the mud, however, had little to encourage high spirits. Their letters written during this period reflected an overwhelming sense of weariness. There were many references to the last time they had been able to get more than two hours or so of undisturbed sleep (usually the night of 2 May). They listed their casualties, and many, especially in the Fifth Corps, began to show a scornful distaste for what they described as reckless assaults in the open against prepared field fortifications. Warren's men blamed their high casualties on these unprofitable assaults.[3]

Lt. Col. Rufus R. Dawes, acting commander of the Sixth Wisconsin, mentioned in a letter to his wife the order of the evening of 15 May. That order alerted the Fifth and Sixth corps to charge the Confederate entrenchments opposite their positions in the event that the Ninth Corps were attacked. He explained that no attack was made and that, as a result, he and his comrades were spared another scene of horrible slaughter. Dawes reminded his spouse that his term of service would expire two months from that day and that he then would be able to leave forever his present occupation of killing and enduring hardships, having done his share for his country. This letter does not appear to reflect the feelings of a man who is "in the best of spirits" and who feels "the greatest confidence in ultimate success."[4]

Most of the reinforcements for which the commanding general thanked Halleck were still at Belle Plain. For the most part they consisted of regiments of heavy artillery troops who had been converted to infantrymen. As gunners they had been manning the maze of forts in Virginia and Maryland that surrounded the nation's capital. Now Grant had asked Lincoln for their services with the army and the President had acquiesced. This was a significant departure from previous administration policy, which insisted upon a strong defense around Washington. Lincoln apparently felt safer with Grant, in person, confronting Lee.

The first unit to join the Federal army had been the First Vermont Heavy Artillery Regiment, fifteen hundred strong, which arrived on the evening of 14 May. On the following day it reported to Lewis Grant's brigade of the Sixth Corps along with two companies of conscripts. This regiment and the heavy artillery regiments that followed usually drew a large crowd of spectators when they arrived at the front, because they were as large as or larger than the brigades to which they were assigned. On 15 May, the Second New

York Mounted Rifles (dismounted) arrived and were assigned to Colonel Marshall's Provisional Brigade of the Ninth Corps.[5]

On the evening of the sixteenth, the Irish Legion, which consisted of four New York regiments, the 155th, 164th, 170th, and 182d, and which was under the command of Col. Mathew Murphy, reported and the following day joined Gibbon's division of the Second Corps. The Honorable Charles A. Dana, assistant secretary of war, was traveling with Grant's headquarters and forwarding daily reports and observations directly to Secretary Stanton in Washington. He claimed that, when Murphy arrived, he reported sixteen hundred troops present and the rest drunk along the road. There were several other units, mostly heavy artillery regiments, accumulating at Belle Plain, and at 6:30 P.M. Grant wired their commander, Brig. Gen. Robert O. Tyler, to get them to the front by the following evening at the latest.[6]

That day Mr. Dana forwarded to the secretary of war field-return figures for the Federal force as of the morning of 13 May. These figures, which did not include those of the Cavalry Corps of the Army of the Potomac or any reinforcements, indicated that, in nine days of campaigning, Meade's army and Burnside's corps had sustained casualties numbering 36,872. Of these, slightly more than 10,700 were designated as missing. This category, which represented prisoners as well as unrecovered dead and wounded battle casualties, also included stragglers, shirkers, and deserters. In addition to casualties, the army was due to lose more of its members. The three-year terms of enlistment for some regiments were beginning to expire. On the morning of 12 May, those members of the Seventy-ninth New York of the Ninth Corps who chose not to reenlist were ordered to report to corps headquarters. They left the area of the armies on the following day as an escort for some of the Confederates captured at the salient.[7]

The Pennsylvania Reserves regiments were a special case. Before the opening of the campaign, there was disagreement as to the specific dates that began these regiments' terms of service. Threats of mutiny were reported until the issue was resolved in the troops' favor. On 4 May the Ninth Regiment had marched away from the opening campaign and headed for home. On 16 May, in response to a question from Warren, Meade said that Warren was authorized to muster out and discharge, effective 31 May, the officers and men of the Pennsylvania Reserves whose terms of service were about to expire. One condition was that those troops whose time was up before the thirty-first must agree to serve until that date. Warren made inquiries and reported back that the members of the Eighth Regiment, whose time had expired on the fifteenth, refused to accept the stipulation and that Crawford doubted whether the remaining troops would accept it either. Warren stated that there were only seventy-five men remaining in the Eighth Regiment, and he received permission to send these troops home.[8]

Finally, Grant's directive to Halleck to assure President Lincoln and Secretary Stanton that the temporary suspension of operations was due strictly to the elements, not to a lessening of his resolve or of the army's physical ability, indicated his intention to maintain pressure on Lee either in the vicinity of Spotsylvania Court House or elsewhere.

The rain continued to fall intermittently.

Confederate First Corps Assumes a New Position

At daylight on 16 May, the troops of Field's five brigades marched south on the road from the village and assumed their position as the right element of the Army of Northern Virginia. The right of the division line extended to the Po River approximately four hundred yards downstream from Snell's Bridge. The Southerners immediately threw up fieldworks. Kershaw's division arrived and remained in reserve to the west of the road. The area in front of the southern half of Field's line consisted of open fields extending to the east for more than a mile in places. Alexander arrived with the corps artillery, and he placed Haskell's entire battalion south of the river, where the gunners would have an enfilading fire on any Yankees who attempted to cross the field. Huger's battalion was positioned north of the river, and Cabell's was held in reserve.[9]

Federal Operations in the Afternoon

At 11:00 A.M. Warren and Wright received orders to advance skirmishers to feel the enemy in front and to determine whether the Confederates had changed their positions there. The order was rescinded at 1:40 P.M. because skirmishers were not needed. The Confederates were obviously still there. They were part of the Third Corps, whose line extended perhaps three-fourths of a mile south from the courthouse. Field's troops farther south were too far away to be spotted by the Yankees.[10]

Late in the afternoon, pickets from Bartlett's and Ayres's brigades, in conjunction with some Sixth Corps troops on their left, moved forward and occupied the spur of a ridge. Major Roebling and Brigadier General Hunt examined this position and convinced Meade that it offered a good position for artillery. After dark, details began to cut roads and to construct two small bridges to make the ridge more accessible from the rear. At 6:00 P.M. Warren was ordered to place batteries on the ridge and to support the position with at least one division of infantry.[11]

Meanwhile, the Federal cavalry beyond the Union left had been busy.

Lieutenant Colonel Hammond and a portion of his Fifth New York Regiment scouted to within two miles of Guinea Station on the railroad. One of his squadrons was also active on the Telegraph Road south from Smith's Mill on the Ni. They might have advanced as far as Stanard's Mill on the Po. Under prodding from Meade, Wright dispatched a body of horsemen west on the Massaponax Church Road from Anderson's Mill about 1½ miles. Their commander reported seeing only Confederate cavalry pickets and described the area they had scouted as being heavily wooded all of the way to the village.[12]

The area beyond the other Union flank also witnessed activity, as the Federal high command decided to retrieve the wounded men of the Fifth and Second corps still at Couse's. Gibbon's division was selected for the mission. Early in the afternoon it left the vicinity of the Stevens house accompanied by one section of Edgell's battery. Approximately two hundred ambulances and some corps headquarters wagons completed the cavalcade. The rescue party arrived and the process of loading began. The wounded soldiers were under fly tents in the yard and crammed into all of the outbuildings. While the loading went on, Mrs. Couse prepared tea for Gibbon and the members of his staff. The staff took tea, but the general would only sip hastily from a cup of coffee handed to him through a window of the house. Obviously he was nervous about the exposed position of his command. The loading was finally completed, and the caravan departed at dusk. The Federals left Mrs. Couse some sugar, coffee, and fresh milk, and the doctors promised to send her a calico dress for her kindness.[13]

After the last Yankee disappeared from view, Katherine Couse noticed that a solemn, deathly stillness hung over the area, the first such in many days: "It seems as if some great funeral procession had lately passed through."[14] She gazed around the grounds and viewed the waste which an army leaves in its wake. Debris of all kinds, especially clothing, was scattered in all directions. And the graves were everywhere.

During the day Burnside ordered Crittenden and Potter to advance heavy lines of skirmishers from their positions opposite to the eastern face of the salient to feel out the enemy. Potter reported that his men discovered a heavy concentration of enemy troops after having moved forward into the woods to the east of the Harrison house before retiring. Birney sent two sections of Lt. John W. Roder's battery to fire as a distraction during Burnside's reconnaissance. Roder's men fired fifty-eight rounds and returned to their camp after dark.[15]

Henry Jackson Hunt and the Artillery Reserve

On 11 May, Grant had advised Meade to send back to Belle Plain at his discretion all of the Artillery Reserve that was then with the army. Because there had been no opportunity to use these batteries to date, Grant thought them a useless encumbrance, which clogged the roads and wasted horseflesh and forage. Meade did not act upon the suggestion, and late on the afternoon of 16 May, he and Burnside each received the following message: "GEN - ERAL: You will send to Belle Plain early to-morrow morning all your Reserve Artillery and the ammunition belonging to it, trains, etc. by command of Lieutenant-General Grant."[16]

This order must have caused one of the lowest points in the wartime career of Brigadier General Hunt. He sadly entered in his journal: "So goes an organization which it has required nearly three years to bring to its present condition of efficiency. Let us now see what will come of it all."[17]

The Artillery Reserve of the Army of the Potomac consisted of twelve batteries totaling sixty-two pieces, their crews, and the ammunition supply, plus an additional special ammunition train. Hunt had secretly created this special train in 1863 and had been using it rather surreptitiously since then. There were also two large infantry regiments, the Sixth and Fifteenth New York Heavy Artillery, which were intended to escort and to guard the batteries. They had not seen the guns, however, since early on the morning of 6 May in the Wilderness, when they had been ordered to the front line rifle pits to shoot and be shot at. Since then, they had spent much of their time constructing or strengthening fieldworks for other troops to use.[18] On 15 May, their commander, Col. J. Howard Kitching, had written to army headquarters requesting either that his command be placed in a different position or that he be relieved of responsibility for it. He had listed his grievances. Since 6 May he and his troops had been assigned temporarily to and had fought with all three infantry corps of the army. These constant movements throughout the army made it impossible for him to get supply wagons or rations for his men. Twice his command had been engaged heavily with no ambulances or stretchers available for his wounded. He and his officers had nothing to eat except what they could obtain from their enlisted men. Kitching had closed by stating that he would never be able to provide for his troops until he was assigned permanently to some command, and he asked to be relieved in some way from his awkward position. Meade had asked for an explanation of this from the Artillery Reserve commander and had ordered supplies and ambulances to be forwarded to the Sixth and Fifteenth New York.[19]

On the sixteenth, Meade told Hunt that Grant wanted the entire wheeled portion of the Reserve detached from the army and sent to the rear. Hunt asked about the special ammunition train, and Meade told him to keep it. The gunner then began to look for some way of retaining as many of his experienced personnel as possible and of keeping adequate numbers of horses and a sufficient supply of ammunition. He prepared an alternate proposal to Grant's order that would fulfill its requirements to some extent.[20] Hunt recommended that all of the corps batteries and those of the Reserve be reduced from six pieces to four and that the surplus guns be sent to Belle Plain. The six caissons of each battery and their supply of ammunition would be retained to function as ammunition wagons, thus reducing the size of the army's trains. The batteries of the Reserve would be distributed among the three army corps, so that each corps's complement of guns would consist of twelve batteries, or forty-eight guns. The result would be that the Second Corps would lose six pieces of artillery while the Fifth and Sixth kept their original number.[21]

Hunt's alternate plan was approved and placed into effect on the following morning. Naturally, the worst horses were selected to pull the surplus guns and limbers to Belle Plain. Colonel Wainwright watched the sorry-looking cavalcade pull out at noon of the following day and wondered whether the teams would be able to make it to their destination.[22]

Hunt's plan, of course, applied only to the Army of the Potomac. In the Ninth Corps, Burnside dutifully sent all of his Artillery Reserve to the rear as ordered by Grant. Thus, the Federal force lost the services of six more field batteries and of Lt. Samuel N. Benjamin, whom Hunt considered one of the finest artillery officers in the service.[23]

Hunt had juggled his resources brilliantly in order to maintain what would be, in his opinion, an acceptable and adequately supplied field artillery force, but he always felt resentful for what he had been forced to do as a result of Grant's peremptory order. In 1883 he recorded his opinion that the decision to break up his Artillery Reserve organization was a stupid blunder.[24]

Operations of 17 May

On the seventeenth the rain subsided slightly, and the sun appeared intermittently during the morning, then shone for the rest of the day. The roads slowly began to dry. At 8:00 A.M. Meade instructed Hancock to prepare to move his command to the left of the Sixth Corps after dark in anticipation of the combined assault by the two corps at dawn. The decision to execute the attack was to depend upon the arrival of Tyler's division of heavy artillery regiments in the evening. Burnside was ordered to have his troops in readiness thirty minutes before the assault and to move by the left flank behind Warren in support of Wright and Hancock. Warren's troops were to remain in position and to support batteries that would be positioned during the night.[25]

Hancock's staff worked out the details for the move and issued a circular describing the order of march. Tyler's division, or as much of it as arrived on the field, was to follow Gibbon's troops. Hancock asked Burnside what time Birney's division could be spared from its position on the right of the Ninth Corps. Hancock stated that, while Birney's pickets were to remain in position until relieved by Ninth Corps authority, those of Gibbon's farther to the right across the Ni at the Stevens house were going to depart at dark. Second Corps headquarters would be relocated to a flat area immediately to the east of the Anderson house.[26]

Since the Fifth Corps would become the right element of the Federal line, Warren spent a busy day attempting to strengthen the position there. The right of Cutler's line north of the Fredericksburg Road was thrown back, so that the line extended to the Ni River. Cutler complained that it required his entire force to man this line, and that he was left with no reserve. At dark Griffin's division moved forward, occupied its former picket line, and immediately dug entrenchments approximately twelve hundred yards from the Confederate line opposite. Griffin's position was on the northern segment of the spur, which offered a good artillery position. Later, Crawford's men moved up on Griffin's left and entrenched. Wainwright managed to position three batteries on the spur between Griffin and Crawford before daylight.[27]

Cavalry Operations

The Federal cavalry was again busy beyond the left of the Union line. Wright sent a scouting party from the Thirteenth Pennsylvania Regiment back to Hamilton's Crossing south of Fredericksburg. The party commander advised that Southern cavalry were reported to have been in that area on the previous evening but had since departed. At 1:30 P.M. Meade sent Colonel Hammond twelve hundred cavalrymen from the dismounted camp. He ordered Hammond to attempt to drive the enemy's cavalry from the Telegraph Road and to destroy the supply depot at Guinea Station. Hammond declined to use the troopers from the dismounted camp but personally led two battalions of the Thirteenth Pennsylvania to within one mile of Guinea Station. There the Federals encountered a Confederate cavalry force estimated to be of brigade strength, and the Yankees withdrew. Meantime, two battalions of the Fifth New York proceeded across the Ni at Smith's Mill, skirmished south to the Po where they engaged a Southern force entrenched on the south bank, and eventually withdrew after sustaining approximately fifteen casualties.[28]

From the opposite end of the battle lines, Wade Hampton sent Cobb's Georgia Legion of cavalry on a reconnaissance north of the Rapidan. They had started out on the previous day but had been unable to cross the river, which was high due to the recent rains. This day they made it across at Raccoon Ford. A member of the Jeff Davis Legion visited Hampton's headquarters during the day and read a recent Richmond newspaper that contained extracts from Northern journals. One of these stated that Lincoln had proclaimed a day of thanksgiving for the Federal victories south of the Rapidan. The Mississippian had just ridden along the recent battle lines of Laurel Hill. He thought that, if the President could have seen the scores of dead Federals rotting in the sun and rain, he would not have proclaimed any victory.[29]

News from Other Fronts

During the morning of the seventeenth, Grant and Meade relocated their headquarters to the vicinity of the Anderson house, east of the Fredericksburg Road. Halleck had been forwarding progress reports from Sherman to Grant as they were received in Washington. They reflected satisfactory results to date. Nothing much had been heard from the other army commanders. That day, Grant asked Halleck whether Sigel, who was in the Valley, could advance to Staunton and destroy the railroad there. This would hamper the Confederates' efforts to supply their armies from that area. Late that night Halleck replied that Sigel had been defeated at New Market on 15 May and that he was in full retreat north. On 16 May, Butler had been defeated below Richmond and had withdrawn to Bermuda Hundred, where he was soon pinned down by a relatively small enemy force. On the sixteenth Grant had suggested to Halleck that Banks be immediately relieved from command of the Department of the Gulf because of incompetence and the resulting loss of morale of his soldiers.[30]

Thus it seems that the incompetence of political generals contributed significantly to the early failures of three of Grant's subsidiary operations against the military forces of the Confederacy. These setbacks did not lessen his resolve. Lee was naturally relieved by these Southern victories, which meant he could anticipate the receipt of reinforcements for his army from the Valley and from the vicinity of Richmond.[31]

Confederates Probe the Federal Right

Early in the morning of the seventeenth, Birney replaced Brewster's and Mott's brigades in the rifle pits on the right of the army's line with the brigades of Crocker and Egan. These entrenchments lay in a line from the east angle in a generally northeast direction beyond the Landrum house.

Late in the afternoon a picket force from Mott's brigade was sent back out to the right of the picket line. From there the Yankees could see the abandoned works lying to the southwest of the Brown house. Just before dark they noticed Confederates massing behind these works. Since their orders were not to fire unless attacked, they remained passive. Suddenly, the Southerners climbed over the works and advanced against Egan's pickets, driving them back to their main line. A force also approached Mott's troops, who retired. The Southerners advanced to within approximately two hundred yards of Egan's main line northeast of the Landrum house, where they skirmished briefly and then withdrew.[32]

These Confederates were from Rodes's division, who were succeeding in locating the right of the main Federal line. After dark the Yankees reestablished their picket lines. Birney ordered the Twentieth Indiana and Ninety-ninth Pennsylvania regiments from Egan's brigade to cross the Landrum clearing and to occupy a segment of the abandoned works lying to the southeast of the Shelton house. They accomplished this without encountering Rodes's retiring troops in the darkness.[33]

Federals Return to the Salient

Wright had employed scouts and staff officers to reconnoiter the area where the assault was planned for the following morning. In the afternoon they reported that the area was entirely unsuited for the passage of troops and so the intended attack there was cancelled.[34]

Wright and Humphreys had been discussing the possibility that Lee might have weakened the left of his line to the rear of the salient in order to counter the Federal buildup east of the Fredericksburg Road. Wright believed that if his command could attack the Confederate position there at first light, the prospects for success would be good. Humphreys agreed, and they suggested the plan to Meade and Grant, who accepted it and decided to use the Second Corps also. At 7:00 P.M. Meade directed Hancock to move his corps back to the vicinity of the Landrum house and to make arrangements for a vigorous assault on the enemy's works at 4:00 A.M. The Sixth Corps was to join the right of the Second and to advance with that corps.[35]

Grant informed Burnside of the change in plan and ordered him to be prepared to follow Hancock's and Wright's troops, should they succeed in penetrating the enemy's line. He was also to be prepared to assist Warren if he were attacked east of the Fredericksburg Road. The Fifth Corps's artillery would open fire at the scheduled time for the advance and enfilade the enemy's works on Burnside's front.[36]

Some, if not all, of Barlow's division had already moved to the left behind the Sixth Corps when the change of orders was received. Colonel Tidball had led all of the Second Corps batteries, except for the three with Birney, almost as far as Anderson's Mill. At 11:00 P.M. he headed back toward the right.[37]

Thus, after dark the infantrymen of the Federal Second Corps started back toward the area where they had fought on 12 May. This time they knew where they were going and the roads were passable. Gibbon's Second Division was joined by the Irish Legion. Col. Thomas A. Smyth and Col. H. Boyd McKeen reported to Gibbon and were assigned to the commands of Webb's and Carroll's brigades respectively. Tyler's five huge regiments of heavy artillery troops began to arrive from the direction of Fredericksburg and were marshalled in fields near the Harris house. With Murphy's Irish Legion, they would add approximately eight thousand muskets to Hancock's command.[38]

The segment of the Confederate line that Hancock and Wright were to attack was still manned by Ewell's infantry and artillery, who had had little to do since the thirteenth except increase the strength of their works. This they had done well. A member of Smith's battery remembered that information came that evening warning of a possible enemy attack early in the morning. Orders were issued for one-third of the troops to remain alert all night. The rest were to be aroused just before first light.[39]

Federal Assault of 18 May

Grant and Meade temporarily relocated their field headquarters for the attack to about one-quarter mile south of the Harris house. At 3:00 A.M. Hancock told Meade that his First and Second divisions were formed and that the Sixth Corps was passing to assume its position to the right of the Second. Barlow's and Gibbon's troops were marshalled in the Landrum field between the Landrum lane and the salient works, the area over which they had advanced in the fog six days earlier. Hancock also stated that he had just learned that Tyler's division was near the Harris house. Because it would require some time for the division to be placed in position, Hancock did not expect to get much service from these newly arrived troops during the attack.[40]

At 4:05 A.M. Hancock said that Wright so far had managed to position only one of his divisions because of difficulties of advancing his picket lines, but that another Sixth Corps division had just arrived in the area. Therefore, Hancock decided to delay the start of the attack for a short time. At 4:35 A.M., he reported that he had ordered the advance, even though one of Wright's divisions was not yet formed and Tyler's troops were not yet in place.[41]

Hancock formed his command in a two-division front with Barlow to the left of Gibbon. Barlow positioned his Second Brigade, now commanded by Col. Richard Byrnes, in the front line to the left of his Third Brigade, whose commander, Col. Hiram Brown, had been captured on 12 May. The Third was now under Col. Clinton D. McDougall. Miles's and Brooke's brigades formed a second line.[42]

To Barlow's right, Gibbon also formed his command in a two-brigade front, with Murphy's newly arrived Irish Legion on the left of McKeen's brigade. Smyth's and Owen's brigades constituted the second line. As they arrived, the men of Tyler's heavy artillery were positioned in the rifle pits that extended from the Landrum house southwesterly to the east angle of the salient. Birney's division remained in reserve just east of the Landrum house. The corps's batteries also were massed there to await developments.[43]

On the right of the Second Corps, Wright was able to position only one of his divisions, Neill's, in time for the advance. Neill formed his command in a column of brigades—Wheaton's, Edwards's, Bidwell's, and Grant's, from front to rear. Ricketts's division, which was to have participated, was not yet formed on Neill's right by 8:30 A.M. Russell's division remained in support behind the works that lay to the west of the west angle.[44]

To the left of the Federal Second Corps, Burnside selected Crittenden's and Potter's divisions to participate in the attack. The two batteries assigned to Willcox's division were sent to the right of the corps line to add their weight to the effort.[45]

The Confederate position that the troops of Hancock and Wright would attack was formidable. The line lay along a rise that descended north toward the attackers. The works had traverses every fifteen or twenty feet and in some cases were enclosed across the rear as well. Extensive abatis had been constructed out in front to distances of more than one hundred yards, especially along the eastern half of the line, which was in woods.[46]

In general, the troops of Rodes's division manned the Confederate left half of the line and Gordon's the right. The order of alignment by brigades from left to right, beginning on the left near the Old Court House Road, was Ramseur, Battle, Daniel, and Doles. Gordon's five brigades occupied the remainder of the line to the east. Portions of Wilcox's Third Corps division occupied the segment of the final line that paralleled the Brock Road and lay in the direction of the courthouse. Twenty-nine pieces of artillery were positioned along the line. Three pieces were in the trees on the left. At least seven were in the open on a rise to the left rear, directly behind the Harrison house. The remainder were in the trees along the right half of the line. Because of losses on the twelfth, there had been some patching of equipment and shifting of personnel among the Confederate Second Corps artillery, but they were ready.[47]

Action Begins

Fifth Corps batteries south of the Fredericksburg Road began the hostilities shortly after 4:00 A.M. Visibility was poor because of ground fog, and, as the Confederates did not respond, the Federal gunners ceased firing and waited until they heard the sounds of the infantry attack at the Landrum farm. When they heard this signal, the Yankee artillerymen began again. Wainwright had placed three batteries, including Taft's six twenty-pounders, just off the Fredericksburg Road within fourteen hundred yards of the village. Three more batteries stood on the spur south of the road between Griffin and Crawford. These twenty-six guns concentrated their fire on the Confederate works that lay just south of the village. They also enfiladed the enemy works north of the village opposite Cutler's division. The Confederate artillerymen began to answer this fire, and eventually they had twenty pieces duelling with the Yankees' twenty-six.[48]

Receiving the order to advance, the troops of Barlow's two lead brigades climbed over the works in the vicinity of the east angle and moved into the woods. To their right Murphy's and McKeen's men of Gibbon's division did likewise. The four brigades of the second line halted at the works to wait in support until ordered forward. Gibbon's right probably crossed the works near the fallen oak tree. Between that point and the west angle, Federal burial details had been active. They had used dirt to fill in the pits directly behind the forward walls in order to cover the dead Confederates. As the four brigades continued forward, McKeen's brigade, which was on the right, gradually emerged from the cover of the trees into the McCoull field, near the house. There they were spotted by Confederate gunners posted near the Harrison house, who fired on them and on the other advancing Yankee brigades as they appeared.[49] The Federals continued their advance and arrived at the former reserve line. Confederate pickets stationed there had retired as the Yankees approached. Gibbon now ordered his two support brigades forward. Murphy's and McKeen's commands received punishing artillery fire from their right front as they continued their advance. Two of Murphy's regiments became separated from the other two as a result of interference from one of Gibbon's staff officers. Murphy led his remaining two regiments forward through the trees for perhaps one-quarter mile to the edge of the abatis in front of the final Confederate line. McKeen's troops on the right had kept pace. Here the Yankees halted and lay down to try to protect themselves from the enfilading artillery fire. The time was now 5:30 A.M. Gibbon reported no connection with the Sixth Corps on his right.[50]

To the left of Gibbon's troops, Barlow's two lead brigades advanced to the edge of the abatis in their front, which, Barlow informed Hancock, was over one hundred yards in depth and the thickest that he had ever seen. He said

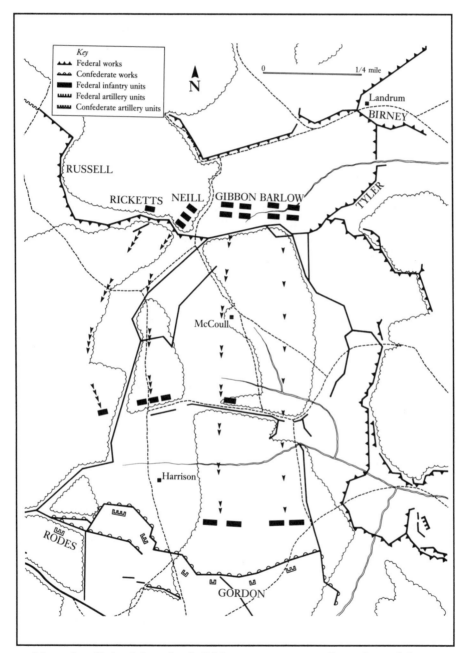

MAP 18-1. Federal Assault of 18 May, 4:30–9:00 A.M. Operations of the Federal Ninth Corps are not shown.

that he did not believe that his men could penetrate it. Many members of Byrnes's Irish Brigade tried and were struck while entangled in the tree limbs. The Northerners were receiving heavy canister fire from directly in front and from their left front. Barlow ordered his men to lie down while he awaited further orders.[51]

On the right of the attacking Federal line, only three brigades of the Sixth Corps became engaged. These were the commands of Wheaton, Edwards, and Bidwell, all of Neill's division. It is uncertain at what time Neill's troops began their advance. Wheaton's brigade led the movement forward along the works on the west face of the salient, with his two left regiments extending out into the McCoull field. Southern gunners concentrated their fire on these two clearly visible regiments. Because of this fire and the difficulty of maintaining a formation while marching along a line of works that had pits in the rear and abatis in front, Wheaton drew the left of his force in under the cover of the trees. The remaining operations of Neill's force are unclear, because of fragmentary and conflicting accounts by the participants.

Wheaton apparently halted his men in the edge of the trees at the abandoned reserve line approximately 220 yards north-northwest of the Harrison house. Oliver Edwards, whose brigade followed Wheaton's, claimed that the leading body of troops sidled to the right and that his own men continued straight ahead to within a few yards of the enemy position. There they lay behind a protective ridge, pinned down by heavy artillery fire, until they were ordered to retire. Edwards claimed that he was ably supported by Bidwell's brigade. Bidwell, for his part, reported that during the advance the right flank of Gibbon's line to the left gave way. Wheaton and Edwards then changed their direction of movement obliquely to the left. This brought Bidwell to the front line with no troops on his right, and as a result, his command suffered severely from artillery fire from front and flank.[52]

Whatever the relative alignment of these three Federal brigades, it appears certain that none of them came within two hundred yards of the Confederate works in their front. A member of Smith's battery remembered that the Southern infantrymen were ordered not to fire until the Yankees were within that distance of the line, and none of them fired. Some of Neill's men might have attempted to advance beyond the reserve line, but if they did, they could not have proceeded far before being struck or driven back by the canister. At 8:00 A.M. Smith's brigade of Ricketts's division reportedly moved up and assumed a position on Neill's right. It appears that they merely hugged the ground until ordered to withdraw.[53]

At 6:50 A.M. Hancock informed Meade that Gibbon's right and the left of the Sixth Corps had given way under a severe fire of canister. Gibbon was unable to reestablish the advanced position on his right. When he ordered his two support brigades forward, Owen, who was on the right, led his troops only a short distance before returning to the safety of the works. (See Chapter 17, note 6.) Smyth moved ahead obliquely through the trees to the right as far as the reserve line, from which his men could see the Harrison house.[54]

On Barlow's front, a portion of his division fell back because of a severe enfilading fire of canister from an enemy battery to the left. Barlow reestablished the troops in their forward position, which Hancock described to Meade as being "in the enemy's rifle pits close to the abatis and in plain sight of their main line."[55] At 8:30 A.M. Hancock informed headquarters that Barlow, after a close personal examination, deemed it impracticable to attempt to take the position in front because of the abatis and because of seven artillery pieces which were visible on his immediate front. Hancock added that, if nothing were going to be done for an appreciable period of time, he would like to withdraw Barlow's men from their exposed position. Upon receipt of this message Meade called off the operation. Wright also had advised against continuing the attack because of the impregnable Confederate position and because Ricketts had reported his inability to advance.[56]

On Burnside's front, portions of Potter's and Crittenden's divisions advanced against the line of works that lay to the right of the line manned by Gordon's division. The Yankees were opposed by troops from Cadmus Wilcox's Third Corps division, principally Thomas's and Scales's brigades. There were patches of thick ground fog on this part of the field, and in some cases, the Federals were able to approach fairly close to the Southern pickets before being seen. However, when the infantrymen and artillerymen in the main line of works saw them, Confederate fire brought the advance to a halt. After firing a few volleys, the Federals withdrew. Potter's troops apparently assumed a new position in advance of their former one, which, the division commander claimed, rendered segments of the Confederate line untenable. Burnside repeated this claim although its validity appears questionable. Burnside was notified that the operation had ceased at 9:00 A.M.[57]

Thus, the final planned Union attack of the battle resulted in complete failure. The advances of the troops from the Army of the Potomac had been halted and broken up by artillery fire alone. The medical director of the army reported that the injuries of the 522 wounded Federal infantrymen were severe in most cases, as most of them had been hit by shell and canister. In the afternoon some Southern artillerymen walked down to the positions where the Yankee formations had been struck by the missiles. The sights were gruesome; bodies had been blown apart or crushed into pulp. It had been a triumphant day for the Confederate Second Corps artillery. Ewell's infantrymen, who had watched the action with admiring, if critical, gaze, later crowded around the gunners, shaking their hands and affectionately patting the warm tubes of the guns.[58]

In round numbers, excluding Tyler's division, Meade had had available for the assault the services of twenty-two thousand troops from his Second and Sixth corps. It is doubtful whether half this number advanced beyond the salient works. Given the formidable nature of the Confederate position, however, it might not have mattered how many Yankees were used. Some of Hancock's batteries supported the attack, but the Confederate gunners paid no attention to their fire and concentrated their efforts against the Yankee infantry.[59]

One result of the attack was that the Federals learned that Lee had neither weakened nor abandoned his left flank in order to buttress his right. The idea for the operation had been Wright's and Humphreys's, and Grant had apparently approved the plan as being worth a try while the army waited for the roads to dry. Now that the attempt had failed, Grant began preparations for his next operation, which he had apparently been considering for a number of days.

Grant's Plan to Move Farther South

On the afternoon of 18 May, Tyler's division of heavy artillery regiments, followed by the Sixth Corps, was sent back to the area of the Anderson house east of the Fredericksburg Road. Burnside's and Hancock's corps remained in position, with Hancock manning the works along the north face of the salient and Birney's division occupying the line west from the west angle nearly to the Shelton house. Grant informed Meade that, after dark, he intended to move the Second and Ninth corps back to the left and to position the Ninth to the left of the Sixth. These two corps were to advance, to establish themselves as close up to the enemy's position as possible, and to entrench. They were to avoid a general engagement unless the Confederates came out of their works to fight.[60]

Hancock was to post his Second Corps to the rear as if in support of the Sixth and Ninth. On the following night, however, he was to move his command as far as possible down the railroad toward Richmond and to fight any enemy force encountered. Some cavalry were to be sent with him. If Lee pursued Hancock with a sizeable portion of his army, the three remaining Union corps would follow and attempt to engage the Confederates before they had time to entrench.[61] If Lee did not follow Hancock, the rest of the Union army would move south toward Richmond, and force Lee into the open.[62]

In the evening, Burnside once more became apprehensive about the security of his right flank. Birney's division was again posted in the pits south from the Landrum house until the Ninth Corps had departed.[63]

Meade sent Warren word of the proposed movements of the other corps to his left flank and advised him to move all of his trains to the east side of the Fredericksburg Road. Meade also suggested that Warren send a brigade to the vicinity of the Harris house to watch for any Confederates who might follow, so Warren ordered Colonel Kitching to have his two regiments of heavy artillery troops at the Harris house by daylight.[64]

There had been a considerable amount of straggling by the Federal forces in the campaign. Gibbon sent a note to headquarters that called attention to this and suggested that these stragglers be collected by patrols and that one out of every one hundred be shot. This suggestion was not adopted. On 17 May, however, Meade issued a special order directing corps and division commanders to bring to immediate trial these deserters from the field and to forward to headquarters the action of the courts, so that punishment could be inflicted where warranted. While waiting for the arrival of darkness, Barlow convened a Field Court Martial and appointed Miles's aide-de-camp, Lieutenant Robertson, as Judge Advocate. Hancock's gunners were still duelling with Confederate artillerymen, and the court conducted its proceedings to the sounds of exploding shells. As the members of the court were all staff officers, interruptions in the proceedings occurred when someone was ordered to deliver a message or perform some other assignment. The court adjourned at dark, when the firing ceased.[65]

That day, in compliance with instructions from Grant, Ferrero moved his Ninth Corps division east from near Chancellorsville to Salem Church on the Orange Turnpike. There had been reports during the preceding two days of mounted Confederate probes toward the western outskirts of Fredericksburg and toward Belle Plain. These reports might have referred to Cobb's Legion, which was on reconnaissance north of the rivers.[66]

The Sixth Corps took up its line of march at 11:00 A.M. on 18 May. Passing behind the Ninth Corps, the corps crossed the Fredericksburg Road and arrived in the vicinity of the Anderson house. From there they crossed the Ni to the Myers farm, where Russell's and Ricketts's divisions assumed defensive positions for the night. At 5:00 P.M. Neill's troops extended the corps line to the east-southeast to the Ni River near Anderson's Mill. At 6:00 P.M. Warren informed Meade that the left of the Fifth Corps's line was about six hundred yards in advance of the recently returned Sixth Corps at the Myers farm and suggested that Wright's men be moved forward to protect the exposed left flank of the Fifth Corps. He was informed that his left was covered adequately as things stood. Wright must have advanced some pickets, however, because he later informed Warren that a connection with Crawford's troops had been made and that all was well.[67]

The Pennsylvania Bucktail Regiment occupied an advanced position on Crawford's picket line within perhaps 350 yards of the Massaponax Church Road. The Eighty-third New York Regiment of Coulter's brigade had just arrived there as a relief at 9:00 P.M. when a Confederate force assaulted the position and drove the Yankees back. Coulter personally moved up to the forward position to reestablish the line and was wounded. The Federal picket line there was reinforced and moved back a short distance. The Southerners entrenched on the slight crest from which they had driven the Yankee pickets. The remainder of the night passed quietly.[68]

19

The Artillery Fired at the Whole D—d Lot

19–21 May

Federal Operations in the Morning

During the evening of 18 May, Hancock's original three divisions marched to the left of the Federal line and went into camp near Anderson's Mill. Tyler's division was east of the Fredericksburg Road, reportedly not far from army headquarters near the Anderson house.[1]

Burnside's troops began to march at approximately 2:00 A.M. on the nineteenth, and he informed Grant at 5:45 A.M. that the head of his column had arrived at the Myers house, where the route was blocked by troops from the Sixth Corps. At 5:00 A.M. Wright's men had begun to move out, following the order to advance as close as possible to the Confederate main line southwest of the Myers farm.[2]

Russell's division moved forward warily and assumed its position north of the Massaponax Church Road, where it connected on the right with Crawford's Fifth Corps division. Neill's division formed on Russell's left across the road. Ricketts's two brigades occupied the left of the corps line, which included the Carter house and extended beyond it three hundred yards southwest. They began to dig in.[3]

Burnside's three divisions moved south from the Myers farm and formed a line on the left of the Sixth Corps. They faced generally south while Wright's line faced west. Willcox's division joined the left of Ricketts's, and the troops of these two commands were aligned nearly back to back. Crittenden's division assumed a position to the left of Willcox's. Potter's regiments completed the line to the left and extended to the Massaponax Church Road. Some of the corps batteries were placed on the front line. Burnside was able to man this position adequately, unlike his earlier line north of the Fredericksburg Road. Col. John Hartranft reported that he had placed only two of his six regiments in the front line of works. Burnside's men constructed strong breastworks and felled trees in front of their positions.[4]

At 10:00 A.M. the Fourth and Tenth United States Regular regiments of

Brig. Gen. James H. Ledlie's First Brigade advanced on a reconnaissance mission to pinpoint the location of the Confederate line. As a result of this mission, Burnside was able to provide Grant with a reasonably accurate description of the terrain to the south of the Ninth Corps's position and to notify him that the Confederate entrenchments ended at the Po River. In the afternoon Grant directed Burnside to occupy the area in the vicinity of the Quisenberry house with a brigade and to establish pickets along the Po if possible. Most importantly, he should attempt to position troops where they could observe the right of the enemy's line in order to detect immediately any Confederate movement south across the river. At 5:00 P.M. Crittenden received orders from Burnside to comply with Grant's instructions and to use Ledlie's brigade for the operation.[5]

Afternoon Operations

At 1:30 P.M. Hancock received orders to begin to move his corps at 2:00 A.M. on the twentieth. He was to proceed south via Guinea Station to Bowling Green and Milford Station and to take a position on the south side of the Mattaponi River if possible. Brig. Gen. Alfred T. A. Torbert was to report to him with a small cavalry force including a battery of horse artillery. The services of an engineer officer and guides were also to be provided. In addition, canvas pontoons would be available.

Torbert, the regular commander of the First Cavalry Division, had reported back from sick leave on the eighteenth and had been placed in command of the Union cavalry remaining with the army. That afternoon he had led a mounted force south to Guinea Station, where the Federals burned the depot, post office, and a small bridge. This mission, Burnside's reconnaissance report, and cavalry scouting reports of conditions beyond the Federal left flank and south led Grant and Meade to feel certain that Hancock would be able to get away without hindrance.[6]

Upon receipt of his order, Hancock informed army headquarters that his chief of staff, Colonel Morgan, had gone that morning as far south as Guinea Station, where he had spotted the first enemy pickets. He said, however, that there was a Confederate observation and signal station on the south side of the Ni from which the march of the Second Corps could be detected early on. Hancock requested permission to depart before the designated time of 2:00 A.M. in order to be well beyond Guinea by daylight. Permission was granted.[7]

Ewell's Reconnaissance and the Battle of Harris's Farm

The Confederates should have detected the movement of the Federal Sixth Corps on the eighteenth from the Landrum farm back to the Myers farm. It is not certain, however, that they did. They definitely were aware of Wright's and Burnside's probing advances on the morning of the nineteenth. The Yankees appeared to be sidling toward the Confederate right. In the afternoon Lee ordered Ewell to advance his corps from its position along the base of the salient and to locate the right of the Federals' main line. Ewell assumed that the Yankees were still in his front along the outside of the works on the north face of the salient.[8]

They were not. Hancock's troops had been gone for at least twelve hours. Not wishing to move against the entrenched Federal force in his front, Ewell obtained permission to lead his six thousand infantrymen on a short swing to the west of the salient before proceeding to the northeast. Lieutenant Colonel Braxton was ordered to accompany the movement with six artillery pieces.[9]

The movement began at 2:00–3:00 P.M. Ramseur's brigade led, followed by Battle's, Grimes's, and Doles's. Gordon's five brigades brought up the rear. The route of march was northwest via the Brock Road to the intersection immediately north of Alsop's, then northeast on the Gordon Road past Couse's toward Armstrong's. When they passed the Spindle farm clearing, they saw many Federal Fifth Corps corpses that the rains had washed from their shallow graves. The bodies had begun to decompose, and the stench was sickening. The Southerners hurried forward as quickly as possible. Kershaw's division moved from its position in reserve behind Field's troops to man the works of the Second Corps while Ewell and his command were away.[10]

Union Dispositions West of the Fredericksburg Road

Warren's Fourth Division under Cutler occupied a position with its left on the Fredericksburg Road. The line extended rightward through the area of the deserted Beverley house and ended on the Ni approximately one-quarter mile west of the road. Wainwright placed Stewart's and Mink's batteries on either side of the deserted house.[11]

North of the river, to Cutler's right, Kitching continued the line with portions of his Sixth and Fifteenth New York Heavy Artillery regiments and the Second Battalion, Fourth New York Heavy Artillery. These three companies, totaling about 440 men, had recently been assigned to his command. The fourth company of the battalion was on escort duty with the corps ammunition trains. The Sixth connected with Cutler's right at the Ni, with

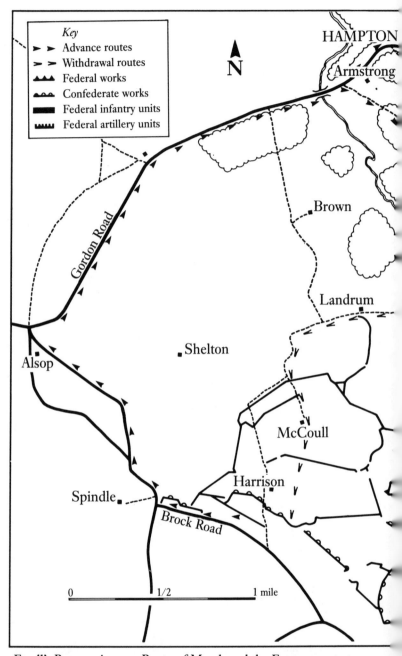

MAP 19-1. Ewell's Reconnaissance Route of March and the Engagement at Harris's Farm, 19 May, 2:00–8:30 P.M.

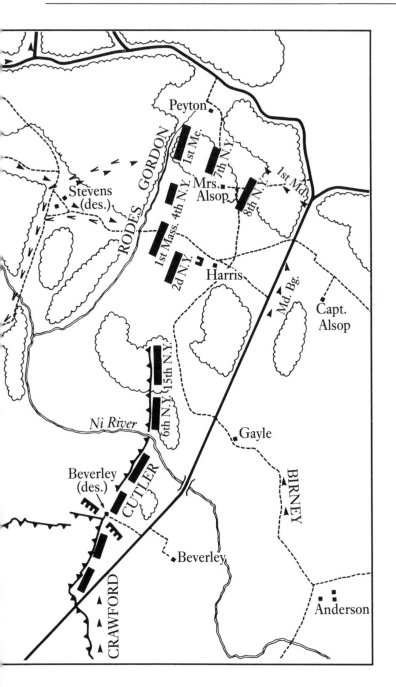

the Fifteenth on its right. The precise location of the Fourth New York battalion is not known. Half of it was placed on picket, and the other half was kept in reserve near Mrs. Alsop's house, about five hundred yards north of the Harris house. The picket line probably extended from about four hundred yards west of the Alsop house to the right along the bank of a small creek. It did not connect on the left with the Fifteenth Regiment, as much of the Harris farm clearing intervened between the two units.[12] At 9:00 A.M. Kitching reported that his main line and picket lines had finally been established. This had been difficult because the artillerymen were unfamiliar with infantry tactics, especially those pertaining to picketing and skirmishing. At midday Capt. Almont Barnes's four three-inch rifles were positioned near the Harris house.[13] In addition to the infantry force, there was a detachment of approximately 450 Federal cavalrymen under the command of Maj. George A. Forsyth posted near the right front of the picket line. A few mounted vedettes were established west of the Ni, possibly opposite the deserted Stevens house. However, the precise locations of Forsyth's main and picket lines cannot be determined.[14]

The morning continued to pass quietly. At 10:15 A.M. Warren reported that Confederates had closely followed the withdrawal of the Ninth Corps during the night and had been spotted in the evacuated Federal works. Later, he confirmed that Kitching's picket line on the right was well posted and was connected with the cavalry detachment.[15]

Toward noon some men of the Fourth New York Heavy Artillery were seating themselves in a picket post for a friendly game of cards when suddenly a squad of mounted Confederates galloped out of the woods from the west. The Yankees jumped to their feet and fired a hasty volley at the Southerners. The riders wheeled and galloped away, firing their revolvers as they went. Their identity is unknown. A short distance to the Federal right, a lone Confederate was captured at about noon. Some believed that he was a scout, but he accepted the offer to take the oath of allegiance and afterwards he was released. Because of these events, Kitching formed his troops into a line of battle. When nothing further developed, he permitted them to fall out again, although he advanced his pickets farther west into the trees.[16]

Contact Is Made and the Battle Opens

Somewhere along Ewell's route of march, the six artillery pieces accompanying the corps were sent back because of the poor condition of the roads. While it cannot be determined where or by whom this decision was made, Ewell must bear the ultimate responsibility for the action.[17]

Lee directed Hampton to cooperate with Ewell's mission. Hampton moved with Rosser's brigade. Mrs. Couse saw them passing her home and recorded that they had artillery with them. This consisted of the four pieces of Capt. James W. Thomson's Horse Artillery battery. When these mounted Southerners arrived in the vicinity of the Armstrong house, they continued straight ahead on the road instead of turning right as the foot soldiers were doing.[18]

The Confederate infantry advance arrived at a clearing around the abandoned Stevens house, where the men halted briefly. During this pause the troops of Gordon's division moved upon Ramseur's left and then continued to march east. Ramseur soon resumed his advance southeast to the point where his skirmishers made contact with the pickets of the Fourth New York, probably at 4:30–5:00 P.M. After his skirmishers drove the Yankee pickets back a short distance, Ramseur halted the main body of his brigade and awaited further orders. Apparently, neither Rodes nor Ewell was near the head of the column at this time.

As Ramseur waited behind his skirmishers, he observed a large body of Federal infantry standing in mass in the Harris farm clearing just off the Fredericksburg Road. He estimated this group to be a brigade. He became concerned that, if his immediate superiors waited much longer before deciding to do something, the isolated Second Corps could find itself in trouble. He dispatched a courier to the rear with a request for permission to attack and was granted the permission by Rodes or Ewell or both.[19]

The Federals whom Ramseur had spotted were soldiers of the First Massachusetts Heavy Artillery Regiment. Notification of the Confederate cavalry probe of Kitching's position, which had occurred at noon, had immediately been forwarded to army headquarters. As a result, Tyler's five large regiments were alerted and soon started northwest toward the Fredericksburg Road. The First Massachusetts arrived just off the road southwest of the Harris house at approximately 2:30 P.M. Looking to the west, they could see only the gunners of Barnes's battery lying on the east side of a small knoll behind their pieces.

When the firing between Ramseur's skirmishers and the pickets of the Fourth New York began, after 4:00 P.M., the First Regiment marched toward the sound of the firing. Passing between the main Harris house and some outbuildings, the men arrived at the knoll on which a section of Barnes's battery rested. Here two companies of the Second Battalion were ordered forward into the woods. Company F proceeded as ordered, but, for some reason, Company D moved a little to its right, halted along the edge of the trees, and awaited further orders. The First Battalion, consisting of 360 troops under the command of Maj. Frank R. Rolfe, moved around to the front of the knoll. The Third and the rest of the Second extended the line to the right in the direction of Mrs. Alsop's house. This was probably the time

Ramseur started his brigade forward in the attack. As the firing in the woods ahead increased, the members of the First Massachusetts Regiment were understandably nervous, as this was their initiation into combat. Word of the unit's first fatality filtered back. Suddenly, Rolfe was directed to advance his battalion into the woods to discover the size of the enemy force in front. The Yankees moved down the slope and about fifty yards through the trees, where they were racked by a volley from Ramseur's troops that shattered their ranks. Rolfe fell from his horse, mortally wounded, pierced by several balls. Most of the Federals retreated toward the knoll. Those who remained firing were killed, wounded, or captured.[20]

The North Carolinians of Ramseur's left front drove the advanced pickets of the Fourth New York back on their reserve near the buildings of Mrs. Alsop's farm. Here the firing became intense, with many casualties. The New Yorkers were hard-pressed to hold on. The Confederates of Ramseur's right front followed the retiring troops of the late Major Rolfe's First Battalion out into the open field. There they were halted by flank fire from the Second Battalion to their left and by canister fire from Barnes's two pieces on the knoll. The Carolinians fell back into the trees. They attempted two or three more times to advance into the clearing, but each time they were driven back by the fire of the Massachusetts troops, who stood nearly shoulder to shoulder atop a slight hill on the skyline and suffered cruel losses in their exposed position. Suddenly, Ramseur realized that both of his flanks were being partially enveloped. He withdrew his men approximately two hundred yards, where Grimes's brigade joined on their left and Battle's on their right.[21]

The Federal unit that Ramseur believed was beginning to envelop his right flank might have been the Second New York Heavy Artillery, although this is not certain. The unit to his left was the First Maine Heavy Artillery. As the Maine troops had moved toward the Fredericksburg Road, they were informed that enemy troops had penetrated to the road and were attempting to capture or destroy a supply train there. When these troops and those of the Seventh New York Heavy Artillery arrived at the road, they discovered that the report was true. They began to receive fire from woods to the west of the road, and the Seventh Regiment was ordered to proceed in that direction. At that time, the supply train was probably due east of Mrs. Alsop's farm, where the road swings to the east. The Yankees dashed up both sides of the road into the train and drove away the Confederates, whom they then pursued to the west. A little more than half a mile from the road, the Yankees arrived at a small stream where they halted and formed a defensive line. Their left rested just northwest of Mrs. Alsop's house, and their line extended north in the direction of the Peyton house.[22]

Facing them across the stream was the major portion of Gordon's division, some of whom had overrun the supply train. After their halt at the Stevens clearing, these troops had resumed a line of march to the east. When they had passed north of Mrs. Alsop's house, some of them had continued on to the road, where they had discovered the defenseless supply train. Realizing that they would be unable to bring off the wagons because of distance to their lines, they had begun to shoot the horses and mules. They had also captured a few teamsters and quartermaster personnel, but most of the Yankees had taken off down the road at first sight of the Rebels. Some of Gordon's men had continued across the road into the woods to the east.[23]

At about this time the main body of Gordon's troops was flanked on its left and fell back in disorder. This exposed Rodes's left brigade, which Grimes commanded. Through skillful maneuvering, Grimes averted further disaster, earning a promotion in the process. Rodes withdrew his three brigades to a new position. The Virginia regiments of Hoffman's brigade moved up on Gordon's left, halted, and drove back the flanking Federals, whoever they were. They might have been members of the First Maryland Regiment Veteran Volunteers.[24]

Welcome Back, Boys

The men of the First Maryland who had reenlisted had been granted a furlough home. On their return they had arrived at Belle Plain by ship on the morning of 12 May. The next day they had been detailed to guard the road between Belle Plain and Fredericksburg, over which Federal supplies and Federal wounded were proceeding in opposite directions. Finally, they had been ordered to rejoin their brigade at the front, and they had taken up the march at 7:00 A.M. on the nineteenth of May. The cavalcade included 140 reenlisted veterans of the Eighty-seventh Pennsylvania of Ricketts's Sixth Corps division, who were also returning to the army, all under the command of Col. Nathan T. Dushane of the First Maryland. Sometime after leaving Fredericksburg, the party had passed a body of troops from the First Maryland who had not reenlisted and were beginning the trip home to be mustered out. One wonders what remarks, if any, passed between the two groups of soldiers.

As they had approached the position of the armies, the returnees had heard the sounds of the fighting ahead. Reaching the bend in the road east of Mrs. Alsop's farm, Dushane realized that the action was relatively close to the road. On his own volition he faced his command to its right and ordered the troops forward into the trees. After advancing approximately fifty yards, they became engaged with some Confederates and were driven back to the road. Dushane reformed his men and advanced again in company with one of the heavy artillery regiments, possibly the Eighth New York, and this time the

Confederate force retired to the west side of the stream south of the Peyton house. There the opposing forces fired at each other until after nightfall. During the fighting Dushane's horse was killed, and the colonel was injured when he fell from the dying animal.[25]

A gap existed between the First Maryland's left and the right of the First Maine Heavy Artillery. After a time this gap was filled by the arrival of the remainder of the Maryland brigade of the Union Fifth Corps. The reenlistees doubtless were happy to see their comrades.

Meade Forwards Reinforcements

Those at Meade's headquarters heard firing between Ramseur's troops and the Fourth New York Heavy Artillery Battalion, followed shortly by that of the First Massachusetts. Meade immediately ordered troops to the threatened area on the right of the line. At the first indication of the enemy's presence there, Hancock, whose troops lay in reserve behind the left of the line waiting to move off to the south at night, was directed to hold his command in readiness to move toward the Fredericksburg Road. At 5:30 P.M. Meade ordered him to send a division on the run and to follow it with his other troops. Birney's division, which was the closest, was dispatched immediately.[26]

Warren was also ordered to forward troops to the threatened sector, and he immediately sent his independent Maryland brigade. Major Roebling led it up the Fredericksburg Road to a location opposite Mrs. Alsop's farm. There they plugged the gap between the First Maine and First Maryland regiments. Warren also sent Crawford's division from the left of the corps line. Wright sidled a portion of Russell's division to its right to man the segment of the Union line vacated by Crawford's troops.[27]

Meade ordered Hunt to forward two batteries each from the Second and Fifth corps to the scene of the fighting. Colonel Wainwright had already started Hart's and Richardson's batteries, under the command of Maj. Robert H. Fitzhugh. Hart's four Napoleons were placed in position near Barnes's pieces and reportedly helped to keep Ramseur's and Battle's infantrymen at bay. Four batteries were sent from the Second Corps but did not become engaged. In fact, the Maryland brigade and Hart's battery were the only reinforcements that did become engaged before the firing ceased a short time after dark.[28]

Until then the fire of the opposing forces had been heavy and continuous. On the left of the Union line north of the Ni, both the Sixth and Fifteenth New York heavy artillery reported being engaged, with the Fifteenth suffering ninety-eight casualties. Toward the end of the fighting, the Second New

York was positioned to the left and rear of the First Massachusetts; the Seventh New York was behind the First Maine; and the Eighth New York was farther back, in the rear of the two front line units, the First Massachusetts and First Maine.[29]

When Birney's troops arrived near the right of the Union line, Major Roebling helped Birney place his men in position behind the Maryland brigade and the First Maine. Later in the evening this division moved forward and replaced the two New England regiments in the line.[30]

From the Federal viewpoint the engagement had been very confusing, because of the inexperience of the heavy artillery troops, their unfamiliarity with infantry tactics, and the fact that, for most, this was their initial ordeal under fire. Moreover, not all of the fire came from their front. In his journal Wainwright recorded a humorous account of the Federal operation as described by a quartermaster who witnessed the fighting: "First there was Kitching's brigade firing at the enemy; then Tyler's men fired into his; up came Birney's division and fired into Tyler's; while the artillery fired at the whole d—d lot." While somewhat exaggerated, this version does contain elements of truth.[31]

Accounts by members of the First Massachusetts complain that members of the Second New York fired a destructive volley into their rear. In addition, some artillery shells from Barnes's or Hart's guns landed among the First Massachusetts. Toward the end of the action members of the Seventh New York blindly fired a volley to their left front at some woods into which the Second New York had just moved. After Birney had placed his infantrymen into position behind the line, he ordered a battery up and directed its crew to open fire. A member of Hunt's staff who happened to be nearby persuaded the general that they should not fire, because the intended target was some of Tyler's men.[32]

Yet, while Tyler's artillerymen were confused in their first combat experience, they were also, for the most part, game. The First Massachusetts lost 398 of its members to musket fire and the First Maine more than 400. Many of these men had received little or no instruction in infantry combat techniques. Instead of taking advantage of irregularities of the terrain, most of them stood upright, shoulder to shoulder, in the open and took their losses.[33]

Lee's Concern

When the commander of the Army of Northern Virginia became aware that his Second Corps, on its mission beyond the protection of the remainder of the army, was without artillery, he feared for its safety and tried to alleviate the danger as much as possible. He ordered Early to advance some troops against

Cutler's position south of the Ni as a diversion to help Ewell. The entire Third Corps was alerted for a possible advance. Early dutifully advanced infantrymen from the left of his line. Most, if not all, of these were from Cadmus Wilcox's division. They drove in a segment of Cutler's picket line but retired soon after coming under artillery fire. The men of Lane's brigade moved to their left rear to guard the Second Corps artillery batteries, which were near the right end of that corps's vacant line. Brown's South Carolinians were placed in the works to the left of Lane's troops. After dark they moved farther to their left along the base of the salient.[34]

Ewell had indeed permitted his command to get into a potentially dangerous situation. While the Yankee foot artillerymen were inexperienced, they did significantly outnumber their Southern antagonists. The Federals under Tyler's and Kitching's commands must have totalled close to ten thousand. Moreover, some of them became highly aggressive toward the close of the action.[35]

After Hoffman's Virginians stopped the Federals who had flanked Gordon's division, they followed the retiring Yankees a short distance, halted, and established a defensive line. Gordon's troops moved forward again and formed on Hoffman's right. Rodes's troops continued the line farther to the right. Sometime during the action Ewell rode up to the rear of Gordon's troops, where he came under fire and his horse was shot. He suffered a severe jolt when he struck the ground, falling from the stricken animal.

The Confederates were determined to hold their position until after dark and then to return to their lines at the base of the salient. Shortly after dark, some of the heavy artillery regiments attempted to advance against the Confederates and to drive them off. These attempts failed but caused concern to the Southerners. A member of Hoffman's Thirteenth Virginia Regiment, which was situated on the left of Ewell's line, recorded that, at about dark, an officer from the rear of the brigade shouted forward the information that, if the Virginians could hold on a short time longer, General Hampton would attack the Federals in flank with artillery. At 8:00 P.M. the Virginia infantrymen heard some artillery that sounded about five miles away.[36]

Operations of Rosser's Cavalry Brigade

Hampton had led his horsemen straight ahead at Armstrong's while the infantrymen marched off to the southeast. Continuing for approximately three miles, the cavalrymen crossed Massaponax Creek and shortly thereafter became engaged with the Union picket outpost of troopers from the Second Ohio cavalry. This meeting occurred less than one-half mile south of the Orange Plank Road, near the point where it crossed the unfinished railroad bed. At the first sound of firing, the off-duty men of the Ohio regiment hurried forward to the scene. After some skirmishing, during which one of Thomson's artillery pieces was used, Hampton withdrew.[37]

During his withdrawal Hampton directed two of Thomson's pieces to a position somewhere north of the Harris farm, where they opened fire at dark. This was the firing which George Peyton of the Thirteenth Virginia heard. It is not known how long these pieces were engaged or even their approximate location. Sometime after the battle, Ewell informed Hampton that the two guns had done good service.[38]

While the Second Ohio was engaged with Rosser's troopers, they heard the sounds of Ewell's battle three miles to the south. Grant had notified Ferrero, whose headquarters were near Salem Church on the Orange Turnpike, that a Confederate force had crossed the Ni River on the right of the army's position. He had warned Ferrero to be ready for trouble and to report to headquarters immediately the appearance of enemy infantry and artillery moving in his direction. At the first sound of firing between the troopers of the Second Ohio and Rosser's Virginians, Ferrero assembled the infantrymen of his Colored Division, but they were not needed. Ferrero also sent back to Fredericksburg Grant's directive that, until further notice, all trains and couriers reporting to the army from the city were to use the road to Massaponax Church rather than the Spotsylvania Court House Road.[39]

Movements after Dark

The infantry firing ceased by 9:00 P.M., and approximately one hour later the Confederates were ordered to return to their lines. It appears to have been a haphazard movement at best. Many of Ewell's infantrymen had fallen asleep after the firing ceased. Near the left of the line, George Peyton and his comrades were awakened and told to sneak away singly, so as not to attract attention. Members of units reunited in the rear and groped their way back, many of them crossing the Ni at the ford east of Landrum's. A number of the Southern infantrymen were too exhausted to move without rest, however, and remained where they were. Most of these were captured in the morning.[40]

At the time when the firing died out, Grant still intended to adhere to his plan to start the Second Corps south during the night. Crawford's Fifth Corps division was to relieve Tyler's heavy artillery regiments so they might join Hancock for the move. Russell's division and Wheaton's brigade from the Sixth Corps moved toward the Fredericksburg Road to relieve Birney's troops. At 9:15 P.M., however, Warren informed Meade that Major Roebling had advised that it would be extremely difficult to extract Birney's men from the line and to have them in condition for an efficient march early in the morning. At 10:15 P.M. Grant and Meade relented and decided to keep Birney's troops in their present position. They were to attack from that position at daylight, however, in conjunction with Kitching's and Crawford's troops on their left.[41]

Earlier in the day Grant had informed Halleck of the intended move and had suggested that Port Royal replace Fredericksburg as the next supply depot. He urged Halleck, who was known as "Old Brains," to ensure cooperation from the navy to open the Rappahannock River to Fredericksburg. Halleck replied that the navy would try to come up the river to Fredericksburg, if the army would clear enemy guerrillas from its south bank. At 10:00 P.M. Grant informed Washington of Ewell's sortie and explained that, because of the potential danger to the Union trains at Fredericksburg, he would not start Hancock south until the whereabouts and intentions of Ewell's command were known.[42]

After the cessation of the firing, the Federals in line from the Ni River right to the road east of Mrs. Alsop's farm threw up crude protective works. There was some shifting along the line as the Maryland brigade was pulled back to report to Crawford on the left near the river. From there Crawford advanced his men a short distance along the river bank, where they picked up a few Confederate stragglers. The uninjured Confederates out in front of the Yankee line were asleep, wandering around lost in the woods, or moving back to their main line. At about midnight, some of them began to arrive in scattered groups at their works along the base of the salient. They described their recent experiences to Brown's men, then lay down in the mud, and went to sleep in the rain.[43]

Some of Ewell's exhausted infantrymen must have wondered what they had accomplished. Without doubt they had discovered that Yankee infantry was located on the right of the Union line near the Fredericksburg Road. The method used to obtain this information had cost them nine hundred casualties, more than half of whom were unwounded prisoners. Col. Samuel H. Boyd of the Forty-fifth North Carolina of Grimes's brigade had been killed while leading his men in an attack against the First Massachusetts. One company of the Forty-fifth had emerged from the battle with not a single commissioned or non-commissioned officer remaining on his feet. Bryan Grimes's old regiment, the Fourth North Carolina of Ramseur's brigade, had suffered a loss of sixty-five killed and wounded, proof that some of the heavy artillery troops had aimed accurately.[44]

Ewell must bear the major share of responsibility for these casualties. If he had reconnoitered the area to his front inside the salient, he would have discovered that the Yankees were no longer there. This, in turn, would have permitted his Second Corps to cross the Ni at the ford east of Landrum's, which would have reduced the marching distance considerably. If Ewell or Rodes had been at the head of the column led by Ramseur, a more judicious reconnaissance might have been executed.

In his report of the action at the Harris and Alsop farms, Ewell claimed that, after charting the Federal position there, which was the object of his mission, he was preparing to retire when he was attacked. This certainly is a remarkable claim in view of Ramseur's report. Ewell's force was not attacked by anybody until nearly dark. At the time when Ramseur requested and received permission to attack, one battalion and a separate company of heavy artillery men with muskets constituted the entire Federal force that was advancing on his immediate front.[45]

As reported by Grant, Federal losses were slightly more than fifteen hundred: 196 killed, 1,090 wounded, and 249 missing. Seventy-eight of these were in the Maryland regiments and the remainder among Tyler's and Kitching's foot artillerymen. In addition to battle casualties, one of the heavy artillery regiments sustained other losses as well. As Birney's division approached the Fredericksburg Road on the double-quick, the leading troops came upon a pile of knapsacks which the men of one of Tyler's large regiments had deposited unguarded on the ground as they hurriedly moved into position. Without diminishing speed, the members of Birney's lead brigade fanned out, and each Federal scooped up a knapsack, examining his prize on the run and confiscating whatever he desired before dropping the rest on the ground. In truth, for the artillerymen turned infantrymen it had been a day of severe indoctrination into the hazards of active field campaigning in the Army of the Potomac.[46]

The indoctrination continued after nightfall. Some of Birney's regiments camped along the edge of the field where the New England heavy artillery troops had fought and died. The bodies lay unattended where they had fallen. No provision had been made to secure their personal effects. Stephen Chase of the Eighty-sixth New York remembered seeing two youthful drummer boys with their caps filled with money, watches, rings, and other valuables that they had stolen from the dead Federals. The New Yorker disgustedly recorded that no one condemned this villainous behavior.[47]

20 May

At first light Crawford and Birney advanced their troops in forced reconnaissances to their fronts. At 4:40 A.M. Crawford informed Warren that his advancing skirmishers had discovered that the Confederates were gone. Some more stragglers were captured near the Ni River.[48] On the right of the Federal line, Birney's skirmishers, composed of troops from Egan's, Crocker's (commanded since 18 May by Col. Elijah Walker), and Mott's brigades, had advanced to positions beyond the abandoned Stevens house. In the process the Federals had picked up more than four hundred Confederate stragglers, many of whom were asleep. In the dark woods some of them had mistakenly joined the ranks of the advancing Federals, assuming they were friendly troops withdrawing.[49]

At 5:30 A.M. Meade informed Grant of the results of these reconnaissances into Ewell's former position. He stated his intention to withdraw Birney's and Tyler's divisions from west of the Fredericksburg Road and to return them to Hancock behind the left of the army's line, east of Anderson's. The two Second Corps divisions withdrew between 10:00 and 11:00 A.M. and marched back to their former positions.

Before departing, the members of the First Massachusetts, First Maine, and Fourth New York buried their slain comrades. This was a new and trying experience for the former gunners. In addition, a number of the First Massachusetts were detached to remain behind and to inter the Confederate dead lying in the area immediately to the west of Mrs. Alsop's farm buildings. Some of this operation was recorded by photographer Timothy H. O'Sullivan. The four brigades of Russell's division and Wheaton's brigade replaced their Second Corps comrades in the line west of the road.[50]

Meade ordered Hancock to use the plan developed for the previous evening and to leave anytime after dark, preceded by Torbert's horsemen. He ordered Warren to have his command ready to follow the enemy at anytime during the night, should any of the Confederates immediately pursue the Federal Second Corps. If the enemy did not move, Warren was to lead his command along Hancock's route, departing at 10:00 A.M.[51]

Meade informed Wright that, after Warren's withdrawal in the morning, the Sixth Corps with Russell's division returned would be responsible for the protection of the right flank of the Union position. He advised Wright to consider the establishment of a new line to the rear of his present one, which would extend due south from the Myers hill and north perhaps as far as Anderson's. Burnside's troops were to extend the line to the left. This new line was to be occupied in the morning when the Fifth Corps departed.[52]

In the morning, detachments from Burnside's First and Second divisions conducted reconnaissances to their front on the Massaponax Church Road and to the left front as far as Smith's Mill on the Ni River. They reported only Confederate cavalry vedettes south of the Ni.[53]

Back at Salem Church, Ferrero was advised of the proposed move and was ordered to dispose his troops so as to cover the city of Fredericksburg and the Telegraph Road south. He had been pleading constantly for more cavalry, but he was told only that Sheridan was expected to arrive soon from his raid and then his force would be augmented or relieved. Torbert, who would lead Hancock's advance, was concerned about the inexperience of some of his troopers. He expected to become engaged before daylight and requested that five hundred experienced horsemen who had reported to the army on the previous day be assigned to him. It is doubtful that his wish was granted.[54]

Confederate Operations

That day, as Lee watched for indications of what his opponents intended to do next, he received from his president the welcome news that Maj. Gen. George E. Pickett's division and Maj. Gen. Robert F. Hoke's former brigade were being sent to reinforce him from south of the James River. In addition, a force under Maj. Gen. John C. Breckinridge was en route from the Shenandoah Valley to join him. Lee ordered Breckinridge, the former vice-president of the United States, to halt at Hanover Junction with his twenty-four hundred troops and to await further orders.[55]

Late in the morning, Kershaw's troops were returned to their positions in reserve behind Field on the right of the line. During the day, Lee received few definite indications of Federal intentions. The return of Birney's troops from west of the Fredericksburg Road to the left of the Federal line might have been spotted. At 2:30 P.M. Rooney Lee reported that his pickets had been driven in at Smith's Mill on the Ni by dismounted cavalrymen followed by infantry. This force was Burnside's reconnaissance. When he received this information, Lee asked Ewell if he could discern any enemy movement in his front and, if so, whether the rear of the Federal column was weak enough to warrant an attack upon it.[56]

At 8:30 P.M. Lee advised Ewell that the Federals appeared to be extending their line to the south. He ordered Ewell to move his command at daylight and to assume a position south of the Po to Field's right, as long as no threat to his present front prevented him. Soon thereafter, Lee concluded that more troops were needed immediately on the right of the line, and before daylight Gregg's Texas brigade was moved from the left of Field's line to a position south of the Ni. Two regiments of the Third Corps filled the vacated segment of the line.[57]

At 11:00 P.M. Hancock's column moved off in the direction of Massaponax Church. Barlow's division led, followed by Gibbon's, Tyler's, and Birney's. When he arrived near the church, Hancock discovered that the cavalrymen were being issued rations and that many of the horses were still unsaddled. He pulled the head of his column off to the side of the road and waited for the horsemen to assume the lead. They did so at approximately 1:30 A.M., at which time Hancock ordered his troops to resume the march, informing Meade of the reason for the delay. The Yankees moved south in the darkness.[58]

Federal Second Corps Breaks Away Cleanly, 21 May

After leaving the vicinity of Massaponax Church, Hancock's men followed Torbert's cavalrymen along the Telegraph Road for more than half a mile, until the horsemen turned left onto a side road that led southeast to the Richmond, Fredericksburg, and Potomac Railroad. Hancock's instructions were to proceed along a road parallel to the railroad, via Guinea Station and Bowling Green, to Milford Station. At Milford he was to cross to the west bank of the Mattaponi River if possible and to assume a defensive position there. The Mattaponi is formed by the merging of four streams, which are, from south to north, the Mat, Ta, Po, and Ni Rivers, with the major stream beginning about two miles south of Guinea. Hancock's arrival at his destination opposite Milford would place his command fifteen to twenty miles from the rest of the Federal army. He would be slightly more than halfway between Spotsylvania Court House and the North Anna River, about eight miles to the east of a straight line connecting the two sites.[59]

Frank Wilkerson, a member of the Eleventh New York artillery battery who marched with the Second Corps infantrymen that night, remembered that the foot soldiers growled and swore as they moved along. While he did not list the complaints of the Federal soldiers, one complaint might have been that their superior officers, who were supposedly intelligent, did not seem to understand that darkness was intended for sleeping, not marching.[60]

At about first light, Torbert's cavalrymen arrived at Guinea Station, where they were fired on by a half dozen or so Confederate cavalry pickets, who then immediately departed. At 4:30 A.M. Hancock informed army headquarters of this encounter and of the fact that the head of his infantry column was 1½ miles beyond Guinea Station. At 5:30 A.M. Meade was informed that Torbert had sent a small detachment of horsemen to hold the bridge over the Poni River about one-half mile southwest of the station, but that these Federals had been driven back from the area of the bridge by a Confederate force that was probably just cavalry. By noon Hancock's lead division had crossed the Mattaponi opposite Milford and was establishing a defensive position beyond the stream. Hancock's command had executed this movement as planned and had experienced no significant enemy opposition.[61]

Federal Operations in the Morning around Spotsylvania Court House

At 1:30 A.M. the pickets of Griffin's Fifth Corps division reported hearing in their front the sounds of Confederate drummers beating reveille and of wood being chopped. At 2:00 A.M. Ricketts's division pickets on the left of the Sixth Corps line heard bugles, and one hour later they detected the sounds of drumming followed by sounds of a Confederate infantry move to the south. These noises were caused by the movement of Gregg's brigade south of the Po and its replacement in line by two Third Corps regiments. The movement heard at 3:00 A.M. might have been Ewell's departure from the base of the salient to his new position south of the Po.[62]

Probably as a result of these picket reports, Meade ordered Warren and Wright at 5:30 A.M. to advance their pickets and to attempt to drive in those of the enemy in their fronts. Both commanders were loath to comply with this order, because they felt certain that no change in enemy strength had occurred during the night. They thought that the operation would result only in more casualties with no compensating gain. At 6:00 A.M. Wright asked Warren whether any enemy movement had been observed opposite the Fifth Corps. No reply has been found. At this same time a signal officer, who was positioned at the Beverley house, notified army headquarters, probably at Warren's urging, that there had been no change in the enemy's artillery or troops in front of the Fifth Corps's position. At 6:30 A.M. Warren received a message from Griffin, which he immediately forwarded to Meade. It read:

> General Warren:
> The enemy is in force in my front, his artillery in plain sight, and before I advance my pickets, I desire this fact to be known. A far stronger force than my picket-line is visible.
> Chas. Griffin
> Brigadier-General[63]

It appears that Griffin and Warren were ensuring that the responsibility for any casualties incurred in these probing operations, which they seem to have considered unnecessary, would rest with army headquarters. Meade replied by advising Warren that the purpose of the order was to ascertain the force and position of the enemy. If Warren was indeed satisfied that the enemy troops in his front were as strong as they had been the day before and could be certain of this without advancing his pickets, then they need not be advanced. Meade closed by sarcastically stating that, even under this condition, headquarters had no objection to the pickets being advanced anyway. When he received this message, a disgusted Warren directed Griffin to order his pickets to "fire away occasionally at the enemy's, and ascertain all they can and report."[64]

At 7:30 A.M. Warren received his movement orders. If not attacked by
10:00 A.M., he was to move his command east to Massaponax Church on the
Telegraph Road and then south on that road as far as Stanard's Mill on the Po
River, where he was to cross the river and establish a position on the bank of
the stream. Meade told Wright of Warren's orders and instructed him to
occupy his newly prepared line, which was about three-quarters of a mile to
the east of his current position, when Warren's troops departed. At 8:25 A.M.
Meade sent word to Wright that he would probably move that night and
would follow Hancock's route. Simultaneously, Grant told Burnside that, if
Warren got away in the morning without interference, the Ninth and Sixth
corps would move at night, the Sixth following Hancock's route and the
Ninth following Warren on the Telegraph Road.[65]

Thus, the Federal plan had one corps, the Second, moving about twenty
miles southeast of the army's position, as bait. Another corps, the Fifth,
would move three or four miles southeast and wait there to see whether Lee
would detach any portion of his army to pursue and engage Hancock. If
nothing occurred during the rest of the day, the Sixth Corps would follow the
Second, and the Ninth would follow the Fifth.

At 9:45 A.M., fifteen minutes before his command was scheduled to depart, Warren got word that his route and destination were changed. Instead of
marching down the Telegraph Road to Stanard's Mill, he was to follow
Hancock's route east to the railroad, then to Guinea Station, and finally
southwest to Guinea Bridge over the Po. Upon arrival he was to report what
he found at the bridge, as headquarters personnel believed that it was held by
enemy cavalry. At 5:30 A.M. Hancock had informed Meade that a small
detachment of Torbert's cavalry had been driven back from the bridge, but
apparently no further intelligence had been received concerning the situation
there. Burnside was informed of the change in Warren's instructions. He was
also told that his own route of march remained unchanged and that Wright's
Sixth Corps was to follow the Ninth.[66]

Federal Fifth Corps Departs

Promptly at 10:00 A.M. Colonel Wainwright started the corps artillery east
from corps headquarters at the Beverley house. Crawford's division, Kitching's brigade, and the Maryland brigade were slated to leave their positions
west of the Fredericksburg Road (at the site of the engagement of 19 May) at
10:00 A.M. They were ready to march at the scheduled time. Russell's
division and Wheaton's brigade on the right of the line, however, were late in
marching to rejoin their corps south of Myers hill, and consequently Warren's troops were one-half hour late in starting. By 11:30 A.M. they passed the

Anderson house, accompanied by their artillery. Grant, Meade, and their staffs moved with the van of the Fifth Corps.[67]

At noon Griffin and Cutler were ordered to depart from their positions on either side of the Fredericksburg Road. As they withdrew, the Confederates opposite Cutler's men spotted the movement. They lobbed a few shells, and the troops of Lyle's brigade were sent back to see if the Rebels intended to follow in force. The Confederates did not, although some of Cutler's pickets were captured during the extraction process.[68]

When Griffin's troops began to withdraw, they received some scattered fire from Confederates opposite, causing some of the Federal pickets to desert their posts and run through the lines to the rear. General Bartlett shouted forward from the rear to Maj. William C. Hopper, commanding the First Michigan Regiment on picket, to hold his men steady, and Hopper reminded his troops to stand fast.[69] More pickets ran through the ranks of the Michigan regiment, and Bartlett told Hopper that he must keep his men in their places. The major rode back to his brigade commander and angrily informed him that his men were maintaining their proper positions. The pickets running to the rear without orders were from Ayres's brigade, who probably believed that they were being left behind. This news made Bartlett furious. He ordered Hopper to face his troops about and to have them fire on any more of Ayres's men who came back. Hopper turned his men around but did not order them to fire. Ayres and Griffin rode in among the panicky Federal pickets and cuffed them. Major Hopper dismounted and, with one of his captains, helped to stop the flight. They halted some of Ayres's men physically and laughed in their faces, shaming them into returning to their duty.

As the rear of Cutler's division passed east of the Anderson house, Russell's and Neill's Sixth Corps divisions on either side of the Massaponax Church Road retired to a new position approximately one-half mile to their rear. Strong picket detachments remained behind in the old works. Wheaton's brigade rejoined Neill's division north of the road, and Russell's division extended the line farther right, to the vicinity of the Myers house. By now this building had been torn down, so that the material could be used for reinforcement of the works. Four artillery batteries, which consisted of twelve Napoleons and four three-inch rifles, supported the new line.[70]

Lee Analyzes the Federal Movements

Lee was undoubtedly informed of the clash between Torbert's cavalry and Chambliss's pickets that occurred in the vicinity of Guinea Station at first light. This engagement did not necessarily presage a change in the tactical situation, because there had been a similar skirmish there a few days previ-

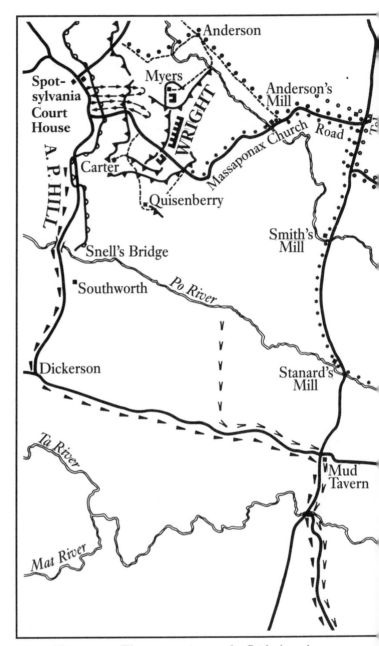

MAP 19-2. Routes of Departure. The reconnaissance by Scales's and Lane's brigades at 6:00–6:30 P.M. is shown. Wright's Sixth Corps and Hill's Third Corps are moving out. The battle is over.

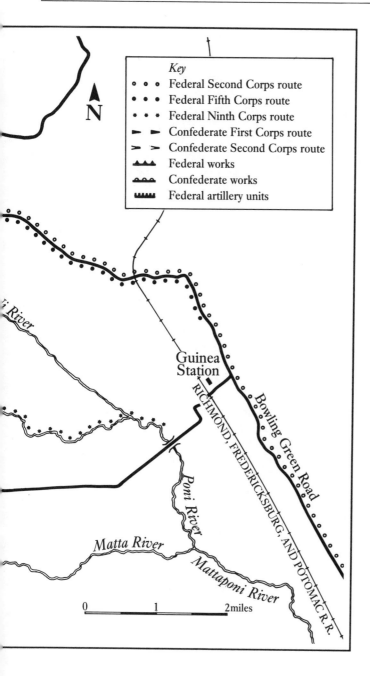

Key
o o o Federal Second Corps route
• • • Federal Fifth Corps route
· · · Federal Ninth Corps route
▬ ▬ Confederate First Corps route
➤ ➤ Confederate Second Corps route
▲▲▲ Federal works
▰▰▰ Confederate works
⚏⚏ Federal artillery units

N

Guinea
Station

RICHMOND, FREDERICKSBURG, AND POTOMAC R.R.

Bowling Green Road

Poni River

Matta River

Mattaponi River

i River

0   1   2 miles

ously. However, from west of the river the Southern horsemen soon spotted the van of Barlow's division marching past the station and proceeding along the Bowling Green Road. The cavalrymen immediately notified army head-quarters and continued to send sighting reports every fifteen minutes throughout the morning. Some of these messages were intercepted by Fed-eral signal officers, who informed Meade of their contents.[71]

Lee did not attempt to attack the detached Federal Second Corps. Instead, he pushed his army due south toward the North Anna River. His goal was to establish a defensive position on the south bank of the river and to await the arrival of the Federals. In this position he could protect the all-important line of the Virginia Central Railroad, which would be immediately to his rear and on which the Confederates depended for the transportation of foodstuffs from the Valley of Virginia.

A detailed analysis of why Lee chose this course of action instead of attempting to destroy Hancock's isolated command is not a part of this work, even though Lee arrived at his decision while still in the vicinity of Spotsyl-vania Court House. However, one reason appears to be that Hancock's route was so far east that he did not present an enticing enough target. Any force which Lee sent south and then east in pursuit of the Union Second Corps would be vulnerable to flank attack from the north for an unacceptably long period of time during its march.[72] Lee might have been tempted to pursue and to strike Hancock had Hancock's route been straight down the Telegraph Road rather than east of the Mattaponi River. If he had moved along the Telegraph Road, Lee could still have ignored him and could have moved south on roads farther west if he wished, but with Hancock's head start and better road, Lee might have felt compelled to stop him before he arrived at the North Anna and the important Hanover Junction, which was defended by Breckinridge's force and a scattering of Pickett's and Hoke's troops. (In 1883, Gen. A. A. Humphreys belatedly suggested that the route along the Tele-graph Road would have been the proper one, and that Warren's Corps should have accompanied Hancock.)[73]

Lee Reacts

At 8:40 A.M. General Lee informed his government that the Federals were apparently changing their base again. He reported the sighting of Barlow's infantrymen at Guinea Station and the progress of Torbert's horsemen along the Bowling Green Road. He stated his belief, which was in fact correct, that the Federals would open communication with Port Royal. He reported that he would regulate his movements according to incoming information about the Federal route of march, and he registered his disappointment that the route chosen would apparently secure the enemy from attack for awhile. He also said that he was "extending on the Telegraph Road."[74]

Lee's statement meant that Ewell's corps was assuming a position along the south bank of the Po River, from Snell's Bridge east toward Stanard's Mill. Southern cavalry pickets were near the mill. Throughout the morning, Lee continued to receive sighting reports of Hancock's column passing Guinea. The 10:30 A.M. departure of the Union Fifth Corps from the vicinity of the Harris farm east to Anderson's and beyond was probably noted by the Confederates. The departures of Griffin's and Cutler's divisions at about midday provided further evidence of a Federal movement.[75]

By this time Lee had reached a decision. Between noon and 1:00 P.M. he ordered Ewell to move his command east, then south on the Telegraph Road. His destination was to be Hanover Junction. It is assumed that Ewell started his men promptly, but this is not certain. They went south to an east-west road that intersected the Telegraph Road at a site known as Mud Tavern, the present-day Thornburg. An infantryman in Gordon's division, which probably led the march, recorded that his unit reached the Telegraph Road and turned south at 2:00 P.M. It marched as fast as it could in the heat and dust for the rest of the afternoon.[76]

The intersection at Mud Tavern is about one mile south of Stanard's Mill. If Warren's route of march had not been changed, his lead division, Crawford's, would have arrived at Stanard's between 3:00 and 3:30 P.M. Crossing to the south bank of the stream, his advancing pickets would have sighted Ewell's column less than three-quarters of a mile ahead. This sequence of events might have precipitated a modified version of the collision for which Grant and Meade had been hoping. But this was not to be. Crawford had turned left below Massaponax Church and headed east toward the railroad. Ewell's men, as well as Anderson's who followed, would pass unmolested.

Anderson was alerted in early afternoon to prepare his command for movement at a moment's notice. Early and Field were directed to sweep their fronts in order to determine if the Yankees were still there. By 3:00 P.M. Early reported finding only some skirmishers in advance of the Third Corps's position. Field was a little tardy in complying with Lee's order, and Lee rebuked Anderson slightly for the delay. Finally, the First Corps was cleared to depart late in the afternoon, and Anderson's men marched south from Snell's Bridge to Dickerson's. Turning left, they moved east to Mud Tavern and headed south from there behind their comrades of the Second Corps. They were to march until 3:00 A.M. before stopping to rest.[77]

Federal Ninth Corps Departs

At midday or shortly thereafter, Grant, who was at Massaponax Church, directed Burnside to move his corps as soon as possible. His destination was to be the intersection at Mud Tavern, and he was to travel the Telegraph Road. If the enemy strongly resisted his crossing of the Po River at Stanard's Mill, however, he was not to cross there but to proceed down the left bank to Guinea Bridge, where he would receive additional orders.[78]

When he received this order, Burnside directed Potter to send one of his brigades ahead to secure the crossing at Stanard's Mill. Curtin's six regiments moved out, accompanied by one artillery battery. Potter departed soon after with Griffin's brigade, one battery, and the division trains. Curtin's skirmishers encountered Confederate pickets less than one mile north of the Po and drove them back across the river at the mill. The Yankee skirmishers came under fire of Confederate artillery pieces positioned south of the stream. Potter reported finding the enemy strongly entrenched across the stream.

While examining the terrain and searching for a ford other than the one at the mill, Potter received orders from Burnside to suspend his advance. He was directed to leave one brigade and battery there to cover the crossing. Behind them the remainder of the corps was to pass down the north bank to Guinea Bridge. It is not known whether the commander of the Ninth Corps was aware of the situation at the mill crossing when he decided upon the alternate route of march and destination.[79]

Crittenden's division followed Potter's and was in turn followed by Willcox's. Willcox's troops had scarcely proceeded one mile from their works when the sounds of heavy firing were heard to their rear, from the position of the Sixth Corps. Burnside returned to Wright's headquarters and discovered that the Sixth Corps pickets had been driven in by an advancing force of Confederate infantry. He ordered Willcox to return with his division and to assist the Sixth Corps if necessary.[80]

The Final Engagement

Late in the afternoon Early decided to execute a more extensive reconnaissance in force in the area to the southeast of the village. Having ascertained that no Federals remained north of the Fredericksburg Road, he selected Wilcox's division from the left of his line for the assignment. At about 6:00 P.M. Scales's and Lane's troops marched south through the village to just north of the Massaponax Church Road intersection. There they turned east and advanced a little beyond the Confederate works. Then they formed a line of battle and continued forward toward the Union entrenchments.[81] When he was within eighty yards of the works, Lt. J. P. Rainey of Scales's Thirteenth Regiment said to a comrade, R. S. Williams, "I'll bet five dollars there isn't a Yankee in those works." No sooner had Rainey spoken when two lines of Union skirmishers rose from behind the works and fired a volley. Most of the balls passed over the heads of Scales's troops, who charged forward to the works and found that the Yankees had departed.[82]

The two brigades of Southern infantrymen crossed the vacant works and continued forward as a thundershower arrived and a drenching rain fell. Suddenly four Federal batteries opened fire in the darkness from behind the new line and were joined by the fire of the entrenched Sixth Corps infantrymen. A chaplain in Russell's New Jersey brigade on Myers hill watched with fascination as artillery shells flew down the slope and burst with brilliant flashes that lit up the forest. Wilcox's men retired rapidly, having discovered that there were still Yankees in the area in force. Both sides suffered only light casualties in this final engagement.[83]

Near the close of the action, Lee ordered Early to return the command of the Third Corps to A. P. Hill, who had reported himself fit for duty. The transfer of command was duly executed. Early had commanded the corps for all of the operations around Spotsylvania Court House.[84]

Shortly after noon Lee had ordered his headquarters camp near the courthouse broken up. He and his staff moved to the Southworth house, which was a little less than half a mile south of Snell's Bridge on the road to Dickerson's. There he awaited the results of Early's and Field's reconnaissance sweeps and the outcome of Wilcox's engagement with the Union Sixth Corps. From there he directed Anderson to start the First Corps south. He ordered Hill to withdraw his last units at 9:00 P.M. unless the enemy's rear guard departed before then. Finally, as darkness arrived, he asked the members of his staff and the guides who had been assigned to headquarters to mount their horses. Lee led the way south toward Dickerson's.[85]

The infantrymen of Neill's Sixth Corps division left their works between 8:00 and 9:00 P.M. Ricketts's two brigades reportedly moved out between 9:00 and 10:00 P.M. Russell's command did not start until 10:30 P.M. These Yankees encountered many delays and detours in the darkness, and the head of the column did not cross the Ni River at Smith's Mill until 5:30 A.M. The troops reached Guinea Station at 8:00 A.M.[86]

Soon after dark, when he was certain that the last of the Union army was beginning to leave the area, A. P. Hill started his Third Corps south from the courthouse toward Snell's Bridge. By midnight the tail of the column had disappeared from sight. The battle of Spotsylvania was over.[87]

20 If It Takes All Summer

After a military operation, analysis of the relative success of the opposing forces is always interesting. As in the case of the Wilderness battle, the results for Spotsylvania are elusive. An understanding of the precise objectives of the opposing commanders is crucial. Nowhere are these objectives explained concisely.

If Grant's intention was to defeat and even destroy the Army of Northern Virginia, he was assuredly unsuccessful at Spotsylvania. His troops stung the Confederates fairly hard but did not seriously impair the fighting efficiency of Lee's army. At Spotsylvania, however, Grant acquired the tactical initiative that he retained until the end of the war. As a result, Lee was kept too busy during his two weeks there to consider assisting the Southern forces defending Richmond and the Valley. The failure of the two political generals, Butler and Sigel, was not Grant's fault. He regretted these failures, but they did not lessen his resolve.

Assuming that Lee's primary objective was to hold the line of the Rapidan River, keeping the enemy out of central Virginia, the battles of the Wilderness and Spotsylvania can be considered strategic defeats. After each battle, Lee was unable to restrict the Union freedom of action. By delaying Grant for two weeks at Spotsylvania, however, Lee prevented Grant from assisting Butler south of the James River. Other Confederate forces frustrated Butler and Sigel, and, as a result, they were able to reinforce Lee after he left Spotsylvania. Lee was to need these reinforcements. His troops had inflicted severe casualties, but his own losses were in some respects more costly. His Second Corps had been nearly wrecked.

Military operations during the Civil War seldom evolved precisely as planned, especially if they involved movements at night. The Federal night march from the Wilderness toward Spotsylvania Court House on the seventh and eighth of May is illustrative. The plan was adequate considering the poor quality of the maps being used. If the various Union corps could have adhered to their scheduled times of departure, the Fifth Corps should have been in position near the courthouse before any Confederate infantry force arrived. A major factor in the Federal failure was Sheridan's decision late on the afternoon of 7 May to withdraw his troopers on the Brock Road to the area of Todd's Tavern instead of staying closer to the courthouse.

The Union efforts on 8 May, beginning with Robinson's arrival at the Spindle farm in the morning, consisted of unprepared piecemeal attacks by newly arrived units against Confederate troops who had also just arrived. The combined attack in the evening was an abysmal failure because of the poor coordination among the exhausted Yankees and the opportune arrival of Ewell's Confederate Second Corps. Fortunately for the Confederates, Richard H. Anderson performed very creditably in his initial assignment as a corps commander. His decision to leave the Wilderness earlier than planned was judicious, and his handling of his force at Spindle's farm and at the courthouse was exemplary. So, the Union movement fell short of its goal. The ninth of May was spent by the opposing commanders in concentrating their armies and attempting to become familiar with the terrain. Burnside's position on the left of the Union line caused constant concern for Grant and Meade until 14 May. Again the poor quality of the available maps precluded an adequate understanding of terrain and distances without extensive reconnaissance. By permitting Sheridan to leave the area with most of the Union horsemen, Grant severely limited his own ability to gain intelligence information by reconnaissance. Lee had better intelligence sources, because although Stuart accompanied Fitz Lee and his division in pursuit of Sheridan, he left behind Hampton and Rooney Lee to support the army.

On 9 May the Union Second Corps might have done better had its three divisions crossed to the south of the Po River in early afternoon rather than later in the day. Grant and Meade probably delayed the operation in order to ensure that the Confederate Third Corps under Early had moved west and was no longer a threat to the Todd's Tavern area. Once again, cavalry could have supplied the desired information to the Union commanders by midmorning.

When Lee was informed of the Federals south of the Po, late in the day of 9 May, he reacted immediately to the threat to the left flank and rear of his infantry by sending Mahone's division to the Block House Bridge and Heth's to oppose Hancock's troops farther west. This, of course, left the eastern approaches to the village, opposite the Federal Ninth Corps, defended by only one Confederate division, but neither Burnside nor anyone else in the Union high command became aware of this until too late.

On the morning of 10 May, when Hancock reported Mahone's defensive position upstream and downstream from the Block House Bridge, Grant decided to abandon the operation south of the Po. He opted instead for an assault against Anderson and Ewell. The prospects of success for this combined attack collapsed when Meade permitted Warren to attack in midafternoon merely because Warren believed he could succeed. Meade may have been overreacting to impress Grant, who must have begun to notice that no attacks by Meade's army seemed to succeed.

The Federal attacks late in the afternoon by the Fifth Corps and portions of Gibbon's and Birney's divisions of the Second against the Laurel Hill position were disjointed affairs that produced nothing but more casualties. What coordination there was between Warren and Hancock is not known. If Meade had been on hand to direct the operation personally (instead of designating Hancock, who knew little of Warren's troop positions or the enemy front), something beneficial might have been accomplished, because the Confederates under Anderson had little or no reserve force available to counter a breakthrough.

Upton's attack achieved a temporary success but was not supported by any other troops. Once again, the absence of an overall directing hand was obvious. Wright, in his first full day in command of the Sixth Corps, apparently oversaw Mott's and Upton's operations with no assistance from higher headquarters. He seems to have felt that he could not spare any troops from his entrenchments to exploit any breakthrough that might occur. Thus Lee's defensive reserves were able to stop Upton's men and force them back. Upton's operation did make one contribution to the Union cause: it gave Grant an idea. Upton's column had penetrated Ewell's line of works relatively easily, so an assault by an entire corps should punch a gigantic hole in the Confederates' line. This, in turn, might lead to a crushing defeat of Lee's army. The plan seemed reasonable, but there were problems. The initial assault was to be executed jointly by Hancock's Second Corps and three divisions of Burnside's Ninth. Burnside's front, from south of the Fredericksburg Road north to a point due east of the east angle of the salient, was too long to be manned adequately by his troops, even for defensive purposes. The Federal map was practically useless. Grant and Burnside were unaware of the distances involved. They did not know the terrain from the front of Heth's salient north to the east angle, because it had not been reconnoitered.

Thus, no matter where along the east face of the salient Burnside attacked, there would still be unaffected brigades from Early's Third Corps to counter any Federal successes. This is why Lee could use Perrin's, Harris's, and McGowan's troops on Ewell's front. It also explains why, in the afternoon, Lane's troops could be extracted safely from the line to make a flank attack. At 1:45 P.M., in an effort to increase the pressure on the Confederates, Grant advised Burnside to abandon the Fredericksburg Road if necessary in order to transfer his Provisional Brigade north to augment the attack on the east face of the salient. Burnside did not move the brigade. If he had, the Confederate reconnaissance up that road late in the afternoon might have led to some interesting operations in the Ninth Corps's left rear.

Hancock's initial success appears to have been due primarily to luck:

dampness and reduced visibility, and the fact that the Confederates were unable to return their artillery pieces to the front line in time to use them against Barlow's mass of troops. The progress of the assault had all of the guns been in position can only be estimated. The eight pieces in Birney's target area do not appear to have affected the result there significantly, if they were fired at all.

Barlow selected a massed formation for his division because of the lack of detailed information concerning the Confederate defenses. This formation assured initial success, but once the works were crossed, the troops became unmanageable. Barlow and the members of his staff had advanced on foot, and both he and Gibbon were unable to control their men until they had been driven back to the first line of works by Gordon's counterattack. For the same reason, Birney's troops on the right were driven back out of the McCoull field by Ramseur's counterattack, although they fought hard and inflicted fairly heavy casualties upon the North Carolinians.

In a postwar letter, Hancock stated that the major obstruction to success after the establishment of the Federal position on the outside of the captured works was that no single officer was in command of that portion of the front. If Meade or even Grant had come up and directed operations, much more might have been accomplished. There would have been no need to ask Wright, whose attention was fixed on the area of the west angle, to suggest a point where he thought that another massed assault would be successful. Moreover, Wright would not have been permitted to squander the services of Cutler's men in relief of his own.

A promising location for a successful Union attack in the afternoon might have been against the area immediately to the west of the east angle. All of Gibbon's and many of Birney's troops lay several lines deep on the outside of this stretch of the works with very little to do during the afternoon. Hancock apparently believed that the Confederate troops of Gordon's three brigades who had driven Barlow's men back out of the salient in the morning were still positioned in force in the woods immediately to the east of the McCoull house. They were not, however. They were scattered in a thin line along the eastern face of the salient, facing Burnside's troops. During the afternoon there were few, if any, Confederate infantrymen in the works south from the east angle to the reserve line of works. (Hancock may have sent scouting parties into this area during the afternoon, but the results of these reconnaissances are not known.) Had Grant or Meade or Humphreys come forward and observed the fighting along the northern face for any appreciable amount of time, they would have realized that most, if not all, of the enemy opposition was coming from the area of the west angle and practically none was coming from behind the east angle, so a Union attack there might have been effective. Hancock certainly must have been aware of the difference in the amounts of firing at the two points. From the time his men were driven back out of the salient in the morning, however, he appears to have thought only in terms of defensive operations.

In his behalf it should be said that he and his troops were operating in unfamiliar, unmapped territory and that the connection with the Ninth Corps on his left throughout the morning had been tenuous at best. Many of his men lay dead or wounded within the salient. Higher headquarters had sent very little constructive advice, mostly admonishing him to hold on to what he had gained. Given the uncertainties of his situation, Hancock chose to operate strictly within the confines of his orders and to secure what his troops had gained.

When analyzing the operations and the judgment of Robert E. Lee on that hectic day, the obvious question is why he did not reinforce Brown's and Harris's brigades at the west angle in the afternoon. Perhaps he did not feel that he could safely withdraw any more troops from their positions elsewhere. After McGowan's South Carolinians entered the works, no attempt was made to reoccupy this line farther to the Confederate right. This made no difference, however, because the Federals did not attempt to come through there in force after early morning operations. When Lee ordered Humphreys's and Bratton's troops to Ewell's support immediately before dark, they were not sent to the firing line but were placed in the reserve line of works to the rear. Lee probably believed that, if the troops at the west angle could hold out until dark, the danger there would be over.

Even so, the question arises as to whether Lee realized the peril of the afternoon's battle at the west angle. His apparent surprise at learning that trees had been cut down by the firing there is described in Appendix C. He would subsequently award to Ramseur's brigade the major credit for saving the army that day. Colonel Brown reported no contact with anyone in the rear until he personally located Harris after dark. Brown's and Harris's men had fought apart from their parent commands because their division commanders, Wilcox and Mahone, were busy with operations on the right flank of the army. In December, Ewell wrote a letter to Harris in which he expressed his gratitude and admiration for the services of the Mississippians on 12 May. In his formal report of March 1865, however, he awarded only faint praise to the Carolinians and Mississippians for what they had accomplished on his front.

The competence of Ewell during the morning operations is suspect. In a postwar conversation, Lee informed William Allan, who had been ordnance officer of the Confederate Second Corps, that immediately after Hancock's breakthrough, Ewell was overwhelmed by the disaster and incapable of functioning efficiently. Also, when Lee learned of the breakthrough from Major Hunter, he went with Hunter to Gordon, who commanded the reserve force, and not to Ewell, although this might have been done to save time. Ewell's hesitant behavior when Perrin was awaiting instructions has been described. That day Ewell undoubtedly missed the presence of Early, upon whom he appeared to have relied heavily for advice and support.

With Longstreet absent indefinitely, A. P. Hill too ill to exercise command, and Ewell proving to be less and less reliable under pressure, the weakness of Lee's corps command was critical. And Stuart was gone. The stress and responsibility of Lee's position were staggering. His army had survived a near disaster, however, and was still intact, if somewhat reduced in numbers. His valiant troops still faced the enemy from a solid line.

The opposing forces were near exhaustion after 12 May. Both armies rested during the thirteenth as much as possible, although the Federals reconnoitered south into the salient and located the Confederates' new line.

Grant decided to transfer Meade's Fifth and Sixth corps from the right of the Union line around to the left of Burnside, where they would become the left element of the line. The move was to be made during the night of 13 May. These two units were then to assault Spotsylvania at dawn from the east. With the Confederates now entrenched in a strong position across the base of the salient, Grant probably hoped for success against Lee's right flank, which he thought might be weaker since 10 May.

Lee was obliged to juggle officers and units within his Second Corps because of the large number of casualties, especially prisoners, therein. The losses among regimental commanders and deputy commanders became a great concern for Lee and for his corps commanders. The replacements in these key positions would need time to gain experience.

The Federal movement on the night of 13 May was a miserable affair because of the muddy roads and paths and the exhaustion of everyone concerned. Slow rates of march and straggling by members of the Fifth Corps caused the intended attack to be called off.

Lee was not informed by Anderson that the Union Fifth Corps had left Laurel Hill until 3:30 on the afternoon of 14 May, sixteen hours after the Federals had begun to march away. In response, Lee began to transfer his First Corps from the left of his line to the right that night.

On 15 May, Hancock's corps left its position along the northern line of the salient and moved around to the left of the army. Thus, the Federal line now ran north and south, facing west. Grant must have been considering a move farther south, because cavalry reconnaissance activity south from the army's left flank increased at this time.

While waiting for the roads to dry and expected reinforcements to join the army, Grant and Meade decided to attempt an attack down the Massaponax Church Road against the Confederate right using Hancock's and Wright's corps. Reconnaissance officers reported, however, that the terrain was un-suitable for such an operation. Then Wright, seconded by Humphreys, recommended that the Sixth Corps return to the Landrum farm and attack down the salient against the left of the Confederate line, which they hoped had been weakened to buttress the right, south of the Fredericksburg Road. Grant and Meade agreed and included the Second Corps in the plan, with Hancock in command of the operation. This attack on 18 May was a complete failure. The Yankee infantrymen enjoyed little artillery support and were repulsed by Southern artillery fire alone.

Grant now issued directives for the army's move farther south, which was intended to begin at 2:00 A.M. on 20 May. Hancock's Second Corps would lead the march. It was to function as a lure to entice Lee to pursue with all or a portion of his army, so the Confederates might be successfully engaged in the open field before they could construct entrenchments.

This Union movement was delayed for twenty-four hours, however, because of Ewell's reconnaissance mission on the nineteenth and the resulting engagement in the vicinity of the Harris farm. Lee had become aware that the Federals appeared to be sidling toward his right and he had asked Ewell to move forward from his position along the base of the salient and locate the right of the Union line. Ewell had erroneously believed that Hancock's troops were still in his front, and, without making an effort to substantiate this belief, he had requested and received permission from Lee to swing somewhat to the west of the salient before proceeding to the northeast. The subsequent collision and engagement at Harris's was a disjointed affair that eventually cost the Confederate Second Corps over nine hundred casualties.

The Federals began to leave the vicinity of Spotsylvania Court House at 11:00 P.M. on 20 May. Lee's forces started on the following afternoon, heading for Hanover Junction to protect the all-important Virginia Central Railroad line from the Valley. The opposing forces would meet again at the North Anna River.

Federal battle casualties for the two weeks of operations were reported as being slightly less than eighteen thousand. Surprisingly, this figure is similar to the number reported for the two days of fighting in the Wilderness. It is difficult to determine an accurate figure for the Confederates. It must have been less than their opponent's, because for most of the time the Southerners fought defensively from behind fieldworks. Approximately forty-six hundred of Ewell's command are known to have been captured on the tenth, twelfth, and twentieth of May. An estimate of nine thousand to ten thousand Confederate casualties appears to be reasonable.

These losses generated an increased sense of despondency on both home fronts. In the North this could affect the Presidential election that was slated for later in the year. From a strictly military viewpoint, however, the Yankees could make good their losses. The Confederates could not.

Lee rode south hoping that a situation would develop that would enable

Revisiting the scene of battle, 12 May 1887. Nearly three hundred Union veterans of the Sixth Corps returned to Spotsylvania to dedicate a monument to their beloved commander, John Sedgwick, on the site where he had fallen twenty-three years before. After the ceremonies, a few wandered over to the field out in front of the west angle, where they had fought so hard and so long. Once again they confronted the Confederate works.

(Sedgwick Memorial Association, Sixth Army Corps, Spotsylvania Court House, Va. 11, 12, 13 May 1887. Philadelphia: Dunlap & Clarks, Printers.)

him to cripple or even destroy a portion of the numerically superior enemy force. He felt that he must prevent a siege of Richmond, or the Confederate cause would be doomed.

Similarly, Grant was hoping to defeat a portion of the Army of Northern Virginia. He had sent Hancock's corps ahead as bait with this in mind. If this ruse proved unsuccessful, he would continue to move south, attempting, if possible, to destroy Lee's army if it halted to make a stand. Nevertheless, he would keep moving south. If siege operations became necessary, the Confederates would eventually have to come out. In this way Grant would attempt to defeat Lee's Army of Northern Virginia. It would take all summer.

APPENDIX A

Order of Battle

This appendix gives the order of battle as of 7:00 A.M., 8 May 1864, but it includes subsequent major command changes and unit additions.

ARMY OF THE POTOMAC—Maj. Gen. George G. Meade
Oneida (New York) Cavalry Company

Provost Guard
Brig. Gen. Marsena R. Patrick
1st Massachusetts Cavalry, Companies C and D
80th New York
3d Pennsylvania Cavalry
68th Pennsylvania
114th Pennsylvania

Artillery
Brig. Gen. Henry J. Hunt
Reserve Artillery
Col. Henry S. Burton
First Brigade
Col. J. Howard Kitching
6th New York Heavy Artillery
15th New York Heavy Artillery

Second Brigade
Maj. John A. Tomkins
  5th Maine, Battery (E)
  1st New Jersey, Battery (A)
  1st New Jersey, Battery (B)
  5th New York Battery
  12th New York Battery
  1st New York, Battery (B)

Third Brigade
Maj. Robert H. Fitzhugh
  9th Massachusetts Battery
  15th New York Battery
  1st New York, Battery (C)
  11th New York Battery
  1st Ohio, Battery (H)
  5th U.S., Battery (E)

First Brigade Horse
Artillery
Capt. James M. Robertson
  6th New York Battery
  2d U.S., Batteries (B and L)

Second Brigade Horse
Artillery
Capt. Dunbar R. Ransom
  1st U.S., Batteries (E and G)
  1st U.S., Batteries (H and I)

2d U.S., Battery (D)	1st U.S., Battery K
2d U.S., Battery (M)	2d U.S., Battery A
4th U.S., Battery (A)	2d U.S., Battery G
4th U.S., Batteries (C and E)	3d U.S., Batteries (C, F, & K)

Volunteer Engineer Brigade
50th New York Engineers (11 companies)
Lt. Col. Ira Spaulding
Battalion U.S. Engineers
Capt. George H. Mendell

SECOND ARMY CORPS—Maj. Gen. Winfield S. Hancock
1st Vermont Cavalry, Company M

First Division, Brig. Gen. Francis C. Barlow

First Brigade	Second Brigade
Col. Nelson A. Miles	Col. Thomas A. Smyth[1]
26th Michigan	Col. Richard Byrnes
61st New York	28th Massachusetts
81st Pennsylvania	63d New York
140th Pennsylvania	69th New York
183d Pennsylvania	88th New York
	116th Pennsylvania

Third Brigade	Fourth Brigade
Col. Paul Frank	Col. John R. Brooke
Col. Hiram L. Brown[2]	2d Delaware
Col. Clinton D. MacDougall	64th New York
39th New York	66th New York
52d New York	53d Pennsylvania
57th New York[3]	145th Pennsylvania
111th New York	148th Pennsylvania
125th New York	
126th New York	

Second Division, Brig. Gen. John Gibbon
2d Company Minnesota Sharpshooters

First Brigade	Second Brigade
Brig. Gen. Alexander S. Webb[4]	Brig. Gen. Joshua T. Owen
Col. H. Boyd McKeen	152d New York
19th Maine	69th Pennsylvania
1st Company Sharpshooters	71st Pennsylvania
15th Massachusetts	72d Pennsylvania
19th Massachusetts	106th Pennsylvania

20th Massachusetts
7th Michigan
42d New York
59th New York
82d New York (2d Militia)

Third Brigade
Col. Samuel S. Carroll[5]
Col. Theodore G. Ellis
Col. Thomas A. Smyth
  14th Connectivut
  1st Delaware
  14th Indiana
  12th New Jersey
  10th New York Battalion
  108th New York
  4th Ohio
  8th Ohio
  7th West Virginia

Fourth Brigade[6]
Col. Mathew Murphy[7]
Col. James P. McIvor
  155th New York
  164th New York
  170th New York
  182d New York

Third Division, Maj. Gen. David B. Birney

First Brigade
Brig. Gen. J. H. Hobart Ward
Col. Thomas W. Egan[8]
  20th Indiana
  3d Maine
  40th New York
  86th New York
  124th New York
  99th Pennsylvania
  110th Pennsylvania
  141st Pennsylvania
  2d U.S. Sharpshooters

Second Brigade
Col. John S. Crocker
Col. Elijah Walker[9]
  4th Maine
  17th Maine
  3d Michigan
  5th Michigan
  93d New York
  57th Pennsylvania
  63d Pennsylvania
  105th Pennsylvania
  1st U.S. Sharpshooters

Fourth Division, Brig. Gen. Gershom Mott[10]

First Brigade
Col. Robert McAllister
  1st Massachusetts
  16th Massachusetts
  5th New Jersey
  6th New Jersey
  7th New Jersey
  8th New Jersey
  11th New Jersey
  26th Pennsylvania
  115th Pennsylvania

Second Brigade
Col. William R. Brewster
  11th Massachusetts
  70th New York
  71st New York
  72d New York
  73d New York
  74th New York
  120th New York
  84th Pennsylvania

Fourth Division (Heavy Artillery)[11]
Brig. Gen. Robert O. Tyler
1st Maine
1st Massachusetts
2d New York
7th New York
8th New York

Artillery Brigade
Col. John C. Tidball
6th Maine, Battery (F)
10th Massachusetts Battery
1st New Hampshire Battery
1st New York, Battery (G)
4th New York Heavy, 3d Battalion
1st Pennsylvania, Battery (F)
1st Rhode Island, Battery (A)
1st Rhode Island, Battery (B)
4th U.S., Battery (K)
5th U.S., Batteries (C and I)

FIFTH ARMY CORPS—Maj. Gen. Gouverneur K. Warren
12th New York Battalion

First Division, Brig. Gen. Charles Griffin
First Brigade
Brig. Gen. Romeyn B. Ayres
140th New York
146th New York
91st Pennsylvania
155th Pennsylvania
2d U.S. (Companies B, C, F, H, I and K)
11th U.S. (Companies B, C, D, E, F and G, 1st Battalion)
12th U.S. (Companies A, B, C, D and G, 1st Battalion)
12th U.S. (Companies A, C, D, F and H, 2d Battalion)
14th U.S. (1st Battalion)
17th U.S. (Companies A, C, D, G and H, 1st Battalion)
17th U.S. (Companies A, B and C, 2d Battalion)

Second Brigade
Col. Jacob B. Sweitzer
9th Massachusetts
22d Massachusetts[12]
32d Massachusetts
4th Michigan
62d Pennsylvania

Third Brigade
Brig. Gen. Joseph J. Bartlett
20th Maine
18th Massachusetts
1st Michigan
16th Michigan
44th New York

83d Pennsylvania
118th Pennsylvania

Second Division, Brig. Gen. John C. Robinson[13]
Col. Richard Coulter

First Brigade
Col. Peter Lyle
  16th Maine
  13th Massachusetts
  39th Massachusetts
  104th New York
  90th Pennsylvania
  107th Pennsylvania[14]

Second Brigade
Col. Richard Coulter
Col. James L. Bates
  12th Massachusetts
  83d New York
  97th New York
  11th Pennsylvania
  88th Pennsylvania

Third Brigade
Col. Andrew W. Denison[15]
Col. Charles E. Phelps[16]
Col. Richard N. Bowerman
  1st Maryland
  4th Maryland
  7th Maryland
  8th Maryland

Third Division, Brig. Gen. Samuel W. Crawford

First Brigade
Col. William McCandless[17]
Col. William C. Talley[18]
Col. Wellington H. Ent
  1st Pennsylvania Reserves
  2d Pennsylvania Reserves
  6th Pennsylvania Reserves
  7th Pennsylvania Reserves
  11th Pennsylvania Reserves
  13th Pennsylvania Reserves

Third Brigade
Col. Joseph W. Fisher
Col. Silas M. Bailey
  5th Pennsylvania Reserves
  8th Pennsylvania Reserves[19]
  10th Pennsylvania Reserves
  12th Pennsylvania Reserves

Fourth Division, Brig. Gen. Lysander Cutler

First Brigade
Col. William W. Robinson
  7th Indiana
  19th Indiana
  24th Michigan
  1st New York Battalion Sharpshooters
  2d Wisconsin
  6th Wisconsin
  7th Wisconsin

Second Brigade
Brig. Gen. James C. Rice[20]
Col. Edward B. Fowler
  76th New York
  84th New York
  95th New York
  147th New York
  56th Pennsylvania

Third Brigade
Col. Edward S. Bragg
  121st Pennsylvania
  142d Pennsylvania
  143d Pennsylvania
  149th Pennsylvania
  150th Pennsylvania

Artillery Brigade
Col. Charles S. Wainwright
  3d Massachusetts, Battery (C)
  5th Massachusetts, Battery (E)
  1st New York, Battery (D)
  1st New York, Batteries (E and L)
  1st New York, Battery (H)
  4th New York Heavy, 2d Battalion
  1st Pennsylvania, Battery (B)
  4th U.S., Battery (B)
  5th U.S., Battery (D)

SIXTH ARMY CORPS—Maj. Gen. John Sedgwick[21]
Brig. Gen. Horatio G. Wright
8th Pennsylvania Cavalry, Company A

First Division, Brig. Gen. Horatio G. Wright
Brig. Gen. David A. Russell

First Brigade
Col. Henry W. Brown
  1st New Jersey
  2d New Jersey
  3d New Jersey
  4th New Jersey
  10th New Jersey
  15th New Jersey

Second Brigade
Col. Emory Upton
  5th Maine
  121st New York
  95th Pennsylvania
  96th Pennsylvania

Third Brigade
Brig. Gen. David A. Russell
Brig. Gen. Henry L. Eustis
  6th Maine
  49th Pennsylvania
  119th Pennsylvania
  5th Wisconsin

Fourth Brigade
Col. Nelson Cross
  65th New York
  67th New York
  122d New York
  82d Pennsylvania

Second Division, Brig. Gen. Thomas H. Neill

First Brigade
Brig. Gen. Frank Wheaton
  62d New York
  93d Pennsylvania
  98th Pennsylvania
  102d Pennsylvania
  139th Pennsylvania

Second Brigade
Col. Lewis A. Grant
  1st Vermont (Heavy Artillery)[22]
  2d Vermont
  3d Vermont
  4th Vermont
  5th Vermont
  6th Vermont

Third Brigade
Col. Daniel D. Bidwell
  7th Maine
  43d New York
  49th New York
  77th New York
  61st Pennsylvania

Fourth Brigade
Brig. Gen. Henry L. Eustis
Col. Oliver Edwards
  7th Massachusetts
  10th Massachusetts
  37th Massachusetts
  2d Rhode Island

Third Division, Brig. Gen. James B. Ricketts

First Brigade
Brig. Gen. William H. Morris[23]
Col. John W. Schall
Col. William S. Truex[24]
  14th New Jersey
  106th New York
  151st New York
  87th Pennsylvania
  10th Vermont

Second Brigade
Col. Benjamin F. Smith
  6th Maryland
  110th Ohio
  122d Ohio
  126th Ohio
  67th Pennsylvania
  138th Pennsylvania

Artillery Brigade
Col. Charles H. Tompkins
  4th Maine, Battery (D)
  1st Massachusetts, Battery (A)
  1st New York, Independent Battery
  3d New York, Independent Battery
  4th New York Heavy, 1st Battalion
  1st Rhode Island, Battery (C)
  1st Rhode Island, Battery (E)
  1st Rhode Island, Battery (G)
  5th U.S., Battery (M)

CAVALRY CORPS—Maj. Gen. Philip H. Sheridan
6th U.S.

First Division, Brig. Gen. Wesley Merritt

First Brigade
Brig. Gen. George A. Custer
  1st Michigan
  5th Michigan
  6th Michigan
  7th Michigan

Second Brigade
Col. Thomas C. Devin
  4th New York [25]
  6th New York
  9th New York
  17th Pennsylvania

Reserve Brigade
Col. Alfred Gibbs
  19th New York
  6th Pennsylvania
  1st U.S.
  2d U.S.
  5th U.S.

Second Division, Brig. Gen. David McM. Gregg

First Brigade
Brig. Gen. Henry E. Davies, Jr.
  1st Massachusetts
  1st New Jersey
  6th Ohio
  1st Pennsylvania

Second Brigade
Col. J. Irvin Gregg
  1st Maine
  10th New York
  2d Pennsylvania
  4th Pennsylvania
  8th Pennsylvania
  16th Pennsylvania

Third Division, Brig. Gen. James H. Wilson

First Brigade
Col. John B. McIntosh
  1st Connecticut
  2d New York
  5th New York
  18th Pennsylvania

Second Brigade
Col. George H. Chapman
  3d Indiana
  8th New York
  1st Vermont

NINTH ARMY CORPS—Maj. Gen. Ambrose E. Burnside
8th U.S.
First Division, Brig. Gen. Thomas G. Stevenson[26]
Col. Daniel Leasure
Maj. Gen. Thomas L. Crittendon[27]

First Brigade
Lt. Col. Stephen M. Weld, Jr.
Brig. Gen. James H. Ledlie[28]
  35th Massachusetts
  56th Massachusetts
  57th Massachusetts

Second Brigade
Col. Daniel Leasure
  3d Maryland
  21st Massachusetts
  100th Pennsylvania

59th Massachusetts
4th U.S.
10th U.S.

Artillery
2d Maine Battery (B)
14th Massachusetts Battery

Second Division, Brig. Gen. Robert B. Potter

First Brigade	Second Brigade
Col. John I. Curtin	Col. Simon G. Griffin
36th Massachusetts	31st Maine
58th Massachusetts	32d Maine
51st New York	6th New Hampshire
45th Pennsylvania	9th New Hampshire
48th Pennsylvania	11th New Hampshire
7th Vermont	17th Vermont

Artillery
11th Massachusetts Battery
19th New York Battery

Third Division, Brig. Gen. Orlando B. Willcox

First Brigade	Second Brigade
Col. John F. Hartranft	Col. Benjamin C. Christ
2d Michigan	1st Michigan Sharpshooters
8th Michigan	20th Michigan
17th Michigan	79th New York
27th Michigan	60th Ohio
109th New York	50th Pennsylvania
51st Pennsylvania	

Artillery
7th Maine, Battery (G)
34th New York Battery

Fourth Division, Brig. Gen. Edward Ferrero

First Brigade	Second Brigade
Col. Joshua K. Sigfried	Col. Henry G. Thomas
27th U.S. Colored Troops	30th Connecticut (Colored)
30th U.S. Colored Troops	19th U.S. Colored Troops
39th U.S. Colored Troops	23d U.S. Colored Troops
43d U.S. Colored Troops	

Artillery
Pennsylvania Independent Battery (D)
3d Vermont Battery

Cavalry
3d New Jersey
22d New York
2d Ohio
13th Pennsylvania

Artillery Reserve
Col. John Edwards, Jr.
27th New York Battery
1st Rhode Island, Battery (D)
1st Rhode Island, Battery (H)
2d U.S., Battery (E)
3d U.S., Battery (G)
3d U.S., Batteries (L and M)

Provisional Brigade[29]
Col. Elisha G. Marshall
2d New York Mounted Rifles (dismounted)[30]
14th New York Heavy Artillery
24th New York Cavalry (dismounted)
2d Pennsylvania Provisional Heavy Artillery

ARMY OF NORTHERN VIRGINIA—Gen. Robert E. Lee
FIRST ARMY CORPS—Maj. Gen. Richard H. Anderson

Kershaw's Division, Brig. Gen. Joseph B. Kershaw

Kershaw's Brigade
Col. John W. Henagan
  2d South Carolina
  3d South Carolina
  7th South Carolina
  8th South Carolina
  15th South Carolina
  3d South Carolina Battalion

Wofford's Brigade
Brig. Gen. William T. Wofford
  16th Georgia
  18th Georgia
  24th Georgia
  Cobb's (Georgia) Legion
  Phillip's (Georgia) Legion
  3d Georgia Battalion Sharpshooters

Humphreys's Brigade
Brig. Gen. Benjamin G. Humphreys
  13th Mississippi
  17th Mississippi
  18th Mississippi
  21st Mississippi

Bryan's Brigade
Brig. Gen. Goode Bryan
  10th Georgia
  50th Georgia
  51st Georgia
  53d Georgia

Field's Division, Maj. Gen. Charles W. Field

Jenkins's Brigade
Col. John Bratton
  1st South Carolina
  2d South Carolina (Rifles)
  5th South Carolina
  6th South Carolina
  Palmetto Sharpshooters

Anderson's Brigade
Brig. Gen. George T. Anderson
  7th Georgia
  8th Georgia
  9th Georgia
  11th Georgia
  59th Georgia

Gregg's Brigade
Brig. Gen. John Gregg
  3d Arkansas
  1st Texas
  4th Texas
  5th Texas

Benning's Brigade
Col. Dudley M. DuBose
  2d Georgia
  15th Georgia
  17th Georgia
  20th Georgia

Law's Brigade
Brig. Gen. E. McIver Law
  4th Alabama
  15th Alabama
  44th Alabama
  47th Alabama
  48th Alabama

Artillery
Brig. Gen. E. Porter Alexander

Haskell's Battalion
Maj. John C. Haskell
  Flanner's (North Carolina) Battery
  Garden's (South Carolina) Battery
  Lamkin's (Virginia) Battery
  Ramsay's (North Carolina) Battery

Cabell's Battalion
Col. Henry C. Cabell
  Callaway's (Georgia) Battery
  Carlton's (Georgia) Battery
  McCarthy's (Virginia) Battery
  Manly's (North Carolina) Battery

Huger's Battalion
Lt. Col. Frank Huger
  Fickling's (South Carolina) Battery
  Moody's (Louisiana) Battery
  Parker's (Virginia) Battery
  Smith's, J. D. (Virginia) Battery
  Taylor's (Virginia) Battery
  Woolfolk's (Virginia) Battery

SECOND ARMY CORPS—Lt. Gen. Richard S. Ewell

Early's Division, Brig. Gen. John B. Gordon

Pegram's Brigade
Col. John S. Hoffman
  13th Virginia
  31st Virginia
  49th Virginia
  52d Virginia
  58th Virginia

Gordon's Brigade
Col. Clement A. Evans
  13th Georgia
  26th Georgia
  31st Georgia
  38th Georgia
  60th Georgia
  61st Georgia

Johnston's Brigade
Brig. Gen. Robert D. Johnston[31]
  5th North Carolina
  12th North Carolina
  20th North Carolina
  23d North Carolina

Johnson's Division, Maj. Gen. Edward Johnson

Stonewall Brigade
Brig. Gen. James A. Walker[32]
  2d Virginia
  4th Virginia
  5th Virginia
  27th Virginia
  33d Virginia

Steuart's Brigade
Brig. Gen. George H. Steuart
  1st North Carolina
  3d North Carolina
  10th Virginia
  23d Virginia
  37th Virginia

Jones's Brigade
Col. William Witcher
  21st Virginia
  25th Virginia
  42d Virginia
  44th Virginia
  48th Virginia
  50th Virginia

Louisiana Brigade (Consolidated)[33]
Brig. Gen. Harry T. Hays[34]
  1st Louisiana
  2d Louisiana
  5th Louisiana
  6th Louisiana
  7th Louisiana
  8th Louisiana
  9th Louisiana
  10th Louisiana
  14th Louisiana
  15th Louisiana

Rodes's Division, Maj. Gen. Robert E. Rodes

Daniel's Brigade
Brig. Gen. Junius Daniel[35]
Col. Bryan Grimes
  32d North Carolina
  45th North Carolina
  53d North Carolina
  2d North Carolina Battalion

Ramseur's Brigade
Brig. Gen. Stephen D. Ramseur
  2d North Carolina
  4th North Carolina
  14th North Carolina
  30th North Carolina

Battle's Brigade
Brig. Gen. Cullen A. Battle
  3d Alabama
  5th Alabama
  6th Alabama
  12th Alabama
  61st Alabama

Doles's Brigade
Brig. Gen. George Doles
  4th Georgia
  12th Georgia
  44th Georgia

Artillery
Brig. Gen. Armistead L. Long

Braxton's Battalion
Lt. Col. Carter M. Braxton
  Carpenter's (Virginia) Battery
  Cooper's (Virginia) Battery
  Hardwicke's (Virginia) Battery

Nelson's Battalion
Lt. Col. William Nelson
  Kirkpatrick's (Virginia) Battery
  Massie's (Virginia) Battery
  Milledge's (Georgia) Battery

Page's Battalion
Maj. Richard C. M. Page
  Carter's, W. P. (Virginia) Battery
  Fry's (Virginia) Battery
  Page's (Virginia) Battery
  Reese's (Alabama) Battery

Hardaway's Battalion
Lt. Col. Robert A. Hardaway
  Dance's (Virginia) Battery
  Graham's (Virginia) Battery
  Griffin's, C. B. (Virginia) Battery
  Jones's (Virginia) Battery
  Smith's, B. H. (Virginia) Battery

Cutshaw's Battalion
Maj. Wilfred E. Cutshaw
  Carrington's (Virginia) Battery
  Garber's, A. W. (Virginia) Battery
  Tanner's (Virginia) Battery

THIRD ARMY CORPS—Maj. Gen. Jubal A. Early
Anderson's Division, Brig. Gen. William Mahone

Perrin's Brigade	Mahone's Brigade
Brig. Gen. Abner Perrin[36]	Col. David A. Weisiger
8th Alabama	6th Virginia
9th Alabama	12th Virginia
10th Alabama	16th Virginia
11th Alabama	41st Virginia
14th Alabama	61st Virginia

Harris's Brigade	Wright's Brigade
Brig. Gen. Nathaniel H. Harris	Brig. Gen. Ambrose R. Wright
12th Mississippi	3d Georgia
16th Mississippi	22d Georgia
19th Mississippi	48th Georgia
48th Mississippi	2d Georgia Battalion

Perry's Brigade
Brig. Gen. Edward A. Perry
  2d Florida
  5th Florida
  8th Florida

Heth's Division, Maj. Gen. Henry Heth

Davis's Brigade	Cooke's Brigade
Brig. Gen. Joseph R. Davis	Brig. Gen. John R. Cooke
2d Mississippi	15th North Carolina
11th Mississippi	27th North Carolina
42d Mississippi	46th North Carolina
55th North Carolina	48th North Carolina

Walker's Brigade	Archer's Brigade
Brig. Gen. Henry H. Walker[37]	Brig. Gen. James J. Archer
40th Virginia	13th Alabama
47th Virginia	1st Tennessee (Provisional)
55th Virginia	7th Tennessee
22d Virginia	14th Tennessee

Kirkland's Brigade
Brig. Gen. William W. Kirkland
11th North Carolina
26th North Carolina
44th North Carolina
47th North Carolina
52d North Carolina

Wilcox's Division, Maj. Gen. Cadmus M. Wilcox

Lane's Brigade
Brig. Gen. James H. Lane
7th North Carolina
18th North Carolina
28th North Carolina
33d North Carolina
37th North Carolina

McGowan's Brigade
Brig. Gen. Samuel McGowan[38]
Col. Joseph N. Brown
1st South Carolina (Provisional)
12th South Carolina
13th South Carolina
14th South Carolina
1st South Carolina (Orr's Rifles)

Scales's Brigade
Brig. Gen. Alfred M. Scales
13th North Carolina
16th North Carolina
22d North Carolina
34th North Carolina
38th North Carolina

Thomas's Brigade
Brig. Gen. Edward L. Thomas
14th Georgia
35th Georgia
45th Georgia
49th Georgia

Artillery
Col. R. Lindsay Walker

Poague's Battalion
Lt. Col. William T. Poague
Richard's (Mississippi) Battery
Utterback's (Virginia) Battery
Williams's (North Carolina) Battery
Wyatt's (Virginia) Battery

McIntosh's Battalion
Lt. Col. David G. McIntosh
Clutter's (Virginia) Battery
Donald's (Virginia) Battery
Hurt's (Alabama) Battery
Price's (Virginia) Battery

Pegram's Battalion
Lt. Col. William J. Pegram
Brander's (Virginia) Battery
Cayce's (Virginia) Battery
Ellett's (Virginia) Battery
Marye's (Virginia) Battery
Zimmerman's (South Carolina) Battery

Richardson's Battalion
Lt. Col. Charles Richardson
Grandy's (Virginia) Battery
Landry's (Louisiana) Battery
Moore's (Virginia) Battery
Penick's (Virginia) Battery

Cutts's Battalion
Col. Allen S. Cutts
Patterson's (Georgia) Battery
Ross's (Georgia) Battery
Wingfield's (Georgia) Battery

CAVALRY CORPS—Maj. Gen. James E. B. Stuart
Hampton's Division, Maj. Gen. Wade Hampton

Young's Brigade
Brig. Gen. Pierce M. B. Young
  7th Georgia
  Cobb's (Georgia) Legion
  Phillips's (Georgia) Legion
  20th Georgia Battalion
  Jeff. Davis (Mississippi) Legion

Rosser's Brigade
Brig. Gen. Thomas L. Rosser
  7th Virginia
  11th Virginia
  12th Virginia
  35th Virginia Battalion

Butler's Brigade
Brig. Gen. Matthew C. Butler
  4th South Carolina
  5th South Carolina
  6th South Carolina

Fitzhugh Lee's Division, Maj. Gen. Fitzhugh Lee

Lomax's Brigade
Brig. Gen. Lunsford L. Lomax
  5th Virginia
  6th Virginia
  15th Virginia

Wickham's Brigade
Brig. Gen. William C. Wickham
  1st Virginia
  2d Virginia
  3d Virginia
  4th Virginia

William H. F. Lee's Division
Maj. Gen. William H. F. Lee

Chambliss's Brigade
Brig. Gen. John R. Chambliss
  9th Virginia
  10th Virginia
  13th Virginia

Gordon's Brigade
Brig. Gen. James B. Gordon
  1st North Carolina
  2d North Carolina
  5th North Carolina

Horse Artillery, Maj. R. Preston Chew
Breathed's Battalion
Maj. James Breathed
  Hart's (South Carolina) Battery
  Johnston's (Virginia) Battery
  McGregor's (Virginia) Battery
  Shoemaker's (Virginia) Battery
  Thomson's (Virginia) Battery

Sheridan versus Meade

The acrimonious exchange between Meade and Sheridan at army headquarters about midday of 8 May was caused in part by their opposing views about the proper use of cavalry during a campaign. Moreover, the temper of each man, always fiery, had been brought close to the detonation point by the military operations of the morning and previous night.

In his formal report written in 1866, Sheridan stated that, when he joined the Army of the Potomac in April 1864 to assume command of the Cavalry Corps, he discovered that its horses "were thin and very much worn out by excessive, and, it seemed to me, unnecessary picket duty; the picket line almost completely encircling the infantry and artillery camps of the army, covering a distance, if stretched out on a continuous line, of nearly sixty miles."[1] Sheridan had personally told Meade of the poor condition of the horses, and Meade had immediately relieved the horsemen of much of this picket duty.[2] During this meeting, Sheridan explained his opinion of the proper use of the mounted arm. He believed that the cavalry corps should not be fragmented in order to support the movements and tactical operations of the remainder of the army. Instead the corps should remain concentrated, with its primary mission to be fighting the enemy's cavalry. Meade, incredulous, asked who, under this arrangement, would protect the army trains and artillery reserve, cover the front of moving infantry columns, and protect the flanks of the infantry force? Sheridan coolly replied that, with his force concentrated, he could keep the enemy's cavalry so busy that it would pose no danger to the army's flanks or rear. Furthermore, he believed that moving columns of infantry should take care of their own fronts.[3]

Meade refused to consider these suggestions. For the movement through the Wilderness, he assigned the task of escorting the army trains to two of his three divisions of cavalry. As a result, the army received little tactical assistance from the mounted arm during the two-day battle there.

The instructions for the movement to take place on the night of 7 May were released from army headquarters at 3:00 P.M. Sheridan's assignment was to "have a sufficient force on the approaches from the right to keep the corps commanders advised in time of the appearance of the enemy."[4] The Federal corps for which this surveillance was intended were Warren's and Hancock's, which were to move in closest proximity to the enemy, directly down the Brock Road. When darkness fell, two of Sheridan's divisions were in excellent position to comply with Meade's instructions, one at Todd's Tavern and one approximately one mile southeast of the tavern just off the Brock Road.

Meade's instructions for Sheridan were general. He was granted full latitude to devise a plan by which to comply with his assignment, after studying the timing and the routes of the other contingents of the Federal force. He was still unaware of his orders, however, at the time when the movement began.

The order should have been delivered to cavalry headquarters at Alrich's on the Orange Plank Road no later than 4:30 P.M. At that time Sheridan was in the vicinity of Todd's Tavern, monitoring the operations of his two divisions there. His last message to Meade from the tavern was sent at 8:00 P.M. and contained no reference to the movement. From this it can be assumed that the staff officer who received the message at Alrich's had held it there for Sheridan's return.[5]

Sheridan should have arrived back at his headquarters by 9:30 P.M. at the latest. He did not compose the orders to his division commanders for support of the movement until 1:00 A.M. on the eighth. Apparently he spent the intervening three hours getting something to eat and studying the details of the movement order. If so, he did not study the details thoroughly, or else his maps were faulty, because the time at which he determined to move out his troopers on their assignments was 5:00 A.M.!

When Meade arrived at Todd's Tavern at midnight, he discovered that Generals Merritt and Gregg had received no orders to support the army's movement and were, in fact, unaware of the movement itself. Realizing that there was insufficient time to coordinate matters with Sheridan at Alrich's, Meade personally wrote orders for the two cavalry divisions. Merritt was directed to proceed down the Brock Road through Spotsylvania Court House and to position one brigade west of the village at the Block House. He was to picket all of the roads which led to the courthouse and to cover the trains located to the north. Gregg was instructed to move out to the west on the Catharpin Road to a point near Corbin's Bridge and to watch the roads leading north in the direction of Parker's Store.[6]

Meade's order to Gregg was already too late. The van of Anderson's Confederate infantry column had entered the Catharpin Road west of Todd's Tavern by 1:00 A.M. Merritt's troopers did not get started until 3:00 A.M. and almost immediately encountered opposition in the darkness on the Brock Road.

According to Sheridan's orders of 1:00 A.M., Merritt and Gregg were directed to move west on the Catharpin Road to Shady Grove Corner and then east on the Shady Grove Road. One division was to have assumed a position at the Block House Bridge over the Po and the other further to the east at the Block House. Wilson's Third Division of cavalry was to enter Spotsylvania Court House from the east and then proceed two miles south to Snell's Bridge over the Po.[7]

In his plans, Sheridan ignored the presence of Fitz Lee's troopers on the Brock Road. He apparently expected the moving infantry columns to protect and control their own fronts. He might also have believed that his troopers had shattered the effectiveness of the Southern cavalry in the fighting of the previous day. His decision to position two divisions west of the courthouse was judicious, as this was the direction from which the Confederate infantry would probably (and did actually) approach. Whatever merits his plan possessed, however, were nullified by the planned starting time of 5:00 A.M. By that time the Union Fifth Corps was expected to have been in the vicinity of the village digging in. In whatever manner Sheridan interpreted his instructions, he did not adequately consider the factor of time when designing his plans.

The support by the Federal cavalry corps of the Union march from the Wilderness on the night of 7–8 May was inadequate. The evidence appears to place most, if not all, of the responsibility for this failure on Sheridan. It is not known whether he ordered the members of his staff at Alrich's to refrain from bothering him with any more messages from army headquarters until he returned. If he did, he was insubordinate. If not, the staff officer who decided not to forward such an important directive is culpable, although his commander must bear the ultimate responsibility. The failure of this Federal movement was just one of many such unsuccessful night maneuvers by both Union and Confederate forces throughout the war. One might expect that by 1886, the Federals would have downplayed the errors of that night in the satisfaction of victory. This was not the case with Phil Sheridan.

Postwar Accounts

Meade wrote his report of the operations of May 1864 in November of that year. Concerning cavalry operations, he mentioned only that Wilson's division had managed to occupy the courthouse but had been forced to withdraw because the infantry could not get close enough to support him.[8]

In his report of July 1865, Grant did not mention cavalry operations at all for the seventh or eighth of May. He stated only that Sheridan started on his raid on the morning of 9 May.[9]

In his report on the operations of 7 May, Sheridan, after describing the cavalry combat operations, stated that "Gregg's and Merritt's divisions encamped in open fields in the vicinity of Todd's Tavern with orders to move in the morning, at daylight, for the purpose of gaining possession of Snell's Bridge, over the Po River."[10] He recorded his instructions to his division commanders and said he believed his orders would have enabled the Federal infantry to reach the courthouse area before the Confederates. Then, "but upon the arrival of General Meade at Todd's Tavern the orders were changed and Gregg was simply directed by him to hold Corbin's Bridge, and Merritt's division ordered in front of the infantry column, marching on the road to Spotsylvania in the darkness of the night, the cavalry and infantry becoming entangled in the advance causing much confusion and delay."[11] He complained that he had not been advised of these changes and that he had developed fears for the safety of Wilson's Third Division at the courthouse. This division had captured the village and held it "until driven out by the advance of Longstreet's corps."[12]

Obviously, Sheridan was attempting to convey the impression in this formal report that Gregg and Merritt had received their orders from him and that Meade had arrived at midnight and had changed them. This is patently untrue. There is incontestable evidence that Meade found the cavalry officers without orders and unaware of the army's movement, which was in progress. Sheridan's contention that following his orders would have precluded interference by Confederate infantry is unconvincing in view of the starting time of 5:00 A.M. His statement that Union infantry and cavalry became entangled along the Brock Road was refuted later by witnesses. Finally, his concern for the safety of Wilson's division at the courthouse, while genuine at the time, appears to have received a disproportionate emphasis in his report, to ensure that Meade would be given all of the blame for the failures. At 9:00

A.M. Wilson had informed Sheridan that he had driven some Confederate cavalrymen through the village and that "everything was all right."[13] When two Confederate infantry brigades led by Kershaw approached the village from the south, Wilson withdrew his men to the village and was positioning them for a defensive engagement at the time when Sheridan's message arrived ordering him to retire to the north toward the Orange Plank Road. Sheridan did not mention this message in his report. He claimed instead that Wilson's command was driven out by an enemy force.

The cavalry commander wrote his report in 1866 from New Orleans, and one might charitably credit these false statements to a lapse of memory. However, he repeated them twenty-two years later in his memoirs.

Grant's Memoirs

In his *Personal Memoirs* Grant, when explaining the failure of Warren's corps to reach Spotsylvania Court House on the morning of 8 May, appears to have relied heavily upon the account of his former staff officer, Adam Badeau, who in 1881 completed a military history of his former commander. In this work Badeau admitted that, when Meade arrived at Todd's Tavern, he found that Merritt and Gregg had received no orders. But, ignoring the factor of time, as had Sheridan in 1864, Badeau claimed that the cavalry leader's orders—one division at the Block House and one at the Block House Bridge—adequately provided for the advance of the Confederate infantry, while Meade's orders did not.[14] The bridge in question is where R. H. Anderson permitted Kershaw's infantrymen of the First Corps to fall out and to rest after their march from the Wilderness. This occurred at 4:00 to 4:30 A.M. By Sheridan's orders Merritt and Gregg were to move out from Todd's Tavern at 5:00 A.M.

According to Grant's account, which was published in 1885, Sheridan "issued the necessary orders for seizing Spottsylvania and holding the bridge over the Po River, which Lee's troops would have to cross to get to Spottsylvania. But Meade changed Sheridan's orders to Merritt—who was holding the bridge—on his arrival at Todd's Tavern, and thereby left the road free for Anderson when he came up."[15] The succeeding portion of the account continues to deplore the change in Merritt's orders and asserts that, under Sheridan's plan, two brigades of Union horsemen at the bridge would have detained Anderson long enough for Warren to reinforce Wilson and to hold the village.

It is a sobering experience to be obliged to dispute the accuracy of even a minute portion of what was once considered by some to be the greatest military writing since Caesar's *Commentaries*. As he courageously labored to complete his work, while fatally ill with cancer, Grant apparently got his information about this episode solely from the Federal military records, which included Sheridan's report, and Badeau's work. These accounts castigated Meade for everything that went wrong. By this time, however, other sources of information were available. For example,
A. A. Humphreys's *The Virginia Campaign of 1864 and 1865* was published in 1883. This work exposed the errors in Badeau's explanation of the events in question. If Grant was aware of Humphreys's work, he chose not to draw from it.[16]

It is impossible to imagine how Grant conceived the idea that Merritt ever held the

Block House Bridge or any other bridge. Merritt's report and those of his subordinates explain clearly that, after the end of their engagement with Fitz Lee's troopers on the Brock Road, they retired to within one mile of Todd's Tavern and went into camp.[17]

Sheridan's Memoirs

The account in Sheridan's *Memoirs*, published in 1888, follows the explanation contained in his 1866 report. In amplifying his instructions to Merritt and Gregg, however, he revealed his ignorance of the terrain in question. "In view of what was contemplated, I gave orders to Gregg and Merritt to move at daylight on the morning of the 8th, for the purpose of gaining possession of Snell's Bridge over the Po River, the former by the crossing at Corbin's Bridge and the latter by the Block House."[18] In fact, both Federal divisions were to use the identical route of march, and neither was ordered to go to Snell's Bridge.

The *Memoirs* explained again that Sheridan's intention was to concentrate his three divisions at or near Snell's Bridge over the Po River. If this was, indeed, his intention, his orders to Merritt and Gregg were faulty. Finally, Sheridan complained that his "three divisions of cavalry remained practically ineffective by reason of disjointed and irregular instructions."[19] Two of his divisions were ineffective because they received no operating instructions until four hours after the movements of the army had begun. The instructions they followed were written by Meade, not by Sheridan.

Humphreys's Appraisal

General Humphreys claimed that the primary reason for the failure of Warren's infantrymen to reach Spotsylvania Court House on the morning in question was the presence of Fitz Lee's troopers on the Brock Road. After offering his opinion that, in the darkness, Federal infantrymen would have made only slightly better progress than did the cavalrymen and that the result would have been the same, Humphreys stated, "The presence of Fitzhugh Lee's cavalry on the Brock Road, and Hampton's cavalry and Longstreet's corps on the Shady Grove road, settled the question as to who should first hold the Court House with infantry, whatever might have been the disposition of our cavalry."[20]

Humphreys was undoubtedly correct about Fitz Lee's troopers on the Brock Road. That was the route used by Warren's corps, and these Confederate cavalrymen were the ones who delayed the Federal rate of advance long enough for Anderson to arrive first. However, the accuracy of Humphreys's assertion that things would have happened as they did regardless of the disposition of the Federal cavalry is questionable, unless he was using the time of 1:00 A.M. on the eighth as the starting point.

Warren's infantry had replaced the cavalry in the advance at approximately 6:30 A.M. of the eighth on the Brock Road next to the Hart farm, one-quarter mile west of the Piney Branch Church Road intersection. This was also the general area in which the fighting between Gregg's and Fitz Lee's troopers had ended at dusk on the previous day. At that time Sheridan had considered it judicious to withdraw his forces to the vicinity of Todd's Tavern for the night.[21]

Had Sheridan received the movement order late in the afternoon and been given time to digest its contents, he should have realized the paramount importance of the Brock Road. Under these circumstances, he might have, although this is by no means certain, retained Gregg's horsemen at their advanced position, at least until the head of the infantry column arrived at approximately 3:45 A.M. In this situation, Robinson's Federal and Kershaw's Confederate divisions would have been at nearly equal marching distance from the courthouse at that time.

In all of the postwar writings, Meade is absent. He was aware of Sheridan's official report but chose not to become involved in a dispute over the matter. The last commander of the Army of the Potomac died in 1872, and thus he was spared the frustration of reading the accounts of Badeau, Grant, and Sheridan, which were written in the 1880s. Grant's version would have been especially painful.[22]

The Oak Stump of Spotsylvania

On the morning of 13 May, a few members of the First South Carolina returned to the area of the west angle from their new position in the rear and examined the fallen oak tree. One of these men, B. F. Brown, who was no relation to Col. Joseph Brown, found a piece of twine on the ground with which he measured the circumference of the stump just below the point where it had been severed. The measurement was sixty-three inches, indicating a diameter of approximately twenty inches. Brown kept the piece of string, and, as late as 1901, he had it along with his Appomattox parole in a dust-proof glass case.[1]

Captain W. W. Old of Edward Johnson's staff, who had escaped capture in the morning and had carried orders for Ewell the remainder of the day, also visited the oak tree on either the thirteenth or fourteenth. Later in the day he described the severed tree to a group of officers that included General Lee. Lee appeared slightly skeptical about the story and quietly asked Old if he could show the generals the tree. Old led the party to the site. Here General Lee viewed the tree and the area where two of his brigades had served him as had few others.[2]

Approximately one year later, on 10 May 1865, the Army of the Potomac was marching north to Washington, D.C. The First Division of the Second Corps camped in the general area of the Landrum farm near Spotsylvania Court House. Everyone in the division, which was now commanded by Nelson A. Miles, went sightseeing over the battlefield. Arriving at the west angle, Miles and the members of his staff discovered that the oak stump had been removed from the ground. The remainder of the tree still lay where it had fallen and was soon cut to pieces by Yankee relic hunters. Miles and his staff rode to Spotsylvania and had dinner at the hotel. They asked the proprietor, a gentleman named Sanford, if he knew who had removed the tree stump and what had become of it. Sanford professed ignorance of anything about the tree, and throughout the meal the table conversation centered around the missing stump.[3]

As the members of the party left the hotel and prepared to mount their horses, an orderly reported to Miles that he had overheard a waiter saying to the cook that he could tell the general something about the tree. Miles sent for the waiter, who said that the stump was locked up in the smokehouse of the hotel. Sanford refused to unlock the door, so the Federals broke it with an axe and liberated the tree stump. In Washington, Miles presented it to Secretary of War Stanton.[4]

Today the stump is on display in the Armed Forces History Section of the Smithsonian Institution's National Museum of American History in the nation's capital. It is an authentic identifiable casualty of the battle.

NOTES

ABBREVIATIONS

AL: Alabama Department of Archives and History
Arty: Artillery
Bg: Brigade
BRU: Brown University
Btln: Battalion
Btry: Battery
BU: Boston University
Cav: Cavalry
CHS: Cincinnati Historical Society
Confed: Confederate
CU: Cornell University
CV: *Confederate Veteran* Magazine
Div: Division
DU: Duke University
DUMC: Duke University Medical Center
Fed: Federal
FCHS: *Bulletin of the Fluvanna County Historical Society*
FSNMP: Fredericksburg and Spotsylvania National Military Park
GA: Georgia Department of Archives and History
HHL: Henry E. Huntington Library
HJC: Hill Junior College
Hq: Headquarters
HSC: Hampden-Sydney College
HSD: Historical Society of Delaware
HSP: Historical Society of Pennsylvania
ILSHL: Illinois State Historical Library
IN: Indiana State Library
Inf: Infantry
INHS: Indiana Historical Society
INU: Indiana University
LC: Library of Congress
LSU: Louisiana State University

MAHS: Massachusetts Historical Society
MC: Museum of the Confederacy
MEHS: Maine Historical Society
MNBP: Manassas National Battlefield Park
MOLLUS: Military Order of the Loyal Legion of the United States War Library and Museum
NA: National Archives
NC: North Carolina Department of Archives and History
NHHS: New Hampshire Historical Society
NY: New York State Library
OCHS: Oswego County Historical Society
OR: *War of the Rebellion: A Compilation of the Official Records of the Union and Confederate Armies*
PCHS: Potter County Historical Society
PSU: Pennsylvania State University
Res: Reserve
RIHS: Rhode Island Historical Society
RU: Rutgers University
SCHS: South Carolina Historical Society
SHSP: *Southern Historical Society Papers*
SHSW: State Historical Society of Wisconsin
TN: Tennessee State Library and Archives
UMI: University of Michigan
UNC: Southern Historical Collection, University of North Carolina
USAMHI: United States Army Military History Institute

USC: University of South Carolina
USMA: United States Military
  Academy
UV: University of Virginia
V: Virginia State Library
VHS: Virginia Historical Society
WCM: Waukesha County Museum

WHGS: Wyoming Historical and Ge-
  nealogical Society
WHS: Winchenden Historical Society
WLU: Washington and Lee University
WVU: West Virginia University
YU: Yale University

INTRODUCTION

1. *OR*, 33:795, 828, 904, 1017.
2. Steere, *Wilderness Campaign*. It is recommended that the reader consult this work, which provides an excellent résumé of Grant's strategic plan.
3. This is the author's estimate based upon an appraisal of the few surviving Confederate reports that mention losses in the battle of the Wilderness. Previous estimates range from a low of 7,700 to a high of more than 11,400.
4. Lyman, Journal, 6 May 1864, MAHS.
5. *OR*, 36 (1):480.
6. Grant, *Personal Memoirs*, 2:211.
7. Cleaves, *Meade of Gettysburg*, 252–55.
8. Atkinson, *Grant's Campaigns*, 210.
9. Grant, *Personal Memoirs*, 2:116.
10. Steere, *Wilderness Campaign*, 119.
11. Humphreys, Field Dispatches, chief of staff, 1–31 May 1864, HSP.

CHAPTER 1

1. Halsey, Diary, 6 May 1864, USAMHI.
2. *OR*, 36 (1):136.
3. Schaff, *Battle of the Wilderness*, 301. A telegraph line that ran from Washington to Rappahannock Station had not been considered important by Union commanders (and when actually tested on the evening of 6 May had proved inoperative).
4. Steere, *Wilderness Campaign*, 459; *OR*, 36 (1):317.
5. Hannaford, Memoirs, 6, 7 May 1864, CHS.
6. *OR*, 36 (1):988; Baird, Memoirs, 16, UMI.
7. *OR*, 36 (1):317.
8. Ibid., 608.
9. Myers, *The Comanches*, 275.
10. *OR*, 36 (2):486.
11. Ibid., 480–81.
12. Sorrel, *Recollections of a Confederate Staff Officer*, 238–39; *OR*, 36 (2):967.
13. Jacob Heater, "Battle of the Wilderness," *CV* 14 (1906):262–64.
14. *OR*, 36 (2):970.
15. Green, Diary, 7 May 1864, UNC; Marshall, *Company K, 155th Pennsylvania*, 7 May 1864.

16. "Incidents In the War of Secession."

17. Gordon, *Reminiscences of the Civil War*, 267–69. Some of Gordon's account of alleged statements by Lee during this ride defies belief. For a tactful treatment of this passage in Gordon's work see Freeman, *R. E. Lee*, 3:302 n. 47.

18. *OR*, 36 (1):1041. Unfortunately, the exact time at which Lee determined to have this road work done cannot be determined. Pendleton stated that it was ordered simultaneously with a Second Corps reconnaissance mission to Germanna Ford, which may have been the one reported by a Union Fifth Corps signal officer at 10:50 A.M. in *OR*, 36 (2):500.

19. *OR*, 36 (2):969.

20. Ibid., 487. The operations of the cavalry forces which were separate from those of the infantry on this date are described in Chapter 3.

21. *OR*, 36 (2):494; Walker and Walker, *Diary of the War*, 165.

22. Walker and Walker, *Diary of the War*, 165; *OR*, 36 (2):969.

23. *OR*, 36 (2):489, 494.

24. Aschmann, *Memoirs of a Swiss Officer*, 151; Ripley, *First United States Sharp Shooters*, 154; Paine, Diary, 7 May 1864, 77–78, ILSHL; Grosport, Diary, 7 May 1864, USAMHI; *OR*, 36 (2):495.

25. Benedict, *Vermont in the Civil War*, 1:437; *OR*, 36 (1):700.

26. *OR*, 36 (2):511.

27. Ibid., 499.

28. Ibid. Grant later recorded that, in addition to possessing this fault, Warren also was often reluctant to permit subordinate officers to act except under his personal supervision. See Grant, *Personal Memoirs*, 2:214–15.

29. *OR*, 36 (1):555.

30. Report of Maj. Robert T. Elliott, commanding Sixteenth Michigan Veteran Volunteers dated 10 May 1864 to Lieutenant Colonel Herring, 118th Pennsylvania Volunteers, Charles P. Herring Papers, MOLLUS.

31. J. L. Smith, *Corn Exchange Regiment*, 405.

32. Report of Maj. Robert T. Elliott, commanding Sixteenth Michigan Veteran Volunteers dated 10 May 1864 to Lieutenant Colonel Herring, 118th Pennsylvania Volunteers, Charles P. Herring Papers, MOLLUS; *OR*, 36 (1):584.

33. Glover, *Bucktailed Wildcats*, 245–46.

34. Schaff, *Battle of the Wilderness*, 330–31.

35. *OR*, 36 (1):308.

36. Ibid., (2):507.

37. Phisterer, *New York in the War of the Rebellion*, 2:1066.

38. Boudrye, *Fifth New York Cavalry*, 126.

39. *OR*, 36 (2):513.

40. Ibid., 513, 878; Wilson, Diary, 7 May 1864, HSD.

41. *OR*, 36 (2):507.

42. Humphreys, *Virginia Campaign*, 53. The author has used Humphreys's figures because, as Meade's chief of staff, he had a day-to-day interest in such things and his postwar efforts to produce accurate figures appear to have been at least as comprehensive as those of other writers.

43. *OR*, 36 (2):483.

44. Ibid., (1):220.

CHAPTER 2

1. Humphreys, *Virginia Campaign*, 57; Atkinson, *Grant's Campaigns*, 214–16; *OR*, 36 (2):529. Atkinson offers an interesting conjectural analysis of Grant's thinking about the projected move.

2. Humphreys, *Virginia Campaign*, 425. The author was unable to locate the original copy of this order. Of four different versions examined, Humphreys's appeared to be the most logically worded.

3. *OR*, 36 (1):293.

4. Theodore Lyman, "Uselessness of the Maps Furnished to the Staff of the Army of the Potomac previous to the Campaign of May 1864," *Papers of Massachusetts*, 79–80.

5. Humphreys, *Virginia Campaign*, 425.

6. *OR*, 36 (2):482, 512.

7. Ibid., 513.

8. Ibid., 508.

9. Ibid.

10. Ibid., 508–9.

11. Hannaford, Memoirs, 43, CHS; *OR*, 36 (1):893.

12. *OR*, 36 (1):995.

13. Hannaford, Memoirs, 43, CHS.

14. Sparks, *Inside Lincoln's Army*, 369.

15. Boudrye, *Fifth New York Cavalry*, 126–27.

16. *OR*, 36 (2):509.

17. Ibid., 512.

18. *OR*, 36 (1):907; Bosbyshell, *The 48th In the War*, 149; Burrage, *Thirty-Sixth Regiment*, 160.

19. Cutcheon, *Twentieth Michigan Infantry*, 110.

20. *OR*, 36 (1):1085.

21. See Chapter 1, n. 18.

22. *OR*, 36 (1):1085; Worsham, *Foot Cavalry*, 205; Toney, Diary, 7 May 1864, TN. Long reported the results of the reconnaissance in a message to Ewell marked noon, which time appears to have been an error by either Long or the government copier of the *Official Records*.

23. *OR*, 36 (2):968. This contradicts Union engineers' postbattle reports claiming that the bridge was gone by 6:00 A.M. The Confederate officer's report is substantiated to some degree by an account of the Third New Jersey Cavalry Regiment saying that the regiment was ordered in the afternoon to escort a pontoon train downriver. The account is in Foster, *New Jersey and the Rebellion*, 662.

24. *OR*, 36 (2):970. The contents of Fitz Lee's message are suggested in *OR*, 51 (2):897–98.

25. *OR*, 36 (2):969–70. The exact time at which this important message was composed cannot be determined. It was sometime between 1:30 and 2:30 P.M.

26. Ibid., 51 (2):897–98.

27. Ibid., 36 (2):490.

28. Ibid.

29. Ibid., 493; (1):490, 493, 502, 504. This ridge had exerted a subtle influence upon the battle of Chancellorsville one year earlier. Stonewall Jackson, during his movement to Hooker's right flank on 2 May, had extended his route of march approximately three-quarters of a mile to pass west of the ridge and screen his troops from possible detection by the Federals. This appears now to have been an unnecessary precaution on Jackson's part. It is interesting to contemplate how much more effective his assault might have been with twenty to thirty more minutes of daylight in which to operate.

30. Ibid., (2):491.

31. Walker and Walker, *Diary of the War*, 165–66; *OR*, 36 (2):492. Hancock's message to Meade stated that Miles had led the operation and had examined the extent of Kershaw's line before retiring. This seems unlikely if Robertson's account, which does not mention Miles, is correct. Miles did not mention the reconnaissance in his official report of the campaign.

32. See this chapter, at n. 2.

33. *OR*, 36 (2):483–84.

34. Ibid., 483.

35. Ibid., (1):277–78.

36. Ibid., 114, 994.

37. Charles E. Pease to commanding officer, Artillery Reserve, Letter Book, Vol. 4, 4 May to 30 May 1864, George G. Meade Papers, HSP.

38. *OR*, 36 (1):287, 289.

39. Ibid., (2):491–93, 495.

40. Ibid., 512.

41. Winne, Journal, 4, DUMC.

42. Randall, Reminiscences, 7–9 May 1864, UMI.

43. Royall, *Some Reminiscences*, 35. The author has been unable to identify the guns that Palmer reported seeing. At least three Ninth Corps batteries were in park a short distance northwest of the Lacy house, but these were not moved until later in the evening. It is possible that the batteries sighted were those of the Ninth Corps Reserve moving to join the Army of the Potomac Reserve near Dowdall's Tavern on the Orange Turnpike. If these moved at 4:00 P.M. or later, they would have probably been routed southeast on the Germanna Plank Road to its intersection with the Orange Plank and then east to their destination in order to keep the pike clear for the Sixth Corps trains. In this case they would have moved initially toward the Confederate right as Palmer stated.

44. Richard H. Anderson to James Longstreet, n.d., Anderson Papers, DU; Anderson, Report of Operations, Lee Headquarters Papers, VHS; Richard H. Anderson to Edward B. Robins, 14 May 1879, *Papers of Massachusetts*, 227–30. The author will use these three sources as the basis for the general description of the Confederate First Corps's movement to the vicinity of Spotsylvania Court House. Unfortunately, Anderson retained few personal wartime military papers and his memory was anything but reliable, which he readily admitted in his letter to Robins in 1879. Pendleton remembered Anderson's stating that his instructions were to begin the movement by 3:00 A.M. rather than punctually at that time. This may have been the case. There is no known written copy of this order, which may have been spoken by Lee to Anderson in Pendleton's presence. Pendleton's report is in *OR*, 36 (1):1041.

CHAPTER 3

1. *OR*, 36 (1):788.
2. Ibid., (2):481.
3. Ibid., 516.
4. Ibid., (1):833.
5. Ibid., (2):513. Sheridan may have already been so informed by a staff officer of Ferrero's who could have arrived at Dowdall's Tavern as early as 9:30 A.M.
6. Ibid., 969, 487, 494.
7. Ibid., 514; (1):816–17, 826, 827. It is difficult to resolve the conflicting accounts in the reports of Custer and his regimental commanders. The author has presented a description of probable events based upon these records.
8. Ainsworth, First New York Dragoons, 74, USAMHI.
9. Pyne, *Ride to War*, 192.
10. Ainsworth, First New York Dragoons, 75, USAMHI.
11. Lee, Report of Operations, 4, MC.
12. Preston, *Tenth Regiment*, 172.
13. Myers, *The Comanches*, 277.
14. Tobie, *First Maine Cavalry*, 252.
15. Ressler, Diary, 7 May 1864, USAMHI.
16. Preston, *Tenth Regiment*, 172.
17. *OR*, 36 (1):867.
18. William McDonald, *Laurel Brigade*, 237.
19. Ainsworth, First New York Dragoons, 75–76, USAMHI.
20. Gracey, *Sixth Pennsylvania Cavalry*, 235.
21. Carter, Diary, 7 May 1864, HSC.
22. Ainsworth, First New York Dragoons, 76, USAMHI.
23. Ibid.
24. Gracey, *Sixth Pennsylvania Cavalry*, 235–36.
25. Ainsworth, First New York Dragoons, 77, USAMHI.
26. Gill, *Reminiscences*, 94–95.
27. Cheney, *Ninth Regiment New York Volunteer Cavalry*, 158. The Volunteer regiments of this brigade often disparaged the fighting efforts of the Regulars. In fairness to the First U.S. Cavalry it should be noted that six of its eight officers received wounds on this day.
28. Lloyd, *First Reg't Pennsylvania Reserve Cavalry*, 91.
29. *OR*, 51 (1):249.
30. Tobie, *First Maine Cavalry*, 253.
31. Waring, Diary, 7 May 1864, UNC.
32. *OR*, 36 (2):515.
33. Ibid., 51 (1):248–49. Many Federal and Confederate postwar accounts insist that the enemy forces encountered on both the Brock and Catharpin roads consisted of infantry.
34. Ibid., 36 (2):515.

CHAPTER 4

1. See Chapter 1.

2. Frederick H. Fields, Report of 22d Massachusetts Regiment picket detachment, 9 May 1864, Charles P. Herring Papers, MOLLUS.

3. Various postwar accounts by Fifth Corps personnel offer different orders of march. The one presented in the text is based upon the order of arrival in the morning and takes into account one change in the order en route.

4. Phelps, "Seventh Regiment," 269.

5. Fowle, *Letters to Eliza*, 82; Schaff, *Battle of the Wilderness*, 342, 344.

6. Humphreys, *Virginia Campaign*, 58 n. 2.

7. John L. Parker, *Henry Wilson's Regiment*, 426–27.

8. Caldwell, *Brigade of South Carolinians*, 135–36; Schaff, *Battle of the Wilderness*, 342–43.

9. Agassiz, *Meade's Headquarters*, 102.

10. Fowle, *Letters to Eliza*, 82. They were also cheered by Hancock's men further south.

11. Farley, "Reminiscences," 246–47; Marshall, *Company K, 155th Pennsylvania*, 7 May 1864.

12. Nevins, *Diary of Battle*, 355.

13. Humphreys, *Virginia Campaign*, 58 n. 2.

14. *OR*, 36 (1):540.

15. Robert S. Robertson, "The Escape of Grant and Meade," 248–51. Robertson provided this account of the incident after the publication of Grant's memoirs, which advanced an entirely different version of the affair, containing no mention of Robertson and awarding credit for the discovery of the incorrect route to one of Grant's staff. This staff officer, Lt. Col. Cyrus B. Comstock, did not mention the incident in a journal that he kept during the war. Robertson's explanation appears to be the more plausible. Grant's accounts of some events, at least in this portion of his memoirs, should be checked carefully. For example, he wrote that when the headquarters group arrived at the aforesaid fork in the road the officers attempted to determine which road Sheridan had taken with his cavalry earlier in the day. Neither Sheridan himself nor any of his cavalry had been on this part of the Brock Road earlier on that day or the day before. It appears that Grant was no more familiar with this section of the army's line than was Meade. Neither commander had visited the left flank during the battle. See also Appendix B.

16. Sparks, *Inside Lincoln's Army*, 370.

17. See Chapter 1.

18. Rawle et al., *Third Pennsylvania Cavalry*, 421–22. The authors of this work convey the impression that the progress of the Fifth Corps was delayed by this fracas in the darkness. This appears to be unlikely because Grant and Meade arrived at Todd's Tavern at approximately midnight, which was the earliest time at which Warren's troops could have left the Orange Plank crossing.

19. Humphreys, *Virginia Campaign*, 70.

20. *OR*, 36 (2):552.

21. Ibid.

22. Ibid., 551.

23. Ibid., 553.

24. See Chapter 2, n. 44.

25. *OR*, 36 (2):968.

26. Ibid.

27. Ibid., 51 (1):248–49. The contents of Lee's message of 7:00 P.M. can be surmised from this reply from Stuart, which was probably sent shortly after 8:00 P.M.

28. Ibid., 36 (1):1041. The location of this road cannot be precisely defined. In March 1944 Douglas S. Freeman asked National Park Service personnel at Fredericksburg, Virginia, to investigate and attempt to establish the location of the first part of Anderson's route, which was referred to as the "Pendleton Road." A report prepared by Francis F. Wilshin, Historical Technician, dated 28 August 1944, concluded that the work performed by Confederate artillerymen under Pendleton's supervision was to widen and clear of obstructions the path that already existed as an extension of Kershaw's line to the south, rather than to cut a completely new road through the forest. The author, after extensive investigation, including traversing the area in question on foot, as did Wilshin, believes this conclusion to be correct.

29. *OR*, 36 (1):1041.

30. Dame, *From the Rapidan to Richmond*, 96–97; Alexander, Personal Narrative, 59, UNC.

31. Anderson to Longstreet, 2, DU. This area was approximately one mile south-southwest of the Stevens and Trigg houses. Hancock's pickets had reported smoke and fire there early in the afternoon.

32. Freeman, *Lee's Lieutenants*, 3:380.

33. Anderson to Robins, 14 May 1879, *Papers of Massachusetts*, 227–30; Anderson to Longstreet, 2–3, DU. Anderson remembered that the guide said the road stayed bad until near Spotsylvania Court House, but this was obviously an error. Apparently what was meant was the part of the road from the beginning of march to the intersection with the Catharpin Road.

34. Waring, Diary, 8 May 1864, UNC.

35. Alexander, Personal Narrative, 59, UNC. Alexander recorded that the infantrymen of the First Corps passed undetected within a little more than one mile from Todd's Tavern. The artilleryman learned this important piece of information from someone else, because he did not accompany the infantry. The distance from Kershaw's right flank in his Wilderness position to the Catharpin Road was just short of three miles by this route, with another mile and two-tenths to Corbin's Bridge. With a rate of march of one and one-half miles per hour in the darkness to the Catharpin Road and slightly higher from that point to the bridge a time of 1:00–1:30 A.M. appears to be reasonable. While most accounts state that the First Corps's departure time was 11:00 P.M., it may have been earlier. In his undated letter to Longstreet, Anderson stated that he moved at 10:00 P.M., and some other Confederate accounts intimate that the march began before 11:00 P.M.

36. Anderson to Robins, 14 May 1879, *Papers of Massachusetts*, 227–30; Alexander, Personal Narrative, 59, UNC.

37. Roebling, Report of Operations, 20, NY; Carswell McClellan, *Memoirs of Sheridan*, 17–18.

38. *OR*, 36 (2):538–39.

39. Wainwright, Journal, 221, HHL.

40. Ibid., 222.

41. Ainsworth, "First New York Dragoons," 81, USAMHI.

42. *OR*, 36 (1):834.

43. Veil, Reminiscences, MOLLUS.

44. *OR*, 36 (2):538–39.

45. Cook, *Twelfth Massachusetts Volunteers*, 129; Theodore Lyman, "Extract from Diary of Colonel Theodore Lyman, A.D.C. to General G. G. Meade, giving an account of a visit to the Wilderness battle-field in April 1866, by General Peirson and himself," *Papers of Massachusetts*, 238.

46. Fowle, *Letters to Eliza*, 88.

47. Charles E. Davis, Jr., *Three Years in the Army*, 333.

48. Lee, Report of Operations, 5–6, MC.

49. Ibid.; Charles E. Davis, Jr., *Three Years in the Army*, 333; Stearns, *Three Years with Company K*, 263; "The War In Virginia."

50. Stone, Personal War Sketch, WHS. From the evidence available it is not possible to pinpoint the precise location of this action. It may have occurred farther south on the clearing of the Spindle farm.

51. *OR*, 36 (2):539. Warren's messages to headquarters that morning intimate that he may have been berated by Meade at Todd's Tavern for the slow rate of his corps's progress. In addition, Wainwright may have informed him that headquarters personnel were aware of the poor march discipline displayed by his troops.

52. Charles H. Porter to Charles L. Peirson, 18 April 1879, BU; Roe, *Thirty-Ninth Regiment*, 182. In Federal accounts the term "Laurel Hill" is used to designate the entire area of the Spindle farm and is so used by the author. However, in 1886 a local inhabitant informed a visiting Union veteran that the true Laurel Hill was located to the northeast of here. See Robert G. Carter, *Four Brothers in Blue*, 393.

53. Govan and Livingood, *Haskell Memoirs*, 67.

54. *OR*, 36 (1):1036; J. W. Eggleston to George S. Bernard, 1895, Bernard Papers, UNC. Artillery personnel from James N. Lamkin's Virginia battery, armed with Enfield rifles, accompanied the battalion. These gunners had joined the army from South Carolina in the fall of 1863, but by the time they reported, their guns and horses had been assigned elsewhere.

55. Govan and Livingood, *Haskell Memoirs*, 67.

56. Dickert, *Kershaw's Brigade*, 357.

57. Joseph B. Kershaw to Edward B. Robins, 7 Oct. 1886, *Papers of Massachusetts*, 231.

58. Anderson, Report of Operations, 3, VHS; Carter, Diary, 8 May 1864, HSC.

59. *OR*, 36 (2):553.

60. Kershaw to Robins, 7 Oct. 1886, *Papers of Massachusetts*, 231; Anderson, Report of Operations, 3, VHS.

61. *OR*, 36 (1):878; Carter, Diary, 8 May 1864, HSC. Many accounts state that it was Rosser and all or a portion of his brigade who were at the courthouse, but he and his troopers were west of Todd's Tavern that morning.

62. Freeman, *Lee's Lieutenants*, 3:384 n. 40.

63. Dickert, *Kershaw's Brigade*, 357; Coxe, "Last Struggles."

64. H. B. McClellan, *J. E. B. Stuart*, 408–9; Govan and Livingood, *Haskell Memoirs*, 67. The reader is again reminded that this narrative of the arrival of Anderson's troops at Laurel Hill and the description of the opening of the infantry fighting that followed are based upon the analysis and merging of various sources, most of which are contradictory.

65. Porter to Peirson, 18 April 1879, BU.

66. Lyman, Journal, *Papers of Massachusetts*, 239; Porter to Peirson, 18 April 1879, BU.

67. Coxe, "Last Struggles"; Charles L. Peirson, "Operations of the Army of the Potomac May 7–11, 1864," *Papers of Massachusetts*, 215.

68. Phelps, "Seventh Regiment," 271. The precise location of Coulter's brigade in the advance is uncertain. It was probably to the left rear of the Maryland brigade.

69. *OR*, 36 (1):641.

70. Phelps, "Seventh Regiment," 271–73.

71. Ibid., 272.

72. Today a visitor to Laurel Hill will find only one monument, ten yards in front of the Confederate works, near the site where Captain Anderson was hit. An inscription on the south face of the stone reads: "Nearest Approach On This Front / 7th Md. Inf." On the east face is inscribed: "2nd Div. 5th Corps / U.S.A. / Never mind cannon! / Never mind bullets! / Press on and clear this road!"

73. Phelps, "Seventh Regiment," 272–73. Anderson survived his wounds.

74. Charles E. Davis, Jr., *Three Years in the Army*, 334. An engraving of this scene made from a pencil drawing by A. R. Waud appeared in the 11 June 1864 edition of *Harper's Weekly*.

75. Phelps, "Seventh Regiment," 274.

76. *OR*, 36 (1):602.

77. McKnight, Diary, 8 May 1864, HSP; *OR*, 36 (1):599.

78. *OR*, 36 (1):141.

79. Ibid., (2):820–21. In a regimental history composed for the state of Maryland in 1898, Colonel Phelps suggested that, when an attack such as the one at Laurel Hill is executed by exhausted troops, without artillery preparation, directly against the front of veteran soldiers behind cover, then the officer ordering such an attack should be held responsible for the results. He should not be permitted to place the blame for unfavorable results upon his soldiers. This statement appears to have been an obvious reference to Warren.

80. Peirson, "Operations of the Army of the Potomac May 7–11, 1864," *Papers of Massachusetts*, 215–16.

81. Roe, *Thirty-Ninth Regiment*, 182–83.

82. Phelps, "Seventh Regiment," 272.

83. Roe, *Thirty-Ninth Regiment*, 188; Porter to Peirson, 18 April 1879, BU; Small, *Road to Richmond*, 136.

84. Nash, *Forty-Fourth Regiment*, 187–88.

85. Hopper, Reminiscences, 5, UMI.

86. Judson, *Eighty-Third Regiment*, 95; *OR*, 36 (1):576; Nash, *Forty-Fourth Regiment*, 188.

87. Hopper, Reminiscences, 6, UMI. The distance between the two advancing

columns cannot be determined. It was close enough to enable a captain in Bartlett's brigade to recognize Robinson, who had been his regimental commander earlier in the war.

88. Judson, *Eighty-Third Regiment*, 95.

89. Ibid., 95–96; Nash, *Forty-Fourth Regiment*, 188–90. The members of these two regiments enjoyed a close relationship based upon mutual respect, throughout the war. Moving into position on Little Round Top at Gettysburg on 2 July 1863, the regimental alignment within the brigade was altered at the request of the commander of the Forty-fourth, so the two units could fight side by side as they had in all previous engagements. See Norton, *Strong Vincent*, 52–53.

90. *OR*, 36 (1):576, 581. The First Michigan claimed that one of its members had carried the regimental colors of the Eighty-third Pennsylvania (which had been found lying on the ground) in two separate assaults and afterward returned them to the Pennsylvania regiment.

91. Ibid., 570.

92. Ibid., 560.

93. Farley, "Reminiscences," 248–49.

94. John L. Parker, *Henry Wilson's Regiment*, 428–29.

95. *OR*, 36 (1):560; Porter to Peirson, 18 April 1879, BU.

96. Nevins, *Diary of Battle*, 356–57.

97. *OR*, 36 (2):539–40.

98. Holmes, *Touched With Fire*, 108–9.

99. Haines, *Fifteenth New Jersey*, 156.

100. Wainwright, Journal, 225, HHL.

101. Sypher, *Pennsylvania Reserve Corps*, 522; Glover, *Bucktailed Wildcats*, 248.

102. Abernathy, *Our Mess*, 42; Watson, Diary, 7–8 May 1864, VHS; Kershaw to Robins, 7 Oct. 1886, *Papers of Massachusetts*, 231; Seventeenth Mississippi Regiment Record of Events, May 1864, NA.

103. *OR*, 36 (1):124–25; Irwin, Diary, 6 May 1864, HSP. Stone's brigade appears to have deteriorated in efficiency after its gallant performance at Gettysburg on 1 July 1863. The fact that an officer from outside the brigade was placed in command is significant. Col. Edmund L. Dana of the 143d Pennsylvania would probably have been a competent replacement for Stone, but he had been wounded and captured on 6 May. Stone may have been drunk at the time he sustained his injury. See Pearson, *James S. Wadsworth*, 270.

104. Irwin, Diary, 7 May 1864, HSP; A. P. Smith, *Seventy-Sixth Regiment*, 295; Curtis, *Twenty-Fourth Michigan*, 238–39.

105. *OR*, 36 (1):625; Marquis and Tevis, *Fighting Fourteenth*, 118–19.

106. Chamberlin, *One Hundred and Fiftieth Regiment*, 225–26; *OR*, 36 (1):637.

107. *OR*, 36 (1):619; Cheek and Pointon, *Sauk County Riflemen*, 93–94.

108. Oates, *War Between the Union and Confederacy*, 354–55.

109. Ibid.; Field, "Campaign of 1864 and 1865."

110. Field, "Campaign of 1864 and 1865"; *OR*, 36 (1):1065–66; Oates, *War Between the Union and Confederacy*, 355; Collier, *They'll Do To Tie To*, 182.

111. Croffut and Morris, *History of Connecticut*, 572; Carter, Diary, 8 May 1864, HSC.

112. *OR*, 36 (2):554–55; (1):878, 1042.

113. Ibid., (1):878, 788.
114. Ibid., (2):545.
115. Ibid., 526.

CHAPTER 5

1. *OR*, 36 (2):510; (1):753–54.
2. Holmes, *Touched With Fire*, 108.
3. Halsey, Diary, 7 May 1864, USAMHI; Newell, *Ours*, 261.
4. Wilkerson, *Recollections of a Private Soldier*, 77–80.
5. Rhodes, Diary, 7–8 May 1864, RIHS.
6. Holmes, *Touched With Fire*, 108.
7. *OR*, 36 (1):702.
8. Baquet, *First Brigade New Jersey Volunteers*, 118–19; Robert Powrie to Father and Mother, 6 May 1864, WCM.
9. *OR*, 36 (2):545, 530.
10. Haines, *Fifteenth New Jersey*, 156; Foster, *New Jersey and the Rebellion* 1:395.
11. *OR*, 36 (1):907–8.
12. Burrage, *Thirty-Sixth Regiment*, 160; Lord, *Ninth Regiment*, 369; Jones, Diary, 8 May 1864, NHHS.
13. Cutcheon, *Twentieth Michigan Infantry*, 110–11; Burrage, *Thirty-Sixth Regiment*, 161; *OR* 36 (1):908.
14. Boudrye, *Fifth New York Cavalry*, 127.
15. *OR*, 36 (2):530. The Fifth New York apparently moved east behind the Ninth Corps rather than reporting to army headquarters.
16. Hannaford, Memoirs, 8 May 1864, CHS.
17. *OR*, 36 (1):1071.
18. Dunlop, *Lee's Sharpshooters*, 43; Freeman, *Lee's Lieutenants*, 3:353.
19. Peyton, *Record*, 23; Dozle, Reminiscences, 3, LC; McMurran, Diary, 8 May 1864, V.
20. *OR*, 51 (2):902; *Official Atlas*, Plate 81, Map 1. The route of march was probably from Chewnings a short distance toward the Tapp clearing and then onto a newly opened woods path that ran southwest and intersected the Orange Plank Road approximately one mile east of Parker's Store. The march continued southwest on a path that intersected the road from Parker's Store to White Hall approximately one mile south of the store. The existence of the path south from the Plank Road is verified in *OR*, 29 (1):902–3.
21. Howard, *Recollections*, 282; Green, Diary, 8 May 1864, UNC; Peyton, *Record*, 24.
22. *OR*, 36 (2):974–75; (1):1071; Daniel Papers, DU.
23. *OR*, 36 (2):974; Field Telegrams, Lee Headquarters Papers Collection, VHS. The VHS copy of this important message is the only one found which contains a time of composition. It contains neither the name of the person addressed nor a signature. The copy used by the U.S. War Department for inclusion in the *Official Records* cannot be located. It said it was received in Richmond at 4:29 o'clock. On

8 May the telegraph instrument used by the Army of Northern Virginia was located at Orange Court House.

24. Grant, *Personal Memoirs*, 2:215.

25. *OR*, 36 (2):495–96, 530; (1):329.

26. This order of march is a guess based upon various accounts of departure and arrival times. Hancock's circular of instructions did not include Birney's division in the order of march.

27. *OR*, 36 (2):531.

28. Tobie, *First Maine Cavalry*, 254. See Chapter 3.

29. *OR*, 36 (2):552.

30. Tobie, *First Maine Cavalry*, 254; Preston, *Tenth Regiment*, 172–73; Waring, Diary, 8 May 1864, UNC.

31. *OR*, 36 (1):329, 370; (2):521.

32. Walker and Walker, *Diary of the War*, 167; *OR*, 36 (1):355.

33. *OR*, 36 (2):974; Early, *Narrative*, 351–52; Badeau, *Military History of U. S. Grant*, 2:569, 332. Badeau declined to use any of Early's Confederate strength figures unless they could be substantiated by at least one separate source.

34. Early, *Narrative*, 352. Some biographers of Grant have used this order as evidence that Lee was still ignorant of the whereabouts of the Union army. In fact Lee ordered this route for Early because it was the shortest to the courthouse. He knew that if this route were not available Early would have enough sense to use another.

35. Dunlop, *Lee's Sharpshooters*, 44–46.

36. Clark, *A Glance Backward*, 49.

37. Ibid., 50.

38. *OR*, 36 (2):494.

39. Ibid., 535.

40. Ibid., (1):995–96; (2):537–38; Ripley, *First United States Sharp Shooters*, 156; Marbaker, *Eleventh New Jersey Volunteers*, 167; William M. Harris, *Movements of the Confederate Army*, 26.

41. Wilcox, Report of Operations, VHS; Early, *Narrative*, 352.

42. *OR*, 36 (1):905, 987; Willis, Diary, 8 May 1864, V; Rawleigh Dunaway to My Dear Sister, 12 May 1864, V.

43. Lyman, Journal, 8 May 1864, MAHS.

44. Sheridan, *Memoirs*, 1:368–69; Porter, *Campaigning With Grant*, 83–84. The subject of this argument, the designated mission and actual operations of Sheridan's cavalry on the night of 7–8 May, is discussed in Appendix B.

45. Sheridan, *Memoirs*, 1:369.

46. *OR*, 36 (2):553.

47. Ibid., 536.

48. Walker and Walker, *Diary of the War*, 170.

49. Ibid., 170–71; Early, *Narrative*, 352.

50. Walker and Walker, *Diary of the War*, 171–72; Hampton, Connected Narrative, 32, USC.

51. Walker and Walker, *Diary of the War*, 172; Mulholland, *116th Regiment*, 182–83; *OR*, 36 (1):329; Early, *Narrative*, 352.

CHAPTER 6

1. Nevins, *Diary of Battle*, 357.
2. Wainwright, Journal, 8 May 1864, HHL.
3. Nevins, *Diary of Battle*, 357; Dame, *From the Rapidan to Richmond*, 112–19.
4. *OR*, 36 (2):531–32.
5. Ibid., 540–41, 543.
6. Ibid., 541; Warren to Cutler, 8 May 1864, NY.
7. Agassiz, *Meade's Headquarters*, 104; Lyman, Journal, 8 May 1864, MAHS.
8. *OR*, 36 (2):542. Meade obviously believed that the Sixth Corps would be an adequate reinforcement for Warren. At the time of this message, 3:05 P.M., Union headquarters personnel did not know the locations of the Confederate Second and Third corps.
9. *OR*, 36 (2):546, 529.
10. Lyman, Journal, 8 May 1864, MAHS.
11. Ibid.; Agassiz, *Meade's Headquarters*, 105; Humphreys, Field Dispatches, chief of staff, 1–31 May 1864, HSP; James C. Biddle to wife, 17 May 1864, Meade Collection, HSP.
12. Haines, *Fifteenth New Jersey*, 157.
13. *OR*, 36 (1):660, 666.
14. Ibid., 723–24; Read, Diary, 8 May 1864, Ricketts Papers, MNBP.
15. *OR*, 36 (1):683, 702; Benedict, *Vermont in the Civil War*, 1:439.
16. Lee, *Forget-Me-Nots*, 114; Howard, *Recollections*, 282–83; Dozle, Reminiscences, 3, LC.
17. *OR*, 36 (2):974.
18. Lee, *Forget-Me-Nots*, 114.
19. Cyrus B. Watson, "Forty-Fifth Regiment," in Walter Clark, *Histories from North Carolina*, 3:45–46.
20. Howard, *Recollections*, 284. Jones had been killed in the Wilderness fighting.
21. Peyton, *Record*, 24.
22. Warren to Humphreys, 9 May 1864, NY.
23. Foster, *New Jersey and the Rebellion*, 110–11, 397; Haines, *Fifteenth New Jersey*, 158–59.
24. Westbrook, *49th Pennsylvania Volunteers*, 188.
25. Brewer, *Sixty-First Regiment*, 89.
26. Prowell, *Eighty-Seventh Regiment*, 127.
27. Newell, *Ours*, 262.
28. Edwards, Reminiscences, 138, ILSHL. In the shake-up of commanders following Sedgwick's death, Eustis was transferred the next day to the command of a brigade in the First Division.
29. Thomson, *History of the Bucktails*, 301.
30. *OR*, 36 (1):591; Bennett, *Musket and Sword*, 218; J. L. Smith, *Corn Exchange Regiment*, 408.
31. Foster, *New Jersey and the Rebellion*, 272.
32. Urban, *Battle Field and Prison Pen*, 407–8; *OR*, 36 (1):1065–66; Mixson, *Reminiscences*, 73–74. Many Federals who were captured on or before the eighth

were liberated on the following day by Sheridan's cavalry near Beaver Dam Station. This may explain why the prisoners among the Pennsylvania Reserves are not recorded on the casualty lists in the *Official Records*.

33. Bennett, *Musket and Sword*, 219–20.
34. Ibid., 220–21; Field to Herring, 9 May 1864, Herring Papers, MOLLUS.
35. *OR*, 36 (1):1083.
36. John L. Parker, *Henry Wilson's Regiment*, 431–32.
37. Pullen, *Twentieth Maine*, 198; Gerrish, *A Private's Reminiscences*, 175–78.
38. J. L. Smith, *Corn Exchange Regiment*, 408–11; *OR*, 36 (1):1083–84.
39. Edwards, Reminiscences, 138–39, ILSHL; Newell, *Ours*, 262.
40. Brewer, *Sixty-First Regiment*, 89.
41. *OR*, 36 (1):660; Robert G. Carter, *Four Brothers in Blue*, 393.
42. Cyrus B. Watson, "Forty-Fifth Regiment," in Walter Clark, *Histories from North Carolina*, 3:46–47.
43. Howard, *Recollections*, 285; Dozle, Reminiscences, 4, LC.
44. Alexander, *Military Memoirs*, 512; Krick, *Parker's Virginia Battery*, 236–39.

CHAPTER 7

1. *OR*, 36 (2):546.
2. Ibid., 548.
3. Ibid., 550, 549.
4. Cutcheon, "To Ny River and Spottsylvania," 9 May 1864, UMI; *OR*, 36 (1):943.
5. Cutcheon, "To Ny River and Spottsylvania," 9 May 1864, UMI.
6. *OR*, 36 (2):581.
7. Cutcheon, "To Ny River and Spottsylvania," 9 May 1864, UMI.
8. *OR*, 51 (2):905–6.
9. Ibid., 36 (1):979, 967–68, 948–49.
10. Ibid., 968, 949; (2):584.
11. Ibid., (2):580.
12. Ibid., 580–81, 583.
13. Ibid., 581.
14. Ibid., 584; Lee, Report of Operations, 7, MC; *OR*, 51 (2):905–6.
15. Prowell, *Eighty-Seventh Regiment*, 132; *OR*, 36 (2):580.
16. Read, Diary, 9 May 1864, MNBP.
17. *OR*, 36 (2):576–77, 574. In his journal entry for 9 May, Theodore Lyman recorded his supposition that Meade assigned this command responsibility to Sedgwick because of the delay of the combined attack on the previous afternoon. Meade probably suspected that Sedgwick had deferred to Warren's judgment too long because he believed that Warren, having arrived in the area first, would be more familiar with the terrain and enemy dispositions.
18. *OR*, 36 (1):660; Westbrook, *49th Pennsylvania Volunteers*, 189.
19. Halsey, Diary, 9 May 1864, USAMHI.
20. *OR*, 36 (1):755; Prowell, *Eighty-Seventh Regiment*, 132.

21. Halsey, Diary, 9 May 1864, USAMHI; Haines, *Fifteenth New Jersey*, 161.

22. Martin T. McMahon, "The Death of General John Sedgwick," in Buel and Johnson, *Battles and Leaders*, 4:175.

23. Ibid. The author feels that this account of Sedgwick's death and the events immediately preceding it is reasonably accurate. Many versions abound, all differing in detail. For example, Dr. John Shaw Billings, who helped to embalm General Sedgwick's body, claimed that Sedgwick was still alive when brought to army headquarters at 11:00 A.M. but died a few minutes later; see Garrison, *John Shaw Billings*, 81, and Westbrook, *49th Pennsylvania Volunteers*, 189. For an excellent description of Sedgwick's death and analyses of its circumstances, the reader is encouraged to consult Stuart G. Vogt's "The Death of Major-General John Sedgwick, U.S.A., May 9, 1864," in the files of the Fredericksburg and Spotsylvania National Military Park. This excellent study considers various Confederate postwar claims as to who fired the fatal shot, from what location, using what type of weapon.

24. Porter, *Campaigning With Grant*, 90; Edwards, Reminiscences, 141, ILSHL.

25. McMahon, "The Death of General John Sedgwick," 175; *OR*, 36 (2):577.

26. Humphreys, *Virginia Campaign*, 73.

27. Dozle, Reminiscences, 5, LC.

28. Varina D. Brown, *Colonel at Gettysburg and Spotsylvania*, 256; Joseph N. Brown, *The Bloody Angle*, 4.

29. Cadwallader Jones, "Trees Cut Down by Bullets."

30. Howard, *Recollections*, 286–87.

31. *OR*, 36 (1):1072; Peyton, *Record*, 24.

32. Krick, *Parker's Virginia Battery*, 238–39.

33. *OR*, 36 (1):1066.

34. Pomeroy, War Memoirs, 78, HJC.

35. Dame, *From the Rapidan to Richmond*, 143, 137; Macon, *First Company of Richmond Howitzers*, 39; *OR*, 36 (1):1042. Dame's account claims that the final line occupied by Gregg's brigade was manned by only sharpshooters until late in the afternoon of 9 May, when Napoleons under Lieutenant Anderson arrived, followed after dark by the infantrymen.

36. Fifth Army Corps Battle Record, NA; Winne, Journal, 8, DUMC.

37. *OR*, 36 (2):574; John L. Parker, *Henry Wilson's Regiment*, 434.

38. *OR*, 36 (2):576; John L. Parker, *Henry Wilson's Regiment*, 434; Judson, *Eighty-Third Regiment*, 98; *OR*, 36 (1):581.

39. Stearns, *Three Years with Company K*, 264; Porter to Peirson, 18 April 1879, BU.

40. *OR*, 36 (1):625.

41. Woodward, *Our Campaigns*, 312.

42. Roebling, Report of Operations, 28, NY.

43. *OR*, 36 (1):642, 655.

44. Warren to Humphreys, 9 May 1864, NY.

45. Ibid. Warren discovered this letter in his files later in the year in November and endorsed upon it that since he had not altered his opinions concerning the contents he was forwarding it at that time. The author has searched Meade's and Humphreys's papers without success for any indication of its receipt and reaction to it.

46. Early, *Narrative*, 353; James H. Lane, "Lane's North Carolina Brigade," 145.

47. *OR*, 36 (1):330, 356; (2):564–66.

48. Ibid., (2):566.

49. Grant evidently assumed that Willcox was misspelling the word, because Grant continued to use the expression "Gate" throughout the day.

50. Grant, *Personal Memoirs*, 2:218.

51. *OR*, 36 (2):561–62.

52. Ibid., 584, 582, 562.

53. Ibid., 586, 682; (1):891, 893; Return of the 2nd Ohio, 9 May 1864, NA.

CHAPTER 8

1. *OR*, 36 (2):566–67.

2. Ibid., (1):330; Walker and Walker, *Diary of the War*, 175.

3. Lyman, Journal, 9 May 1864, MAHS; Landon, "Letters From Camp," 90; Schaff, *Battle of the Wilderness*, 319. According to Lyman, the generals discussed the possibility of crossing the river and attacking the wagons but did not attempt it.

4. *OR*, 36 (1):408; (2):569; Walker and Walker, *Diary of the War*, 175; Waring, Diary, 9 May 1864, UNC; Neese, *Confederate Horse Artillery*, 265.

5. *OR*, 36 (2):570; Waring, Diary, 9 May 1864, UNC.

6. *OR*, 36 (1):430, 439; (2):567, 569.

7. Ibid., (2):567–68.

8. Dunlop, *Lee's Sharpshooters*, 444–45, states that two brigades of Mahone's Confederate division arrived near the bridge as early as 7:00 P.M. Meade informed Humphreys in a message (*OR*, 36 [2]:562) that at 1:30 P.M. Gibbon had been directed to take his division across and attempt to capture the bridge. Meade observed how slowly things were progressing. Grant also saw but apparently did not prod Meade. For an accounting of the misunderstandings among Grant, Meade, and Hancock on this day see Atkinson, *Grant's Campaigns*, 252–57.

9. John L. Parker, *Henry Wilson's Regiment*, 434; *OR*, 36 (1):555.

10. Farley, "Reminiscences," 250; Judson, *Eighty-Third Regiment*, 98.

11. *OR*, 36 (1):561, 570.

12. Ibid., 611; Donald L. Smith, *Twenty-Fourth Michigan*, 194; Cheek and Pointon, *Sauk County Riflemen*, 95.

13. *OR*, 36 (1):642, 657. Some of this fire may have been directed against Cabell's battalion of guns, which stood on a slight hill to the rear of Field's infantry line.

14. *OR*, 36 (2):576.

15. Ibid., 578.

16. Ibid.

17. Paul, Diary, 9 May 1864, USAMHI; Halsey, Diary, 9 May 1864, USAMHI; Haines, *Fifteenth New Jersey*, 162–63.

18. *OR*, 36 (1):660, 683.

19. Ibid., 775, 765; Rhodes, Diary, 9 May 1864, RIHS.

20. *OR*, 36 (1):1086.

21. Ibid., 1072; Seymour, Journal, 10 May 1864, UMI. Seymour, a volunteer

aide-de-camp to Hays, said Hays was wounded on the morning of 10 May by a Yankee skirmisher's bullet.

22. Dozle, Reminiscences, 4, LC.

23. Worsham, *Foot Cavalry*, 209–10.

24. *OR*, 36 (1):949, 977.

25. Ibid., (2):584–85.

26. Ibid., 582, 585, 583.

27. Ibid., (1):908.

28. Ibid.; Bosbyshell, *48th In the War*, 149; *OR*, 36 (2):583.

29. Lane, "Lane's North Carolina Brigade," 145.

30. Benson, *Civil War Book*, 68.

31. Early, *Narrative*, 353.

32. *OR*, 36 (2):610.

CHAPTER 9

1. *OR*, 36 (1):1043.

2. Ibid., 330.

3. Billings, *Tenth Massachusetts Battery*, 226 n. 2.

4. *OR*, 36 (1):330–31.

5. Walker and Walker, *Diary of the War*, 176.

6. Ibid.

7. *OR*, 36 (1):1043.

8. Ibid., 408.

9. Ibid., 331; Waring, Diary, 10 May 1864, UNC; Green, "From the Wilderness to Spotsylvania," 95. Hancock reported that the purpose of Birney's movement was to provide a cover for Brooke's operations.

10. *OR*, 36 (2):599; Comstock, Diary, 10 May 1864, LC.

11. Grant, *Personal Memoirs*, 2:222; *OR*, 36 (2):600, 604, 609, 610; (1):331.

12. *OR*, 36 (1):331, 447, 509.

13. Ibid., 36 (2):604.

14. Nevins, *Diary of Battle*, 363; Collier, *They'll Do To Tie To*, 184–85; *OR*, 36 (1):643.

15. Roebling, Report of Operations, 31–32, NY.

16. *OR*, 36 (1):651, 655.

17. Bennett, *Musket and Sword*, 227.

18. Ibid., 227–29; Wylie, Diary, 10 May 1864, BU; John L. Parker, *Henry Wilson's Regiment*, 435; Robert G. Carter, *Four Brothers in Blue*, 395–96; Krick, *Parker's Virginia Battery*, 237; *OR*, 36 (1):561, 568, 570.

19. *OR*, 36 (2):606.

20. Marquis and Tevis, *Fighting Fourteenth*, 121.

21. *OR*, 36 (2):606–7; (1):541.

22. Ibid., (2):568, 573.

23. Ibid., (1):755.

24. Ibid., 755, 285, 608.

25. Ibid., (2):607–8.
26. Ibid., (1):1043; Return of Hardaway's Battalion, 10 May 1864, NA.
27. *OR*, 36 (1):1072.
28. Haines, *Fifteenth New Jersey*, 163; *OR*, 36 (2):608.
29. Lyman, Journal, 10 May 1864, MAHS.
30. Foster, *New Jersey and the Rebellion*, 399 n. 9; Halsey, Diary, 10 May 1864, USAMHI; Holmes, *Touched With Fire*, 111; Seymour, Journal, 10 May 1864, UMI.
31. *OR*, 36 (2):582, 609.
32. Ibid.
33. Coco, *Through Blood and Fire*, 81–82.
34. *OR*, 36 (2):612; Lane, "Lane's North Carolina Brigade," 145.
35. Porter, *Campaigning With Grant*, 93–94; *OR*, 36 (2):610.
36. *OR*, 36 (2):612.
37. Ibid.
38. Ibid.; (1):954.
39. Richards to Colonel Leasure, 10 May 1864, BU.

CHAPTER 10

1. Croft, *One Hundred Forty-First Regiment*, 189, 191; Green, "From the Wilderness to Spotsylvania," 95, 96.
2. *OR*, 36 (2):600.
3. Ibid., (1):330; Walker and Walker, *Diary of the War*, 177.
4. *OR*, 36 (1):330.
5. Ibid. The precise location of this line is uncertain. Hancock's report is dated September 1865. Brooke's final report, dated 1 November 1865, says that the line was approximately 100 paces north of and parallel to the road.
6. Ibid., 409, 427; Sixty-fourth New York Regiment Diary, 10 May 1864, INU.
7. Simons, *One Hundred and Twenty-Fifth New York*, 204; Muffly, *148th Pennsylvania Volunteers*, 121.
8. *OR*, 36 (1):331–32; Walker and Walker, *Diary of the War*, 178.
9. Muffly, *148th Pennsylvania Volunteers*, 120, 853; Simons, *One Hundred and Twenty-Fifth New York*, 204.
10. *OR*, 36 (1):332.
11. Favill, *Diary of a Young Officer*, 294; Ryno, Diary, 10 May 1864, CU.
12. *OR*, 36 (1):332, 509, 333.
13. Ibid., 357; Chase, Memoirs, 103, USAMHI.
14. *OR*, 36 (1):332; Early, *Narrative*, 354.
15. Sixty-fourth New York Regiment Diary, 10 May 1864, INU.
16. Muffly, *148th Pennsylvania Volunteers*, 120–21, 854; *OR*, 36 (1):427–28.
17. *OR*, 36 (1):332–33.
18. Ibid., 333.
19. Ibid., 509, 1043.
20. Hunt, Journal of Siege Operations, 14, LC.
21. *OR*, 36 (1):332, 408; Reichardt, *Diary of Battery A*, 128–29.

22. *OR*, 36 (1):333; Walker and Walker, *Diary of the War*, 178.

23. Dunlop, *Lee's Sharpshooters*, 449–50; Early, *Narrative*, 354; *OR*, 36 (1):333, 334.

24. Dame, *From the Rapidan to Richmond*, 170.

25. *OR*, 36 (2):606, 607; Galwey, *The Valiant Hours*, 205; Dame, *From the Rapidan to Richmond*, 145–47; Locke, *Story of the Regiment*, 336.

26. *OR*, 36 (2):600.

27. Humphreys, *Virginia Campaign*, 81; Marshall, *Company K, 155th Pennsylvania*, 10 May 1864; *OR*, 36 (1):576, 587.

28. Coles, "History of the 4th Regiment," 2–3, AL; Oates, *War Between the Union and Confederacy*, 356; "Incidents In the War of Secession."

29. Krick, *Parker's Virginia Battery*, 241–42; Chamberlin, *One Hundred and Fiftieth Regiment*, 229–31; Porter to Peirson, 18 April 1879, BU.

30. Chamberlin, *One Hundred and Fiftieth Regiment*, 229–30.

31. Humphreys, *Virginia Campaign*, 81.

32. Wise, *Long Arm of Lee*, 781–82.

33. Chamberlin, *One Hundred and Fiftieth Regiment*, 230–31; "Death of General Rice and Captain Dorr"; Bristol, Diary, 10 May 1864, OCHS; Coles, "History of the 4th Regiment," 4, AL.

34. *OR*, 36 (1):439, 447; Galwey, *The Valiant Hours*, 206.

35. Dame, *From the Rapidan to Richmond*, 161–62.

36. Ibid., 141; Smither, Letter, May 1864, HJC.

37. *OR*, 36 (1):334.

38. Ibid.; Walker and Walker, *Diary of the War*, 179; Lyman, Journal, 10 May 1864, MAHS.

39. Meade to Barlow, 10 May 1864, Barlow Papers, MAHS; *OR*, 36 (1):509, 334; Tidball, Report of Campaign, 9, USMA.

40. Chamberlin, *One Hundred and Fiftieth Regiment*, 235; Donald L. Smith, *Twenty-Fourth Michigan*, 195; Coles, "History of the 4th Regiment," 4, AL.

41. Porter to Peirson, 18 April 1879, BU; Bradford, Account of Service, Small Papers, MEHS.

42. Charles E. Davis, Jr., *Three Years in the Army*, 338. This regiment's term of enlistment was nearly up, which might explain why its members were assigned less hazardous duty.

43. *OR*, 36 (1):430.

44. Banes, *Philadelphia Brigade*, 243–44; *OR*, 36 (1):439.

45. Thomson, *History of the Bucktails*, 303; Nevins, *Diary of Battle*, 364.

46. *OR*, 36 (1):470; Weygant, *One Hundred and Twenty-Fourth Regiment*, 309–10.

47. Dame, *From the Rapidan to Richmond*, 164–65.

48. Ibid., 165; Collier, *They'll Do To Tie To*, 185; Stiles, *Four Years*, 254; *OR*, 36 (1):470.

49. Weygant, *One Hundred and Twenty-Fourth Regiment*, 310–11; Croft, *One Hundred and Forty-First Regiment*, 190–91; Newburger, Diary, 10 May 1864, LC; *OR*, 36 (1):334.

50. Dame, *From the Rapidan to Richmond*, 165–69; Chase, Memoirs, 102, USAMHI; Hanks, Captain B. F. Benton's Company, 40, HJC; Minor, "Rallying With a Frying Pan," 72–73.

51. Macon, *First Company of Richmond Howitzers*, 39.
52. *OR*, 36 (1):139; Chase, Diary, 10 May 1864, USAMHI.
53. Hanks, Captain B. F. Benton's Company, 40, HJC.
54. Dame, *From the Rapidan to Richmond*, 168–69.

CHAPTER 11

1. *OR*, 36 (1):712.
2. Ibid., 297.
3. Ibid., 667. The figures for the strength of Upton's force are an estimate based upon several sources of incomplete information.
4. Ibid., 667; Westbrook, *49th Pennsylvania Volunteers*, 189.
5. *OR*, 36 (1):667, 1086.
6. Ibid., 667.
7. Atkinson, *Grant's Campaigns*, 267; Morse, "Rebellion Record," 78–79.
8. *OR*, 36 (2):602–3.
9. Ibid., 603.
10. Ibid.; (1):514. The efforts of Mott's pickets to locate the right of the Ninth Corps were probably hampered by the Twenty-first Virginia Regiment of Jones's brigade, which lay across their route. Mott's men may have crossed to the east bank of the Ni River and moved downstream, where two regiments from the Ninth Corps joined them at 3:00 P.M.
11. Hamlin, *Old Bald Head*, 177.
12. *OR*, 36 (2):609–10.
13. Humphreys, *Virginia Campaign*, 81; Holmes, *Touched With Fire*, 112; *OR*, 36 (1):765.
14. Most accounts of the action state that Upton's men were inadequately supported by Mott's division on their left, which is true. These accounts imply, however, that the two Federal forces advanced simultaneously, which is not obvious to the author. The reports from Mott's division are in *OR*, 36 (1):490, 494, 499, 502. The author is indebted to Edmund Raus of the Manassas National Battlefield Park for first suggesting the possibility that Mott may have attacked one hour earlier than Upton.
15. *OR*, 36 (1):490; Halsey, Diary, 10 May 1864, USAMHI.
16. *OR*, 36 (1):490, 494, 499.
17. Marbaker, *Eleventh New Jersey Volunteers*, 168–69; *OR*, 36 (1):494, 499.
18. *OR*, 36 (1):490, 514.
19. Ibid., 765; Return of Hardaway's Battalion, 10 May 1864, NA.
20. *OR*, 36 (1):1072; White, "Diary of the War," 243; Dozle, Reminiscences, 5, LC.
21. *OR*, 36 (1):668; Atkinson, *Grant's Campaigns*, 265.
22. Morse, "Rebellion Record," 78.
23. *OR*, 36 (1):668.
24. Morse, "Rebellion Record," 78.
25. White, "Diary of the War," 244.
26. Return of Hardaway's Battalion, 10 May 1864, NA; [Hardaway], "Operations

of General Lee's Army," in Frank Moore, *Rebellion Record*, 11:479; White, "Diary of the War," 244–45.

27. Boyle, Diary, 10 May 1864, UNC.

28. Dozle, Reminiscences, 6, LC.

29. Some accounts of the action claim that Mott's troops refused to move forward when ordered. It is possible that after the initial repulse officers rallied them and attempted to send them forward again at 6:10 P.M. as support for Upton but were unsuccessful.

30. Taylor, *General Lee*, 240.

31. Toney, Reminiscences, 10 May 1864, TN; George P. Hawes, "A Week With the Artillery, A.N.V.," *CV* 31 (1923):370; Thomas H. Carter, "The Bloody Angle," 239. This seems unlikely had Mott also been attacking at the time.

32. Howard, *Recollections*, 287–89; Thurston, "General George H. Steuart's Brigade," 150–51.

33. Cyrus B. Watson, "Forty-Fifth Regiment," in Walter Clark, *Histories from North Carolina*, 3:48.

34. Westbrook, *49th Pennsylvania Volunteers*, 191.

35. I. G. Bradwell, "Spotsylvania, Va., May 8 and 9, 1864," *CV* 28:56; Walter A. Montgomery, "Twelfth Regiment," in Walter Clark, *Histories from North Carolina*, 1:41.

36. *OR*, 36 (1):1078; Daniel Papers, DU.

37. A. W. Garber, "Artillery Work at Wilderness"; [Hardaway], "Operations of General Lee's Army," in Frank Moore, *Rebellion Record*, 11:479–80; Herndon Fife to Major J. McDowell Carrington, 11 September 1905, 4, Daniel Collection, UV.

38. Westbrook, *49th Pennsylvania Volunteers*, 192.

39. *OR*, 36 (1):668. Upton reported that his men retired without molestation. Some Confederate accounts state that the Federals were driven from the works. The role of Ramseur's brigade in the action is uncertain. A member of Jones's battery related that when the Federals retired Ramseur leaped atop the works and ordered his men to charge but they refused. See Creed Davis, "Diary," 10. In his official report Ramseur was uncharacteristically reticent concerning the activities of his command that day.

40. *OR*, 36 (1):668; Westbrook, *49th Pennsylvania Volunteers*, 193, 197; Watson, "Forty-Fifth Regiment," 48; Keiser, Diary, 10 May 1864, USAMHI.

41. *OR*, 36 (1):1072, 668; Sparks, *Inside Lincoln's Army*, 371; Dozle, Reminiscences, 6, LC; Watson, "Forty-Fifth Regiment," 49; Harden Papers, DU.

42. *OR*, 36 (2):983; Dozle, Reminiscences, 6, LC.

43. Grant, *Personal Memoirs*, 2:224–25; Tyler, *Recollections*, 169; Agassiz, *Meade's Headquarters*, 110 n. 1.

44. *OR*, 36 (2):611. Burnside's concern for the safety of Mott's division was probably caused by the faulty map.

45. Burrage, *Thirty-Sixth Regiment*, 162; *OR*, 36 (2):613–14.

46. *OR*, 36 (1):908, 949, 977, 928; Bosbyshell, *48th In the War*, 149.

47. Porter, *Campaigning With Grant*, 95; Lyman, Journal, 10 May 1864, MAHS; *OR*, 36 (2):611–12. Grant, in his *Personal Memoirs*, 2:225, states that Burnside at this time had completely turned Lee's right, a questionable assertion. He also says that

Burnside was unaware of the advantage he had gained. Grant did not find out in time to take advantage of it, but he did not blame Burnside for this. He faulted himself for failing to have a staff officer with Burnside who could have reported the position. He evidently forgot that Porter was with Burnside.

48. Caldwell, *Brigade of South Carolinians*, 139; Early, *Narrative*, 554; *OR*, 36 (2):982–83.

CHAPTER 12

1. *OR*, 36 (2):630, 640–41.
2. Ibid., 595–96.
3. Ibid., 627.
4. Ibid., 628.
5. Ibid., 628, 629–30. This order by Grant appears to reflect the expertise in problems of resupply he had garnered during service in the Mexican War. It also reflects his apparent inability to refrain from usurping Meade's and Burnside's authority, caused by his strong desire for efficiency. If in this campaign Grant had chosen to travel with, say, Sherman, one can only wonder how Meade and Burnside would have handled this instance of resupply if indeed their forces were facing the Army of Northern Virginia near Spotsylvania Court House.
6. *OR*, 36 (1):490; (2):634, 635, 641, 644–55; Humphreys, *Virginia Campaign*, 88.
7. Lyman, Journal, 11 May 1864, MAHS.
8. *OR*, 36 (1):334.
9. Early, *Narrative*, 354.
10. Lane, "Lane's North Carolina Brigade," 145–46. Lane's second move may have occurred in the afternoon.
11. Anderson, "Major D. W. Anderson's Relation," 252; Varina D. Brown, *Colonel at Gettysburg and Spotsylvania*, 262 n. 1.
12. "Battle's Brigade"; Cyrus B. Watson, "Forty-Fifth Regiment," in Clark, *Histories from North Carolina*, 3:49; Bone, Diary, 11 May 1864, NC; Seymour, Journal, 11 May 1864, UMI. For references to Battle's brigade see above, Chapter 6, and *OR*, 36 (1):1083–84.
13. Dozle, Reminiscences, 6, LC.
14. White, "Diary of the War," 249–50.
15. Pomeroy, War Memoirs, 80, HJC.
16. *OR*, 36 (1):334, 373; (2):635–36; Walker and Walker, *Diary of the War*, 179–80.
17. *OR*, 51 (2):917; Early, *Narrative*, 355; George H. Mills, "Sixteenth Regiment," in Clark, *Histories from North Carolina*, 4:193.
18. McDonald, *Make Me A Map*, 203.
19. *OR*, 51 (2):916–17. In addition to Rooney Lee's cavalry scouts, other Confederates obtained a splendid view of the area behind the Ninth Corps's line from the upper windows of a church near the courthouse.
20. Ibid., 36 (1):909.

21. Burrage, *Thirty-Sixth Regiment*, 163; Comstock, Diary, 11 May 1864, LC.

22. Bliss, Reminiscences, 4:116, USAMHI; *OR*, 36 (1):928; Coco, *Through Blood and Fire*, 83.

23. Charles S. Venable, "General Lee in the Wilderness Campaign," in Buel and Johnson, *Battles and Leaders*, 4:243. Whether or not Lee intended to abandon the salient voluntarily and reform on this rear line is not certain.

24. Marbaker, *Eleventh New Jersey Volunteers*, 169; Junkin and Norton, *Life of Winfield Scott Hancock*, 170.

25. Morrison, *Memoirs of Henry Heth*, 186. Heth mentioned three separate assaults supposedly conducted by Union Ninth Corps troops against his division's position near the courthouse on 11 May. He maintained that Burnside's men sustained three hundred fatal casualties in these attacks. No additional evidence has been found to corroborate this assertion.

26. Ibid.; Alexander, Personal Narrative, 68, UNC.

27. Alexander, *Military Memoirs*, 518.

28. *OR*, 36 (1):1044, 1086, 1088–89, 1079–80.

29. Howard, *Recollections*, 293.

30. *OR*, 36 (1):1086; J. McDowell Carrington to Wilfred E. Cutshaw, October, 1905, 5, Daniel Collection, UV.

31. Brown, Memoranda, TN.

32. [Hardaway], "Operations of General Lee's Army," in Frank Moore, *Rebellion Record*, 11:480.

33. Cutshaw to Carrington, October 7, 1905, p. 2, Daniel Collection, UV.

34. *OR*, 36 (1):1086.

CHAPTER 13

1. *OR*, 36 (2):629.

2. Ibid., 629, 643.

3. Grant, *Personal Memoirs*, 2:228.

4. *OR*, 36 (2):635.

5. Humphreys, *Virginia Campaign*, 90; *OR*, 36 (1):334; Walker, *History of the Second Army Corps*, 468.

6. *OR*, 36 (2):642, 638.

7. Ibid., 637–38, 639.

8. Francis C. Barlow, "Capture of the Salient May 12, 1864," *Papers of Massachusetts*, 4:245–46.

9. Simons, *One Hundred and Twenty-Fifth New York*, 205; Gilbreath, Reminiscences, IN, 93.

10. Barlow, "Capture of the Salient May 12, 1864," 246; Humphreys, *Virginia Campaign*, 90.

11. *OR*, 36 (1):509; Tidball, Report of Campaign, 11, USMA; Holmes, *Touched With Fire*, 113.

12. *OR*, 36 (2):635.

13. Barlow, "Capture of the Salient May 12, 1864," 246–47.

14. Ibid.

15. Ibid., 4:248–49; Junkin and Norton, *Life of Winfield Scott Hancock*, 171–72.

16. Black, "Reminiscences," 423.

17. *OR*, 36 (1):335.

18. Junkin and Norton, *Life of Winfield Scott Hancock*, 171 n. 1.

19. *OR*, 36 (1):440, 373.

20. Ibid., 335; Black, "Reminiscences," 424; William R. Driver, "The Capture of the Salient at Spottsylvania May 12, 1864," *Papers of Massachusetts*, 4:278.

21. *OR*, 36 (1):335.

22. Ibid., 514.

23. Howard, *Recollections*, 294–95. Johnson may have also received reports from those pickets of Walker's brigade who were opposite the treeless corridor facing north toward the Brown house.

24. Hunter, "Major-General Johnson at Spotsylvania," 337.

25. Thomas H. Carter, "The Bloody Angle," 240; Anderson, "Major D. W. Anderson's Relation," 253.

26. *OR*, 36 (1):1086. Johnson's staff officer involved in this episode may have been Henry Kyd Douglas. See Douglas, *I Rode with Stonewall*, 281.

27. Thomas H. Carter, "The Bloody Angle," 240; Page, "Captured Guns at Spotsylvania," 535.

28. Page, "Captured Guns at Spotsylvania," 535–36; Thomas H. Carter, "The Bloody Angle," 240–41.

29. *OR*, 36 (2):656.

30. Ibid., (1):335; Junkin and Norton, *Life of Winfield Scott Hancock*, 173.

31. *OR*, 36 (1):409, 421.

32. Ibid., 358; Sawyer, *8th Regiment*, 83.

33. Worsham, *Foot Cavalry*, 134–35.

34. *OR*, 36 (1):470; Junkin and Norton, *Life of Winfield Scott Hancock*, 174; Gilbreath, Reminiscences, IN.

35. Black, "Reminiscences," 425.

36. *OR*, 36 (1):1078; Funkhouser, "General Lee to the Rear."

37. *OR*, 36 (1):1080; Howard, *Recollections*, 295; Anderson, "Major D. W. Anderson's Relation," 252; Hunter, "Major-General Johnson at Spotsylvania," 337.

38. Worsham, *Foot Cavalry*, 130; *OR*, 36 (1):672; Archer, "Letter to Editor of the *Times*."

39. In his reminiscences, L. L. Dozle, a junior officer in the Thirty-third Virginia, which was positioned next to the left of Walker's brigade line, stated that the troops were awakened by the firing to their right and stood to arms. It is uncertain whether the troops referred to were those of the Thirty-third Regiment only or of the entire brigade.

40. Barlow, "Capture of the Salient May 12, 1864," 250. Barlow maintained that his infantrymen instinctively executed this slight change of direction solely to ensure enveloping the east angle. This may have been the case of those on the left who spotted this angle, but it would appear that most of the Yankees corrected their course to get to the enemy's works in the shortest possible time.

41. *OR*, 36 (1):491.

42. Ibid., 335, 410.

43. Dozle, Reminiscences, 7, LC; Alinson Moore, *Louisiana Tigers*, 139–40; James A. Walker, "The Bloody Angle," 235–36; R. G. Cobb to A. J. Balchelor, 14 June 1864, LSU; Miles to Brother and all, May 25, 1864, USAMHI.

44. Thomas H. Carter, "The Bloody Angle," 240–41.

45. Mulholland, *116th Regiment*, 198.

46. *OR*, 36 (1):410.

47. Howard, *Recollections*, 296. Edward Johnson in his official report (*OR*, 36 [1]:1080) treats this brief encounter as a prolonged assault and repulse. The identity of these Yankees presented in this narrative is the author's opinion. They could have been troops from the Second Division of Burnside's Ninth Corps.

48. Toney, *Privations of a Private*, 79–80; John Cowan and James I. Meets, "Third Regiment," in Walter Clark, *Histories from North Carolina*, 1:204; Howard, *Recollections*, 296; *OR*, 36 (1):373.

49. Smith, Letter to mother, 13 May 1864 and 8 June 1864, USAMHI.

50. Purifoy, "Jeff Davis Artillery."

51. Return of Page's Battalion, 12 May 1864, NA.

52. Lane, "Lane's North Carolina Brigade," 146; William H. McLaurin, "Eighteenth Regiment," in Walter Clark, *Histories from North Carolina*, 2:50, 52–54. It is possible that Lane's men were also engaging some of Burnside's troops at this time.

53. Muffly, *148th Pennsylvania Volunteers*, 122–23; Howard, *Recollections*, 301; Hunter, "Major-General Johnson at Spotsylvania," 338.

54. Lyman, Journal, 12 May 1864, MAHS; *OR*, 36 (1):359; Sparks, *Inside Lincoln's Army*, 372.

55. In a letter home, McAllister claimed that his brigade captured the eight guns of Cutshaw's battalion. See James I. Robertson, *Letters of General Robert M. McAllister*, 420–21.

56. Green, "From the Wilderness to Spotsylvania," 99; Dozle, Reminiscences, 7–8, LC; Casler, *Four Years in the Stonewall Brigade*, 320; Seymour, Journal, 12 May 1864, UMI.

57. Chase, Memoirs, 107, USAMHI.

58. Webb to Father, 14 June 1864, YU; *OR*, 36 (1):440; Bruce, *Twentieth Regiment*, 376.

59. Cyrus B. Watson, "Forty-Fifth Regiment," in Walter Clark, *Histories from North Carolina*, 3:50–51.

60. *OR*, 36 (2):656; Agassiz, *Meade's Headquarters*, 110.

61. Venable, "Wilderness to Petersburg," 529; Hunter, "Major-General Johnson at Spotsylvania," 338–39.

62. *OR*, 36 (1):1078–79; James C. MacRae, "Fifth Regiment," in Walter Clark, *Histories from North Carolina*, 1:289; Bradwell, "Spotsylvania, Va.," 102.

63. *OR*, 36 (1):1079; Peyton, *Record*, 25–26; Gibson, "Battle of Spotsylvania Courthouse," 200–201; Snider, Diary, 12 May 1864, WVU. At one time the Forty-ninth Virginia was nearly cut off. See Hale and Phillips, *Forty-Ninth Virginia*, 113–14.

64. J. William Jones, "General Lee to the Rear," 33–35; W. Smith, "General Lee to the Rear," 565; Gibson, "Battle of Spotsylvania Courthouse," 201–2, 212; Stringfellow, "The Bloody Angle," 246. The account in the narrative is a composite

constructed from portions of these sources. See Freeman, *R. E. Lee*, 3:319 n. 74.

65. The strength figure is an estimate. It is uncertain whether any members of Evans's three shattered regiments or of Johnston's North Carolina brigade participated in the initial advance.

66. *OR*, 36 (1):470–71, 474.

67. Gibson, "Battle of Spotsylvania Courthouse," 204–5; Snider, Diary, 12 May 1864, WVU; Stringfellow, "The Bloody Angle," 248; Peyton, *Record*, 27, 29; *OR*, 36 (1):137.

68. Nichols, *Soldier's Story*, 151–54; Gibson, "Battle of Spotsylvania Courthouse," 205.

69. Brown, Memoranda, TN.

70. *OR*, 36 (1):1082, 1072.

71. Ibid.

72. Ibid.; Bryan Grimes to Wife, 14 May 1864, UNC; R. T. Bennett, "Fourteenth Regiment," in Walter Clark, *Histories from North Carolina*, 1:723.

73. Early, *Narrative*, 355.

74. Scott, Memoirs of Service, 19–20, VHS.

75. Ibid., 20–22; Roche, "The Bloody Angle"; Peyton, *Record*, 27.

76. *OR*, 36 (2):656–57.

CHAPTER 14

1. *OR*, 36 (2):642; (1):679, 669; Haines, *Fifteenth New Jersey*, 174. As will be seen, later in the day the Federals drew in the right flank of their army further still, and Lee found time to consider flank attacks.

2. Tyler, *Recollections*, 178–79; Edwards, Reminiscences, 144, ILSHL; Agassiz, *Meade's Headquarters*, 111.

3. Varina D. Brown, *Colonel at Gettysburg and Spotsylvania*, 248, 253. The distances presented were obtained by the writer with a tape measure. These figures, however, are conjectural, because today it is impossible to determine the precise sites of the west angle, oak tree, and east angle. Brown's work is valuable for an understanding of the fighting along McGowan's brigade front. It helped to clear up much of the confusion of the two angles in postwar accounts of this fighting. Its description of the terrain is excellent. The writer feels, however, that Brown mislocated the east angle by ninety yards. The distance from west angle to east angle is approximately 365 yards and not 276 as Brown stated.

4. Tyler, *Recollections*, 365; Bowen, "The Bloody Angle"; Edwards, Reminiscences, 144, ILSHL.

5. *OR*, 36 (1):681, 720; Tyler, *Recollections*, 180.

6. *OR*, 36 (1):703, 359, 336; Lewis A. Grant, "Review of Major-General F. C. Barlow's Paper on the Capture of the Salient at Spotsylvania May 12, 1864," *Papers of Massachusetts*, 4:265–66.

7. *OR*, 36 (1):1044–45; Stiles, *Four Years*, 261; Agassiz, *Meade's Headquarters*, 112–14; Lyman, Journal, 12 May 1864, MAHS.

8. *OR*, 36 (1):1091.

9. Ibid., 1091–92; Venable, "Wilderness to Petersburg," 531; Venable to General N. H. Harris, 24 November 1871 in "General Lee to the Rear," supplement to J. William Jones, "General Lee to the Rear," 107; Freeman, *R. E. Lee*, 3:320.

10. Roche, "The Bloody Angle"; Venable to Harris, 24 November 1871, 107; *OR*, 36 (1):1091–92.

11. *OR*, 36 (1):494; Roe, *Tenth Regiment*, 276; Williams, "From Spotsylvania to Wilmington, North Carolina," 5; Edwards, Reminiscences, 145, ILSHL. The source for the time the Tenth Massachusetts was driven from the works is Lt. Col. Joseph B. Parsons, who was in command of the regiment. Another account by someone who was not present during the battle stated that the Tenth was forced to withdraw later in the morning. The withdrawal will be mentioned again when other actions occurring at the later time are explained.

12. Williams, "From Spotsylvania to Wilmington, North Carolina," 5–6.

13. *OR*, 36 (1):336, 410–11.

14. Ibid., 1093.

15. Caldwell, *Brigade of South Carolinians*, 140; *OR*, 36 (1):1093.

16. Caldwell, *Brigade of South Carolinians*, 141–43.

17. Varina D. Brown, *Colonel at Gettysburg and Spotsylvania*, 126–27.

18. Ibid., 127; Caldwell, *Brigade of South Carolinians*, 143.

19. Varina D. Brown, *Colonel at Gettysburg and Spotsylvania*, 128.

20. Ibid., 273 n. 2, 253–54, 258 n. 2.

21. Grant, "Review of Barlow's Paper," 267; *OR*, 36 (1):703–4. It is uncertain whether Grant arrived behind Wheaton's troops before or after Brooke. The writer has been unable to determine an accurate chronology of arrival times for Sixth Corps units opposite to the west angle. Meade's aide-de-camp Theodore Lyman compounded the confusion in a message to army headquarters (*OR*, 36 [2]:672) marked 8:45 A.M., where he reported that Russell was hard pressed and that Neill was going to his support, when in actuality Russell was moving to Neill's support.

22. *OR*, 36 (1):669; Upton, "Upton to Galloway."

23. Roe, *Tenth Regiment*, 276–77; Joseph B. Parsons, "The Bloody Angle," *Philadelphia Weekly Press*, October 12, 1887, pt. 1, col. 2. These dissimilar accounts illustrate the difficulty of determining a coherent sequence of events during this phase of the action. Parsons indicated that the regiment that Upton did not order over the crest but instead placed under Edwards's command was the Eleventh Massachusetts of Mott's division. These newly arrived Federals, however, may have been Upton's own regiments and they may have reached the works and fought there for a short time before being driven back to the crest. See Morse, "Rebellion Record," 79.

24. Varina D. Brown, *Colonel at Gettysburg and Spotsylvania*, 289 n. 2.

25. *OR*, 36 (1):411.

26. Ibid.

27. Ibid., 720.

28. Haines, *Fifteenth New Jersey*, 174–75.

29. Ibid.; Halsey, Diary, 12 May 1864, USAMHI.

30. Foster, *New Jersey and the Rebellion*, 115 n. 27.

31. Barber, Diary, 12 May 1864, BRU.

32. Ibid.; *OR*, 36 (1):509, 537.

33. *OR*, 36 (1):537, 539; G. Norton Galloway, "Hand-to-Hand Fighting At Spotsylvania," in Buel and Johnson, *Battles and Leaders*, 4:171–72; Sanborn, Scrapbook, 39, LC; Brewer, *Sixty-First Regiment*, 94–95.

34. Breech, Diary, 12 May 1864, USAMHI.

CHAPTER 15

1. *OR*, 36 (1):909; Early, *Narrative*, 355.

2. *OR*, 36 (1):909.

3. Burrage, *Thirty-Sixth Regiment*, 164–65.

4. *OR*, 36 (1):928.

5. Waite, *New Hampshire in the Great Rebellion*, 416–17.

6. Comstock to Grant, 12 May 1864, 7:00 A.M., Burnside Official Correspondence, NA.

7. *OR*, 36 (1):935; Gould, *Story of the Forty Eighth*, 179–80.

8. Gould, *Story of the Forty Eighth*, 179–80.

9. Burrage, *Thirty-Sixth Regiment*, 165–68. The authors of this regimental history maintain that the Confederates who marched across the front of the regiment and flanked its left were Lane's troops. If so, this incident probably occurred as Lane was withdrawing his regiments after having been flanked by Hancock's troops (see Chapter 10).

10. *OR*, 36 (1):677–78.

11. Comstock, Diary, 12 May 1864, LC.

12. *OR*, 36 (1):677–78; Comstock, Diary, 12 May 1864, LC.

13. It can be argued that the Federal Second Corps executed a similar night movement successfully under the identical difficult conditions and the Ninth Corps should have been able to also. In a general sense this contention possesses some merit. It should be remembered, however, that the Second Corps knew its route and destination in advance, because Federal troops had occupied these areas previously. In the case of the Ninth Corps, the Federals were completely in the dark as to what lay to their right, between the deserted Beverley house and the Landrum farm. No one had been sent to scout the area.

14. *OR*, 36 (1):574, 581, 584, 587, 591; Roebling, Report of Operations, 34–35, NY.

15. *OR*, 36 (2):666–67, 661.

16. Ibid., 662; (1):581, 591; Roebling, Report of Operations, 35, NY; Burger and Bouton, Diary and Leaves, 3, 16, FSNMP.

17. *OR*, 36 (2):662, 658; (1):1057; Anderson, Report of Operations, 4, VHS.

18. *OR*, 36 (2):658.

19. Warren, Diary, 12 May 1864, Warren Papers, NY; Roebling, Report of Operations, 36, NY.

20. *OR*, 36 (1):562, 570, 555; Francis J. Parker, *Thirty-Second Regiment*, 214–15.

21. Donald L. Smith, *Twenty-Fourth Michigan*, 196; *OR*, 36 (1):143; Return of 2nd Wisconsin, 11 May 1864, NA.

22. Woodward, *Our Campaigns*, 313–14; Vautier, *88th Pennsylvania Volunteers*, 182.

23. *OR*, 36 (2):662, 663.

24. Ibid., 663; Meade to Rawlins, 21 June 1864, Meade Papers, HSP. In this letter Meade asked that Grant relieve Warren from duty with the Army of the Potomac. In general terms, Meade's complaint was that Warren appeared to be constitutionally incapable of obeying a direct order from higher authority without first analyzing the order to determine whether or not it coincided with his own military judgment. Meade conceded that appraisal of an order was all right, so long as the subordinate, whether agreeing with the order or not, nevertheless initiated immediate action to obey it fully. He could simultaneously forward the reasons for his objections to higher headquarters with the statement that he was proceeding to obey unless ordered otherwise. Meade claimed that on 12 May Warren stated his objections but did not press the attack. Meade cited three instances to justify his request: Mine Run, 12 May at Spotsylvania, and 18 June before Petersburg. In the latest case Warren's action contributed to the Federals' failure to capture Petersburg before Lee could man the defenses there with the Army of Northern Virginia. Meade did not forward this letter to Grant. Instead he informed Warren of its contents and lectured him thoroughly on his shortcomings. See Porter, *Campaigning With Grant*, 251–52.

25. *OR*, 36 (2):663.

26. Ibid., 664.

27. Ibid., 668, 669, 671.

28. Ibid., (1):1057, 1066.

29. Ibid.; Farley, "Reminiscences," 252; Fuller, Diary, 12 May 1864, LC.

30. *OR*, 36 (1):562.

31. Pattison, Diary, 12 May 1864, INHS.

32. Donald L. Smith, *Twenty-Fourth Michigan*, 196; Chamberlin, *One Hundred Fiftieth Regiment*, 237; *OR*, 36 (2):671; Bradford, Account of Service, 12 May 1864, MEHS.

33. McKnight, Diary, 12 May 1864, HSP; Field, "Campaign of 1864 and 1865," 547; *OR*, 36 (2):669–70.

34. *OR*, 36 (2):668; (1):749.

35. Ibid., (2):654–55. Humphreys, in *Virginia Campaign*, 101 n. 3, claimed that he personally monitored Warren's attacks and when satisfied that they would not succeed directed the transfer of these troops to the left.

36. Ibid., 654.

37. Ibid., 655, 665, 676.

38. Ibid., 655, 665.

39. Ibid., (1):909, 941, 944.

40. Ibid., 954, 982, 939.

41. Ibid., 955, 949–50.

42. Ibid., 969.

43. Ibid., 950.

44. Ibid., 950, 944.

45. Wilcox, Report of Operations, 12 May 1864, VHS; Lane, "Lane's North Carolina Brigade," 147.

46. Wilcox, Report of Operations, 12 May 1864, VHS; Freeman, *R. E. Lee*, 3:322.

47. J. H. Moore, "At Spottsylvania"; Heth, Report of Operations, MC; Early, *Narrative*, 356; *OR*, 36 (1):1093, 1037–39, 1045; Charles M. Stedman, "Forty-Fourth Regiment," in Walter Clark, *Histories from North Carolina*, 3:28; Brock, "General John Rogers Cooke."

48. Peyton, *Record*, 27; Gibson, "The Bloody Angle," 206–7, 209.

49. Lane, "Lane's North Carolina Brigade," 147–48; Wilcox, Report of Operations, 12 May 1864, VHS.

50. Wilcox, Report of Operations, 12 May 1864, VHS; Lane, "Lane's North Carolina Brigade," 148.

51. Octavius A. Wiggins, "Thirty-Seventh Regiment," in Walter Clark, *Histories from North Carolina*, 2:667; Lane, "Lane's North Carolina Brigade," 148–49; *OR*, 36 (1):939, 954–55.

52. Wiggins, "Thirty-Seventh Regiment," 667; *OR*, 36 (1):939, 954–55. Lane claimed to have captured a battery of six guns, which he relinquished because there were no horses available nor roads on which to withdraw the pieces by hand.

53. Bolton, Journal, 593, MOLLUS.

54. Lane, "Lane's North Carolina Brigade," 149.

55. *OR*, 36 (1):969, 954; Cockrell, *Gunner With Stonewall*, 92.

56. *OR*, 36 (1):958.

57. Ibid., 964, 970.

58. Ibid., 970, 977.

59. Ibid., 974.

60. Ibid., 969, 974; Lanman, *Red Book of Michigan*, 402–3.

61. Dunlap, Diary, 12 May 1864, PSU.

62. Wallace, *Memorial of Patriotism*, 352–53.

63. Lane, "Lane's North Carolina Brigade," 149–50; Wiggins, "Thirty-Seventh Regiment," 667. The writer has been unable to discover any movement of Federal troops in this direction. A few Confederate writers claimed that this sighting by Lane indicated that the action of his North Carolinians compelled Grant to shift troops from in front of Ewell to Burnside and thus Confederate defeat was averted. There is no evidence to date to support this contention.

64. Lane, "Lane's North Carolina Brigade," 148, 151; James A. Weston, "Thirty-Third Regiment," in Walter Clark, *Histories from North Carolina*, 2:572.

65. Lane, "Lane's North Carolina Brigade," 151–52; Early, *Narrative*, 356. The correspondence pertaining to this controversy is located in the Cadmus Wilcox Papers in the Library of Congress and has been published in *OR*, 36 (3):802–3.

66. Early, *Narrative*, 356–57; Lane, "Lane's North Carolina Brigade," 156; Return of Company D, 61st Virginia Infantry Regiment, 12 May 1864, NA; *OR*, 36 (1):944, 982; Samuel Hoey Walkup, Letter, UNC. Walkup, who was colonel of the Forty-eighth North Carolina Regiment of Cooke's brigade, claimed that both Cooke and Mahone protested vigorously to Early, who was drunk, against making the movement unsupported. Weisiger lost two colonels and a major from his brigade in this action.

67. *OR*, 36 (1):148, 911.

CHAPTER 16

1. Varina D. Brown, *Colonel at Gettysburg and Spotsylvania*, 273 n. 2.
2. Ibid., 96.
3. Ibid.
4. *OR*, 36 (2):673.
5. Ibid., 672–73.
6. Ibid., (1):373, 422; Walker and Walker, *Diary of the War*, 185.
7. *OR*, 36 (1):373.
8. Ibid.
9. Ibid., 373–74.
10. Joseph N. Brown, *The Bloody Angle*, 7, 10.
11. Ibid.; Cadwallader Jones, "Trees Cut Down by Bullets"; *OR*, 36 (1):373–74. In his report Church claimed that at the first token of surrender the Confederates were invited to cross over to the Yankee line and that a number of them had started to when a line of supporting troops sidled in to their rear in the works, whereupon most of the Southerners turned around and jumped back behind the protection of their earthworks, and the firing resumed.
12. Caldwell, *Brigade of South Carolinians*, 144–45.
13. Roche, "The Bloody Angle." These incidents probably occurred simultaneously during the cessation of firing along the line.
14. *OR*, 36 (1):374.
15. Edwards, Reminiscences, 147–49, ILSHL; Chase, Memoirs, 105–6, USAMHI.
16. Edwards, Reminiscences, 149–50, ILSHL.
17. Morse, "Rebellion Record," 80; Marbaker, *Eleventh New Jersey Volunteers*, 176.
18. Ibid., 174; Tyler, *Recollections*, 191.
19. *OR*, 36 (1):509; Tidball, Report of Campaign, 11, USMA.
20. Ames to Home Circle, May 16, 1864, NY; *OR*, 36 (1):514, 524.
21. *OR*, 36 (1):771.
22. Hyde, *Following the Greek Cross*, 200; Swinfern, *122nd New York Volunteers*, 39.
23. Hyde, *Following the Greek Cross*, 200; Chamberlin, *One Hundred and Fiftieth Regiment*, 238–39; Mason, "Through the Wilderness," 307; Westbrook, *49th Pennsylvania Volunteers*, 198. The battery to which the two guns were assigned cannot be identified.
24. *OR*, 36 (1):611–12; (2):674. The 126th Ohio of Ricketts's division, less some skirmishers left behind, shortly after midday relieved a portion of Wheaton's brigade approximately one hundred yards north of the oak tree. The Ohio troops fired fifty rounds apiece here and had approximately seventy men (one-fourth of their number) killed or wounded before being ordered to retire. In his formal report Lt. Col. Aaron W. Ebright claimed that in moving forward into position the regiment passed over several lines of battle.
25. Ibid., (2):673–74.
26. Ibid., 675.
27. Ibid.
28. Edwards, Reminiscences, 150–51, ILSHL.

29. Ibid., 151.

30. Ibid., 152; Roe, *Tenth Regiment*, 227–28.

31. Edwards, Reminiscences, 152–53, ILSHL.

32. Ibid., 153. Edwards did not fault the enlisted men or company officers of this brigade, who were willing to stay and fight, only the commanding officer.

33. *OR*, 36 (1):669, 491; Bardeen, *Little Fifer's War Diary*, 308. The members of the First Massachusetts who chose not to reenlist departed for home on 20 May.

34. Bicknell, *Fifth Regiment Maine Volunteers*, 321; Campbell, Diary, 12 May 1864, WHGS; *OR*, 36 (2):1092.

35. *OR*, 36 (1):570, 574, 577, 584; (2):670, 671.

36. Varina D. Brown, *Colonel at Gettysburg and Spotsylvania*, 273; Cadwallader Jones, "Trees Cut Down by Bullets."

37. Joseph N. Brown, *The Bloody Angle*, 5; Caldwell, *Brigade of South Carolinians*, 146.

38. Joseph N. Brown, *The Bloody Angle*, 5–6; Varina D. Brown, *Colonel at Gettysburg and Spotsylvania*, 95.

39. Caldwell, *Brigade of South Carolinians*, 143; *OR*, 36 (1):1094.

40. Caldwell, *Brigade of South Carolinians*, 147; Old, "Trees Whittled Down at Horseshoe."

41. *OR*, 36 (1):1092; Hunt, "Hunt to Brown."

42. *OR*, 36 (1):1067; Anderson, Report of Operations, 4, VHS; Fuller, Diary, 12 May 1864, LC.

43. Edwards, Reminiscences, 152, ILSHL; Tyler, *Recollections*, 193.

44. Cheek and Pointon, *Sauk County Riflemen*, 97; Donald L. Smith, *Twenty-Fourth Michigan*, 197–98.

45. *OR*, 36 (2):660, 680.

46. Varina D. Brown, *Colonel at Gettysburg and Spotsylvania*, 265.

47. *OR*, 36 (2):675–76.

48. Ibid., 676, 723–24.

49. Ibid., 722–23, 666.

50. Ibid., 680–81.

51. Varina D. Brown, *Colonel at Gettysburg and Spotsylvania*, 128–29; Joseph N. Brown, *The Bloody Angle*, 6.

52. Varina D. Brown, *Colonel at Gettysburg and Spotsylvania*, 134–35, 136, 258 n. 2; Old, "Trees Whittled Down at Horseshoe."

53. Joseph N. Brown, *The Bloody Angle*, 5, 7–8; Varina D. Brown, *Colonel at Gettysburg and Spotsylvania*, 273, 277; *OR*, 36 (1):1094.

54. Edwards, Reminiscences, 154, ILSHL; Varina D. Brown, *Colonel at Gettysburg and Spotsylvania*, 136.

55. *OR*, 36 (1):1067, 1082; Peyton, *Record*, 28.

56. Lyman, Journal, 12 May 1864, MAHS; Tyler, *Recollections*, 195; Varina D. Brown, *Colonel at Gettysburg and Spotsylvania*, 253 n. 2.

57. Sanborn, Scrapbook, 41, LC; *OR*, 36 (1):669.

58. Black, "Reminiscences," 13–14; Varina D. Brown, *Colonel at Gettysburg and Spotsylvania*, 254 n. 1.

59. Roe, *Tenth Regiment*, 278.

60. *OR*, 36 (1):626, 704; Edwards, Reminiscences, 154, ILSHL; Varina D. Brown, *Colonel at Gettysburg and Spotsylvania*, 294.

61. Gilbreath, Reminiscences, 95, IN.

62. Albert L. Harvey to My Dear Kate and friends at home, 19 May 1864, PCHS.

63. Charles E. Wheldon, Letter, 14 May 1864, SCHS; John J. Dillard to a friend, 20 May 1864, DU.

64. Joe Shaner to Dear Sisters, 17 May 1864, typescript copy at FSNMP.

65. Humphreys, *Virginia Campaign*, 104–6. Humphreys estimated the Confederate losses for that day to be as high as 9,000 to 10,000 by including 3,700 troops of Ewell's corps who could not be accounted for after the twentieth of April. This writer would credit many of these to Ewell's losses in the Wilderness fighting, which were reported as being only 1,250. Of the eight Confederate brigades that are known to have been heavily engaged on the twelfth, Harris's, McGowan's, and Lane's suffered a combined total of 1,321 casualties. Gordon reported that the losses in Hoffman's and Evans's brigades were not heavy. The numbers of casualties sustained by Ramseur's, Daniel's, and R. D. Johnston's brigades are not known.

66. McCabe, "Major Andrew Reid Venable, Jr."

CHAPTER 17

1. *OR*, 36 (1):19.

2. Edwards, Reminiscences, 154, 158, ILSHL.

3. James Denton to brother, 19 May 1864, RU.

4. *OR*, 36 (2):724, 702, 713–14.

5. Ibid., 704.

6. Ibid., (1):448. In his formal report Gibbon did not explain why Owen was superceded by Carroll for the reconnaissance mission. Lt. Col. William Davis, who commanded the Sixty-ninth Pennsylvania Regiment, reported that late in the afternoon of the twelfth he was placed in temporary command of the brigade and ordered to report to Carroll. In a postwar publication, *Personal Recollections of the Civil War*, 221, Gibbon stated that Carroll executed the reconnaissance with his own brigade reinforced by other troops, which does not appear to have been the case. These writings appear to be attempts to gloss over or cover up some deficiency of Owen's. Owen was mustered out of the service on 18 July 1864, after having been accused of disobeying orders on 18 May at Spotsylvania and 3 June at Cold Harbor. See *OR*, 36 (1):435–36.

7. *OR*, 36 (2):706, 705.

8. Ibid., (1):374, 386, 425.

9. Ibid., 749, 765; Read, Diary, 13 May 1864, MNBP; *OR*, 36 (2):725, 726, 727.

10. Edwin Emery to sister, undated, DU.

11. Bone, Diary, 12–14 May 1864, NC.

12. *OR*, 36 (2):698, 705; Grant, *Personal Memoirs*, 2:234.

13. Ibid., 726, 718, 716, 720, 728.

14. Ibid., 1001; Freeman, *Lee's Lieutenants*, 3:434–35; *OR*, 36 (3):813–14.

15. Krick, *Lee's Colonels*, 34–344.

16. *OR*, 36 (2):654, 714, 698.

17. Ibid., 730, 795.

18. Porter, *Campaigning With Grant*, 114–15.

19. *OR*, 36 (1):471.

20. Muffly, *148th Pennsylvania Volunteers*, 265.

21. Birney and Hancock to Walker, FSNMP.

22. *OR*, 36 (2):703, 709, 711–12.

23. Ibid., (1):1079, 371, 374, 517; (2):708; Walker and Walker, *Diary of the War*, 186–87.

24. *OR*, 36 (2):700, 731–32.

25. Ibid., 720, 721; Roebling, Report of Operations, 40, NY; Nevins, *Diary of Battle*, 368.

26. *OR*, 36 (2):721–22.

27. Ibid., 721.

28. Roebling, Report of Operations, 40, 41, NY; *OR*, 36 (2):755.

29. Stearns, *Three Years with Company K*, 267; *OR*, 36 (2):762.

30. Roebling, Report of Operations, 40–41, NY.

31. *OR*, 36 (2):755.

32. Wainwright, Journal, 249, 247, HHL; Nevins, *Diary of Battle*, 369–70.

33. *OR*, 36 (2):756; Nevins, *Diary of Battle*, 371; Roebling, Report of Operations, 41, NY.

34. This house was erroneously labelled on various military maps and in postbattle reports and postwar narratives as the Jett house, Gayle house, Gate house, and Galt house.

35. Willis, Diary, May 10, 13, 14, 1864, V.

36. *OR*, 36 (1):555–56; Roebling, Report of Operations, 41–42, NY; Nevins, *Diary of Battle*, 371.

37. Willis, Diary, 14 May 1864, V; Beale, *Ninth Virginia Cavalry*, 117–18.

38. *OR*, 36 (1):685.

39. Ibid., (2):762; Holmes, *Touched With Fire*, 120–21; Agassiz, *Meade's Headquarters*, 115–16; *OR*, 36 (1):669.

40. *OR*, 36 (1):669–70.

41. Ibid., (2):757.

42. Holmes, *Touched With Fire*, 118; *OR*, 36 (1):670; Beale, *Ninth Virginia Cavalry*, 119; Oestreich, Diary, USAMHI; James C. Biddle to Wife, 16 May 1864, Meade Collection, HSP. Lee and A. P. Hill witnessed this action from the rear near a church. Hill became furious at what he perceived to be bungling tactics by Wright and threatened to hold a court of inquiry. Lee explained that this would result in more harm than good and that Hill must be patient and attempt to get the best results possible with the officers assigned to him. This beautiful passage by Lee is in Freeman, *Lee's Lieutenants*, 3:331.

43. *OR*, 36 (2):758, 764; (1):767, 768, 738; Early, *Narrative*, 357.

44. *OR*, 36 (2):750, 761.

45. Fuller, Diary, 14 May 1864, LC; *OR*, 36 (1):520, 526; Thomas Allcock, Record of the 4th New York Heavy Artillery, 3rd Battalion, 14 May 1864, Union Reports, NA.

46. *OR*, 36 (1):484; (2):751; Allcock, Union Reports, NA.

47. Hampton, Connected Narrative, 37, USC; *OR*, 36 (1):228.

48. *OR*, 36 (2):701; (1):231–32.

49. Ibid., (1):232; (2):753; Hampton, Connected Narrative, 37, USC; Katherine Couse to Friends, 14 May 1864, UV. This twelve page letter, written by an ardent Unionist originally from New Jersey, describes events which occurred near the Couse homestead during the period 4–22 May 1864.

50. *OR*, 36 (1):232; (2):752.

51. Ibid., (2):760, 747, 750. Two more Confederate artillery pieces were secured during the day by Barlow's troops.

52. Ibid., 51 (2):929; Sorrel to Alexander, 14 May 1864, Alexander Papers, UNC; Anderson, Report of Operations, 5, VHS.

53. *OR*, 36 (2):754, 787, 785.

54. Ibid., (1):1057.

55. Ibid., (2):786, 785, 784, 787; Marbaker, *Eleventh New Jersey Volunteers*, 177.

56. *OR*, 36 (2):795, 782.

57. Ibid., 752; Livingston, Diary, 15 May 1864, RU; Couse to Friends, 15 May 1864, UV.

58. *OR*, 36 (2):733; Hannaford, Memoirs, 15 May 1864, CHS.

59. William J. Smith, "Just a Little Bit," 113–14.

60. Hannaford, Memoirs, 15 May 1864, CHS. Hannaford believed that if the Confederates had remained silent they could have captured the entire encampment.

61. William J. Smith, "Just a Little Bit," 114; *OR*, 36 (1):893–94.

62. Hannaford, Memoirs, 15 May 1864, CHS; *OR*, 36 (1):986, 1098. Hannaford expressed doubt as to whether many of his trooper colleagues had any complaints to make about the color of the infantry relief.

63. *OR*, 36 (1):991; Cuffel et al., *History of Durell's Battery*, 183.

64. *OR*, 36 (1):1098.

65. Ibid., 1098, 303; Couse to Friends, 15 May 1864, UV.

66. *OR*, 36 (1):1098; (2):795.

67. Ibid., (2):795, 782, 788–89.

68. Ibid., 796; (1):431, 1098.

69. Ibid., (2):794.

70. Boudrye, *Fifth New York Cavalry*, 129; *OR*, 36 (2):790, 797; Wright to Humphreys, undated, Army of the Potomac Correspondence, Box #70, NA.

71. *OR*, 36 (2):749.

72. C. Marshall to R. S. Ewell, undated, Ewell Order Book, TN; *OR*, 51 (2):933.

73. Worsham, *Foot Cavalry*, 138.

74. *OR*, 36 (1):1057; Anderson, Report of Operations, 5, VHS; Alexander, Personal Narrative, 82, UNC; Watson, Diary, 16 May 1864, VHS.

CHAPTER 18

1. *OR*, 36 (2):809–10.

2. Ibid., 812.

3. Meacham, *Empty Sleeve*, 15–16; John L. Smith, Letter, 19 May 1864, HSP; Marshall Phillips to Wife, 11–13 May 1864, MEHS.

4. Rufus Dawes to Wife, 16 May 1864, SHSW.

5. *OR*, 36 (1):70, 704.

6. Ibid., 72; (2):828–29.

7. Ibid., (1):71, 149, 969.

8. Bates, *Pennsylvania Volunteers*, 1:792; *OR*, 36 (2):631, 818–19.

9. *OR*, 36 (1):1057, 1067, 1047; Fuller, Diary, 16 May 1864, LC; Alexander, Personal Narrative, 82, UNC.

10. *OR*, 36 (2):816–17, 823.

11. Ibid., 818; Roebling, Report of Operations, 44–45, NY.

12. *OR*, 36 (2):824–25; Gordon, Memoirs, 164–65, WLU; Beale, *Ninth Virginia Cavalry*, 119.

13. *OR*, 36 (1):431, 520; (2):815, 817, 819, 826; Couse to Friends, 16 May 1864, UV.

14. Couse to Friends, 16 May 1864, UV.

15. *OR*, 36 (1):910, 929, 534; (2):825, 811–12, 827.

16. Ibid., (2):628, 811, 826.

17. Hunt, Journal, 21, LC.

18. Ibid., 26–27, LC.

19. J. Howard Kitching to S. Williams, Hunt Papers, LC.

20. Hunt, Journal, 27, LC.

21. Ibid., 21.

22. Nevins, *Diary of Battle*, 375.

23. Hunt, Journal, 21, LC.

24. Ibid., 27.

25. *OR*, 36 (1):72; (2):849–50.

26. Ibid., (2):845, 849, 846.

27. Roebling, Report of Operations, 45–46, NY; *OR*, 36 (2):847; (1):562, 577, 581; Nevins, *Diary of Battle*, 377.

28. *OR*, 36 (2):848; Boudrye, *Fifth New York Cavalry*, 129–30; *OR*, 36 (1):892.

29. Brooks, Diary, 17 May 1864, UNC; Waring, Diary, 17 May 1864, UNC.

30. *OR*, 36 (2):843, 840–41; (3):615.

31. Freeman, *R. E. Lee*, 3:334–35.

32. *OR*, 36 (2):815; (1):494, 484.

33. Ibid., (1):471.

34. Ibid., 73.

35. Humphreys, *Virginia Campaign*, 110; *OR*, 36 (2):844.

36. *OR*, 36 (2):850; Humphreys, *Virginia Campaign*, 110.

37. *OR*, 36 (1):705, 425, 510; Walker and Walker, *Diary of the War*, 188.

38. *OR*, 36 (1):431, 459, 337.

39. White, "Diary of the War," 254.

40. *OR*, 36 (1):303; (2):866.

41. Ibid., (2):866.

42. Walker and Walker, *Diary of the War*, 189.

43. *OR*, 36 (1):431, 361, 338.

44. Ibid., 679, 661.

45. Ibid., 910–11, 982–83, 985.

46. Ibid., (2):867–68; Theodore Lyman, "Extract from Diary," in *Papers of Massachusetts*, 4:237.

47. *OR*, 36 (1):1082; White, "Diary of the War," 252–54.

48. *OR*, 36 (1):644; Nevins, *Diary of Battle*, 377.

49. *OR*, 36 (1):431.

50. Ibid., 431, 459; (2):867.

51. Ibid., (2):867; Mulholland, *116th Regiment*, 222.

52. *OR*, 36 (1):685–86, 720; Edwards, Reminiscences, 159, ILSHL; Pettit, William B., to My Dear Bell, 19 May 1864, *FCHS*, 73–74.

53. White, "Diary of the War," 256–57.

54. *OR*, 36 (2):868; Galwey, *The Valiant Hours*, 217–18.

55. *OR*, 36 (2):868.

56. Ibid., 868, 869, 878.

57. Ibid., (1):910–11, 917–18; Fitzpatrick, *Letters to Amanda*, 128.

58. *OR*, 36 (1):232; White, "Diary of the War," 256.

59. *OR*, 36 (1):510, 520, 524.

60. Ibid., (2):869, 864–65, 872.

61. Ibid., 865.

62. Ibid., 910, 931; Humphreys, *Virginia Campaign*, 119.

63. *OR*, 36 (2):873, 876, 878.

64. Ibid., 872, 880.

65. Gibbon, *Recollections of the Civil War*, 223; *OR*, 36 (2):843; Walker and Walker, *Diary of the War*, 189.

66. *OR*, 36 (2):989, 881–82.

67. Ibid., (1):686, 713, 725; (2):875, 876, 874.

68. Ibid., (2):877.

CHAPTER 19

1. Shaw, *First Maine Heavy Artillery*, 109.

2. *OR*, 36 (2):927.

3. Ibid., 924; (1):670, 686, 705.

4. Ibid., (1):911, 945, 918, 939, 983, 951.

5. Ibid., 918; (2):927, 928, 929.

6. Ibid., (1):803, 74; Wynn, Diary, 18 May 1864, FSNMP.

7. *OR*, 36 (2):910.

8. Ibid., 1022; (1):1073.

9. Ibid., (1):1073, 362, 1088.

10. Ibid., 1082, 1058; White, "Diary of the War," 253; Peyton, *Record*, 32.

11. Nevins, *Diary of Battle*, 378.

12. Burger and Bouton, Diary and Leaves, 18, 19 May 1864, FSNMP; Wainwright, Journal, 263, HHL; Kirk, *Heavy Guns and Light*, 218–19.

13. *OR*, 36 (2):923; Wainwright, Journal, 263, HHL.

14. *OR*, 36 (2):913, 931.

15. Ibid., 914, 915.

16. Kirk, *Heavy Guns and Light*, 219–20; *OR*, 36 (2):931–32.

17. *OR*, 36 (1):1046, 1073, 1088; Venable, "Wilderness to Petersburg," 533; Couse to Friends, 19 May 1864, UV. Brig. Gen. A. L. Long, chief of artillery of the

Second Corps, who did not accompany the column, claimed that the guns were returned after traveling two or three miles. Venable, who likewise was not along, stated that the guns were sent back because of difficulties of the route along the flat ground adjacent to the Ni River. Katherine Couse mentioned no guns with the infantry that she saw passing along the road in front of her house.

18. Hampton, Connected Narrative, 37, USC; Couse to Friends, 19 May 1864, UV; McDonald, *Laurel Brigade,* 242.

19. *OR,* 36 (1):1082–83; Freeman, *Lee's Lieutenants,* 3:440.

20. Gardner et al., *Souvenir,* 22–23; Roe and Nutt, *First Regiment Heavy Artillery,* 34, 153, 156.

21. Kirk, *Heavy Guns and Light,* 220–27; Gardner et al., *Souvenir,* 25–26; *OR,* 36 (1):1083.

22. Shaw, *First Maine Heavy Artillery,* 110; Gardner et al., *Souvenir,* 23.

23. Benjamin F. Wilder to Mrs. Larouque, 20 May 1864, GA.

24. *OR,* 36 (1):1083; Archbell, "Major General Bryan Grimes," 13; Peyton, *Record,* 32–33.

25. Camper and Kirkley, *First Regiment Maryland Infantry,* 141–44; Prowell, *Eighty-Seventh Regiment,* 139–40; *OR,* 36 (1):600, 462. It is uncertain with whom and when Dushane's troops fought. They may have been fighting Gordon's, Hoffman's, or even Ramseur's men. Major Roebling, who led the Maryland brigade to its position on the firing line, claimed that Dushane's contingent arrived after the brigade was in position and engaged. Much of the account of this engagement, especially its chronology, is conjectural because of vague and conflicting sources.

26. *OR,* 36 (2):911.

27. Ibid., 915, 916, 917.

28. Ibid., (1):288, 510; Wainwright, Journal, 263–64, HHL.

29. *OR,* 36 (1):609; Dailey, Diary, 19 May 1864, USAMHI.

30. Gardner et al., *Souvenir,* 23; Roebling, Report of Operations, 50, NY; *OR,* 36 (1):478, 481.

31. Nevins, *Diary of Battle,* 379.

32. Roe and Nutt, *First Regiment Heavy Artillery,* 34, 156; Miller, *Drum Taps In Dixie,* 90; Hunt, Journal, 25, LC.

33. Roebling, Report of Operations, 50–51, NY.

34. Early, *Narrative,* 357–58; Venable, "Wilderness to Petersburg," 533; Harris, *Historical Sketches,* 49; Stearns, *Three Years with Company K,* 269; Small, *Road to Richmond,* 142–43; Caldwell, *Brigade of South Carolinians,* 151–52; *OR,* 36 (2):908.

35. *OR,* 36 (1):285, 337.

36. Ibid., 1073, 1083; Peyton, *Record,* 33.

37. Hannaford, Memoirs, 55–56, CHS.

38. Hampton, Connected Narrative, 37, USC. Peyton in his diary claimed that the Confederate guns were fired for from one to two hours. One of the gunners, George Neese, stated that his piece was fired only twice in this action.

39. *OR,* 36 (2):930. A few accounts claim that the Colored Troops became engaged on the Fredericksburg Road and saved the wagon train. In fact they did not leave their bivouac near Salem Church. On 21 May, a captain from Ewell's command surrendered himself and five of his men to pickets of the Second Ohio Cav-

alry near where Rosser's troopers had collided with Ferrero's outposts on the nine-teenth. The Southerners had really become lost! The account is in Hannaford, *Memoirs*, 56.

40. Peyton, *Record*, 33.

41. *OR*, 36 (2):918, 926, 919, 921.

42. Ibid., 906, 907.

43. Ibid., (1):600–601; Sypher, *Pennsylvania Reserve Corps*, 536; Peyton, *Record*, 33; Caldwell, *Brigade of South Carolinians*, 152.

44. Gardner et al., *Souvenir*, 30–31; Cyrus B. Watson, "Forty-Fifth Regiment," in Walter Clark, *Histories from North Carolina*, 3:54; Osborne, "Fourth Regiment," in Walter Clark, *Histories from North Carolina*, 1:258; *OR*, 36 (3):6, 9, 15.

45. Ibid., (1):1073.

46. Ibid., (3):3; (1):602; William P. Shreve, "The Operations of the Army of the Potomac May 13–June 2, 1864," in *Papers of Massachusetts*, 4:297.

47. Chase, Memoirs, 111, USAMHI.

48. *OR*, 36 (3):11.

49. Ibid., (1):467, 471, 475, 478, 481, 484; Hays, *Under the Red Patch*, 243–44.

50. *OR*, 36 (3):4–5; (1):471, 475, 670, 673; Frassanito, *Grant and Lee*, 111–14.

51. *OR*, 36 (3):8, 13.

52. Ibid., 16, 17, 19.

53. Ibid., 20, 21; (1):911, 918, 929.

54. Ibid., (3):21–22.

55. Ibid., 51 (2):945; Dowdey and Manarin, *Wartime Papers of R. E. Lee*, 734.

56. *OR*, 36 (1):1058; (3):7, 8, 9, 11, 801.

57. Ibid., (3):801, 802. Freeman in *R. E. Lee*, 3:340, intimates that Lee relocated Gregg's troops on the morning of the twentieth but the evidence indicates that the Texans moved during the early hours of the twenty-first.

58. *OR*, 36 (1):362; (3):46.

59. Humphreys, *Virginia Campaign*, 120.

60. Wilkerson, *Recollections of a Private Soldier*, 101.

61. *OR*, 36 (3):46, 47, 48, 49.

62. Ibid., 52, 60.

63. Ibid., 52, 53.

64. Ibid., 53.

65. Ibid., 53, 61, 62, 64.

66. Ibid., 55, 64.

67. Roebling, Report of Operations, 53, NY; *OR*, 36 (3):55; Frassanito, *Grant and Lee*, 116.

68. Roebling, Report of Operations, 53, NY; Stearns, *Three Years with Company K*, 270; Small, *Road to Richmond*, 143.

69. Hopper, Reminiscences, 8–9, UMI.

70. *OR*, 36 (1):679–80, 738, 749, 661, 759, 761, 767, 772; Haines, *Fifteenth New Jersey*, 188.

71. Beale, *Ninth Virginia Cavalry*, 119–20; *OR*, 36 (3):45, 46. Freeman in *R. E. Lee*, 3:340–41 n. 57, emphasized the fact that Lee became aware of the location and route of march of Hancock's corps only six hours after the Federal movement

began and thus was able to react quickly to it. Freeman believed the Union commanders were censurable for permitting this early detection of the movement by Confederate scouts and pickets. On the contrary, once Hancock's command cleared the general area of the army's position, the Federal commanders hoped it would be detected and pursued by all or part of the Army of Northern Virginia. Freeman thought that the movement of Ewell's Corps from Snell's Bridge a short way down the south bank of the Po River was Lee's initial move from the area. The real Confederate move south did not begin until after midday, at which time the head of Hancock's column was arriving at its destination below Milford.

72. It is suggested that the reader interested in analyses of what the Federals hoped to accomplish during the movement and why Lee did not cooperate consult Freeman, *R. E. Lee*, 3:340–42, and Atkinson, *Grant's Campaigns*, 330–37.

73. Humphreys, *Virginia Campaign*, 126–27. Atkinson suggests that the Federals may have chosen the eastern route for Hancock to ensure that the access roads leading farther east to Port Royal would be open and clear of enemy forces.

74. *OR*, 36 (3):812.

75. Ibid., (1):1058; *Official Atlas*, Plate 81, Map 2.

76. McDonald, *Make Me a Map*, 206; Freeman, *R. E. Lee*, 3:343 n. 64; Peyton, *Record*, 34.

77. *OR*, 36 (3):814, 815; (1):1058.

78. Ibid., (3):64–65. Timothy O'Sullivan took five photographs of the headquarters staffs at Massaponax Church. In one of these Grant is seen writing a message, possibly the one containing Burnside's instructions. See Frassanito, *Grant and Lee*, 116–21.

79. *OR*, 36 (1):911, 929.

80. Ibid., 929, 945, 951.

81. Early, *Narrative*, 358; Lane, "Lane's North Carolina Brigade," 153–54.

82. R. S. Williams, "Thirteenth Regiment," in Walter Clark, *Histories from North Carolina*, 1:677.

83. J. H. Lane, "Twenty-Eighth Regiment," in Walter Clark, *Histories from North Carolina*, 2:480; James A. Weston, "Thirty-Third Regiment," in Walter Clark, *Histories from North Carolina*, 2:573; *OR*, 36 (1):686, 705, 738, 743; Haines, *Fifteenth New Jersey*, 188–89; Oestreich, Diary, 51–52, USAMHI.

84. Early, *Narrative*, 358; *OR*, 36 (3):813–14.

85. Freeman, *R. E. Lee*, 3:343–44; Moncure, "A Ride with Gen. Robt. E. Lee," 50–51.

86. *OR*, 36 (1):687, 670; Read, Diary, 21 May 1864, MNBP.

87. Caldwell, *Brigade of South Carolinians*, 152; Dunlop, *Lee's Sharpshooters*, 78.

APPENDIX A

1. Assigned to command Third Brigade, Second Division, 17 May.

2. Assigned 10 May; captured 12 May.

3. Detailed as escort for wounded to Fredericksburg 8 May.

4. Wounded 12 May.

5. Wounded 13 May.
6. Joined 17 May.
7. Wounded 18 May.
8. Assigned 12 May.
9. Assigned 18 May.
10. Division disbanded 13 May.
11. Joined 18 and 19 May.
12. Second Company Massachusetts Sharpshooters attached.
13. Wounded 8 May.
14. Joined 16 May.
15. Wounded 8 May.
16. Wounded and captured 8 May.
17. Wounded 8 May.
18. Captured 8 May.
19. Left army 15 May.
20. Killed 10 May.
21. Killed 9 May.
22. Joined 14 May.
23. Wounded 9 May.
24. Assumed command 14 May.
25. Detached guarding trains and prisoners.
26. Killed 10 May.
27. Assumed command 12 May.
28. Assumed command 13 May.
29. Discontinued as an unattached command and assigned to the First Division 12 May.
30. Joined 15 May.
31. Wounded 12 May.
32. Wounded 12 May.
33. Reverted to two separate brigades 11 May.
34. Wounded 10 May.
35. Mortally wounded 12 May.
36. Killed 12 May.
37. Wounded 10 May.
38. Wounded 12 May.

APPENDIX B

1. *OR*, 36 (1):787.
2. Sheridan, *Memoirs*, 1:356.
3. Ibid., 354–55.
4. *OR*, 36 (2):484.
5. Ibid., 515–16.
6. Ibid., 552.
7. Ibid., 553.
8. Ibid., (1):191.

9. Ibid., 19.

10. Ibid., 788.

11. Ibid., 789.

12. Ibid.

13. Ibid., (2):554.

14. Badeau, *Military History of U. S. Grant*, 2:139.

15. Grant, *Personal Memoirs*, 2:212–13.

16. *Index to the Ulysses S. Grant Papers*, 8, including n. 27, LC; Humphreys, *Virginia Campaign*, 67–70.

17. *OR*, 36 (1):811, 833, 846.

18. Sheridan, *Memoirs*, 1:365.

19. Ibid., 367.

20. Humphreys, *Virginia Campaign*, 70.

21. Sheridan, *Memoirs*, 1:364.

22. For detailed critical analyses of the accuracy of these three postwar accounts and an indictment of the veracity of Sheridan, in general, the reader can consult two works by Carswell McClellan, who at the beginning of the 1864 campaign was an assistant adjutant general on the staff of Brig. Gen. Alfred T. Torbert, commander of the First Cavalry Division. These are, *The Personal Memoirs and Military History of U. S. Grant Versus The Record Of The Army of the Potomac* and *Notes on the Personal Memoirs of P. H. Sheridan.*

APPENDIX C

1. Varina D. Brown, *Colonel at Gettysburg and Spotsylvania*, 134, 294–95.

2. Old, "Trees Whittled Down at Horseshoe," 18–19.

3. Black, "Reminiscences," 14–15; Peirson, "Operations of the Army of the Potomac May 7–11, 1864" in *Papers of Massachusetts*, 4:217.

4. Black, "Reminiscences," 15. The trunk was sawed through immediately above the roots so it could stand upright unsupported and was placed on display at the entrance of the old War Department building facing Pennsylvania Avenue. It was sent to the Centennial celebration at Philadelphia in 1876, where ex-Captain Old viewed it and remonstrated with exhibit personnel because the placard which explained the tree's demise erroneously claimed that it had been felled by Confederate fire. In 1888 the tree stump was donated by the War Department to the Smithsonian Institution. In 1893 it was taken to Chicago for the World's Fair. So this mass of wood has been relatively well traveled for a tree, and all because at one time it stood along the edge of a farmer's field in Spotsylvania County, Virginia.

BIBLIOGRAPHY

Where relevant, the military unit of the author or subject of a work is given in brackets.

MANUSCRIPTS

Alabama Department of Archives and History, Montgomery.
  Coles, R. T. "History of the 4th Infantry Regiment." Chapter entitled "Spotsylvania Ridge to the James River, from May 8th to June 16, 1864."
Boston University.
  Military Historical Society of Massachusetts Collection.
    Porter, Charles H. Letter. [39th Mass. Inf.]
    Richards, J. W. Letter. [3d Div, Fed 9th Corps.]
    [Wylie, O. A.]. Confederate Diary. [6th S.C. Inf.]
Brown University, Providence, R.I.
  Barber, James A. Diary. [Btry G. 1st R.I. Arty, Fed 6th Corps.]
Cincinnati Historical Society.
  Hannaford, Roger. Memoirs. [2d Ohio Cav.]
Cornell University, Ithaca, N.Y.
  Ryno, John L. Diary. [3d Bg, 1st Div, Fed 2d Corps.]
Duke University, William R. Perkins Library, Durham, N.C.
  Anderson, Richard H. Papers. [Hq Confed 1st Corps.]
  Daniel, John W. Papers. Box 1905–1910. Undated file.
    Johnston, Robert D. Notes. [Hq Bg, Early's Div, Confed 2d Corps.]
  Dillard, John J. Letter. [26th Ga. Inf.]
  Emery, Edwin. Papers. [17th Maine Inf.]
  Harden, Edward. Papers.
    Jackson, Asbury. Letter. [44th Ga. Inf.]
Duke University Medical Center Library, Durham, N.C.
  Winne, Charles K. Journal. [Medical Officer, Fed 5th Corps.]
Fredericksburg and Spotsylvania National Military Park.
  Birney, David B., and Hancock, Winfield S. to Lt. Col. Walker, 4 June 1864. Typescript copy. [Fed 2d Corps.]
  Burger, Stephen D., and Bouton, George W. P. Diary and Leaves from Memoranda. Typescript copy. [6th N.Y. Heavy Arty.]
  Shaner, Joe. Letters. [Graham's btry, Confed 2d Corps.]
  Vogt, Stuart G. "The Death of Major-General John Sedgwick, U.S.A., May 9, 1864."
  Wilshin, Francis F. "'The Pendleton Road': Key Route in the Race from Wilderness to Spotsylvania, 1864."

Wynn, B. L. Diary. Reel #6239. [Hq Confed 2d Corps.]
Georgia Department of Archives and History, Atlanta.
    Wilder, Benjamin F. Letter. Civil War Miscellaneous Correspondence, Box 30. [4th Ga. Inf.]
Hampden-Sydney College, Eggleston Library, Hampden-Sydney, Va.
    Carter, William R. Diary. [3d Va. Cav.]
Henry E. Huntington Library, San Marino, Calif.
    Wainwright, Charles S. Wartime Journal 1861–1865. [Fed 5th Corps Arty.]
Hill Junior College, Hillsboro, Texas.
    Hanks, O. T. History of Captain B. F. Benton's Company, 1861–1865. [1st Tex. Inf.]
    Pomeroy, Nicholas. War memoirs. [5th Tex. Inf.]
    Smither, J. Mark. Letter. [5th Tex. Inf.]
Historical Society of Delaware, Wilmington.
    Wilson, James H. Diary. [Hq Div, Fed Cav.]
Historical Society of Pennsylvania, Philadelphia.
    Humphreys, Andrew A. Papers. [Hq Army of the Potomac.]
    Irwin, John. Diary. [149th Pa. Inf.]
    McKnight, Charles. Diary. [88th Pa. Inf.]
    Meade, George G. Papers.
        Official Correspondence.
        Biddle, James C. Letters.
    Smith, John L. Papers. [118th Pa. Inf.]
Illinois State Historical Library, Springfield.
    De Peyster, John Watts. Papers.
        Paine, William H. Diary. [Crocker's bg, 3d Div, Fed 2d Corps.]
    Edwards, Oliver. Reminiscences. [37th Mass. Inf.]
Indiana Historical Society, Indianapolis.
    Pattison, Alexander B. Diary. [7th Ind. Inf.]
Indiana State Library, Indianapolis.
    Gilbreath, Erasmus C. Reminiscences. [20th Ind. Inf.]
Indiana University, Lilly Library, Bloomington.
    Sixty-fourth New York Infantry Regiment. Diary.
Library of Congress, Manuscript Division.
    Comstock, Cyrus B. Diary Oct. 16, 1863–Dec. 7, 1867. [Grant's Hq.]
    Fuller, Joseph P. Diary. [20th Ga. Inf.]
    Hotchkiss, Jedediah. Papers.
        Dozle, L. L. Reminiscences. [33d Va. Inf.]
    Hunt, Henry J. Papers. [Hq Army of the Potomac, Arty.]
        Journal of Siege Operations April 1864 to March 1865.
        J. Howard Kitching to S. Williams, 15 May 1864.
    Newburger, Alexander. Diary. [4th N.Y. Cav, Train Guard.]
    Sanborn, Fred. Papers. [Bg Staff, 1st Div, Fed 2d Corps.]
    Wilcox, Cadmus. Papers. [Hq Div, Confed 3d Corps.]
Louisiana State University, Baton Rouge.
    Balchelor, Albert A. Papers.
        Cobb, R. G. Letter. [2d La. Inf.]

Maine Historical Society, Portland.
  Bradford, Luther. Account of Service, 12 May 1864. [16th Maine Inf.]
  Phillips, Marshall. Papers. [16th Maine Inf.]
  Small, Abner. Papers. [16th Maine Inf.]
Manassas National Battlefield Park.
  Ricketts, James B. Papers.
    Read, James M. Diary of the Movements of the Third Division Sixth Army
      Corps.
Massachusetts Historical Society, Boston.
  Barlow, Francis C. Papers. [Hq 1st Div, Fed 2d Corps.]
  Lyman, Theodore. Journal. [Hq Army of the Potomac.]
Military Order of the Loyal Legion of the United States—War Library and Mu-
    seum, Philadelphia.
  Bolton, William J. Journal. [51st Pa. Inf.]
  Herring, Charles P. Papers. [118th Pa. Inf.]
  Maine Commandery folder, 1865–1896.
  Veil, C. H. Reminiscences. [1st U.S. Cav.]
Museum of the Confederacy, Richmond.
  Heth, Henry. Report of Operations of Heth's Command from May 4, 1864 to
    December 4, 1864. Folder H-480. [Hq Div, Confed 3d Corps.]
  Lee, Fitzhugh. Report of Operations from May 4, 1864 to September 19, 1864.
    [Hq Div, Confed Cav.]
National Archives.
  Record Group 94: The Adjutant General's Office.
    Army of the Potomac Correspondence—1864. Entry 731.
    Burnside, Ambrose E. Official Correspondence, January to May 1864. Entry
      731. Box 30.
    Fifth Army Corps Battle Record. Entry 612. Box 69.
    Return of the 2nd Ohio Cavalry Regiment. Entry 53. Microcopy 594, roll 140.
    Return of the 2nd Wisconsin Infantry Regiment. Entry 53. Microcopy 594, roll
      198.
    Union Reports. Entry 731. Box 69.
  Record Group 109: War Department Collection of Confederate Records.
    Records of Events, 17th Mississippi Infantry Regiment, May 1864. Microcopy
      269, roll 250.
    Return of Hardaway's Battalion. Microcopy 861, roll 64.
    Return of Page's Battalion. Microcopy 861, roll 64.
    Return of Company D, 61st Virginia Infantry Regiment. Microcopy 861, roll
      71.
New Hampshire Historical Society, Concord.
  Jones, J. N. Diary. [6th N.H. Inf.]
New York State Library, Albany.
  Ames, Albert N. Papers. [Fed 2d Corps Arty.]
  Fifth Army Corps Letter Books.
  Roebling, Washington A. Report of Operations of the 5th Corps A. of P. in Gen-
    eral Grant's Campaign from Culpeper to Petersburg as seen by W. A. Roebling,
    Maj. and ADC. 1864.

Warren, Gouverneur K. Papers. [Hq Fed 5th Corps.]
    Correspondence. Box 7, Vols. 7a and 7b, May 8–13, 1864.
    Diary.
North Carolina Department of Archives and History, Raleigh.
    Shuford, Lowry. Papers.
        Bone, J. W. Diary. [30th N.C. Inf.]
Oswego County Historical Society, Oswego, N.Y.
    Bristol, Lansing. Diary. [147th N.Y. Inf.]
Pennsylvania State University, University Park.
    McDowell, Marinus K. Papers.
        Dunlap, Hamilton R. Diary. [100th Pa. Inf.]
Potter County Historical Society, Coudersport, Pa.
    Harvey, Albert L. Letter. [149th Pa. Inf.]
Rhode Island Historical Society, Providence.
    Rhodes, Elisha H. Diary. [2d R.I. Inf.]
Rutgers University, New Brunswick, N.J.
    Denton, James. Papers. [1st N.J. Inf.]
    Livingston, Justus H. Diary. [12th N.J. Inf.]
South Carolina Historical Society, Charleston.
    Whilden, Charles E. Papers. [1st S.C. Inf.]
State Historical Society of Wisconsin, Madison.
    Dawes, Rufus. Papers. [6th Wis. Inf.]
Tennessee State Library and Archives, Nashville.
    Brown-Ewell Papers. [Hq Confed 2d Corps.]
        Ewell, Richard S. Order Book. Box 2, Folder 6.
    Civil War Collection.
        Toney, Marcus B. Diary and Reminiscences. [44th Va. Inf.]
    Ewell-Stewart-Brown Collection. [Hq Confed 2d Corps.]
        Brown, Campbell. Memoranda of the Campaign of 1864.
United States Army Military History Institute, Archives, Carlisle, Pa.
    Bilby, Joseph C. Collection.
        Breech, John P. Diary. [4th N.J. Inf.]
    Bliss, Zenas R. Reminiscences. [Hq Bg, 2d Div, Fed 9th Corps.]
    Civil War Times Illustrated Collection.
        Chase, Stephen P. Papers. [86th N.Y. Inf.]
            Diary.
            Memoirs in the form of articles submitted to the Canisteo, N.Y. *Times* in
                1915.
        Dailey, William J. Diary. [6th N.Y. Heavy Arty.]
        Ressler, Isaac H. Diary. [16th Pa. Cav.]
    Halsey, Edmund. Diary. [15th N.J. Inf.]
    Harrisburg Civil War Round Table Collection.
        Ainsworth, Jared L. Letters. Published in "With the First New York Dragoons," edited by Richard J. Del Vecchio.
        Keiser, Henry. Diary. [96th Pa. Inf.]
        Oestreich, Maurus. Diary. Translated by William Hammeke. [96th Pa. Inf.]

Hawbaker, Gary T. Collection.
  Grosport, Daniel. Diary Oct. 1, 1863 to June 16, 1864. [63d Pa. Inf.]
Leigh, Lewis Collection.
  Smith Brothers Papers. Folder entitled "1864 (1)."
    Smith, William F. Letters to Mother. [1st Del. Inf.]
  Miles, Nelson A. Papers. [Hq Bg, 1st Div, Fed 2d Corps.]
Smith, Murray J. Collection.
  Paul, Charles R. Diary. [N.J. Bg, Fed 6th Corps.]
United States Military Academy Library, West Point, N.Y.
  Tidball, John C. Report of Campaign from Wilderness to Petersburg, May 4–July
    2, 1864. [Fed 2d Corps Arty.]
University of Michigan, Ann Arbor.
  Bentley Historical Library.
    Baird, William S. Memoirs. [23d U.S. Colored Troops.]
    Cutcheon, Byron M. Autobiography. Segment entitled "To Ny River and
      Spottsylvania." [20th Mich. Inf.]
    Hopper, George C. Reminiscences. [1st Mich. Inf.]
    Randall, William H. Reminiscences. [Medical detachment, Fed 9th Corps.]
  William L. Clements Library.
    Schoff, James S. Collection.
      Seymour, Isaac. Journal. [Confed La. bg Staff.]
University of North Carolina, Southern Historical Collection, Chapel Hill.
  Alexander, Edward P. Papers. [Confed 1st Corps Arty.]
    Correspondence.
    Personal Narrative: "Wilderness and Spotsylvania, encompassing May 6–19,
      1864."
  Bernard, George S. Papers. [Lamkin's btry, Confed 1st Corps.]
  Boyle, Francis A. Books 1864–1865.
    Diary. [32d N.C. Inf.]
  Brooks, Noble J. Diary. [Cobb's Ga. Legion, Cav.]
  Green, James E. Diary. [53d N.C. Inf.]
  Grimes, Bryan. Papers. [4th N.C. Inf.]
  Walkup, Samuel H. Papers. [48th N.C. Inf.]
  Waring, Joseph F. Papers. [Jeff Davis Legion, Cav.]
University of South Carolina, South Caroliniana Library, Columbia.
  Hampton Family Papers.
    Hampton, Wade. Connected Narrative of the operation of the Cavalry Corps of
      the Army of Northern Virginia during the last campaign.
University of Virginia, Charlottesville.
  Couse, Katherine. Letter. No. 10441, Manuscripts Dept.
  Daniel, John W. Collection. Box 23, Folder entitled "Civil War material:
    Spotsylvania, 8–21 May 1864."
Virginia Historical Society, Richmond.
  Lee Headquarters Papers Collection.
    Anderson, Richard H. Report of Operations May 7, 1864 to October 19, 1864.
      [Hq Confed 1st Corps.]

Lee, Robert E. Field Telegrams March 18, 1862–October 8, 1864.
Scott, Alfred L. Memoirs of Service in the Confederate Army. [9th Ala. Inf.]
Watson, John S. D. Diary. [17th Miss. Inf.]
Wilcox, Cadmus M. Report of Operations. Roll C59. [Hq Div, Confed 3d Corps.]
Virginia State Library, Richmond.
    Dunaway, Randolph W. Letter. Mary Fanny Dunaway Collection, Miscellaneous
        Reel #517. [9th Va. Cav.]
    McMurran, Joseph. Diary. [4th Va. Inf.]
    Personal Papers Collection.
        Willis, Byrd C. Diary April 7, 1864–May 22, 1865. [9th Va. Cav.]
Washington and Lee University, Lexington, Va.
    Special Collections.
        Allan, William. Conversations with General R. E. Lee.
        Gordon, William A. Memoirs. Collection No. 055; Box No. 1, Folder No. 5.
            [1st Engineers, Confed.]
Waukesha County Museum, Waukesha, Wis.
    Powrie, Robert. Letters. [5th Wis. Inf.]
West Virginia University, Morgantown.
    Snider, Joseph C. Diary. [31st Va. Inf.]
Winchenden Historical Society, Winchenden, Mass.
    Stone, George B. Personal War Sketch. [13th Mass. Inf.]
Wyoming Historical and Genealogical Society, Wilkes-Barre, Pa.
    Dana, Edward L. Papers.
        Campbell, C. H. Diary. [143d Pa. Inf.]
Yale University, New Haven, Conn.
    Webb, Alexander S. Papers. [Hq Bg, 2d Div, Fed 2d Corps.]

MAPS

Fredericksburg and Spotsylvania National Military Park.
    Historical Base Map of Spotsylvania Battlefield, compiled by Michael Jeck, 1981.
Historical Society of Pennsylvania.
    Andrew A. Humphreys Collection.
        Campaign Map of 1864.
Library of Congress, Geography and Map Division.
    Jedediah Hotchkiss Map Collection.
National Archives. Records Group 77. Office of the Chief of Engineers.
    Map of the Battle Field of Spottsylvania C.H. Surveyed under the order of Bvt.
        Col. J. C. Duane, Major of Engineers, Chief Engineer Army of the Potomac.
    Map of the Battlefield of Spottsylvania C.H., compiled from surveys made under
        the direction of N. Michler, Major of Engineers, Bvt. Brig. Gen'l U.S.A. and
        C. W. Howell, Capt. of Engineers, Bvt. Maj. U.S.A. 1867.
    Map of the country in the vicinity of Todd's Tavern. Surveyed under the orders of
        Bvt. Col. J. C. Duane, Major of Engineers, Chief Engineer Army of the Poto-
        mac.

Maps of the Battle Fields of the Wilderness, May 5th, 6th and 7th, 1864. Surveyed under the orders of Bvt. Col. J. C. Duane.
Topographical Sketch of the Battle Field of the Wilderness from Reconnaissances during the Actions of the 5th, 6th and 7th of May 1864 made under the direction of Major N. Michler, Corps of Engineers, U.S.A.
United States Geographic Survey.
United States Topographic Maps; Virginia; 7.5 minute Series.
Quadrangles: Belmont, Bowling Green, Brokenburg, Chancellorsville, Germanna Bridge, Guinea, Ladysmith, Mine Run, Salem Church, Spotsylvania, Woodford.

NEWSPAPERS

Charleston (S.C.) *Sunday News.*
Richmond Daily Enquirer.
Lancaster (Pa.) *Intelligencer.*
Montgomery (Ala.) *Journal.*
Montgomery (Ala.) *Weekly Advertiser.*
Philadelphia Evening and Sunday Bulletin.
Philadelphia Weekly Press.
Philadelphia Weekly Times.
Richmond Sentinel.

ARTICLES, BOOKS, AND PAMPHLETS

Biographies, Memoirs, Personal Narratives, and Campaign and Battle Narratives

Agassiz, George R., ed. *Meade's Headquarters, 1863–1865: Letters of Colonel Theodore Lyman from the Wilderness to Appomattox*. Boston: The Atlantic Monthly Press, 1922.
Alexander, Edward P. *Military Memoirs of a Confederate*. New York: Charles Scribner's Sons, 1907. [Confed 1st Corps Arty.]
Anderson, D. W. "Major D. W. Anderson's Relation." *Southern Historical Society Papers* 21 (1893):252–53. [Witcher's bg, Johnson's div, Confed 2d Corps.]
Archbell, L. V. "Great Men of North Carolina: Major General Bryan Grimes." *Carolina and the Southern Cross* (Kinston, N.C.) 1, no. 1 (November 1912). [4th N.C. Inf.]
Archer, W. S. "Letter to Editor of the *Times*." *Southern Historical Society Papers* 21 (1893): 243. [48th Va. Inf.]
Aschmann, Rudolph. *Memoirs of a Swiss Officer in the American Civil War*. Edited by Heintz-Meier. Bern: Herbert Lang & Co., Ltd., 1972. [1st U.S. Sharpshooters.]
Atkinson, C. F. *Grant's Campaigns of 1864 and 1865*. London: Hugh Rees, Ltd., 1908.

Badeau, Adam. *Military History of U. S. Grant from April 1861 to April 1865.* 3 Vols. New York: D. Appleton and Company, 1881.

Bardeen, C. W. *A Little Fifer's War Diary.* Syracuse, N.Y.: C. W. Bardeen, 1910. [1st Mass. Inf.]

"Battle's Brigade." Montgomery, Ala., *Weekly Advertiser*, 8 June 1864, Vol. 29, 2.

Benedict, George C. *Vermont in the Civil War.* 2 vols. Burlington: The Free Press Association, 1886.

Benson, Susan W., ed. *Berry Benson's Civil War Book: Memoirs of a Confederate Scout and Sharpshooter.* Athens: University of Georgia Press, [1962]. [McGowan's bg, Confed 3d Corps.]

Black, John D. "Reminiscences of the Bloody Angle." In *Glimpses of the Nation's Struggle: Papers Read Before the Commandery of the State of Minnesota, Military Order of the Loyal Legion of the United States.* Fourth Series. St. Paul: H. L. Collins Co., 1898. [1st Div Staff, Fed 2d Corps.]

Bowen, James L. "The Bloody Angle." Philadelphia *Weekly Press*, 12 October 1887, p. 1, col. 1. [37th Mass. Inf.]

Bradwell, I. G. "Spotsylvania, Va., May 8 and 9, 1864" and "Spotsylvania, Va., May 12 and 13, 1864." *Confederate Veteran* 28 (1920): 56, 102. [Evans's bg, Confed 2d Corps.]

Brock, R. A. "General John Rogers Cooke." *Southern Historical Society Papers* 18 (1890): 324. [Hq Bg, Heth's div, Confed 3d Corps.]

Brown, Joseph N. *The Battle of the Bloody Angle May 12, 1864.* Anderson, S.C.: The Advocate Publishing Co., 1900. [McGowan's bg, Confed 3d Corps.]

Brown, Varina D. *A Colonel at Gettysburg and Spotsylvania.* Columbia, S.C.: The State Company, 1931. [McGowan's bg, Confed 3d Corps.]

Buel, Clarence C., and Johnson, Robert U., eds. *Battles and Leaders of the Civil War.* 4 vols. New York: Thomas Yoseloff, 1956.

Carter, Robert G. *Four Brothers in Blue, or Sunshine and Shadows of the War of the Rebellion: A Story of the Great Civil War from Bull Run to Appomattox.* Washington, D.C.: Gibson Bros., Inc., 1913. [22d Mass. Inf and 1st Mass. Heavy Arty.]

Carter, Thomas H. "The Bloody Angle." *Southern Historical Society Papers* 21 (1893): 239–41. [Confed 2d Corps Arty.]

Casler, John O. *Four Years in the Stonewall Brigade.* Guthrie, Okla.: State Capital Printing Company, 1893. [33d Va. Inf.]

Clark, George. *A Glance Backward: Or Some Events in the Past History of My Life.* Houston: Press of Rein & Sons, [1914?]. [11th Ala. Inf.]

Cleaves, Freeman. *Meade of Gettysburg.* Norman: University of Oklahoma Press, 1960.

Cockrell, Monroe, ed. *Gunner With Stonewall: Reminiscences of William Thomas Poague, Lieutenant, Captain, Major and Lieutenant Colonel of Artillery, Army of Northern Virginia, C.S.A.; A Memoir Written for His Children in 1903.* Jackson, Tenn.: McCowat-Mercer Press, 1957. [Confed 3d Corps Arty.]

Coco, Gregory A., comp. and ed. *Through Blood and Fire: The Civil War Letters of Charles J. Mills.* Lanham, Md.: Stanley S. Phillips and Assoc., 1982. [1st Div Staff, Fed 9th Corps.]

Coxe, John. "Last Struggles and Successes of Lee." *Confederate Veteran* 22 (1914): 357. [3d S.C. Inf.]

Croffut, W. A., and Morris, John M. *The Military and Civil History of Connecticut During the War of 1861–1865.* New York: Ledyard Bill, 1869.

Dame, William M. *From the Rapidan to Richmond and the Spottsylvania Campaign.* Baltimore: Green-Lucas Company, 1920. [McCarthy's btry, Confed 1st Corps.]

Davis, Creed. "Diary." *Contributions to the History of the Richmond Howitzer Battalion* no. 3 (1884). [Jones's btry, Confed 2d Corps.]

"The Death of General Rice and Captain Dorr." *Philadelphia Evening and Sunday Bulletin,* 13 May 1864, 4, cols. 2 and 3. [Hq Bg, 4th Div, 5th Corps.]

Douglas, Henry K. *I Rode with Stonewall.* Chapel Hill: The University of North Carolina Press, 1940. [Hq Confed 2d Corps.]

Dowdey, Clifford, and Manarin, Louis H., eds. *The Wartime Papers of R. E. Lee.* New York: Bramhill House, 1961.

Early, Jubal A. *Lieutenant-General Jubal A. Early C.S.A.: Autobiographical Sketch and Narrative of the War Between the States.* Philadelphia: J. B. Lippincott Company, 1912. [Hq Confed 3d Corps.]

Farley, Porter. "Reminiscences of the 140th Regiment New York Volunteer Infantry." *The Rochester Historical Society Publications,* no. 22 (1944).

Favill, Josiah M. *The Diary of a Young Officer.* Chicago: R. R. Donnelly & Sons Company, 1909. [57th N.Y. Inf.]

Field, Charles W. "Campaign of 1864 and 1865." *Southern Historical Society Papers* 14 (1886): 547. [Hq Div, Confed 1st Corps.]

Fitzpatrick, Marion H. *Letters to Amanda.* Compiled by Henry M. Hannock. Culloden, Ga., 1976. [45th Ga. Inf.]

Foster, John Y. *New Jersey and the Rebellion.* Newark: Martin R. Dennis & Co., 1868.

Fowle, George. *Letters to Eliza.* Edited by Margery Greenleaf. Chicago: Follett Publishing Company, n.d. [39th Mass. Inf.]

Frassanito, William A. *Grant and Lee: The Virginia Campaign 1864–1865.* New York: Charles Scribner's Sons, 1983.

Freeman, Douglas S. *Lee's Lieutenants: A Study in Command.* 3 vols. New York: Charles Scribner's Sons, 1944.

————. *R. E. Lee: A Biography.* 4 vols. New York: Charles Scribner's Sons, 1935.

Funkhouser, R. D. "General Lee to the Rear." *Southern Historical Society Papers* 24 (1896): 81. [49th Va. Inf.]

Garber, A. W. "Artillery Work at Wilderness." *Southern Historical Society Papers* 33 (1905): 342. [Garber's btry, Confed 2d Corps.]

Gardner, Joseph W., et al. *Souvenir, First Regiment of Heavy Artillery Massachusetts Volunteers, Excursion to Battle Fields, Dedication of the Monument May 19, 1901.* N.p., [1901?].

Garrison, Fielding H. *John Shaw Billings: A Memoir.* New York: G. P. Putnam's Sons, 1915.

Gerrish, Theodore. *Army Life: A Private's Reminiscences of the Civil War.* Portland, Me.: Hoyt, Fogg, & Donham, 1882. [20th Maine Inf.]

Gibbon, John. *Personal Recollections of the Civil War.* New York: G. P. Putnam's Sons, 1915. [Hq 2d Div, Fed 2d Corps.]

Gibson, J. Catlett. "The Battle of Spotsylvania Courthouse, May 12, 1864." *Southern Historical Society Papers* 32 (1904): 200–207. [49th Va. Inf.]

Gill, John. *Reminiscences of Four Years as a Private Soldier in the Confederate Army,*

1861–1865. Baltimore: Sun Printing Office, 1904. [Fitzhugh Lee's Confed Cav Div.]

Gordon, John B. *Reminiscences of the Civil War*. New York: Charles Scribner's Sons, 1904. [Hq Div, Confed 2d Corps.]

Govan, Gilbert E., and Livingood, James W., eds. *The Haskell Memoirs*. New York: G. P. Putnam's Sons, 1960. [Confed 1st Corps Arty.]

Grant, Ulysses S. *The Personal Memoirs of Ulysses S. Grant*. 2 vols. New York: Charles L. Webster & Company, 1885.

Green, William H. "From the Wilderness to Spotsylvania." *Papers Read Before the Commandery of the State of Maine, Military Order of the Loyal Legion of the United States*. 3 vols. Portland, Me.: Lefanor-Tower Company, 1902, 2:95–96. [10th Mass. Inf.]

Hamlin, Percy C. *Old Bald Head*. Strasburg: Shenandoah Publishing House, Inc., 1940. [Hq Confed 2d Corps.]

Harris, James S. *Historical Sketches: 7th North Carolina Regiment*. Ann Arbor: University Microfilms International, 1978.

Harris, William M., comp. *Movements of the Confederate Army in Virginia and the Part Taken Therein by the Nineteenth Mississippi: From the Diary of Gen. Nat H. Harris*. Duncansby, Miss.: W. M. Harris, 1901.

Holmes, Oliver Wendell, Jr. *Touched With Fire: Civil War Letters and Diary of Oliver Wendell Holmes, Jr., 1861–1864*. Cambridge: Harvard University Press, 1946. [Hq Fed 6th Corps.]

Howard, McHenry. *Recollections of a Maryland Confederate Soldier and Staff Officer Under Johnson, Jackson and Lee*. Baltimore: William & Wilkins Company, 1914. [Steuart's bg, Confed 2d Corps.]

Humphreys, Andrew A. *The Virginia Campaign of '64 and '65*. New York: Charles Scribner's Sons, 1883. [Hq Army of the Potomac.]

Hunt, Isaac F. "Isaac F. Hunt to Joseph N. Brown." *Charleston* (S.C.) *Sunday News*, 28 July 1895, 9, cols. 1 and 2. [McGowan's bg, Confed 3d Corps.]

Hunter, Robert. "Major-General Johnson at Spotsylvania." *Southern Historical Society Papers* 33 (1905): 337–39. [Johnson's div, Confed 2d Corps.]

Hyde, Thomas W. *Following the Greek Cross: Or Memories of the Sixth Army Corps*. New York: Houghton, Mifflin and Company, 1894.

"Incidents In the War of Secession." *Montgomery* (Ala.) *Journal*, 16 January 1908, 2. [15th Ala. Inf.]

Index to the Ulysses S. Grant Papers. Presidents' Papers Index Series, Reference Department, Manuscript Division, Library of Congress, Washington, D.C., 1965.

Jones, Cadwallader. "Trees Cut Down by Bullets." *Confederate Veteran* 34 (1926): 8. [12th S.C. Inf.]

Jones, J. William. "General Lee to the Rear." *Southern Historical Society Papers* 8 (1880): 33–35, 107.

Junkin, D. X., and Norton, Frank H. *The Life of Winfield Scott Hancock*. New York: D. Appleton and Company, 1880. [Hq Fed 2d Corps.]

Krick, Robert K. *Lee's Colonels: A Biographical Register of the Field Officers of the Army of Northern Virginia*, Rev. ed. Dayton: Press of Morningside Bookshop, 1984.

Landon, William. "Letters From Camp, Battlefield and Hospital." *Indiana Magazine of History* 34 (1938). [14th Ind. Inf.]

Lane, James H. "History of Lane's North Carolina Brigade." *Southern Historical Society Papers* 9 (1881): 145–56.

Lanman, Charles. *The Red Book of Michigan*. Detroit: E. B. Smith & Company, 1871.

Lee, Laura E. *Forget-Me-Nots of the Civil War*. St. Louis: A. R. Fleming Co., 1909. [4th N.C. Inf.]

McCabe, W. Gordon. "Major Andrew Reid Venable, Jr." *Southern Historical Society Papers* 37 (1909): 68. [Hq Confed Cav Corps.]

McClellan, Carswell. *Notes on the Personal Memoirs of P. H. Sheridan*. St. Paul: Press of Wm. E. Banning, Jr., 1889.

_____. *The Personal Memoirs and Military History of U. S. Grant Versus the Record of the Army of the Potomac*. Boston: Houghton, Mifflin and Company, 1887.

McClellan, H. B. *The Life and Campaigns of Major-General J. E. B. Stuart*. Richmond: J. W. Randolph and English, 1885. [Hq Confed Cav Corps.]

McDonald, Archie P., ed. *Make Me A Map of the Valley: The Civil War Journal of Stonewall Jackson's Topographer*. Dallas: Southern Methodist University Press, 1973. [Hq Confed 2d Corps.]

Mason, Edwin C. "Through the Wilderness to the Bloody Angle at Spottsylvania Court House." *Glimpses of the Nation's Struggle: Papers Read Before the Commandery of the State of Minnesota, Military Order of the Loyal Legion of the United States*. St. Paul: H. L. Collins Co., 1898. Fourth Series. [2d Div, Fed 6th Corps.]

Meacham, Henry H. *The Empty Sleeve: Or the Life and Hardships of Henry H. Meacham*. Springfield, Mass.: published by the Author, n.d. [32d Mass. Inf.]

Minor, J. B. "Rallying With a Frying Pan." *Confederate Veteran* 13 (1905): 72–73. [3d Ark. Inf.]

Mixson, Frank M. *Reminiscences of a Private*. Columbia, S.C.: The State Company, 1910. [1st S.C. Inf.]

Moncure, E. C. "A Ride with Gen. Robt. E. Lee." Edited by W. W. Scott. *Bulletin of the Virginia State Library* 16 (July 1937) nos. 2 and 3.

Moore, Frank, ed. *The Rebellion Record*. 12 vols. New York: D. Van Nostrand, 1868.

Moore, J. H. "At Spottsylvania." *Philadelphia Weekly Times*, 26 November 1881, 1, col. 1. [7th Tenn. Inf.]

Morrison, James L., Jr., ed. *The Memoirs of Henry Heth*. Westport, Conn.: Greenwood Press, 1974. [Hq Div, Confed 3d Corps.]

Morse, W. E. H. "The 'Rebellion Record' of an Enlisted Man." *The National Tribune Scrapbook*, no. 3. Washington, D.C.: The National Tribune, n.d. [5th Maine Inf.]

Neese, George M. *Three Years in the Confederate Horse Artillery*. New York: The Neale Publishing Company, 1911. [Thomson's Confed btry]

Nevins, Allan, ed. *A Diary of Battle: The Personal Journals of Colonel Charles S. Wainwright, 1861–1865*. New York: Harcourt, Brace & World, 1962. [Fed 5th Corps Arty.]

Norton, Oliver W. *Strong Vincent and His Brigade at Gettysburg, July 2, 1863*. Chicago: n.p., 1909.

Oates, William C. *The War Between the Union and Confederacy and Its Lost Opportunities*. New York: The Neale Publishing Company, 1905. [15th Ala. Inf.]

Official Atlas of the Civil War. New York: Thomas Yoseloff, 1958.

Old, William W. "Trees Whittled Down at Horseshoe." *Southern Historical Society Papers* 33 (1905): 19. [Hq Johnson's div and Confed 2d Corps.]

Page, R. C. M. "The Captured Guns at Spotsylvania—Correction of General Ewell's Report." *Southern Historical Society Papers* 7 (1879): 535–36. [Page's btln, Confed 2d Corps Arty.]

Papers of the Military Historical Society of Massachusetts. Vol. 4, *The Wilderness Campaign, May–June 1864*. Boston: The Military Society of Massachusetts, 1905.

Parsons, Joseph B. "The Bloody Angle." Philadelphia *Weekly Press*, 12 October 1887, p. 1, col. 2.

Pearson, Henry G. *James S. Wadsworth of Genesee, Brevet Major General of United States Volunteers*. New York: Charles Scribner's Sons, 1913. [Hq Div, Fed 5th Corps.]

Peyton, George Q., comp. *A Civil War Record for 1864–1865*. Edited by Robert A. Hodge. Fredericksburg, Va.: Robert A. Hodge, 1981. [13th Va. Inf.]

Phisterer, Frederick. *New York in the War of the Rebellion*. 5 vols. Albany, N.Y.: J. B. Lyon Company, 1912.

Porter, Horace. *Campaigning With Grant*. Bloomington: Indiana University Press, 1965. [Grant's Hq]

Purifoy, John. "The Jeff Davis Artillery At the Bloody Angle." *Confederate Veteran* 24 (1916): 223–24 and 31 (1923): 332. [Reese's btry, Confed 2d Corps Arty.]

Reichardt, Theodore. *Diary of Battery A First Regiment Rhode Island Artillery*. Providence: N. B. Williams, 1865.

Robertson, James I., ed. *The Civil War Letters of General Robert M. McAllister*. New Brunswick, N.J.: Rutgers University Press, 1965. [Hq Bg, 4th Div, Fed 2d Corps.]

Robertson, Robert S. "The Escape of Grant and Meade." *Magazine of American History* 19 (1888): 248–51. [Hq Miles's bg, Barlow's div, Fed 2d Corps.]

Roche, Thomas T. "The Bloody Angle." *Philadelphia Weekly Times*, 3 September 1881, 1, col. 5. [16th Miss. Inf.]

Royall, William L. *Some Reminiscences*. New York: The Neale Publishing Company, 1909. [Hq Confed 3d Corps.]

Schaff, Morris. *The Battle of the Wilderness*. Boston: Houghton, Mifflin Company, 1910. [Hq Army of the Potomac.]

Sheridan, Philip H. *Personal Memoirs of P. H. Sheridan*. 2 vols. New York: Charles L. Webster & Company, 1888. [Hq Fed Cav Corps.]

Small, Harold A., ed. *The Road to Richmond: The Civil War Memoirs of Major Abner R. Small of the Sixteenth Maine Volunteers, together with the Diary Which He Kept When He Was a Prisoner of War*. Berkeley: University of California Press, 1939.

Smith, W. W. "General Lee to the Rear." *Southern Historical Society Papers* 8 (1880): 565.

Smith, William J. "Just a Little Bit of a Civil War, As Seen by W. J. Smith, Company M, 2nd O.V. Cavalry." Edited by Robert W. Hellon. *Ohio History* 84, no. 3 (1975): 113–14.

Sorrel, G. Moxley. *Recollections of a Confederate Staff Officer*. New York: The Neale Publishing Company, 1905. [Hq Confed 1st Corps.]

Sparks, David, ed. *Inside Lincoln's Army: The Diary of Marsena Rudolph Patrick, Provost Marshal General, Army of the Potomac*. New York: Thomas Yoseloff, 1964.

Steere, Edward. *The Wilderness Campaign*. Harrisburg: The Stackpole Company, 1960.

Stiles, Robert. *Four Years Under Marse Robert*. New York: The Neale Publishing Company, 1903. [Confed 1st Corps Arty.]

Stribling, Robert M. *Gettysburg Campaign and Campaigns of 1864 and 1865 in Virginia*. Petersburg: n.p., 1905. [Johnson's div, Confed 2d Corps.]

Stringfellow, M. S. "The Bloody Angle." *Southern Historical Society Papers* 21 (1893): 246, 248. [13th Va. Inf.]

Sypher, Josiah H. *History of the Pennsylvania Reserve Corps*. Lancaster: Elias Burr & Co., 1865.

Taylor, Walter H. *General Lee: His Campaigns in Virginia, 1861–1865, with Personal Reminiscences*. Norfolk: Press of Braunworth & Company, 1906.

Thurston, S. D. "Report of the Conduct of General George H. Steuart's Brigade from the 5th to the 12th of May, 1864, inclusive." *Southern Historical Society Papers* 14 (1886): 150–51. [3d N.C. Inf.]

Toney, Marcus B. *The Privations of a Private*. Nashville: Printed by the author, 1905. [44th Va. Inf.]

Tyler, Mason W. *Recollections of the Civil War*. Edited by William S. Tyler. New York: G. P. Putnam's Sons, 1912. [37th Mass. Inf.]

United States. War Department. *War of the Rebellion: A Compilation of the Official Records of the Union and Confederate Armies*. 70 vols. in 128 parts. Washington D.C.: Government Printing Office, 1881–1902. All references are to Series One.

Upton, Emory. "Emory Upton to G. Norton Galloway, 31 August 1878." *Philadelphia Weekly Times*, 10 August 1887, 1, col. 1. [Hq Bg, 1st Div, Fed 2d Corps.]

Urban, John W. *Battle Field and Prison Pen*. N.p.: Edgewood Publishing Company, n.d. [1st Pa. Res Inf.]

Venable, Charles S. "The Campaign from the Wilderness to Petersburg." *Southern Historical Society Papers* 14 (1886): 529–31. [Hq Army of Northern Virginia.]

Waite, Otis F. R. *New Hampshire in the Great Rebellion*. Concord, N.H.: J. H. Jewett & Co., 1873.

Walker, Charles N., and Walker, Rosemary, eds. *Diary of the War by Robt. S. Robertson, 93d N.Y. Vols. & A.D.C. to Gen. N. A. Miles, Commanding 1st Brigade, 1st Division, 2nd Army Corps, 1861-2-3-4*. [N.p.: Privately printed, 1966?.]

Walker, Francis A. *A History of the Second Army Corps*. New York: Charles Scribner's Sons, 1886.

Walker, James A. "The Bloody Angle." *Southern Historical Society Papers* 21 (1893): 235–36. [Hq Stonewall bg, Confed 2d Corps.]

Wallace, Francis B., comp. *Memorial of the Patriotism of Schuykill County in the American Slaveholder's Rebellion, Embracing a Complete List of the Names of all Volunteers from the County During the War*. Pottsville, Pa.: Benjamin Bannan, 1865. [50th Pa. Inf.]

"The War In Virginia." *Lancaster* (Pa.) *Intelligencer*, 17 May 1864, 19, 2, col. 7.

White, William S. "A Diary of the War, or What I Saw of It." *Contributions to the History of the Richmond Howitzer Battalion*, no. 2 (1883). [Smith's btry, Confed 2d Corps.]

Wilkerson, Frank. *Recollections of a Private Soldier in the Army of the Potomac*. New York: G. P. Putnam's Sons, 1887. [11th btry N.Y. Light Arty.]

Williams, Sidney S. "From Spotsylvania to Wilmington, North Carolina by Way of Andersonville and Florence." *Personal Narratives of Events in the War of the Rebel-*

lion, *Rhode Island Soldiers and Sailors Historical Society*, fifth series, no. 10. Providence: Rhode Island Soldiers and Sailors Historical Society, 1899. [10th Mass. Inf.]

Wise, Jennings C. *The Long Arm of Lee*. Lynchburg: J. P. Bell Company, Inc., 1915.

Worsham, John H. *One of Jackson's Foot Cavalry*. New York: The Neale Publishing Company, 1912. [21st Va. Inf.]

Unit Histories

Abernathy, William M. *Our Mess: Southern Gallantry and Privations*. McKinney, Texas: McKintex Press, 1977. [17th Miss. Inf.]

Banes, Charles H. *History of the Philadelphia Brigade*. Philadelphia: J. B. Lippincott & Co., 1876.

Baquet, Camille. *History of the First Brigade New Jersey Volunteers*. Trenton: MacCrellish & Quigley, 1910.

Bates, Samuel P. *History of Pennsylvania Volunteers, 1861–65*. 5 vols. Harrisburg: State Printer, 1869.

Beale, R. L. T. *History of the Ninth Virginia Cavalry in the War Between the States*. Richmond: B. F. Johnson Publishing Company, 1899.

Bennett, Edwin C. *Musket and Sword: Or the Camp, March and Firing Line in the Army of the Potomac*. Boston: Corburn Publishing Co., 1900. [22d Mass. Inf.]

Bicknell, George W. *History of the Fifth Regiment Maine Volunteers*. Portland, Me.: H. L. David, 1871.

Billings, John D. *The History of the Tenth Massachusetts Battery of Light Artillery in the War of the Rebellion*. Boston: The Arakrlyan Press, 1909.

Bosbyshell, Oliver C. *The 48th In the War: Being a Narrative of the Campaigns of the 48th Regiment, Infantry, Pennsylvania Veteran Volunteers, during the Rebellion*. Philadelphia: Avil Printing Company, 1895.

Boudrye, Louis N. *Historic Records of the Fifth New York Cavalry*. Albany: S. R. Gray, 1865.

Brewer, A. T. *History of the Sixty-First Regiment Pennsylvania Volunteers*. Pittsburgh: Art Engraving & Printing Co., 1911.

Bruce, George A. *The Twentieth Regiment of Massachusetts Volunteer Infantry*. Cambridge, Mass.: Houghton, Mifflin, and Company, 1906.

Burrage, Henry S., ed. *History of the Thirty-Sixth Regiment Massachusetts Volunteers, 1862–1865*. Boston: Rockwell and Churchill, 1884.

Caldwell, J. F. J. *The History of a Brigade of South Carolinians Known First as "Gregg's" and subsequently as "McGowan's Brigade"*. Philadelphia: King & Baird, Printers, 1866. Reprint. Dayton: Press of Morningside Bookshop, 1974.

Camper, Charles, and Kirkley, Joseph W., comps. *Historical Record of the First Regiment Maryland Infantry, with an Appendix Containing a Register of Officers and Enlisted Men, Biographies of Deceased Officers, Etc.* Washington, D.C.: Gibson Brothers, Printers, 1871.

Chamberlin, Thomas. *History of the One Hundred and Fiftieth Regiment Pennsylvania Volunteers, Second Regiment, Bucktail Brigade*. Philadelphia: F. McManus, Jr., & Co., 1905.

Cheek, Philip, and Pointon, Mair. *History of the Sauk County Riflemen, Known as Company "A", Sixth Wisconsin Veteran Volunteer Infantry, 1861–1865.* Madison: Democratic Printing Company, 1909.

Cheney, Newel. *History of the Ninth Regiment New York Volunteer Cavalry.* Poland Center, N.Y.: Martin Mentz & Son, [190?].

Clark, Walter, comp. *Histories of the Several Regiments and Battalions from North Carolina in the Great War, 1861–'65.* 5 vols. Goldsboro: State of North Carolina, 1901.

Collier, Calvin L. *They'll Do To Tie To: The Story of the Third Regiment Arkansas Infantry C.S.A.* N.p.: James D. Warren, n.d.

Cook, Benjamin F. *History of the Twelfth Massachusetts Volunteers.* Boston: Twelfth Regiment Association, 1882.

Croft, David. *History of the One Hundred Forty-First Regiment Pennsylvania Volunteers.* Towanda, Pa.: Published by the author, 1885.

Cuffel, Charles A., et al. *History of Durell's Battery in the Civil War (Independent Battery D, Pennsylvania Volunteer Artillery).* Philadelphia: Craig, Finley & Company, 1903.

Curtis, O. B. *History of the Twenty-Fourth Michigan of the Iron Brigade.* Detroit: Winn & Hammond, 1891.

Cutcheon, Bryon Mac. *The Story of the Twentieth Michigan Infantry, July 15th, 1862, to May 30th, 1865, Embracing Official Documents on File in the Records of the State of Michigan and of the United States Referring or Relative to the Regiment.* Lansing: Robert Smith Printing Company, 1904.

Davis, Charles E., Jr. *Three Years in the Army: The Story of the Thirteenth Massachusetts Volunteers.* Boston: Estes and Lauriat, 1894.

Dickert, D. Augustus. *History of Kershaw's Brigade.* Newberry, S.C.: Ebert H. Aull Company, 1899. Reprint. Dayton: Press of Morningside Bookshop, 1973.

Dunlop, William S. *Lee's Sharpshooters, or the Forefront of Battle: A Story of Southern Valor that Never Has Been Told.* Little Rock: Tunnah & Pittard, 1899. [McGowan's bg, Confed 3d Corps.]

Glover, Edwin A. *Bucktailed Wildcats: A Regiment of Civil War Volunteers.* New York: Thomas Yoseloff, 1960. [13th Pa. Res Inf.]

Gould, Joseph. *The Story of the Forty Eighth: A Record of the Campaigns of the Forty Eighth Regiment Pennsylvania Veteran Volunteer Infantry during the Four Eventful Years of Its Service in the War for the Preservation of the Union.* Philadelphia: Alfred M. Slocum Company, 1908.

Gracey, S. L. *Annals of the Sixth Pennsylvania Cavalry.* N.p.: E. H. Butler & Co., 1868.

Haines, Alanson A. *History of the Fifteenth New Jersey Volunteers.* New York: Jenkins & Thomas, 1883.

Hale, Laura V., and Phillips, Stanley S. *History of the Forty-Ninth Virginia Infantry C.S.A.* Lanham, Md.: Stanley S. Phillips and Assoc., 1981.

Hays, Gilbert A., comp. *Under the Red Patch: Story of the Sixty-Third Regiment Volunteers, 1861–1864.* Pittsburgh: Sixty-Third Pennsylvania Volunteer Regimental Association, 1908.

Judson, A. M. *History of the Eighty-Third Regiment Pennsylvania Volunteers.* Erie: B. F. H. Lynn, 1865.

Kirk, Hyland C. *Heavy Guns and Light: History of the 4th New York Heavy Artillery.*

New York: C. T. Dillingham, 1890.

Krick, Robert K. *Parker's Virginia Battery*. Berryville: Virginia Book Company, 1975. [Confed 1st Corps Arty.]

Lloyd, William P. *History of the First Reg't Pennsylvania Reserve Cavalry*. Philadelphia: King & Baily Printers, 1864.

Locke, William H. *The Story of the Regiment*. Philadelphia: Lippincott & Co., 1868. [11th Pa. Inf.]

Lord, Edward O. *History of the Ninth Regiment New Hampshire Volunteers in the War of the Rebellion*. Concord: Republican Press, 1895.

McDonald, William N. *A History of the Laurel Brigade*. Published by Mrs. Kate S. McDonald, n.d.

Macon, T. J. *Reminiscences of the First Company of Richmond Howitzers*. Richmond: Whellet & Shepperson, [1892?].

Marbaker, Thomas D. *History of the Eleventh New Jersey Volunteers from Its Organization to Appomattox, to Which Is Added Experiences of Prison Life and Sketches of Individual Members*. Trenton: McCrellish & Quigley, 1898.

Marquis, D. R., and Tevis, C. V., comps. *The History of the Fighting Fourteenth*. N.p.: Fourteenth Regiment, 1911. [84th N.Y. Inf.]

Marshall, D. Porter. *Company K, 155th Pennsylvania Volunteer Zouaves*. N.p.: 1888.

Meirs, Earl S., ed. *Ride to War: The History of the First New Jersey Cavalry*. New Brunswick: Rutgers University Press, 1961.

Miller, Delaran. *Drum Taps In Dixie: Memories of a Drummer Boy, 1861–1865*. Watertown, N.Y.: Hungerford-Holbrook Co., 1905. [2d N.Y. Heavy Arty.]

Moore, Alinson. *The Louisiana Tigers: Or the Two Louisiana Brigades of the Army of Northern Virgina, 1861–1865*. Baton Rouge: Ortlieb Press, Inc., 1961.

Muffly, Joseph W., ed. *A History of the 148th Pennsylvania Volunteers*. Des Moines: Kenyon Printing & Mfg. Co., 1904.

Mulholland, St. Clair Augustine. *The Story of the 116th Regiment Pennsylvania Infantry*. Philadelphia: F. McManus & Co., 1899.

Myers, Frank A. *The Comanches: A History of White's Battalion Virginia Cavalry*. Baltimore: Kelly, Piet & Co., 1871. [35th Va. Btln.]

Nash, Eugene A. *A History of the Forty-Fourth Regiment New York Volunteer Infantry in the Civil War 1861–1865*. Chicago: R. R. Donnelly & Sons, 1911.

Newell, Joseph K., ed. *Ours: Annals of the 10th Regiment Massachusetts Volunteers in the Rebellion*. Springfield, Mass.: G. A. Nichols & Co., 1875.

Nichols, G. W. *A Soldier's Story of His Regiment and Incidentally of the Lawton-Gordon-Evans Brigade*. [Jesup?], Ga.: n.p., 1898. [61st Ga. Inf.]

Parker, Francis J. *The Story of the Thirty-Second Regiment Massachusetts Infantry*. Boston: C. W. Calkins & Co., 1880.

Parker, John L. *Henry Wilson's Regiment*. Boston: Press of Rand Avery Co., 1887. [22d Mass. Inf.]

Phelps, Charles E. "Seventh Regiment Infantry." In *History and Roster of Maryland Volunteers, War of 1861–65*, 1:271–75. 2 vols. Baltimore: Press of Guggenheimer, Weilm & Co., 1898.

Preston, Noble D. *History of the Tenth Regiment of Cavalry New York State Volunteers*. New York: D. Appleton and Company, 1892.

Prowell, George W. *History of the Eighty-Seventh Regiment Pennsylvania Volunteers*.

York: Press of the *York Daily*, 1901.

Pullen, John J. *The Twentieth Maine: A Volunteer Regiment in the Civil War.* Philadelphia: J. B. Lippincott Company, 1957.

Pyne, Henry R. *Ride to War: The History of the First New Jersey Cavalry.* New Brunswick: Rutgers University Press, 1961.

Rawle, Willaim B.,et al. *History of the Third Pennsylvania Cavalry, Sixtieth Regiment Pennsylvania Volunteers in the American Civil War, 1861–1865.* Philadelphia: Franklin Printing Company, 1905.

Ripley, William Y. W. *Vermont Riflemen in the War for the Union: A History of Company F, First United States Sharp Shooters.* Rutland, Vt.: Tuttle & Co., 1883.

Roe, Alfred S. *The Tenth Regiment Massachusetts Volunteer Infantry, 1861–1864.* Springfield, Mass.: Tenth Regiment Veteran Association, 1909.

————. *The Thirty-Ninth Regiment Massachusetts Volunteers, 1862–1865.* Worcester: Thirty-Ninth Regiment Veteran Association, 1914.

Roe, Alfred S., and Nutt, Charles. *History of the First Regiment Heavy Artillery Massachusetts Volunteers, Formerly the Fourteenth Regiment of Infantry, 1861–1865.* Worcester: Commonwealth Printers, 1917.

Sawyer, Franklin. *A Military History of the 8th Regiment Ohio Volunteer Infantry: Its Battles, Marches and Army Movements.* Cleveland: Fairbanks & Co. Printers, 1881.

Shaw, Horace H. *The First Maine Heavy Artillery, 1862–1865.* Portland, Me.: n.p., 1903.

Simons, Ezra D. *A Regimental History: The One Hundred and Twenty-Fifth New York State Volunteers.* New York: The Judson Printing Company, 1888.

Smith, A. P. *History of the Seventy-Sixth Regiment New York Volunteers.* Cortland, N.Y.: Truair, Smith & Miles, 1866.

Smith, Donald L. *The Twenty-Fourth Michigan of the Iron Brigade.* Harrisburg: The Stackpole Company, 1962.

Smith, J. L. *History of the Corn Exchange Regiment 118th Pennsylvania Volunteers, From Their First Engagement at Antietam to Appomattox, to which is added a Record of Its Organization and a Complete Roster.* Philadelphia: J. L. Smith, 1888.

Stearns, Austin C. *Three Years with Company K.* Edited by Arthur A. Kent. Rutherford, N.J.: Fairleigh Dickinson University Press, 1976. [13th Mass. Inf.]

Swinfern, David B. *Ruggles' Regiment: The 122nd New York Volunteers in the American Civil War.* Hanover and London: University Press of New England, 1982.

Thomson, D. R. Howard, et al. *History of the Bucktails.* Philadelphia: Electric Printing Company, 1906. [13th Pa. Res Inf.]

Tobie, Edward F. *History of the First Maine Cavalry, 1861–1865.* Boston: Emery & Hughes, 1887.

Vautier, John D. *History of the 88th Pennsylvania Volunteers in the War for the Union.* Philadelphia: J. B. Lippincott Co., 1894.

Westbrook, Robert S. *History of the 49th Pennsylvania Volunteers.* Altoona, Pa.: n.p., 1898.

Weygant, Charles H. *History of the One Hundred and Twenty-Fourth Regiment N.Y.S.V.* Newburgh, N.Y.: Journal Printing House, 1877.

Woodward, Evan M. *Our Campaigns: Or the Marches, Bivouacs, Battles, Incidents of Camp and History of Our Regiment During Its Three Years of Service.* Philadelphia: John E. Potter and Co., [1865]. [2d Pa. Res Inf.]

INDEX

Alabama troops
—artillery, light battery
Reese's, 191; overrun, 196
—infantry regiments
3d, 93
5th, 93
6th, 92
8th, 206
9th, 206, 207
10th, 206, 212
11th, 79
12th, 92
15th, 15, 68
48th, 68
61st, 92
Alexander, E. Porter, 53, 94, 175, 288,
299
Alrich's (farm), 3, 21, 25, 30, 31, 34, 35,
43, 50, 51, 69, 73, 75, 81, 99, 100,
292, 368, 369
Alsop's (house and farm), 56, 60, 61,
63, 64, 65, 66, 67, 83, 85, 91, 94,
100, 101, 108, 109, 126, 152, 153,
184, 254, 258, 278, 279, 282, 287,
317
Alsop's, Captain (house), 99
Alsop's, J. (house), 22, 23, 30, 31, 51,
99, 129, 138, 140, 171
Alsop's, Mrs. (house and farm), 320–21,
322, 323, 328, 329, 330
Anderson, D. W., 193
Anderson, Ephraim F., 61
Anderson, George T., 148, 229
Anderson, Meriwether, 154, 155
Anderson, Richard H., 33, 52, 75, 80,
86, 106, 228, 256, 288, 295, 339,
341, 343, 344, 347, 370, 371; selected to command First Corps, 14;
departs early for Spotsylvania, 53,
382 (n. 35); performs creditably on
8 May, 57–59

Anderson's (house and plantation), 284,
285, 286, 303, 304, 312, 313, 315,
330, 335, 339
Anderson's Mill, 294, 300, 306, 313,
315
Arkansas troops
—infantry regiment
3d, 106, 135; driven from works, 154;
retakes works, 155
Armstrong's (house), 228, 229, 278,
282, 292, 293, 317, 321, 326
Army of Northern Virginia, 1, 2, 15, 16,
42, 77, 88, 173, 199, 268, 271,
299, 342, 349; losses at Spotsylvania, 348; losses on 12 May, 408
(n. 65)
CORPS
First (Anderson's), 2, 14, 15, 16, 33,
46, 52, 69, 86, 87, 101, 106, 107,
109, 135, 148, 202, 278, 299, 341,
347, 368, 369, 371; march to Spotsylvania, 53, 57–60; moves to right
of line, 288–89, 295; departs, 339
Second (Ewell's), 3, 14, 46, 75, 76,
77, 78, 109, 128, 136, 156, 179,
325, 342, 343, 347, 348; march to
Spotsylvania, 76, 86–87; position
in salient, 103, 106, 187; receives
Hancock's attack, 193–99; at Harris's farm, 321–23, 326, 327, 328;
departs, 339
Third (Early's), 3, 4, 16, 46, 75, 76,
77, 78, 82, 101, 128, 131, 141,
168, 233, 275, 299, 326, 343, 344;
march to Spotsylvania, 80, 109; position on right of line, 109, 129;
units used elsewhere, 206–7, 211–
12, 213–15; departs, 341
Cavalry (Stuart's), 275
DIVISIONS
Field's, 53, 75, 106, 146, 232, 286,